D0941368

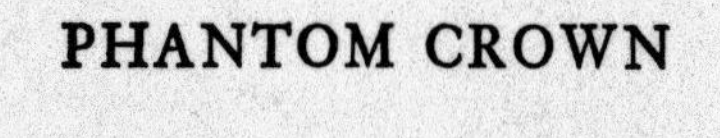
PHANTOM CROWN

Reproduction by Korty, Vienna.

A contemporary and imaginative picture of the reception of the Emperor and Empress on land-

PHANTOM CROWN

THE STORY OF MAXIMILIAN & CARLOTA OF MEXICO

by

BERTITA HARDING

(SEÑORA B. LEONARZ DE HARDING)

"*Die Beseelung . . . da ist es, das schöne Wort. Es ist nicht die Gabe der Erfindung,—die der Beseelung ist es, welche den Dichter macht.*"
—THOMAS MANN

BLUE RIBBON BOOKS
NEW YORK

CL

PRINTED AND BOUND BY THE COUNTRY LIFE PRESS, INC., FOR
BLUE RIBBON BOOKS, INC., 14 WEST 49TH STREET, NEW YORK CITY

Printed in the United States of America

A los míos.
Den Meinen gewidmet.

To
JACK HARDING
who reads to me in the English
known as the King's.

CONTENTS

	PAGE
THE PROLOGUE	13
THE PLOT	55
THE PLAY	127
THE CURTAIN	189
THE EPILOGUE	275
THE STOREHOUSE	353
BIBLIOGRAPHY	365
INDEX	371

I

THE PROLOGUE

PHANTOM CROWN

I

THE PROLOGUE

Chapter 1

Herr Johann Strauss of Vienna was very busy composing waltzes. No easy task, this, after you had furnished some hundred and fifty popular dance hits within two decades and couldn't detect a fresh idea anywhere about your frenzied person. Quite frankly, Herr Strauss had of late begun to plagiarize himself. He did this shrewdly, deftly, with much the same skill his mother had employed when baking her famous *Apfelstrudel* during Johann's infancy.

Apfelstrudel is a cake made from dough that has been stretched over the dining-room table on the family's best dinner cloth and rolled up around a filling of spiced fruits. No matter how little dough one starts out with, the size of the table in the end determines the amount of cake. Frau Strauss never ceased to baffle her doting household by the lengths to which she could make batter go. Already her unrelenting fingers had pulled the mixture out to paper thinness when, to the consternation of her admiring spectators, she would cry suddenly for an extension of the table. True, this procedure left the finished *Strudel* of a consistency at times so fragile and transparent that the compote more often than not broke through the thin walls of its envelope, spreading out shamelessly before the observer's eye.

And it was so, at times, with the waltzes composed by the brilliant Johann in his more crowded moments. After such masterpieces as *Wiener Blut* and *Tales of the Vienna Forest* (dedicated respectively to his Majesty, King Christian IX of Denmark, and Prince Constantin zu Hohenlohe-Schillingsfürst), he gathered up the cuttings, as it were, and with the aid of a few banal diatonics swung into the joyless cliché of *Gypsy Baron* or *The Queen's Shawl.*

To be sure, he had been at this sort of thing for a long time. Events of the greatest historical importance took place during his own childhood. The first Napoleon had conquered and lost Europe and the glorious grenadiers lay dying in the snows about Moscow, while the small Johann stewed over his music lessons and pounded out bright ditties on his mother's harpsichord.

In the spring of 1821 the fierce Corsican languished on St. Helena, fallen and forgotten. But the adolescent Strauss, untroubled by the currents of his era, stood moping blissfully beside the rushing Danube. Its legendary waters were blue—a deep, rich, sapphire blue—and he was wondering what he ought to do about it. Such beauty, he felt, must surely be sung and by this means perpetuated. He did not know that within a single generation steamship navigation would tear up the peculiar underwater growth which lent its cobalt pigment to the ancient stream. Nor did he suspect that his own frivolous muse would wait for another Strauss, another Johann, to preserve the river's classic hue. (How was one to know that one would even have a son, let alone that he would continue the waltz tradition?)

On that bright shore the first Johann stood, the none-too-clean hands of boyhood clasped behind him. His mind was on higher things. Oh, very much higher than the granite-ware basin and flannel wash-cloth with which Frau Strauss was still capable of molesting her precocious seventeen-year-old. Beautiful blue Danube! Some day one must make something very lovely out of that.

When, rather more than a decade later, the captive Duke of Reichstadt—*L'Aiglon,* Napoleon's little "King of Rome"—expired at the palace of Schönbrunn in Vienna, the Austrian capital took scarcely any notice of this pathetic epilogue to a heroic tale. For the heart and the pulse of Vienna belonged to the popular idol of the moment, the opulently hirsute *Kapellmeister* Johann Strauss who carried the social world after him to the ravishing three-quarter beat of his new dance rhythm.

Even in court circles, where for centuries the traditional minuet had only reluctantly given way to an occasional gavotte or a daring mazurka, prejudice was fast surrendering before the onslaught of the shocking and scandalous waltz. Had not Metternich's celebrated Vienna Congress, convoked to repartition the map of Europe, resolved itself into a conference among Talleyrand, the spiritualist clairvoyant Baroness von Krüdener, and Prince Clemens Lothar Wenzel himself, simply because the visiting potentates and their entire retinue had fallen prey to the dance craze? . . . Since the sidelights on history are generally more interesting than history itself, it is not surprising that the famous conference was forever after remembered as the "waltzing congress." For the better part of a year the Viennese had a headache, due only partly to the constant boom of cannon fired for the intermittent arrival or departure of belated royalty, and more specifically to the abandon with which honest burghers kicked up their heels to the tune of:

It was in his more mature years, after serving a short apprenticeship as substitute conductor in Lanner's orchestra, that Johann Strauss formed a band of his own and became the favorite *Ballmusik-Direktor* at the Hofburg. Here, in the drafty imperial residence that rose like a rocky bastion above the heart of the city, the Dowager-Mother Archduchess Frederika Sophie governed her sons—the eighteen-year-old Emperor Franz Joseph and his three cadet brothers—with an energetic if loving hand. It was well that she did so, for their father, Archduke Franz Karl, and his brother, the childless ex-Emperor Ferdinand I, were men of gentle dispositions and even gentler wits.

When the revolutionary year of 1848 swept across the European horizon causing Metternich's creaking old order to totter, "Ferdinand the Good" *(der Gütige)* abdicated. He retired promptly to Innsbruck and later to the noble palace of the Hradschin in Prague. "Goodinand the Finished" *(Gütinand der Fertige),* said the Viennese of their obliging monarch, and permitted him the pleasures of a simple life. So comfortable were these pleasures that the ex-Emperor's brother and heir, Franz Karl, hastily joined in the renunciation. Together the two gentlemen abandoned cares of state and gathered about their favorite meal of dumplings and gravy, a gustatory indiscretion which doctors had long forbidden them.

"I'd like to know who is Emperor," muttered Ferdinand in his Tyrolean dialect as he reached for another helping. *("Möcht' do a wissen, wer Kaiser is, wann i kane Knödeln essen darf!")* If a man couldn't even have a dumpling what good was a crown?

His wife, Maria Anna, a melancholy Sardinian princess, joined the Emperor with equanimity in his self-chosen exile. But not so the indomitable Sophie. The double abdication had cheated this Bavarian lady of a throne, but there were still her children. For them she would not renounce. There was the tried historic formula: Bourbon—Robespierre—Bonaparte—Bourbon. One must wait. . . .

Her judgment was correct. The spark of 1848 died down. The French who had lighted it by throwing out the Bourbons for the second time, were turning in repentance to Louis Napoleon and heading straight for another empire. Europe's periodic infatuation with Dame Democracy had cooled once more, and Austria, bewildered by this outcome, wanted her Hapsburgs back. The Archduchess Sophie returned with her four sons to Vienna and placed the handsome young Franz Joseph on the throne.

Having accomplished this much she bethought herself of a human angle. The Court over which her eldest must preside was essentially a juvenile affair. A monarch still surrounded by his governors and teachers must be permitted the relaxations proper to his age. Accordingly, the Archduchess undertook to supplement the educational program (which was entrusted to Count Heinrich Bombelles) by a series of parties and dance receptions to which the youth of Vienna's aristocracy had been invited.

It was not that the tall and bony Archduchess herself had succumbed, at her ripe age, to the lure of the ever-present dance craze. Heaven forbid! But she was a good Roman Catholic and a wise mother. She knew that four boys in their sultry 'teens were bothered with devilish thoughts. She felt that music, exercise and a refined sort of pandemonium provided a safe outlet for all the suppressed lechery of the truly innocent.

And so she invited the more acceptable offspring of the diplomatic circle and the local élite, together with their chaperoning elders. The latter were not permitted to participate in the youthful goings-on. Instead, these necessary adjuncts to propriety were seated upon the interminable rows of backless settees that encircle the ballrooms of all royal establishments. Here, across the great desert of space that stretched out before them, they watched the youngsters (generally around one hundred couples) disport themselves upon the shining parquet.

Those dance parties were long affairs, beginning at eight o'clock in the evening and ending the following morning at five. During the carnival season festivities went on still longer, until on the night of Shrove Tuesday the music stopped at the stroke of twelve and Lent was ushered in. This always brought a welcome relief to the exhausted chaperons who, while their charges made merry, had gradually frozen into pillars of salt during the endless vigils required by the well-meaning Sophie.

The Archduchess herself suffered no less under the strain but there was that in her which admitted no weakness. Sitting bolt upright on her stool she slumbered on for hours while her children danced, never once relaxing her grip on the jeweled lorgnon which she held before her eyes. Beside her, likely as not, the blowzy Countess Gaby Dietrichstein snored cozily into the brocaded folds of her top skirt which she had pulled up about her neck, thinking it her nightly feather quilt. This lady, who for years made the rounds of the fashionable salons escorting her three ugly ducklings on a futile husband chase, was a veteran ballroom sleeper—her plum-colored petticoats with their twofold mission in life a byword among the gay.

On this subject of fashions it is pertinent to note that silks and fine embroideries played a very small part. Young girls wore flowered percale and crisp tarlatan, while their mothers appeared in damask robes which were preserved from one year to the next in venerable camphor fumes.

The Emperor and the Archdukes of course wore the beautiful

white uniform of the Austrian guard regiments. Cavalry officers from the famous Spanish Riding School of Vienna, L'Équitation, made up the remaining contingent of male guests—fresh, good-looking, beardless youngsters all, whose romantic heads were as dizzy as their waltzing feet.

And Johann Strauss played the violin. Johann Strauss directed. There was scarcely a hostess in Vienna, whether among the nobility or the rich merchant class, who did not deem it a triumph to secure the great *Kapellmeister* for her parties. Naturally a court engagement eclipsed all others. But apart from this the versatile maestro devised a scheme whereby he could meet the vast demand for his services. He moved with his orchestra from party to party, arriving at the most unexpected times between dusk and dawn. Taking up his baton in the middle of a musical phrase, he silenced the rival band and substituted his own players without loss of a single beat. No one had noticed the change. Or rather, every one was suddenly aware of it. For when Strauss conducted there was a new élan, a new savor to the dance. . . .

"Es war eine Lust!" wrote the seventeen-year-old Countess Paula von Linden in her diary. "It was a joy!"

The Emperor Franz Joseph is remembered as one of the best ballroom dancers of his time. Elegant, of medium stature, and with a strange gravity that lent an edge to his charm, he caused many hearts to flutter. The dance partners he chose most frequently were labeled, by their less fortunate contemporaries, the *"Kaiser-Contessen."* Outstanding among these was the lovely Countess Julia Hunyadi, with whom the dashing young Emperor began each cotillion. This little girl, known more intimately as Juppy, is reported to have had "a pert nose, pretty bosom, and the ivory shade of skin peculiar to pure bred Hungarians." Seeing her in a creation of blue tarlatan, with flowers in her burnished hair, Monsieur Talleyrand of the French Embassy exclaimed: "A dream of moonlight in the clouds!"

Juppy disappeared one day and was reported married to a Serbian, Prince Milosh Obrenovitch. Foreigners from "down there" were regarded as a barbarous sort and Juppy's mother found herself besieged with reproaches for consenting to her daughter's union. But that fond parent shrugged her shoulders with gusto. *"Que voulez-vous,"* she declared, *"elle sera couverte de diamants!"* (What would you,—she will be covered with diamonds!)

Since favoritism was inevitable, Franz Joseph soon singled out another young beauty, the flaming, dark Countess Ugarte. His preference for this girl led, many years later, to a strange parallel. Countess Ugarte married Alexander Baltazzi, famous turfman and brother of Countess Vetsera whose daughter Marie brought tragedy into the life of Crown Prince Rudolf, Franz Joseph's only son. Over those guileless Vienna dancing days brooded a dark prophetic future.

The younger Archdukes were not bothered by premonition, however. A sort of radiance was spread over their faces. Unburdened by the weight of an imperial mantle on their happy shoulders, they found everything a great lark. While their elder brother bowed to his dance partner with the utmost formality and *décor,* they contented themselves with grinning straight into the girls' faces. Franz Joseph danced in silence. Breathlessly he whirled through every waltz, choosing always the difficult left turns. His face was serious. Conversation with him was problematical. "Perhaps he is concentrating on those left turns," explained his irrepressible brothers.

The Archdukes, who did a bit of trampling on maidenly toes, made up in boisterous hilarity what they lacked in august reserve. Ferdinand Maximilian, the Dowager Sophie's second son, had also an adolescent fancy. Two years younger than the Emperor, he had only a small share of the latter's handsomeness. (Franz Joseph was one of the few Hapsburgs who did not inherit the well-known Hapsburg lip.) In Maxl's case this family trait combined oddly with a mildly slanting chin. The flaw was offset by a pair of singularly striking blue eyes and bright, wavy, blond hair. He was the tallest of the Archdukes, having taken after the gigantic Sophie.

The object of Maxl's infatuation happened to be the fifteen-year-old Countess von Linden, only daughter of his Excellency, Franz de Paula, Ambassador of Württemberg in Vienna. "That little Linden," said Franz Joseph calmly after meeting her, "is quite nice but too skinny."

Ferdinand Maximilian's romance was lyrical and platonic in the extreme. The little Linden was a great giggler and at that time the Archduke fancied himself an extraordinary wit. This made things very entertaining for both of them. For almost two years the youngsters danced together without anything even remotely resembling an avowal being uttered between them. At last, on one of those Shrove Tuesdays that ushered in a return to sobriety, the Archduke felt a pang. For forty days there was to be no social folderol, no waltzing, no maiden laughing at his corking jokes! He ordered a fiacre and drove to a florist's on the Ringstrasse. By means of an anonymous corsage of orange blossoms Maximilian fired a timid dart.

Through obtuseness on the part of the messenger, Papa Linden received the bouquet. He was astonished. He demanded explanations. Obviously his daughter could not accept flowers, and such expensive flowers, without knowing the identity of their giver. The young vixen sighed and fell to meditating. Her chum, Princess Cara Kinsky, she ventured—the girls sometimes arranged to wear similar corsages. . . .

Count Linden accepted the alibi. That night there was a gala ball at the Hofburg, the last before Prince Carnival was laid to rest. The little Linden wore her best frock made of dull white tulle. At her waist she carried the nosegay of white blossoms.

While the carriages lined up within the palace courtyard a snowstorm raged over the city. The wind howled mournfully through the streets. But inside the great halls the crystal chandeliers were already gleaming with a thousand reflected lights, and candles dripped mercilessly upon the bare shoulders of sitting dowagers.

And now the orchestra had struck up the cotillion. With long strides the Archduke Maximilian rushed across the floor to seize a trembling Countess Linden. They danced a few measures, silent, constrained, oppressed. At last the prince gripped her more closely in his arm. "I'm so happy to see you wear my flowers," he breathed. Of course she had known all along. But now the words had been spoken. After two years of childish play something had happened to them—something that was real. . . .

Outside the storm seemed every minute to grow more furious. Along the entire north front of the great salon the glass doors were suddenly thrown open by the force of the wind. Lackeys rushed through the corridors fetching mattresses, which were held against the cracks where snow-drifts prevented the closing of shutters. Furniture was propped against the lackeys when the latter grew tired of supporting mattresses, and as a last resort the undaunted Archduchess Sophie enlisted the chaperons for storm duty. No one thought of stopping the dance. Johann Strauss was leading the orchestra!

"It was a joy——" wrote Countess Linden in her diary. She also made a note of the foolish behavior of her pet canary on that Lenten morning when she returned to her room rather earlier than usual. "At sight of my lighted candle he began to sing, thinking it was the sun."

As for Papa Linden, there was no singing on the morrow when his daughter reported the true donor of the mysterious bouquet. "I advise you not to imagine anything," was his prudent commentary. He deduced, with wise cynicism, that the Archduke's high station precluded all danger of an entanglement.

At the palace, meanwhile, the matter of the corsage had not gone unnoticed. To begin with, the younger Archdukes, Karl Ludwig and Ludwig Viktor—to whom the fair sex was as yet a subject for vast guffawing scorn—exposed Maxl's condition with a heathenish delight. But younger brothers could be withered into silence by a sufficiently threatening glance. Bombelles, however, was different. The tutor had seen the florist's bill.

Sober words were spoken. The Archduke must not forget that he was brother to a Holy Roman Emperor. What did the Archduke think constituted Majesty? Was it not a sacred aloofness exacted from those to the purple born by their very subjects? Did not the common people themselves demand that the strain of their dynasty remain a sovereign strain? Orange blossoms to a Countess Linden—the Archduke obviously had made a mistake.

The youthful prince was deeply impressed. For the first time in his life it had been brought home to him that he was a Hapsburg and that, being a Hapsburg, he would be expected to differ from other people. To belong to Europe's most ancient dynasty was a sublime privilege for which a sublime price would be exacted. Mercifully, the knowledge that a dynasty can survive only when its members sacrifice personal desire to the interests of their house is not imparted to royal offspring until provocation arises. Until this knowledge came to Maximilian he had been, like most princely children, exceptionally care-free and gay.

He did not take kindly to advice. Count Bombelles frowned. The matter, then, was more serious than had at first been suspected. The Archduchess Sophie was brought into the conference and finally the Emperor himself.

Franz Joseph felt ill-equipped for remonstrances with this brother who was his favorite. Admonitions similar to those which Maxl was now hearing had fallen upon Franz Joseph's head on the eve of his accession. Not in vain was the Boy Emperor noted for his exquisite discretion and tact. "This is the end of my youth," he had said at the moment of his coronation. For he knew that to be Emperor one must forfeit the privilege of being a common man.

In an effort to relieve the tension that was certain to follow his brother's obstinacy, Franz Joseph hit upon a clever plan. He would make a place for Maximilian in the Austrian fleet and thus open up to him the world of travel. At Trieste, the harbor on the Adriatic where the young Archduke could serve a brief apprenticeship, adventure and the sea would beckon. Here the infatuated dreamer might wake from his dream and turn to a life of action.

The plan was promptly carried out. On the day following the episode of the corsage Maxl's career had been decided upon. With neither pomp nor circumstance the young man was dispatched to Trieste, carrying in his pocket a recommendation to the admirals of the fleet.

His first days with the navy proved very painful. He was in love and he had never been away from home. After a fortnight's separation, Franz Joseph—apparently touched by a similar loneliness—summoned him back. Maxl arrived on the afternoon following the summons. He stopped at the florist's in the Ringstrasse, sent a large bunch of roses to the Countess Linden, and drove to his rooms at the Hofburg.

That evening there was a gala performance at the opera. The little Linden sat with her father in the diplomats' loge directly opposite the imperial boxes. Flanked by his nearest kin and the surrounding court attendants sat the unfortunate Maxl. He lifted his binoculars and stared shamelessly across a sea of bobbing heads at the girl he loved. He saw her raise the flowers and bury her face in them. He did not know what opera was being played that night. He remembered only the melody which had filled his heart on that Shrove Tuesday. . . .

The Court was scandalized. Franz Joseph himself could see it wouldn't do. He must devise a more thorough cure for his love-sick brother. Again the family conclave foregathered and this time a more radical scheme was propounded. A sightseeing trip to the Near East, with a possible visit to the Sultan and other Oriental potentates, had roused many another young romantic who took matters of the heart too seriously. A Hungarian *homme du monde,* Count Julius Andrássy, was willing to act as guide for the instructive voyage. And in order that Maxl's pangs of nostalgia might not become too acute it was decided that one of the younger brothers, the complaisant Karl, be added to the baggage. This arrangement served a twofold purpose, for the Archduke Karl might well profit by an opportune ounce of prevention. The pedagogue Bombelles and the parent Sophie nodded owlish heads.

Every one, with the exception of Maxl, was satisfied.

CHAPTER 2

THE Odyssey began in the summer of 1850 and embraced a cruise through Grecian waters to Asia Minor, Egypt and the fabled byways of Capri. At first the two princelets looked timidly backward toward homelier scenes, but soon they began to relish the novelty of each fleeting experience. There was the stormy passage through the Bosporus in the fat Pasha's barge. There was the slave market in Smyrna where the voluptuous bodies of Berber and Nubian beauties were exposed to the haggler's scrutiny. The Archduke Maximilian made notes of his impressions. He was no prude. He wrote down what he saw.

"A naked woman frightens me. I am made to realize that sin is unbearably attractive."

But he remembered Vienna, for he also added: "No matter how stubborn others may be, I am still more headstrong and harder to swerve from my own intentions."

This deep-rooted tenacity, combined with an almost blind sense of loyalty and devotion *ad absurdum* to a cause, largely controlled the pattern of the Archduke's future life. This fault, which is at the same time a virtue, provides the key to his fate.

A great deal happened in Europe during those years of idle roaming. Ambassador Linden and his daughter left Austria for a post in Berlin. The Teutonic capital was becoming Hohenzollern conscious, while across the Channel, a German prince consort to the British Queen urged the building of Albion's navy.

Below the Rhine the Second French Republic changed, by a coup d'état, into a Second Empire and Napoleon III, the *"arriviste* who arrived," scanned the *Almanach de Gotha* for a bride of ancient lineage to buff the newness of his own. He was spurned by every royal pedigree in Europe and thereafter consoled himself with the caresses of a certain Señorita de Montijo, the Spanish granddaughter of a Scotch wine merchant at Málaga. The lady was twenty-seven, well built, and had a bad reputation acquired during years of arduous social climbing. But she would make a fearless sovereign. And, in the words of Lord Palmerston: "He [Napoleon] had no chance of a political alliance of any value, or of sufficient importance to counterbalance the annoyance of an ugly or epileptic wife whom he never saw till she was presented to him as a bride, so it is my opinion that he chose well."

"*Adiós toros!* [Good-by bull-fights!]" wrote Eugenia de Montijo in Spanish to her sister Francisca, Duchess of Alba, whom in the vernacular of the wineshop Kirkpatrick relatives called Paca. The wedding was set for January 30, 1853, at Notre Dame. "I can tell you," continued the glowing bride, "that my heart beats quite fast when I think of the distance we must travel to the church. I do hope nothing happens. . . ." Royal personages are never surprised by the crashing of anarchist bombs; they expect them.

All went well, however. Even so, while the wedding-bells clanged over Paris, stocks at the Bourse dropped to alarming low levels and a European press cackled frostily. But a radiant Eugénie entered the Tuileries, where for seventeen years she was to remain as Empress of the French.

The violence she had feared turned up in Vienna. Within little more than a fortnight the Danube city witnessed the first attempt upon the life of Austria's young monarch. A Hungarian blacksmith named János Libényi had attacked Franz Joseph as the latter took his morning stroll along the Graben. The dagger struck a collar button at the nape of the Emperor's neck, so that the force of the blow was lessened and the direction of the thrust deflected. Franz Joseph bled profusely but he did not collapse.

Investigation disclosed that Hungary, resentful over the persecution of her fanatical patriot, Louis Kossuth, continued to nurture in secret the spark of liberalism released in 1848. Though by no means desirous of a republican form of government the Hungarians, a haughty sovereign people, demanded parliamentary rule after their own pattern. Being of greater size than all the remaining provinces constituting the Empire, Hungary felt entitled to privileges which the latter did not enjoy. The Libényi attempt was a warning coming from the heart of the Magyar nation.

Franz Joseph suffered no physical consequences from the experience, but it completely changed his attitude toward life. He had been serene, happy and trusting. Now he became sensitive and suspicious. Only once did his gentleness and boyish enthusiasm return, in the spring of 1854, when he married the rare and lovely Princess Elisabeth of Bavaria. But the frost had fallen upon his soul. Though, in his own words, he was enamored like a lieutenant and happy as a god, bitterness gnawed at his heart. King Leopold I of Belgium, one of the wedding guests, wrote from Vienna to his niece, the young Queen Victoria of England: "Franzi is transfigured with joy!" Yet Franzi's marriage grew chilled almost from the start by the strange rigidity that had seized the Emperor's whole impressionable being. That was it. Henceforth he was the Emperor. He was the sovereign, and nothing but the sovereign. . . .

Maximilian, immediately upon returning from his enforced travels, sensed this change that had come over his brother. Arriving at the Hofburg, eager and overcome with emotion, he had been received in a formal audience. The old tenderness, the jovial intimacy were gone. Franz Joseph spoke in monosyllables like one who mistrusts words. He asked no questions about Maxl's voyage. Instead he mentioned state affairs and duty. The word duty he pronounced slowly and with unction, as though it were a sublime end in itself. A dagger grazing his spine had focused his whole consciousness upon that word. The millions over whom he ruled, heterogeneous and multilingual as they were, looked to him for its fulfilment. Duty. Or death. He had been shown.

The very atmosphere about the Hofburg was different. The Archduchess Sophie's merry dancing parties were no more. Instead, that benevolent lady had turned her iron will to more serious matters. She was initiating a frightened sixteen-year-old girl who answered to the title of "Kaiserin Elisabeth" into the rigorous precepts of Hapsburg etiquette. For the princess from Bavaria came out of a pastoral environment. In her eyes still shone the memory of rustic freedom on the lakes and hills of her native Possenhofen.

Nor was this the full extent of the Dowager Sophie's activities.

For some time past she had been engaged in furthering a project that lay very close to her ambitious heart. Pleased with Franz Joseph's sober development, she now wished an advantageous marriage for her irresponsible Maxl. Even before the latter's return to Vienna negotiations had been opened with the Portuguese royal house. There was an available Braganza girl, young, a trifle delicate, and—if reports given out by relatives, who wanted to be rid of her, could be trusted—very charming indeed.

The unsuspecting Maximilian was dazed by the news. He hadn't surrendered an inch in his determination to have the little Linden, and here he was suddenly engaged! His mother must be mad. . . . He stewed and fretted over his absurd fate when that same fate came quietly to his rescue. The maid at Lisbon had been more delicate, apparently, than her eager kin would admit. She wilted somewhat abruptly and died before a stitch had been taken in her trousseau.

The Austrian Court wore mourning and Maxl went about with a grave mien. When gravity palled he conversed with his delightful sister-in-law, recounting to her the colorful cycle of his adventures abroad. Elisabeth, herself an incurable romantic who was to spend so much of her restless life roaming over the earth, listened with hungry rapture.

Another thing which these two had in common was their love of sports. Among royalty, to no one's great surprise, excellent horsemanship is the rule. But Franz Joseph had cried, as a baby, when he was put on his pony. Even though in later years he drilled himself into perfect mastery over his mount, he never rode for pleasure. Maxl, on the other hand, was mad about horses and invariably tore along at a wild gallop. "I don't know how to ride slowly," he complained. He found more than his match in the amazon prowess of Elisabeth. At times, carried away by their insatiable thirst for action, they argued about the merits of a new invention then in its experimental stages, the air-balloon. "It must be from flying alone," they raved, "that one can expect an extraordinary sensation."

Speculations of this sort were profoundly distasteful to the earthbound Sophie. She would far rather have seen her daughter-in-law occupied with plans of expectant motherhood. As for Maxl, something had to be done about his equestrian passion. There was actually about him a faint odor of stable.

Perhaps Bombelles had an idea. Sniffing disdainfully, the Archduchess prepared for another conference with the tutor.

Bombelles had an idea. To be sure, not a very novel one. He suggested more travel. *"Sapristi,"* the Archduchess wanted to know, "where to?"

At this the old confidant smiled sagely. "Why not France?" he inquired softly. "They have a new Emperor over there. It might be well to hear how this fresh Bonaparte broom is sweeping. . . ."

The scheme was an admirable one. Franz Joseph submitted it to his ministers, who vouchsafed their unanimous approval. Information regarding the methods employed by other governments might help Austria in her difficult internal policy. The Archduke Maximilian must be groomed at once for his task. He must review his linguistic equipment, take a supplementary peep at history, and above all things grow a beard. For overnight the world had plunged into the era of abundantly decorated male chins. After the long line of clean-shaven Bourbons, Frederick the Great, the first Napoleon, the handsome Romanov (Alexander I—who waltzed through the Vienna Congress), royalty had suddenly consolidated in a defiant gesture against the nude complexions of those giants of yesteryear. Even though they had yet to make history, the gentlemen of the 1850's were determined to flourish the most convincing facial attributes of manhood.

In England the Prince Consort, Albert of Coburg, surprised his doting Vicky by slowly hiding behind an impressive array of whiskers that completely changed his rather pretty young face. Henceforth, though he was barely thirty, the stolid, middle-aged, frocked husband of the Queen became the symbol of respectability.

In France the obscure nephew of a famous uncle strove to give the Bonaparte throne "a new coat of glory paint." Before measuring his strength on the battle-field, however, Napoleon III looked to his figure. Was it cut after the fashionable heroic pattern? His beard, despite coaxing salves and ointments, grew in a disappointing, meager stubble. L'Empereur was perplexed, humiliated. At last his barber hit upon a clever solution. The *impériale,* "a pointed tuft of hair left on a man's upper lip and chin," was devised, the Court rejoiced, and Pliny Beauchamp—the barber—received a medal for his inspiration.

In Prussia sundry Hohenzollerns strutted masterfully behind a hirsute garnish while St. Petersburg was to witness a line of Tsars, beginning with the colossal Nicholas, who looked as alike as the heroes in Sudermann's novels.

Everywhere the masculine note predominated. Butcher-boys and operatic tenors stroked their shirt-fronts, hopefully noting the most insignificant sign of capillary progress. European capitals had presently an ominous dark look about them which seemed to make for romance of a grim and paleozoic order.

It was only natural that the Hapsburgs should have been affected. They, of all people, were as a family self-conscious about their hereditary prognathous jaw. True, this characteristic mark had been noticeably modified after 1736, the year of Maria Theresia's marriage to Francis, Duke of Lorraine. The old Hapsburg stock had died out with Charles VI, father of the great Empress. The present house of "Hapsburg-Lothringen" retained less of the ancient trait than had been given to the French Bourbons by Marie Antoinette, and to the Spanish Bourbons by Charles V, Philip II, or Crazy Jane, the madwoman of Castile.

Even so, Franz Joseph welcomed the new fashion and gave it his ardent approval. It coincided with his self-imposed solemnity, his stern point of view. Promptly the young Emperor stopped shaving. As the growth on his jaw increased, vanity caused him to consider a point. He did not wish people to say that he was concealing the notorious defect of his house. Accordingly, his well-shaped chin was allowed to remain perfectly exposed and the famous *"Kaiserbart"* was originated.

Maxl rather admired his brother's bid for individualism and concentrated on achieving something equally unique. In his own case there was not so much a strong as a weak chin to cover, despite the prominent lower lip. Maxl experimented. He tried out different patterns. At last he emerged with a sort of variation on the Prince Albert theme, with a part in the middle and a small pointed twist at each end. The color of this masterpiece was golden, a shade admirably calculated to work havoc with susceptible maiden hearts.

The necessary preparations for a diplomatic visit to foreign parts having been herewith completed, the Archduke Maximilian was ready to set out. At the last moment his mother was overcome by the illuminating force of another of her staggering schemes. Why not, as long as he was going so far away, make a more exhaustive tour of the Continent and take stock of matrimonial prospects? The Archduke protested in horror. He had just rejoiced in accidentally gaining his freedom from the Portuguese entanglement. But the Dowager Sophie was never known to lose an argument. Maxl's itinerary was changed and amplified to look like a modern Baedeker.

Coincident with his departure from Vienna a pleasant and intriguing rumor spread rapidly through the European capitals. A handsome and unattached Hapsburg prince was traveling about in search, it was murmured, of a suitable bride. The twenty-three-year-old Archduke Ferdinand Maximilian, so the insidious gossip ran, had recently passed through a sad affair of the heart, his betrothed, a Princess of Braganza, falling suddenly ill of a fatal disease. The romantic and disconsolate lover had forthwith been given a furlough from his duties as an admiral in the navy and sent on a pleasure trip to the Orient. From here he had returned, after years of maturing, as a veritable Harun-al-Rashid.

It was not difficult for the tall blond Archduke to ride to glory on the crest of such publicity. He opened his transcontinental tour by first calling on his relative, Spain's regent queen. This spendthrift lady, from whose Court the youthful Eugenia de Montijo had once flounced in disgrace and a pair of provocative trousers, received her imperial guest with lavish honors. But, there being no available princesses about, Maximilian spent his time appropriately visiting the tombs of the Spanish Hapsburgs in the Escorial.

Here, in the dank ill-smelling crypt, the mystery of Philip II's oracle confronted him. In the octagon-shaped chamber at the center of the mausoleum this eccentric monarch had fitted out a permanent abode for his embalmed ancestors. That was not all. After providing accommodation for ten defunct forebears he had added, with dreadful insight, space for as many crowned successors to himself as he deemed probable. Tier upon tier the marble coffins stood, thirty in all. And only three were empty. . . . But the Queen, Isabella II, was fitting up a nursery in her palace at Madrid for the expected heir, Alfonso XII. Would there then be but one more Alfonso? A thirteenth? . . . The Archduke sank into uncomfortable reflection while a phlegmatic guard rattled a bunch of keys.

"When they are all full," the man said, pointing to the coffins, "we will get the Republic."

Maximilian felt a sudden chill. After polite farewells he presently departed from sunny Spain.

Some time later, on May 17, 1856, he bobbed up in Paris. Prince Napoleon "Plon-Plon" (son of King Jerome of Westphalia, and a cousin of Napoleon III) made up the welcoming committee at the station, a fact which emphasized the sulky attitude of the Bonapartes toward the old aristocracies that had scorned them. Maxl's pen described the reception to Franz Joseph in something of a pique. "He [Plon-Plon] conducted himself in a manner so crude and stiff that, as a reprisal, I felt bound to show extreme aloofness."

At the palace of St. Cloud, whither the Court moved every spring, the Emperor of the French awaited his unexpected guest at the top of the steps—another mark of subtle defiance. "Napoleon's stubby, unimposing stature," goes the report to Vienna, "his shuffling walk, ugly hands and sly, inquisitive glance make a most ungainly impression."

Yet, in spite of discoursing so freely on his host's physical shortcomings the Archduke remained in Paris for a total of twelve highly interesting days. For, to tell the truth, he was completely dazzled by the modern advancement of the Ville Lumière.

Those were the elegant days of the Second Empire. The feminine world had skipped swiftly from the clinging fashion of high directoire waists into the hoops of an exaggerated crinoline (invented by Worth for the Empress Eugénie, in order to conceal her pregnancy). It was the era of mechanical discoveries. While a bold architect named Haussmann tore open the narrow thoroughfares of Paris to make room for a colossal system of boulevards, public fancy was dazzled by a tinkling electric telegraph, smoke-belching steamboats, locomotives and the isolation of a "remarkable featherweight metal called aluminium." Very elegant people introduced into their plush-decked parlors an American contraption known as a rocking chair. Adelina Patti sang at the Opera. Taglioni set Paris aflame with her dance *La Sylphide,* only to be eclipsed by Fanny Elssler with her ballet *Le Diable Boiteux.* Zola's *Nana* started on her lurid though diverting career, while in the boulevard cafés Victor Hugo, Sainte-Beuve, Lamartine, de Musset, and Théophile Gautier lamented the lost Republic, upheld *Les Misérables* and protested against the persecution of *Madame Bovary's* radical author, Gustave Flaubert.

After the Biedermeier provincialism of his native Vienna Maxl could not but admit, however grudgingly, that France surpassed in cultural advancement anything he had heretofore seen. In time he also revised his first unflattering impression of Napoleon III, for the latter's simplicity and quick changes of mood revealed engaging and likable qualities. But to Plon-Plon Maxl would not soften. "He absolutely looks like a worn-out basso in an Italian opera," was the final verdict on that sorry figure.

The Crimean War, in which England and France joined forces against the Tsar for the benefit of the Sultan, had been fought out to a Pyrrhic victory only two years before. How the winning parties actually felt was evidenced by a half-joking remark made by Napoleon III in an unguarded moment and promptly committed to paper by the alert Maximilian. "That was a deplorable business," commented L'Empereur, "to have bolstered up the Turks, the stupidest people in the world, but Russia had to be thrust back where she belonged." The formation of alliances was governed, as ever, not by determination of right or wrong but by expediency alone.

Concerning the celebrated Eugénie the Archduke had also something to say. "Her beauty is undeniable, though it owes much to artifice and shows really no trace of the Spanish type. She seems *rassig* [thoroughbred] and educated, but singularly lacking in that august quality one expects of an empress; her charm pales beside that of Sisi. . . . [Franz Joseph's consort, Elisabeth]."

It is possible that Eugénie did not show up to best advantage because the pangs of jealousy—which were to eat into her soul for so many years to come—had already begun. Regardless of her slightly unsavory past, as a wife and mother she had raised herself to a standard of impeccable decorum. But the Emperor, of whom she had written so ardently to Paca: "I love him,—this is a vast guaranty for our happiness; he is devoted and noble of heart" . . . deceived her at every turn, even with her own ladies-in-waiting. A year after the imperial wedding Countess Castiglione was the favorite. Some time later a Countess Walewska (wife of a natural son of Napoleon I) occupied the fickle sovereign's fancy, only to be replaced by a Princess Troubetzkoi from St. Petersburg and, in turn, a vivacious Labedoyère. Both the latter ladies were friends of the Duc de Morny, half-brother to Napoleon III, and love-child of the gay Hortense.

The Spaniard did not take these things lightly. It was her pride which suffered most under the affronts of her husband's conduct. She who had been hailed as an international beauty found the rôle of a discarded wife bitter beyond measure.

The growing marital rift must have been already noticeable during those early years, for the disapproving Maxl wrote:

"A flock of adventurers swarms about this decidedly *parvenu* Court. I should classify among them a certain Countess Castiglione, born a Marchesa Oldoini, whose unusual beauty is matched only by her brazen and impertinent conduct. This creature may harm the domestic relations between Emperor and Empress. Already the courtiers are competing with one another for her favors. . . . Princess Mathilde (Plon-Plon's sister) and the Countess Hatzfeld complained to me furiously—and with that disconcerting candor of the French—about her lack of decency in seizing this opportunity (Eugénie's child, the Prince Imperial, was born only two months ago) for supplanting the Empress. However that mav be, Napoleon's interest in every attractive female is becoming notorious and will greatly diminish his prestige as a sovereign."

Having thus spoken his mind on a variety of subjects the Archduke bethought himself of packing and continuing on his way. The French imperial yacht *Reine Hortense* being placed at his disposal, he was able to make a brief call in London where an enamored little queen fluttered about her royal tasks and kept a fatuous diary. Yorkshire puddings at Osborne, military reviews at Aldershot, as well as a bit of battledore and shuttlecock with Victoria and Albert made up the English sojourn, after which Maximilian hastened eastward to the homeland of his greatest ancestor, the Fleming Charles the Fifth.

Chapter 3

The diminutive kingdom of Belgium, born in the revolutionary year of 1830 (which separated the Catholic from the Protestant Netherlands), marched proudly in the parade of European nations under the capable rule of its first monarch, the German princelet Leopold I of Saxe-Coburg-Gotha. This brilliant Nestor and doyen among sovereigns was rapidly earning for his house the Latin pasquinade applied once exclusively to the Hapsburgs: *Bella gerant alii—tu, felix Austria, nube.* Others wage wars (for power)—you, happy Austria, marry.

For the sweeping rise of the Coburgs to world prominence was due largely to Leopold's machinations as a matrimonial agent. "*Marquis Peu à Peu* [Little by Little]" the Hanoverian Georges called him, unable to fathom the secret of his success since "that fellow, damn it, will drink no wine!"

As for Leopold's healthy opportunism, he himself was the last to make apology for it. Long before the Belgian Crown was offered him he had become a naturalized Briton and married the English Princess Charlotte, only daughter of "Prinny," the Prince Regent (later George IV). Finding himself thus in agreeable proximity to England's throne Leopold at once began to nurse hidden aspirations. But on a chill November night of the year 1817 Charlotte died in childbed at Castle Claremont near Esher, putting an end to his schemes. Leopold returned to the Continent, where in due time he wooed and won Louise Marie of the fallen Orléans and Bourbon line. Politically the union proved a miscalculation since the Bonapartes and not the Bourbons regained the throne of France. For this Leopold hated the Bonapartes.

Some time thereafter he presented a bridegroom to his young niece, Victoria of England, in the person of his favorite nephew Albert, whom the virtuous if not brilliant queen loved devotedly until fate cut short her bliss. Under Leopold's sponsorship a Coburg lad assumed the crown of Portugal as consort to the voluptuous Maria da Gloria, while for his own son—the future Léopold II of Congo fame and infamy—the Belgian monarch chose a frolicsome Archduchess Henriette of Austria. And lastly, in the autumn of 1856, the busy king longed to do as well, if not better, in carving a future for his sixteen-year-old daughter Charlotte.

This slender, impulsive girl whose passionate dark eyes and superior intelligence caused her father to declare that she would grow up to be Europe's most alluring princess, was the child of his second marriage. The tactful or obedient mother had named the baby after her husband's first wife. Little Charlotte's additional names were Marie Amélie Augustine Victoire Clémentine Léopoldine.

At the time of the Archduke Ferdinand Maximilian's announced visit to Brussels Queen Louise, daughter of the exiled Louis Philippe, had been dead for some years. King Leopold, now aged sixty-six, had retired to a quiet existence in the ancient and neglected palace of Laeken. From here he had dispatched his oldest son, the Duke of Brabant, to the coast to receive the nation's exalted guest.

Maxl's visit to Brussels promised many delights. Belgium welcomed this scion of her former ruling house with unrestrained enthusiasm. Even the old palace at Laeken rang with merriment and laughter for King Leopold had planned festivities. Charlotte herself, in the full flush of adolescence, became dazzled by the dashing Austrian prince with whom it was not difficult to fall in love. Romance seemed to be budding in the gloomy mists of Brussels.

But Maximilian had been fortified by his first experience in heart-break. Time and travel had finally dimmed his memory of that adorable Countess Linden whom he had loved so strenuously so many years ago, although he wondered, still with something of a pang, whether his path would ever again cross hers. He wondered, too, with a gnawing curiosity, where in all creation she had disappeared to. Thus it happened that the obvious rapture in Charlotte's innocent eyes never pierced his consciousness.

His letters to Vienna did not even mention her name. He reported with naïve astonishment that one could travel the whole length of King Leopold's realm without difficulty in a couple of hours. "I find this the most cultivated flowering land that I have yet seen. The Court is well managed; in all the towns splendid carriages awaited me. On the other hand, the equipment in the various palaces is pretty bad. The northern suburb of Laeken boasts an interesting residence, but the palace in Brussels has not even a stone staircase. Everything seems to be made of wood."

As a foreign correspondent the Archduke Maxl was disclosing unexpected talents. In still another missive he engaged quite frankly in some family gossip. Cousin Henriette, the Duchess of Brabant, was persisting in the hoydenish habits of her youth and shocking the stolid Coburg relatives. As a girl she had sufficiently exasperated Vienna society by purchasing a milkman's nag, unharnessing the creature in the middle of a crowded thoroughfare and riding off to the cheers of a joyful populace. Such pranks were very well for Henriette's juvenile era, but she was now—Maxl had figured it out—fully twenty years old, and her frivolity would not add to Hapsburg prestige abroad. What was more, Henriette had always been plump, but now she looked positively dumpy and uglier than ever. (Archduke Karl, who had impersonated the Duke of Brabant during the proxy wedding in Vienna, had accepted this office under protest and with the words: "Well, I'll be bridegroom, if I don't have to keep the bride!") But there was the duke. One had to think of the duke.

While these opinions, scattered freely by the philosophical Maxl, should really have made good reading at the Hofburg, their perusal brought nothing but frowns to the brows of his unappreciative kin. The Dowager Sophie, in particular, grew daily more chagrined at her second son's bland evasion of that which had become her principal concern, his marriage.

A stern epistle reached him by return post. After all, Henriette was settled, wasn't she? But what about himself? Had he bothered taking a look at King Leopold's daughter? Or did he intend writing memoirs as a profession? . . .

Even across the distance of a continent maternal authority gripped him. He took a belated look at Charlotte. She was slender, elegant, and it struck him that she gave promise of blossoming into a great beauty. Her eyes were a little strange. The pupils looked large and black, but they were surrounded by a dark green iris. Spaniards called such eyes *ojos garzos* because they resembled the phosphorescent orbs of the tropical heron.

She spoke to him in French, a French that seemed at first peculiar until he realized it was the Belgian accent. With the little Linden he had whispered in Viennese. . . . And now he shuddered with sudden realization. Here was the crux of all dynastic marriages! Unions they must be of alien spirits, alien tongues, otherwise they could be of no value to the State. The State! That greedy monster for whose satisfaction he must now pretend that he was overcome by the fascination of this girl, this child, this stranger who stood before him in her prim lace-covered frock.

His mother's letter, enlarged by a tiresome postscript in the hand of Count Bombelles, rustled thickly in his pocket. The words Duty, Honor, Self-Sacrifice, danced before his eyes in capital letters. But all his instincts yearned automatically for escape. At least he had a right to complete his itinerary and glance over the narrow field assigned to him before he chose—the word was terrifying—a wife.

In Madrid, Paris and London, where no such problems had beset him, it was easy enough to proffer exquisite *adieux*. To face the expectant Leopold was infinitely more difficult. Leopold was too old to remember the human urge for self-preservation. He froze to a stone when he understood. So; the Archduke had yet to visit Holland and Hanover—he did not want to miss anything, the prudent Hapsburg. Trembling with rage the offended King buried his dream. Absently he stroked the head of the infatuated girl who had flung herself weeping into her father's arms.

The object of her sorrow, meanwhile, had scurried to The Hague where again to his vast relief he encountered a childless royal household. The effect upon Maxl's spirits was akin to a tonic. Cheerfully he continued eastward. And then, in Berlin, something happened.

It was at a court ball given in honor of the visiting Archduke. The glittering assembly of royalties and foreign diplomats had gathered under the burning chandeliers and the imported gypsy orchestra had struck up the season's newest waltz hit. Ferdinand Maximilian stood under the high canopy at one end of the great salon and stared at the whirling couples. They looked like a mad pattern of ever-changing colors. Above the din of shuffling feet one could hardly distinguish the orchestra. He wondered what Hohenzollern princess had been selected for his dance partner and how soon he would be obliged to plunge with her into the breathless maelstrom.

He was still wondering when, in the blurred confusion of that crowd, his eyes were caught suddenly by a fine and charming face. He rushed forward a few paces and checked himself at the very edge of that dancing sea. But now he had lost the view afforded by his former position, or else he had been imagining things. . . . With searching glance he regarded the couples that brushed past him, and now he was certain.

"Is that Countess Linden?" he inquired from some one near who didn't matter but who wore a diplomatic ribbon. "Over there beside the mirrors; here, now she is coming toward us!"

The man he had addressed looked up a trifle puzzled. "I don't know, sir, unless you mean Baroness von Bülow," he said slowly, "dancing with her husband——"

"Countess Linden," Maximilian repeated impatiently, "in the black dress, with the silver diadem in her hair——"

"Linden," came the voice again, "yes, her father was a colleague of mine, we served together in——"

But the Archduke was not listening. He had stepped back from the dance floor and at this distance fixed his eyes upon the woman who was Baroness von Bülow. She, too, had seen him. She had known he would be here and had waited in a blissful sort of torment for the sight of him.

He was changed. The unfamiliar beard made him look older, more mature. As he stood there, towering above the others with that arrogant figure equaled only by the Romanov Grand Dukes, she found him more beautiful than ever. And more remote. Her father's voice came back to her: "I advise you not to imagine anything . . ."

The dance brought them closer together; over the shoulder of the man whose name she now bore their eyes met. In hers there quivered an almost angry childlike question: "Why? Why did you leave me?" In his, no answer. Only a deep burning ache.

The music had wound up with a Strauss potpourri. The melody which once had rocked their dream of love to heights of innocent ecstasy returned now in a sad and mellow key:

The pretty Baroness von Bülow danced on in the arms of her unsuspecting husband. The imperial scion returned to the canopy and the shadow of a throne. They had found him a Prussian princess by this time but he declined with profuse apologies. This was, he confessed, the anniversary of a profound loss. He had not wanted to mention it before, but dancing would be out of the question.

While a distressed Potsdam Master of Ceremonies and the highest Privy Councilors of the Prussian King strove for weeks to discover their error in ignoring what seemed to have been a particularly painful Hapsburg bereavement, the restless Maxl had finished his wanderings. Peremptory calls at the remaining major capitals of Europe had ended with his speedy and unheralded return to Vienna. This time he stopped at no florist's shop but drove directly to the Hofburg. The old building engulfed him like a prison. He thought of it as a symbol of his circumscribed and barren life.

The family gathered about him in a flutter of agitation. Well, what had he seen? What had he done for the betterment of the Empire and himself? Were congratulations in order?

Maxl had nothing to say. His head ached, and, anyway, what did they all mean by jumping on him? . . . He felt on the verge of an illness.

For several weeks more he moped about in his rooms, brooding and scheming thoughts of liberty. If he could leave Austria forever and become a new person somewhere in a new world! Had he not relatives in South America? His Aunt Leopoldine (sister of Napoleon the Great's second wife, Marie Louise) had espoused the Emperor of Brazil, Dom Pedro de Braganza. But that was precisely the trouble; he had relatives in every part of the world and being in contact with them meant that he must respect their terms.

The little Linden had treated him very badly, too. She might have waited a bit longer before getting herself tied up in a bourgeois marriage. He had intended finding her all along, she must have known that. But then, a person with such extraordinary and inexplicable eyes, dark in the center, and about the edges of a strange unholy green . . .

Now he knew something must be wrong. The girl of his boyhood romance had no such eyes as his imagination painted. Nor did she have that heart-shaped face with its expression, so bitter-sweet, of a first awakening. . . . He realized slowly that before his unhappy fancy there moved the poignant vision of King Leopold's *petite fille*.

It was not love. His honesty told him that. Besides, he wasn't interested in love at the moment; he was unhappy. And because of this he remembered with an intense clarity that look of desolation on Charlotte's face at the instant of bidding him farewell. Charlotte was unhappy. She was a princess. She knew the fetters, the bondage that were his. Far better than the little Linden who had consoled herself so quickly, Charlotte understood what lay ahead of him, of them all, the blue-bloods! An irrelevant thought struck him. If Charlotte, with whom in his suffering he felt a spiritual kinship, were to know love and to lose love, she might not console herself—ever. It was a strange thought. It was crazy. Because of course he didn't love Charlotte.

Even so, in December of that year a secret messenger, later disclosed as one Count Arquinto, left the Hofburg. He arrived in Brussels bearing the Archduke Maximilian's request for the hand of King Leopold's only daughter.

It was a day of triumph for the Coburg parent. Bursting inwardly with satisfaction at the attainment of this desired end, the

Belgian King concealed whatever rancor he still harbored. But he was to enjoy a sly revenge. Before a date for the marriage could be agreed upon, a serious complication arose in the matter of a royal dowry. King Leopold, whose two wives had brought him noble connections and a generous accumulation of debts, did not believe in dowries. Charlotte was to have her mother's jewels, a small sum of money voted by the Chambers, and an elaborate wedding festival at the church of Sainte Gudule. But, loving father though he might be, he would not agree to impoverish his small constitutional kingdom by parceling its estates among those of his children who married into foreign lands.

This standpoint was very new to Hapsburg ears. One did not enter the sacred and exclusive circle of Europe's most ancient dynasty without bearing gifts worthy of acceptance. The Hofburg favored retreat. But with that impetuosity which characterized him, Maximilian had already announced his troth to the four winds. Retreat was impossible without losing face.

Negotiations with Belgium grew more pressing. Leopold was deluged with diplomatic advice. But the shrewd King gave a shopkeeper's shrug of shoulders and for the rest remained adamant.

The Emperor of Austria was left in an awkward quandary. Wedding invitations having already been issued to the governments of all major powers, Franz Joseph was obliged to save the prestige of his house by providing the prospective newly-weds with a suitable *dot*. After some reflection he appointed his brother to the rank of viceroy over the Upper Italian provinces of Lombardy and Venice, which were at that time subject to the Austrian Crown.

This magnanimous gesture imbued Maximilian with a certain eminence abroad and at the same time removed the ambitious young man from Vienna, where it was feared he might ultimately dabble in politics. Unknown to Maxl, during his prolonged absence from home Hungary had clamored again for a separate king. Rumors were current to the effect that the Archduke Ferdinand Maximilian would make a desirable candidate. Franz Joseph had reason to suspect his debonair brother of Magyar sympathies.

For the moment, however, such alarms were both premature and pointless. After the royal wedding, which took place at Brussels on July 27, 1857, Maxl was far too busy adjusting himself to that which he had done. He had taken a radiant young creature across the Alps and deposited her in a vast medieval palazzo at Milan. He had dreaded being alone with this strange person who, because of a few words spoken in a crowded cathedral, was now a part of him "forever." Yet being alone with her had brought the solution of his ills. Almost from the start Charlotte's strong impassioned nature was able to transform this plainly calculated union into a bond of overpowering happiness.

Oddly enough, she was not a timid doting spouse. Despite her youth (she was seventeen) and her humble surrender to love, she became a compelling goddess at her own hearth.

In time it was Maximilian who virtually knelt at her feet.

CHAPTER 4

CHARLOTTE thoroughly enjoyed Italy. After the dark foggy winters of her native land she basked luxuriously in the southern sun. At night, when the great balconies of the palazzo opened to the caressing breeze, music was wafted upward from the street, lending enchantment to the foreign scene.

A romantic poet stirred the Neapolitans at that time with his ethereal ballads. His melodies were carried from town to town by artists and beggars alike, until they reached Milan and the crooked byways that surrounded the Viceroy's mansion. Here Charlotte heard, for the first time, Tosti's tender love-songs and the full beauty of a language she did not know.

> *"Vola—O serenata: la mia diletta è sola,*
> *E con la bella testa abbandonata*
> *Posa tra le lenzuola—*
> *O serenata vola,*
> *O serenata vola. . . ."*

Under the spell of those accents she presently changed her name to the Italian Carlotta and persuaded her young husband to engage for them a private tutor. Daily, after his government tasks were completed, Maxl found himself perched on an uncomfortable stool of the cinquecento with a Roman grammar propped upon his knees. And soon, with an undeniable thrill, he too was able to make out the madrigals of passing troubadours.

Tosti's songs in time fluttered across Europe and beguiled the sentimental Queen of England. Discounting all major obstacles, the mistress of Windsor summoned the composer for a private hearing before her Court. He came, fell victim to Britannic blandishments, and was knighted. Sir Francesco Paolo Tosti was the impressive title that estranged him forever from the homeland of his earlier muse.

But romancing alone did not fill Carlotta's days. She was in-tent upon becoming her husband's valuable aide in his difficult administration of the provinces. Alas, they were the dangerous heritage of a bloody past. In his mad rush for world power the first Napoleon had torn up the Italian peninsula into small fragments which he distributed among his other vassals. To Austria, over whose fields and woodlands the Corsican must drive his legions en route to Moscow, he had ceded the duchies of Parma, Modena, and the northern regions of the Po. This was a sort of recompense for the rental due on the palace of Schönbrunn in Vienna, where, without a by-your-leave, the conqueror had made his headquarters.

After two generations of military governors and princely despots Austria was still having a bad time with those "gifts." The kindest and most innocuous Hapsburg who might enter Milan or Venice as viceroy was looked upon by rankled natives as a foreign tyrant. However, because of their youth and personal charm, Maximilian and Carlotta were able to overcome much antagonism. Soon their florid carriage was greeted in the streets and public squares with friendly cheers.

For a time Carlotta became a familiar figure in the flower and fruit market. The countless new blossoms and delicacies offered by this sun-drenched country never ceased to interest her, for she had become suddenly absorbed in the complex task of housekeeping.

To royalty, enmeshed in appalling ceremonial, the management of a palace assumes gigantic proportions. Few dynasties in history have attempted to interfere with the autocratic dispositions of their majordomos. But the Coburgs were a recent and almost middle-class edition of royalty. They liked putting fingers in pies. In England the Prince Consort had introduced an expense account for Buckingham Palace. All the prodigal habits of Stuarts, Tudors and burly Hanoverians were frowned upon and discarded. Since time immemorial candles once lighted had been thrown out and never used again by his Lordship, the Keeper of Lights. But Albert the Good condemned this practise. He saved on the candle bill and demanded an exact reckoning of pantry and cellar expenditures.

Even so, neither he nor Cousin Vicky herself had been able to annihilate the demon of tradition. According to an ancient custom which seemed absolutely irrevocable, the Lord Chamberlain had charge of washing the palace windows on the inside, while the Department of Woods and Forestry attended to them from without. Both parties were imbued with an admirable sense of duty and went about their respective tasks with commendable punctilio. But they could not agree on the time when each would function in behalf of the Queen's balconies. If the Lord Chamberlain splashed merrily from within it appeared that Woods and Forestry could not from without, and the same held true when the latter arrived with brandished poles and mops. And so, throughout her long and blessed reign, Victoria's windows were never quite clean.

Carlotta meant to do things very much better. Having only a fraction of her cousin's servant army at her command, she personally supervised each task about the old mansion. It absorbed her active, energetic spirit to perceive the multitude of trivial motions required to keep a domestic establishment alive. At Laeken she had never thought of her environment. It was part of the stilted frame into which she had been born and fitted as the daughter of a king. Nor did years of careful schooling awaken her, for she had been taught to see nothing and never to ask questions. It was a day when royal governesses preached: "*Il faut que les princesses aprennent à s'ennuyer avec grâce.* [Princesses should learn to be gracefully bored.]"

But now she heard from her chatty Tuscan maid that dust must be wiped off peasant tables as well, and dry leaves plucked from the hyacinths. A similarity of joys and needs pervaded all earthly stations. The world must be made fresh each day for each day's living. Even the humble had a part in this, perhaps a greater part than the mighty.

She was beginning to understand so much about the actual flavor of existence. Having been instructed as a child to walk past open doors without peering in, she now unlearned, marching through them eagerly and looking about her with gusto. Everything had acquired a fuller meaning since she herself was allowed to be a part of everything.

And then, at the peak of this newly found happiness, the Venetian honeymoon came to an end.

There lived in Italy an embittered statesman, Count Camillo Benso di Cavour, who dreamed of a united kingdom under Sicilian rule. A few years ago, during the inglorious Crimean War, this prudent patriot had joined the winning side; France was indebted to him. In return for past services Cavour now demanded French assistance in his struggle against Austria.

Napoleon III was not obdurate. In exchange for "Nice and a slice of Savoy" he promised to look into the matter. Secret agents were sent to Lombardy and Venice, there to engage in systematic agitation against Austrian rule. This was followed up by an ominous and decidedly Napoleonic rolling of drums. Although for more than two years Maximilian and his bride had enjoyed warmest sympathies throughout the provinces, their popularity at length could not withstand the gathering storm. Somewhere in the Tyrol a bewildered Austrian sentry was accused of overstepping an invisible border-line. A shot was fired and the tussle began.

"The conflict was contrived," wrote Lord Palmerston in his memoirs, "after some exertion by that meddlesome mediocrity, Napoleon III, in whose brain foolish ideas multiply like rabbits."

It turned out to be a brief imbroglio into which Austria's proud young Emperor Franz Joseph stumbled angrily. His beautiful white cavalry was beaten at Magenta and Solferino. The year 1859 brought panic and flight for Maximilian and Carlotta who, after the dismal news, were forced to retire to their summer castle of Miramar at Trieste. An age-old dictum had once more held true: "France hates Austria and fights her on Italian soil."

The idyl of Milan might well have continued now on the peaceful shores of the Adriatic. Miramar was a palace built of brilliant white limestone and Carrara marble, rising from the sea on a rocky peninsula that overlooked the harbor. It had been started by the Archduke Maximilian shortly after his marriage and had barely reached completion when its owners made a forced occupation.

On first seeing it Carlotta found the place an enchanting paradise. Great care had been devoted to its planning. The soil for the gardens had been brought from far away so that oleanders, olives, myrtles and laurels might grow in wonted profusion. The granite for the terraces had been quarried in the Tatra Mountains; the sphinxes that adorned them were from Egypt.

As for the interior, Maxl's tastes were everywhere apparent. With the exception of Carlotta's sitting-room and boudoir, the marine note predominated throughout, bespeaking the owner's profession. Maximilian's study was a copy of the commandant's quarters on the frigate *Novara*. Here and in the great salons all draperies were of blue damask embroidered with a pattern of anchors. The name Miramar—"View of the Sea"—had long been made famous by Spanish kings in their pleasure haunts along the Bay of Biscay.

But pleasure haunt the palace on the Adriatic did not become. Within its walls the Archduke and his bride experienced the first mental anguish of their wedded life. Their departure from Italy had, after all, been an escape from physical danger. At Miramar they were safe—too safe. They had nothing to do. As viceroy, Maximilian had lost his post in the Austrian fleet. The war, on the other hand, had reduced that modest body to such insignificance that a plea for reinstatement was ridiculous.

Things were easier for Carlotta. She was eager to try out her newly acquired domestic prowess in this fresh environment. Together with the archducal treasurer, Jakob von Kuhacsevich, she inspected the estate. How many flowers she would have for her vases! What luscious oranges, pomegranates, figs, to be picked at sundown and gathered in her little basket of gilt straw with its bow of blue moiré ribbon. She fancied herself a second Marie Antoinette, strenuously busy in a rococo landscape of perfumed rivulets, illumined grottoes and flowering pastures over which scrubbed cows were led on silken bands and milked into Dresden china buckets decorated with the Bourbon crest. Not that her own taste coincided with the atrocious Petit Trianon. The cows, the buckets and the perfume she could do without. But there was in her that same readiness to play house and imitate the outward gestures of living which had beset the ill-fated Queen of France.

She started out bravely enough, reading up on botany and discussing its finer points with her unlettered gardener. Maxl grew stimulated by her energy. Endowed with those unprofitable accomplishments which preserve royalty's amateur standing, he ventured out into fields of his own and improved the shining hours with painting and modeling. The results, be it said to his credit, discouraged him. He next developed literary inclinations. Recalling his early travels, he sat down and penned a series of memoirs, travel sketches, aphorisms and poems. They turned out much better than his sculptural efforts and preserved much that is revealing concerning his youth and later development. But these dilettante activities could not satisfy his innate craving for a man's profession; nor could they still his re-awakened hunger for adventure and the sea.

Carlotta, too, began to grow restless. Music, letter-writing and embroidery, the feminine pastimes of the age, held her attention briefly. She sang now and then, in her beautiful mezzo-contralto voice, the melodies that had lent magic to those vanished Italian nights. . . . She moved about with her quick step through marble corridors. But she knew she was going nowhere.

This went on for months. They were bored, hopelessly bored. They seemed, in fact, to have been forgotten. No one ever came to see them. Once, in the early viceregal days, King Leopold had paid them a short visit at Monza. But that was long ago. In those days they had held—on however small a scale—a Court of their own.

Suddenly, in the early 1860's, Maxl could stand it no longer. He ordered a few bags packed, lifted his wife into a stage-coach, and set out with her for Vienna. The need for human contacts had become acute.

The reception at the Hofburg was not exactly enthusiastic. Apparently the spook of a Hungarian Pretender had not been laid. On the contrary, England, in the person of Lord John Russell, had added to Franz Joseph's misgivings. Government circles in London strongly advised Austria to place the Archduke Ferdinand Maximilian at the head of an independent Hungarian State. It appeared that during Maxl's dash to the British Isles he had made a most favorable impression on the royal household; Victoria and Albert wished him well. But of the above recommendation, made through Count Corti after an interview with Lord Russell, the Archduke knew nothing.

Franz Joseph's aloofness and his suspicious attitude pained the visitors. They scarcely unpacked, not feeling certain of the length of their stay. Things had changed at the Hofburg, even more than during Maxl's earlier absences. Empress Elisabeth had become a mother. Sophie, her oldest child, had died not long ago while the imperial family embarked on a journey to Budapest. But there were the others, Archduchess Gisela, and the baby, Crown Prince Rudolf. The former wore lace pantalettes emerging grotesquely under stiff taffeta garments, while little Rudolf scowled behind a diminutive hussar's regalia.

Carlotta was fascinated by the children but she saw little of them. A silent war seemed to be raging between Elisabeth and the Dowager Sophie over the prerogatives of the nursery. The Emperor's mother, it was reported, had descended upon the babes and mapped out a schedule for their development. Elisabeth, the rebel, objected and defied her mother-in-law at every turn. The air at the Hofburg was icy.

Even so, a favorite tradition of the age was not neglected—the family photograph. Grouped about a hideous baroque sofa the imperial relatives gathered for a pose. The Emperor and his three brothers were lined up manfully in the background, with Carlotta standing beside Maximilian, her very pretty hand resting on his. Upon the couch sat Empress Elisabeth and the Dowager Sophie, with Gisela standing between them and Rudolf squirming on his mother's knee. On an armchair to the right, wearing a silk topper and an exceedingly resigned expression, sat Sophie's husband, the aging Archduke Franz Karl. He had come over from Prague and his brother Ferdinand's dumplings in order to fill his place in the happy scene.

The portrait having been taken, and the photographic plate deposited in the famous archives of Raoul Korty in Vienna, there seemed to be no reason for prolonging the visit further. That which Maximilian and Carlotta had come to seek, the familiar routine and glamour of court life, was banished by a nursery feud.

Dejected and sick at heart, the master and mistress of Miramar departed. They came back to their sea-bordered mansion and the solitude of which poets dream. But neither was a poet, and it was not given them to fill the blessed void with anything but a desperate yearning for fellowship and action. Leisure, craved by men while they are bent in toil, can be fraught with tedium and inertia when attained.

They reentered the white palace where nothing ever happened and time stood still. Drawing the curtains upon their melancholy, they shut out the moaning sea and clung to each other in piteous need. Their love, barren, meaningless like their destiny, must bear them up. Upon their love they must feed.

Clinging thus, the one to the other, they fell into the half-slumber that was their night and the half-waking that was their day. Not sorrow, nor anger, nor illness took pity on them by casting a gleam of reality into their isolated peace. They ate off gold and silver plates and went hungry. Their silken couch brought no relief from weariness. Busy with idle, fruitless tasks, they found their life one gigantic game of double solitaire which in the end, if solved, left nothing.

Was theirs the plight of normality? Did all men who were born to be cog-wheels in a vast related whole grow sickeningly faint when forced into a cul-de-sac where they must face that enervating sense of "going it" alone? And the deserted island, the "away from it all," the castle in thin air—could these make up a goal fit only for the abnormal or the supernormal? Genius must surely break away from the human fold and walk on isolated peaks. But Miramar did not harbor genius. The Archduke and his wife were average people scanning the heavens for their lucky star.

It was not to be wondered at that the flare of an artificial rocket, ignited by the flames of transoceanic passions and tinted by the imagination of a Gallic showman who was obsessed with a *gloire* fixation, should sweep them off their feet.

They were ready to be swept off their feet. Theirs was a heart for any fate. . . .

II
THE PLOT

II

THE PLOT

Chapter 1

The Empress Eugénie did not enjoy thinking about her past. And yet her past was far more colorful than her future. It was bourgeois and richly flavored with the pungent atmosphere of the ancestral "pub." It had all the sparkle and tang of her grandsire's famous Málaga grapes, but Eugénie hated grapes. Her fine aquiline nose sniffed disdainfully at all varieties, and more emphatically at the sweet, full-bodied, white sort from the above named province.

And yet, it was this innocent fruit which had made for her grandfather, the immigrant Caledonian wine merchant, Mr. Kirkpatrick, a handsome fortune which the services of his comely daughter—as dispenser of the paternal beverage—in no way undermined. Nor did the crude tone which prevailed in the jolly tavern prove too much for that young lady. She liked the customers right well, a frame of mind which met with reciprocity. For among the numerous habitués there appeared one day a susceptible elderly Spanish artillery colonel who, though totally unhampered by any matrimonial intentions, fell blindly (he had only one eye) in love with her ripe charms.

Since the girl was intelligent and knew the value of good merchandising, her blushing maneuvers soon drew from the decrepit suitor the well-calculated price she had set upon herself. There was a fine wedding and fortune came to her aid in that the bridegroom's elder brother died. This made her heiress to a string of elegant titles. With a true Spanish flair for nomenclature she was able to call herself Duquesa de Peñaranda, Condesa de Teba, as well as Marquesa de Moya, and in her odd moments she was allowed to play with such additional and sonorous surnames as Guzmán, Puertocarrero, Palafox and de Montijo.

The bridal couple moved to Granada in Andalucía where the duchess promptly and cheerfully gave birth to a daughter, Francisca, and another soon thereafter, María Eugenia. This second child, born on May 5, 1826, first saw the light of day in a rustic garden tent whither the duchess had been carried during an inconvenient earthquake. The happy occasion boasted another distinctive feature over the more ordinary birth of little Paca, the older child. María Eugenia had been born exactly five years—to the day—after Napoleon I was found dead on the island of St. Helena. As soon as this mild historical coincidence became known to idle gypsies of the region a wave of agreeable prophecies was showered upon the infant's cradle, for the Romanies, given a reasonable starting-point, accomplish wonders.

But the future joys of such significant motherhood did not completely absorb the convalescent duchess. For the time being, her aging husband's mental dulness was relieved by the pleasurable conversation of a chance acquaintance, Prosper Mérimée, who was visiting Spain in search of literary inspiration (and would leave it again with the plot of a gypsy cigarette girl whose fickleness ends in bloodshed outside a Sevilla bull-ring).

Since aging husbands also don't wear well romantically, an amiable cavalry general named Narváez supplied more intimate diversion. This gentleman was influential at the Court in Madrid and succeeded in advancing the ambitious duchess to the rank of a first lady-in-waiting to the adolescent Queen Isabella II. But a careless flirtation with an Italian swindler soon deprived the spirited lady of the general's friendship and her position at Court, as well as the assorted family jewels (with the exception of such sentimentally valued pieces as came from the Kirkpatrick side).

At this point the duke, Don Manuel Fernández de Peñaranda, Count of Teba and Montijo, became irritated. He removed his two children from the *Sacré-Cœur* convent and sent them away with their mother. A very attractive life opened now before the enterprising ex-Attendant of the Royal Bedchamber. She divided her time between London or Paris, and the Riviera, making always the most useful acquaintances. Wherever she settled down, her house became at once a center of interest, and in her salon congregated the noblest, most influential and most amusing gentlemen of the age. To be sure, they did not bring their ladies.

In 1839 the old duke had the good taste to die. Polite historians of the romantic school dwelled fondly on the grief of a bereft spouse and her orphaned babies. The sober fact seems to be, however, that with her daughters—who were now fifteen and seventeen years of age—the widow decided to reconquer Madrid.

She arrived in a curtain of black crêpe and swooped down at the feet of her abandoned General Narváez. The retired cavalryman, who had not grown younger with the passing years, attributed this extraordinary outburst of devotion to his own enduring seductiveness and, like most men in a similar predicament, was overcome by the attendant obligation. He promised to do what he could, which was plenty.

This time it was not for herself that the duchess sought advancement. She was well past her prime and she knew it. But a future must be carved for her daughters. Narváez called upon his entire store of eloquence and the Queen, whose youth was short of memory, allowed herself to be persuaded. She accepted both girls as attendants in her suite.

Experience had been a good teacher. While the slender brunette Francisca and the red-haired plump Eugénie (French schools had altered the name) dazzled every one with their fresh exuberance, the shrewd mother surveyed the marriage horizon for such possibilities as it might contain.

Among the more prominent satellites revolving about her beautiful girls was the Duke of Berwick and Alba, one of the first grandees of Spain and a direct descendant of the renowned, if fearsome, Governor of the Netherlands. Since it proved difficult to determine which one of the young ladies had conquered his heart, and "gossip was beginning to imply that he did exceedingly well with both," the duchess arranged a private interview during which she presented his Grace with a curt ultimatum. The embarrassed Alba meditated and decided hastily upon Paca. A door was opened with dignity, and the girls—who had stood behind it, eavesdropping—were notified of the outcome.

While Francisca received a mother's moist congratulations and a prospective bridegroom's formal embrace, the humiliated Eugénie swallowed poison. She was found stretched out on her bed, with glassy eyes and a purple face. Though it was possible to save her life, nothing could soothe her outraged spirit, her injured vanity and flaming pride.

Voluptuous of form and incredibly rash of disposition, she yet was neither a passionate nor an emotional creature. Behind her pale blue eyes lingered a mind as tranquil as it was lacking in brilliance, but a mind that had been fed from earliest childhood on one single substance—ambition. Frustration could mean but one thing: a complete distortion of social values and mental balance.

Henceforth she could not restrain her vain desires. She wished to be first, the most beautiful, the most elegant, the most admired of women. Only thus could her wounded ego erase the shame of having been jilted. With unheard-of extravagance she designed fantastic costumes, bathing suits, hair ornaments—appearing with her creations in startled court circles. When the novelty of this wore off she donned native or gypsy attire, and visited the bull-ring, dressed as a man. Nothing could check her hunger for display. Before very long the baffled Queen was scandalized and, ten years after her mother's unfortunate dismissal, Eugénie was dispatched in haste from the royal entourage.

Her first reaction was one of utter despondency. She would take the veil and bury herself in a convent. But the duchess, armed with a Baedeker and some travel charts, soon dispelled such gloomy notions. London was selected as a temporary residence and into Eugénie's life stepped a short, taciturn gentleman with lengthy waxed moustachios and a melancholy stare. He was Prince Charles Louis Napoleon (son of King Louis of Holland) who, after the failure of his first coup d'état, had just escaped from a six-year imprisonment at the Belgian château of Ham and was now living as an exile in England.

Since nursery days Eugénie had been made familiar with the Napoleonic cult. As a child of eight she had sat on the knees of Stendhal, whom the obliging Mérimée had introduced to the Montijo home, and listened wide-eyed to the glorious legend of the brave Corsican. Later, on the seashore in the South of France, she had caught sight of the Pretender who with his mother, Queen Hortense (née Beauharnais), traveled about in search of supporters for his cause. And now he was in London, still searching.

The possibilities inherent in a well planned "chance" meeting became at once apparent. Despite rumors of a compromising attachment to a certain Miss Howard (whose millions were poured generously into Bonapartist propaganda) the Spanish duchess drew Prince Louis into her circle. His eyes were allowed to rest, a trifle hungrily, upon the white shoulders of Eugénie.

When, in 1848, the Orléans dynasty (a branch of the Bourbons) was overthrown, King Louis Philippe and his Queen Marie Amélie hastened to that haven of royal exiles, Dover. The Pretender in turn floated across the Channel toward Calais while the Montijo ladies packed their trunks, prepared to spend a hectic summer at Spa and the following winter at Brussels, with eyes fixed on Paris. Here, in a deceptive pose of democratic idealism, Prince Louis had meanwhile succeeded in being elected President of the Second Republic, but after a year of oratory and hand-shaking his ultimate goal became apparent. By his second coup of December, 1851, he proclaimed himself Napoleon III, Emperor of the French (a mythical Napoleon II having long since passed into oblivion within the shadows of a Viennese castle).

In the congenial company of a Rothschild banker and an enamored Spanish princelet (de Camerata, who later obligingly committed suicide), Eugénie and her mother arrived in Paris. They refurbished their finery, preened before the dull mirror of an obscure *pension* and set out to drop calling cards. But the Emperor seemed less accessible than in those ardent London days. He had bought an *Almanach de Gotha.* He had sent secret emissaries to the four winds. He was furthermore absorbed in settling earlier obligations. A contralto singer by the name of Gordon must be agreeably pensioned. A little laundress, Alexandrine, la Belle Sabotière (known later as "Madame Sans Gêne") who had comforted the exalted prisoner at Ham, claimed a modest memento. The prodigal Miss Howard who had made those loans must be tactfully induced to accept the coronet of a bachelor *com-*

tesse in place of a cherished sprig of imperial orange blossom. And lastly, there was an actual betrothal to a lovely Miss Rowles of Camden Place, Chislehurst, Kent, to be canceled—for it had been contracted in days when the hope of accession seemed altogether chimerical.

In time, however, all pending business had been discharged and the Emperor's emissaries were returning from their discreet rodeo of European Courts. They brought the astonishing news that every princess between the ages of sixteen and sixty was either engaged or otherwise involved in a manner most remarkable among marriageable competitors whose range of choice was of necessity all too limited.

The forty-five-year-old nuptial candidate took the hint. Making a virtue of his quandary, he composed that exemplary note which ever after was to remain the proudest trophy in the Montijo files. (He addressed the duchess as Countess de Teba, a practise current among the society of the times which did not wish to accord the Kirkpatrick lady quite her due.)

"Palace of the Tuileries
"January 15th, 1853.

"Madame la Comtesse:

"It is for a long time that I have loved mademoiselle your daughter and that I have desired to make her my wife. I come then, to-day, to ask you for her hand, since only she would be capable of bringing me happiness, nor is anyone more worthy of wearing a crown. I shall beg you, in the event of your consenting, not to reveal this project until we have made our arrangements.

"Receive, madame, my assurance of sincere friendship.

"Napoleon."

The mother thus addressed suffered delightful palpitations of the heart. Truly she had come up in the world. Goya had painted her portrait, a duke had married her first child, and an emperor now wooed the second. . . . As for the pretty maid in question, Eugénie experienced the full intoxication of triumph. From the rampant crest of de Montijo the odious snub of Alba had been blotted out. . . .

That the gilt crown surmounting the carriage (which was once used by Josephine and Marie Louise on their way to the altar) tumbled off as Eugénie arranged herself upon the cushions did not lessen her triumph. But the Emperor's subsequent interpretation of marital fidelity did.

Soon after the wedding, while she sat at favorable angles to a gallant painter named François Xavier Winterhalter and smiled benignantly upon her bevy of ladies-in-waiting, her chief preoccupation was to discover which of them betrayed her currently with his Majesty. Winterhalter, whose contribution to the world's art galleries is an assortment of preposterous dynastic belles (all done in oil after a chaste and slightly insipid matrix), remained blissfully unconscious of his sovereign's emotional malaise. He pursued his brushwork charmingly, portraying the court trollops as they gathered in dulcet attendance upon their loved mistress. But the poison that was slowly consuming the heart of his Empress he could not distil. It appears nowhere on his many canvases.

Humiliated as a woman, Eugénie became a politician. She had long ago dropped the old air of frivolity, and, with an eye to the delicate matter of her international prestige, had adopted a reserved and dignified poise. There now remained no trace of the sobriquet "adventuress" which her former conduct had earned for her. If Disraeli commented maliciously on her "Chinese eyes, and that perpetual smile or simper which I detest," the English statesman must have overlooked the superb self-control practised by this woman who henceforth had but one aim in life. With a husband who grew daily more dissipated and diseased, she seized upon every means of strengthening her own position. Wholeheartedly she threw herself into the task of becoming invaluable to France.

Her great hobby was history, and she indulged this satisfying penchant with all the talents at her disposal. Her own checkered career had automatically made her an accomplished linguist. Also, public imagination had focused for years on individual personalities and the power of supermen; the ghost of a superman loomed still darkly from Elba and the South Atlantic over the western world. Eugénie's thinking was colored by the thinking of the age. She read history in its most attractive form, biography. From Josephine Beauharnais (née Tascher) whom the Great Napoleon cast aside for a more profitable match, from playful Marie Antoinette who lost her head, she learned what not to do. The matriarchs of antiquity, the Medici viragoes and the Russian Ekaterinas taught her more positive tricks.

She enriched her idle hours at Fontainebleau, Compiègne, St. Cloud, with study. Always she had detested serious music; now, seeing herself supplanted by ever-changing ballroom rivals, even dancing wearied her. She cut a fine figure in the saddle, but since the birth of a Child of France (the Prince Imperial), court physicians opposed horseback riding for the Empress. Only one passion of her youth remained—she still loved bull-fights. She was a Spaniard still. *"Adiós toros!"* she had once written. "I have become Empress of the French!" But he, Louis, made little of her. And so she returned to bull-fights, the Señorita de Montijo. . . .

At the imperial summer villa in Biarritz, quaintly referred to as "Our Nest," the mortifications endured in Paris fell from her. Just across the frontier, bathed in glaring sunlight, lay the land that was once her home. At Pamplona on the Spanish side, and Bayonne on the French, black Miura bulls were challenged by matadores who wore spangles and satin for their dance with death.

From her box the Empress of France applauded, her eyes glued to the arena.

Chapter 2

It was along the dusty carriage road to Bayonne, one lazy summer afternoon in 1858, that a sallow-faced gentleman waved frantic and persuasive hands in an effort to attract the attention of an imperial coachman. The coachman, it so happened, had a good memory and was not to be attracted. Early that year he had driven *"Moustachu,"* as the Emperor of France was called, to the opera in Paris for a performance of *Wilhelm Tell.* But the Orsini conspirators had posted themselves along the boulevards and pelted the monarch's barouche with silk-wrapped hand grenades. Although the January night was cold, Napoleon and Eugénie had sweated profusely when at length they reached safety and the reassuring strains of Rossini's overture.

No, the Biarritz coachman preferred not to stop. Besides, bullfights began punctually at three-fifteen and the Empress prided herself on never being late. The shiny black horses clop-clopped steadily on.

Just then Eugénie herself caught sight of the swarthy gentleman who was loping across the road, about to be enveloped in a cloud of dust. Something in his face and manner struck her as familiar. She ordered the carriage to halt.

Her keen eye had not been mistaken. The individual with the semaphore arms turned out to be an old acquaintance by name of José Manuel Hidalgo y Esnaurrizar. For reasons now forgotten, his family enjoyed papal benedictions "unto the third generation" and figured prominently in the best Spanish circles. Being related to the large Guzmán clan of Andalucía and Mexico, Señor Hidalgo had frequently visited in the former salon of the Montijo ladies. He once served as secretary to the Mexican Legation in London and was later appointed to a similar post in Paris. But he had more specific interests in private life. For many years he had assumed leadership over a large group of Mexican émigrés who drifted about the watering resorts of the Old World while their far-away country went through one of its violent party upheavals. Slender and slightly foppish in appearance, he was possessed of exquisite manners, talked well and made himself instantly agreeable to ladies. The Empress Eugénie was no exception. She bade Hidalgo at once to step into her black-lacquered landau, while the disapproving Pepa, her Majesty's factotum, was relegated to a collapsible seat upon which she made the remaining journey riding backward.

The injured feelings of a piqued waiting-woman would hardly have rendered that drive to Bayonne worth recording. Yet a drive it was, tremendous and dramatic in its consequences, for the soft rumble of those wheels would one day send an echo from a little town named Querétaro around the civilized world, and the symphony of galloping hoofs would change to the crack of muskets on an execution site.

Not that the Empress of France was troubled by such augury. On the contrary, she felt delighted at the unexpected pleasure of masculine attendance and was more than eager for an exchange of gossip concerning mutual friends in Madrid. Hidalgo humored her, reporting with assiduous attention to detail some of the more juicy scandals that engrossed the capital on the Manzanares. But presently he turned to other matters and the ear of his companion was caught by a mad fantastic outpour of oratory.

Such was the trend of the conversation which now followed that the Empress had difficulty in pursuing her intentions as regarded the Corrida de Toros scheduled for that afternoon. Glowing with suppressed excitement, she drew up a swift plan for the following day. Her husband was coming down to "Our Nest" for the week-end. Two seedy Infantas had stopped at the hotel, and there was a Russian Grand Duke who adored picnics. It would be simple to organize an excursion out to sea, with hard-boiled eggs and everything. When sailing, L'Empereur always sat near the helm, pretending to guide the ship. There was Hidalgo's chance! He must repeat, word for word, the gigantic scheme with which he had just startled her. He must repeat it into the navigating monarch's ear.

According to a letter written by Eugénie to her mother the very next night, as well as Hidalgo's description in his *Notas Secretas,* the picnic was a complete success. While bobbing along over the choppy waves of Biscay the Emperor of the French had listened tensely to a graphic word-picture of conditions in a wretched place called Mexico, where vegetation and population were equally savage in character, and political schisms tore the country in half. As a result of such disorders, innocent people like the émigrés whom the speaker represented (and who seemed invariably to attach themselves to the losing party) were forced to spend an unhappy existence far from their homeland. It was at this stage that Hidalgo, who was born overseas yet burned with a fierce monarchic ardor, cleared his throat for a climax in his speech.

"Does your Majesty realize," he cried, "that an exceptional opportunity beckons here to a monarch of discernment?"

"No," said Napoleon agog, "what for?"

"To build a French empire beyond the Atlantic. To save Catholicism, as well as the Latin races, from being engulfed by uncouth Anglo-Saxons and their mercenary culture!"

This was not all that the eloquent patriot spouted. Warming up to his subject, he skipped from one rebus to another. Who did his Majesty suppose supplied the poor Mexicans with deadly ammunitions for their fratricidal wars?

"Well, who?" asked Napoleon.

"The United States, fittingly termed the Colossus of the North! One must stem the Yankee tide which sweeps downward over the Western Hemisphere."

The idea was well expressed. It struck a response in Eugénie's pious heart and ruffled her Spanish feathers. She could not but resent this allusion to the gradual immolation of her own race on a continent once gloriously a part of Spain. Of course Hidalgo was canny. She noticed that, in addressing a French monarch of Italian and West Indian ancestry, he had chosen a collective term embracing the Latin peoples as a whole. Spain alone did not count nowadays.

If he was canny, Señor Hidalgo was also well informed. He knew that this Napoleon, sometimes referred to as *"Le Petit"* in contrast to his uncle *"Le Grand,"* had been thwarted by the United

States in his project of digging a handy canal through Nicaragua. He recalled that during years of long exile, this Bonaparte had occupied a hall bedroom at the Hotel Washington on Broadway, and that he had left New York after a fortnight, carrying with him the usual tourist's encompassing knowledge of American affairs. In short, no one was ever in doubt but that L'Empereur could always be enticed into a debate on the subject of the New World.

As a sequel to these preliminary causeries the French Court now turned in a body to the pursuit of the Empress's hobby, the perusal of ancient histories. Under Hidalgo's guidance the more readable tomes on Aztec lore and Spanish Conquest were fetched from the Bibliothèque Nationale and spread out on the tables in L'Empereur's study. There were days, nay weeks, of spasmodic reading, and a great many interesting things came to light.

To begin with, no one in the imperial entourage had ever thought that the American continent possessed a history. Charts, codices and chronological tables now laid bare the startling evidence that such a history not only existed but that it seemed to predate all recordings of civilized Europe.

Laboriously bent over a map, the amateur scholars recaptured vaguely familiar landmarks. Here before their eyes, tinted in pastel shades, lay the Cuba of Columbus, the Florida of Ponce de León, Cabeza de Vaca's grim Southwest, Pizarro's high Perú, Valdivia's Chile. . . . And up there in the heart of the great hemisphere the Mexico of Hernán Cortés. That Mexico which centuries ago had known temples and pyramids rivaling those of Egypt, and cities, splendors, riches that equaled the pomp of Oriental potentates. An empire in the true sense of the word, a federation of states, ruled by an elected prince, Motecuhzoma (Severe Man), whom the Spaniards called Moctezuma or Montezuma.

On long strips of woven silk-cotton fiber called *ceibón* the story was told, in graceful hieroglyphics, of how the Aztecs came down from the North and settled in the blue Vale of Anáhuac after conquering all creatures within sight. Their capital, Tenochtitlán, was a city of three hundred thousand inhabitants who rejoiced in aquatic sports, for their streets were the water causeways of a great lagoon. Chapultepec, the Emperor's palace on Grasshopper Hill (Aztec: *chapulin*—insect of the genus Gryllus, which once infested the spot; *tepec*—mound), was a magnificent place. It boasted thousands of beautiful handmaidens, frescoed ball courts where the princes played a kind of jai-alai game, crystal baths, and a menagerie—a thing hitherto unknown in Europe. Gold-dust, preserved in vessels of fixed capacity, was used as ordinary currency, while silver was esteemed so little that streets were paved with it. This prodigality extended to food and other necessities which would elsewhere have been deemed luxuries. Chocolate (Aztec: *chocolatl*) was extracted from the cacao plant and used as a beverage. For centuries past every one smoked tobacco, a luxury introduced into civilized Europe at a comparatively recent date.

Napoleon III loved his cigars and he was impressed by the menagerie. Holding his small son Loulou on the imperial lap, he expounded some of the less complicated data like the cocoa bean, the cisatlantic Deluge which did not agree with that of the Holy Land, and the Aztec Noah who was called Cox-Cox. Eugénie, too, felt her imagination caught by the spell of ancient legend. . . .

"From his couch Motecuhzoma rose,
Descended steps of lapis
Lazuli and pearl,
Slaves hastened to unfurl
The Emperor's robe
And so their God entered the pool
Of crystal waters.

"From his bath Motecuhzoma rose
And stood upon a daïs of amber,
Jeweled daughters
Of princes wiped his splendid form
And dusted it with bronze.

"A tale was told
Over the earth of *El Dorado,*
The Gilded One,
Who bathed in pools of gold!

And from a country poor—
Though not obscure,
As Spain then was,—
There came bold squires,
Rogues, adventurers and friars
Hungry for treasure.

"The Emperor's pleasure
Grew boundless; guileless vanity
Invited the foe her splendor to see!
The stranger stared
And, sullen, glared—
... It need not be told how Anáhuac fared...."

"We have a very *simpático* proverb," announced Señor Hidalgo at this juncture, "which grew out of the fate the Americas suffered."

Eugénie begged to hear it and the Mexican again cleared his throat. He recited:

"Charming lady, be not too bold
Lest you tempt like Aztec gold...."

There was a rustling sound and a little chuckle of delight across the paper-strewn table. Yes, that was very *simpático* indeed. Napoleon, having had enough study for to-day, cheerfully left the room. There he goes, thought Eugénie, at the mere mention of temptation. . . .

Stifling her inevitable chagrin, she forced her mind back to that which was at hand. Fiercely she concentrated on a figure of nobler proportions, a hero of her own race, who "with five hundred infantry, sixteen horsemen, a handful of small cannon with stone cannon balls, and thirteen muskets" had subdued a giant nation several million strong. The exploits of Cortés, beginning on Good Friday, 1519, at La Villa Rica de la Vera Cruz and ending with the establishment of a university at Mexico City in 1551, filled her with an almost personal pride.

And now, with still deeper satisfaction, she discovered for herself the actual statistics involved in the famous "bloody" Conquest of New Spain. She learned that, despite their high degree of material civilization, the Aztecs had already entered upon a period of decline. The chronicler of the *Conquista,* Bernal Díaz del Castillo, found them idolatrous and given to abominable human sacrifice of such enormity that it amounted to race-suicide. Soothsayers moaned:

> "Where is the White God Quetzalcoatl?
> Whence shall he come?
> For Anáhuac is a woman who has slain her children
> And gives birth no more. . . ."

In truth, the entire Conquest did not take a toll of lives comparable to the number of victims slaughtered by debauched priests on a single Aztec holiday. For a while, a considerable portion of the cruel Spaniard's time was spent in opening small cages wherein these sorcerers kept thousands of boys and virgins for the purpose of fattening them to a shapeliness pleasing to the gods. For every flower-garlanded, carved stairway leading up to the summit of the *teocalli,* or temple-pyramids, there was a corresponding steep decline leading back to earth. Here in a never-ending stream of blood the mound of corpses grew. Warriors and little children, dancing upward on one side with ritual chants upon their lips, were tossed over the gore-spattered abyss after the living heart had been torn from their breasts. . . .

And only fifteen years after such happenings Mexico City opened its first printer's shop! In 1537 America's first book, *Escala Espiritual,* by Juan Clímaco, was published.

When contrasted with more efficient Nordic ideas of colonization, Spanish methods seem almost childishly naïve, for the latter favored survival of conquered peoples, while the former started toward colonial prosperity on a slate wiped ruthlessly clean. Except in battle, Cortés did not kill. After the power of the Spanish Crown had been established, Spaniards and Mexicans intermarried.

In New England the pious Pilgrim Fathers, busily shooting bad Indians and wresting their patrimony from them, sent ships back home for their own women. Amalgamation versus extermination.

The logical historic sequence is clear. With the exception of a few decimated Indian tribes living on government reservations, America, north of the Río Grande, was populated by pure-bred Europeans who were able to transplant their customs without undue delay. Only the forcible importation of Africans has marred the salubrity of that picture.

With the Portuguese and Spanish colonies matters took a different course. The sons of the land survived. To-day Latin America is eighty-five per cent. Indian.

The whole question invites a parable. One may move into another man's house and be confronted with the obstreperous owner firmly planted on his door-step, demanding the interloper's evacuation. But one does not wish to evacuate. Here is a dilemma.

It can be solved by either of two very practicable schemes. The owner can be locked up in a closet or reservation (reserved for his very own use). Here, through lack of air and exercise, he will eventually lose his appetite and stop vexing any one. There will be peace and, at the most, the outlay of a sympathetic funeral.

The second scheme seems more humane, although it is untidy and has met with the tolerant scorn of those who practised the first. In the second instance the protesting owner is allowed the freedom of his domain—under one condition—he must assimilate the stranger who has come to share his roof. This does not make for peace. At least, not immediately. It makes for discord which must broil and seethe for generations to come, although at length there should be a rather beautiful truce.

At any rate, the world has "ruthless, cruel Spain" to thank for the national survival of true Americans on the American continent as something more than an exhibit of *homo extinctus*. . . .

In Mexico the above named process of assimilation continued for some three hundred years after the death of Cortés, during which time no fewer than sixty-two viceroys ruled in succession over the colony. These gentlemen had been recruited for the most part from aristocratic families with flamboyant Spanish escutcheons. They introduced into the land of cactus blossoms and obsidian tools the churrigueresque refinements of their caste.

Oxen, horses and even donkeys having been unknown, the Aztecs had regarded the first mounted white men as centaurs of supernatural and godlike power. But horsemanship soon captivated native and conqueror alike. The tight-fitting garb of Castilian *caballeros* was modified into the sturdy *charro* rig, while wide brims of swagger *madrileño* hats were added to the brimless peaks of Toltec and Nahua helmets, thus producing the unique *sombrero jarano* of modern times. The picture of colonial Mexico came into being, with porticoes and archways blending into the pattern of Aztec angles and planes. The arabesques of iron grillework vied with geometric stone-carving of earlier days and, most significant of all, the blood-soaked pyramids crumbled before the advent of the Catholic Church. The Mexico of Montezuma, already doomed to self-destruction, was slowly forced into the mold imposed by strong new masters.

Chapter 3

No government is possible without force. No human society submits to law and order simply because it has been invited to do so, and no formulations of law and order have ever been wholly disinterested. The Spanish viceroys certainly were no different from politicians the world over. They believed in filling their own pockets while proclaiming the wisdom and glory of Spain. They lorded it over awed Indian subjects just as, on their seigniorial estates in Asturias or Aragón, high-born grandees were lording it over the lesser gentry and the tenants of their particular districts. The conquered Aztecs, released from far heavier bondage, bowed meekly to their new tyrants, grateful that at least the constant levy of warriors for battle and new-born babes for sacrificial meat had come to an end.

Three centuries long their meekness endured. Then something happened in the great white country to the north. The English-speaking colonies that had been subject to the British Crown broke suddenly away from the mother country. Their Declaration of Independence, issued on a memorable July 4, 1776, flared across the horizon, lighting the fires of unrest throughout the western world. In France, the giddy Marie Antoinette had been queen for two years and was playing Watteau shepherdess; while at Ajaccio on the isle of Corsica a stubborn lad with a bulging head gave his mother, Donna Lætitia Ramolino Buonaparte, no end of worry because he did not seem to grow. Yet only a dozen years later there was murder and famine on Paris streets, and France rushed headlong into the cataclysm of her Revolution. The tocsin of *Liberté, Égalité, Fraternité* resounded across the seas and Latin America took up the refrain.

Hot-headed counterparts to Washington and Robespierre began to crop up along the full length of the cordilleras. The torch of freedom and the Phrygian cap beguiled the fancy of patriots on the Amazon, the La Plata, at Cuzco, and below the Río Grande.

In Mexico, a sixty-year-old priest, Miguel Hidalgo y Costilla, began the Indian insurrection under the banner of the dark Madonna of Guadalupe. With his loosely assembled proselytes he marched upon the capital, only to be routed by the disciplined troops of the viceroy, who imprisoned the leader and had him executed. But the fight was soon taken up by another priest, José María Morelos; the soldier, Vicente Guerrero; and the cavalier, Don Agustín de Iturbide. The last named of these three was a high-minded nobleman of Spanish parentage, born at Valladolid (now Morelia) in Michoacán. He was destined to become a figure strangely parallel to that other champion of pseudo-liberalism, Napoleon the Great.

Like the stripling from Ajaccio, Iturbide saw the wrongs of inflexible autocracy and fell in with the prophets of a new age. Like Napoleon, he caught up the poorly organized insurgents at a moment when their cause faltered, and led them to victory. Next, at Iguala, on February 24, 1821, Iturbide evolved a Mexican Declaration of Independence with a pleasant clause by the terms of which he, Don Agustín, became constitutional head of the nation.

But soon after, perhaps in unconscious imitation of the First Consul of the French Republic, he had come to doubt the wisdom of government by the masses. He wondered if Mexico's mestizo population would prove anything but a handicap to independent order. Napoleon, facing no racial problem, wondered the same and peremptorily cleared up the matter by declaring himself emperor. May, 1822, saw Iturbide following suit. The palace on the Plaza Mayor, vacated only recently by the last Viceroy, Don Francisco de Novella, was dusted and put in readiness for its new occupant.

Mexico's Second Empire was destined to be short-lived. After a precarious winter of balancing the crown upon his head the usurper was forced to abdicate and flee to Europe. Unable to become reconciled to the life of an exile he returned once more, like Napoleon from Elba, hoping to be met by a crowd of faithful adherents. But on landing in disguise at Soto la Marina he was arrested, brought before the legislature of Tamaulipas, and condemned to death.

During the next thirty years the affairs of the young republic were outrageously mismanaged by a political juggler and unprincipled rogue who had served under Iturbide and later turned upon his benefactor. Antonio López de Santa Ana, a man with a purchase price for any party, became president or dictator no less than six times. Under his arbitrary and wretched rule Mexico lost Texas to the United States. Due to constant bribery and theft the treasury fell into a state of chronic depletion and the government cheerfully saddled the people with a crushing foreign debt. This was indeed worse than anything the country had experienced under the viceregal system. A large group of conservatives, mostly educated and wealthy Creoles, were beginning to wonder whether an absolute and independent monarchy under a prince of royal blood was not after all the only civilized form of authority. Democracy assuredly offered too many temptations to recreant upstarts.

One of the capital's aristocrats, José María Gutiérrez de Estrada, wrote a memorandum in which he warned his fellow-countrymen that "if two more decades pass in the same state of anarchy as the years since the rupture with Spain, the star-spangled banner of North America will float over the National Palace in Mexico City."

To Santa Ana and the various political groups hoping for their turn at the republican coffers, Gutiérrez and his partisans became a serious danger. Steps were immediately taken against the more prominent members of the Conservative Party. Their property was confiscated and countless families were banished to Europe.

Here they settled in the sunnier portions of France and, as the years went by, took a fancy to Continental modes of living. The great cities of the Old World impressed them. They yearned to reconstruct their own semi-savage homeland and develop its resources after similar patterns. Glittering monarchies and empires being the current style, they longed more than ever for an improvement upon the Iturbide experiment, this time with the aid of a genuine European dynasty.

The genteel and verbose José Manuel Hidalgo (no relation to the soldier-priest) whom the Empress Eugénie had spotted on the road to Bayonne was the self-appointed spokesman for Mexico's émigrés. His lucid dissertations on the subject of intervention were causing a stir at the Vatican, in London, Paris and Brussels. They affected the world of finance. European bankers were growing irritable in regard to heavy loans made to constantly changing Mexican administrations, and there was talk of collecting interest on these loans in the form of territorial conquest.

Mexico's principal creditors were England and France. British citizens living in the Aztec capital had invested in government bonds under Santa Ana's régime and that of his successors, Comonfort, Zuloaga, and Miramón. As security for these loans a deposit of six hundred thousand pesos was made with an English financial agent in Mexico City. But Miramón, finding himself in need of funds, caused the Legation seals to be broken and helped himself to the money.

When further need arose he turned to the Swiss banking house of Jecker, Torre and Company, which had for some years operated in Mexico. Jean Baptiste Jecker and his older brother Louis, who was a noted surgeon, lived in the suburb of San Ángel on a picturesque estate called La Bombilla. (Here, almost a century later, General Álvaro Obregón was assassinated.) Both men were extremely wealthy and embroiled in government intrigues of many nations. To the impecunious Miramón they vouchsafed several loans which totaled three million francs in gold. In return for this service they received crisp government bonds which, following their own stipulations, would mature to the value of seventy-five million francs. Miguel Miramón, somewhat backward in mathematics, freely appended his signature.

That such a transaction could under no sane circumstances be considered valid did not stop the firm of Jecker. The bogus bonds were accepted and later put to profitable use in extracting concessions from the harassed Mexican people. A large portion of these bonds went to the younger Jecker's friend, the Duc de Morny, who lived pleasantly in Paris. Through this fortunate concatenation France held suddenly a weapon in her fist which could one day be waved grimly over the struggling Aztec republic.

In the latter, things had gone rapidly from bad to worse. Toward the end of 1858 Mexico was blessed with two presidents at war with each other. In the capital the spendthrift Miramón was bribing the clergy to join his ranks, while at Vera Cruz the Indian, Benito Pablo Juárez, raised the standard of radicalism. The national debt had mounted to inconceivable figures and from Washington came recognition of Juárez as president.

A new era now opened. The Indian from Oaxaca, self-educated and poor, understood the character of his people. With resolute deliberation he located the blind Minotaur that for nearly four centuries had sapped the life, energy and wealth of the nation. He had long noticed with a sort of cynical wonderment that, while each political upheaval drained the State still further and brought it nearer the brink of ruin, the Church seemed to increase daily in power and riches. Fully one-third of the land belonged to the clerics. There were ten thousand churches and one hundred and fifty conventual estates valued at ninety million pesos. While government treasuries had to be replenished by every chicanery, decent and otherwise, the corpulent Archbishop of Mexico enjoyed an annual income of one hundred and thirty thousand pesos. The Bishops of Puebla, Michoacán and Guadalajara "earned" one hundred and ten thousand, one hundred thousand and ninety thousand pesos respectively. With such sums at their disposal were not the friars able, at their pleasure, to establish or upset administrations and to foment whatever schisms most suited their ends? Juárez thought so.

Quietly, but with cold Indian cunning, he cut straight to the heart of the evil. By means of the scathing *Leyes de Reforma* he separated Church and State, wresting from the former the vast feudal possessions which had been amassed through votive endowments and forced tithes. Proclaiming all religions on a footing of equality with Roman Catholicism, he expelled the archbishop, the bishops and all militant fanatics—including the Spanish Minister—who stood in his way of reform. The regeneration of Mexico had begun.

Chapter 4

Thus far went the Empress Eugénie's study of history. Señor Hidalgo had done very well by his pupil and brought things up to date. Now, if her Majesty wished a personal account by Monsignor Pelagio Antonio Labastida y Dávalos, the unfortunate Archbishop who had just been forced to pick up his ecclesiastical robes and float across the Atlantic, a meeting could be arranged. Her Majesty could hear from the disgruntled clergyman's own lips the lamentable story of his persecution.

Eugénie's pious heart was touched. Certainly she must see poor Labastida. If that man Juárez were indeed the Antichrist whom Hidalgo's account had pictured she had at last found a mission to perform, a mission which would be pleasing in the sight of God and highly beneficial to the glorious interests of France.

The interview took place. Rotund Labastida easily caused the Empress to sob at the spectacle of his breathless chase, with Juarista bullets whistling about his skirts, through the less reputable quarters of a city which had turned suddenly godless. All this, the Archbishop added emphatically, went on under the approving eye of Mexico's Protestant neighbor, the United States.

It was really very shocking, and so her Majesty found it. The distressing details must be repeated to the Emperor at breakfast, with an added description of the plight of the two thousand nuns who had had to escape in borrowed petticoats and improvised wigs for their cropped heads, leaving behind them fifty-eight charming convents and a floating capital of four million five hundred thousand dollars.

Napoleon was frightfully interested. He saw at once that something must be done. What a pity that, unlike his famous uncle, he had no collection of Bonaparte relatives from whom to choose the proper instrument for his imperialistic scheme. What a misfortune that his own son, Loulou, was too young to avail himself of this opportunity! A harmless and susceptible prince who could further the ends of France, without himself being French, would be hard to find. Of late, what with regicide in the Balkans, nihilism across the Volga and unrest in Italy, it had become embarrassing to recruit for thrones. Even Lord Derby found himself pursued by a cluster of tenacious Greeks who offered him a scepter.

At best, one could procrastinate and brood about the matter until a happy solution presented itself. Hidalgo must be flattered and entertained in Paris. It would not do to let him drift back over the Pyrenees toward Madrid. The prattling Isabella was a Bourbon and the number of her jobless cousins was legion. But the Bourbons were the avowed foes of Bonapartism. Little patches in the brocade at the Tuileries still showed where the golden bees (symbols of the Napoleonic crest) had been snipped out by a Bourbon Charles X and a Bourbon Louis XVIII after the downfall of the Corsican.—If he was not always sure of his friends, Napoleon III was never in doubt about his enemies.

While yet he tarried over the problem new champions joined the monarchist cause. The fugitive Santa Ana, who had dethroned Iturbide, was growing restless on his West Indian isle of banishment and ready to uphold any party that permitted him to reenter Mexico. Unhappy Miramón cherished similar yearnings, while Juan Nepomuceno Almonte, Mexican Minister in Paris under a half-dozen régimes, trembled for his post and strove to whip up intervention in Mexico before the avenging ax of Juárez reached him. (It was said of Almonte that he was the son of the Independence hero, Padre Morelos. The warlike priest had carried the baby in his saddle whenever he set out for the mountains—*al monte*—and had made him a colonel in the first regiment of *Libertadores*. The little colonel, who was a love-child, had grown up and taken his name from those exciting gallops when, not knowing what else to do with him, his tender parent had hurried him "for safety" into the thick of battle.)

Meanwhile the radical Juárez was cleaning house. Enjoying the full support of the United States, he was able to defy both anathema and papal bull hurled at him from the Vatican. A quarrel with the Church was precisely what he wanted.

Impassive and self-sufficient, he soon wondered whether he

needed diplomatic representatives in Paris or, for that matter, anywhere else. Embassies and legations cost money, whereas he had pledged himself to rehabilitate Mexico both morally and financially. To accomplish this it became necessary to repudiate the outrageous obligations incurred by his predecessors and make a new start. A moratorium must be declared on all foreign loans, suspending payment of interest as well as principal for a period of at least two years. The European powers, Juárez felt, were a long way off. With the Monroe Doctrine in operation they could not do him much harm.

The moratorium was proclaimed during the summer of 1861. It caused a great stir in international banking circles. But, by a quirk of chance, its main support now vanished, for across the Río Grande hostilities were breaking out between the abolitionist North and the slaveholding South. The famous Monroe Doctrine was destined to be temporarily shelved.

In many countries speculation was rife as to the outcome of the impending American War of the Secession. Leading minds in Europe believed that the South would prevail against the North. While such an outcome was eminently desirable to Old World statesmen it also brought up a ticklish problem. The seceding states were known to crave annexation to Mexico and the West Indian island group for the purpose of creating a vast independent Central American empire. Although welcoming the internal rupture of the "Colossus of the North," France, England and Spain could not view complacently the immediate birth of another giant combination. It was therefore essential for these three powers to agree on an overseas policy.

Almost forty years earlier, in December of 1823, President James Monroe had delivered a message to the Congress of the United States. It contained some significant declarations:

> "(1) The American Continents, by the free and independent condition which they have assumed and maintained, are henceforth not to be considered as subjects for future colonization by any foreign power. (2) Any attempt on the part of European Powers to extend their political systems to any

portion of the Western Hemisphere would be considered dangerous to the peace and safety of the United States. . . . Nor would such extension be regarded with indifference."

The gentlemen who had gathered about a round table in Paris to examine a copy of this fearsome document smirked. "Nor would such extension be regarded with indifference." It was really quite amusing.

With their big experiment in democracy going to pieces, where were those formidable Americans now?

Napoleon III was in a particularly sprightly mood. His faith in Napoleon III was at its peak during this period. Hardly more than a year ago the Franco-Italian campaign against Austria had come to a successful close. With two profitable wars to his credit a sovereign could command the attention of his neighbors; accordingly, though not invited, the Emperor had gone calling. His first important visit after the Crimean victory had been to England, where Victoria's fancy had been captivated by pretty courtesies and Latin vocals, although her "garish outmoded garments and purple porkpie hats" contrasted sharply with the Parisian elegance of Eugénie.

So complete was the success of the London visit that only a few weeks later the Queen and the Prince Consort were off to Paris for a return of compliments. It was the first time in more than four centuries that an English ruler had entered the French capital. *"Moustachu's"* triumph was complete. With England's approval so patently established, the truculent Courts of all Europe must follow suit.

As for dear Vicky's diary, what a marvelous occasion it all proved to be! With "Bertie in full Highland dress—he looks so well in green—and a dance at Fontainebleau to the strains of a mechanical handle organ plied by one Bacciocchi" . . . (It was the dawn of the great machine age and any self-respecting élite must scorn mere fiddlers!) The Queen's pen found it all "delightfully *gemuethlich.*"

Yes, Napoleon's star was rising and it pointed overseas toward Vera Cruz. The gentlemen from London and Madrid who sat chuckling about the table in L'Empereur's study might speak freely. This question of Mexican intervention—was it not a simple project, a mere child's play? Each of their governments had something to gain. Together they could plunge ahead as a sort of entente cordiale, which in itself would enlist the sympathy of future historians since public opinion seldom believed majorities to be wrong.

It must be an amicable expedition, of course. Just a friendly little "bondholders' war." The main point was to get a military foothold on Mexican soil and, having consolidated their positions, to checkmate all overtures which might be made by a triumphant Confederacy across the Río Grande. At the same time the warring Confederates must be assured of Europe's sympathy with the South, lest they lose hope and give up the fray. Without an American Civil War in progress the crusade to Mexico lacked allure.

The Juárez moratorium gave each of the three powers a logical pretext for intervention in Mexican affairs. Spain was insulted because her minister had been dispatched back home. England wished compensation for the moneys which the desperate Miramón had snatched from a strong box protected by the Queen's seal. And France had quickly naturalized the Swiss Messieurs Jecker in order to safeguard the interests of their depositors. All three countries were inspired with the kindliest feelings toward Mexico, but each needed a small poultice of petrol, silver-ore, coast-line or cotton to heal a particular wound. Each was, furthermore, prejudiced against mail-order methods and preferred to come across the seas to do her own picking.

In December of 1861, while Prince Albert lay dying at Windsor, three navies were set in motion. The Spaniards, who had a fleet resting intermittently in Cuban waters, were the first to arrive at Vera Cruz under the command of General Juan Prim, Count of Reus. Six thousand men wearing Queen Isabella's buttons put down their marching kits and occupied the empty forts.

With the turn of the year came more ships veering around the dangerous reef of San Juan de Ulúa and an English admiral marched his brigades across a sleepy town. The Union Jack had just been hoisted over the barracks of the British contingent when France unloaded her zouaves under Vice-Admiral Jean Pierre Edmond Jurien de la Gravière.

Up to a certain point the puzzled natives witnessed these goings-on in their harbor with no more than mild astonishment. Spaniards and Englishmen voicing vague excuses about some debts they were going to collect, and meanwhile settling down to wassail and dolce far niente in the tropical sun, caused no pother among the tranquil Veracruzanos. As yet no one had even troubled himself to report the invasion to headquarters in Mexico City. The collecting of moneys was quite patently not a matter of life and death.

But at sight of the zouaves the townsmen became annoyed. African blood was repulsive to Indian and Creole alike, and the fact that France should seek dealings on foreign soil without exposing her own nationals outraged Mexican pride. Angrily the glove was picked up, and the war was on.

It progressed slowly at first, due to uncertainty of purpose among the participants. England and Spain seemed to favor negotiations while France was all for storming the capital, a trifling matter calling for a steady climb (over a distance of one hundred miles) to the plateau, eight thousand feet above the sea. The problem induced some cogitation in the dirty cafés along the water-front where the allied forces sought relief from boredom and heat.

Vera Cruz lay embedded in the yellow fever zone and Admiral Hugh Dunlop complained that some of his tars had caught the *vómito negro*. If they were to have a war, the admiral felt, it ought to be carried on in a decent climate. Furthermore, neither Juárez nor his troops had as yet put in an appearance. Perhaps the best thing to do was to send a message.

Accordingly, after concerted effort spent in the formulation of an impressive text, word was sent to the capital that here they were and what did the President of Mexico propose to do about it? Also, a conference would be granted on condition that the foreign troops be invited to transfer from the *Tierra Caliente* with its fever-laden air to the temperate zone half-way up the Sierras. The mosquitoes were very bad and did Señor Juárez know of a better place?

The assumption that the Indian President suffered any pangs over the health of hostile troops was grotesque, to say the least.

Juárez was nonplussed. He became disturbed. If this was a sample of how the tropics affected the invaders it might be wise to temporize and learn their further object. La Soledad, a pretty spot some miles inland, was suggested as a meeting-place.

If Juárez now expected to hear from the allied spokesmen a clear and honest presentation of their case he was due for a thorough disappointment. France, England and Spain, the presidential representative Doblado was told, harbored the most philanthropic sentiments. Nothing was more remote from their intentions than the violation of Mexican sovereignty. At the same time they wished their respective forces to be stationed in the three healthful towns of Córdoba, Orizaba and Tehuacán, high up in the mountains, where they intended to remain. More conferences would follow.

Not without justice did the Mexican Minister of Foreign Affairs reject these "friendly but indefinite explanations, the real object of which nobody unravels."

One thing alone was clear. The Mexican Government was unprepared for war with anybody. It could only hope for an amicable settlement before further hostilities broke out. Popular demonstrations against the zouaves in Vera Cruz had been as yet the only signs of violence. Juárez racked his brain for some scheme whereby he might dispose of the unwelcome visitors before it was too late.

Fortune came to his aid. The allies were quarreling among themselves. General Prim, the Spanish commander, was known to be vain and ambitious. Murmurs had arisen which hinted at his dream of becoming viceroy over a reconquered colony. With a permanent army stationed in Cuba, Spain might easily support such cabalistic plans before England or France could send new forces across the Atlantic.

A few asperities were exchanged in the course of which Prim challenged Jurien to lay the French cards on the table. This clinched matters; the veil of mystery could be dropped. Jurien made a series of blunt announcements: France was here for the purpose of establishing a Mexican Empire under Napoleonic protection. The Jecker bonds had been a ruse. Mexican royalists in Paris were already negotiating with a possible candidate for the new throne.

This information came as a severe blow to both Spaniards and Britons. General Prim looked hurt. A viceregal coronet having faded into something less than conjecture, the coquettish soldier's interest in the campaign became extinguished. Admiral Dunlop was even more startled when it dawned upon him that his government alone had been prompted by the artless rapacity of a debt-collector. In short, both parties withdrew from the project and, packing up their little armadas, steamed out of the harbor in disgust. Just beyond the choppy Florida waters they encountered a tri-colored flotilla in formation. From its decks a neat conglomeration of shadows cheered lustily. They were the newly arrived French recruits who would bolster up Jurien's unpopular zouaves. Napoleonic diplomacy had won the day.

It remained only for the glorious army of *La Patrie* to march up-hill across the cordilleras toward the City of Palaces built on an Aztec lagoon. The whilom capital of Montezuma had been given warning and Juárez waited, bristling with decrepit republican guns.

Slowly the French columns advanced, buoyed up by the steadfast cheering section of the mother country, and above all by the Emperor, who abounded in gratuitous advice on the rigors of the climate. As a small boy Napoleon III had tended flowers in the garden of his grandmother Josephine, at Malmaison, with a sprinkling can which a solicitous governess kept filled with warm water. He felt a similar concern now for his troops. In the cool comforts of Vichy he drew sketches for a new tropical uniform and discoursed gravely on the importance of insect bites. Tons of mosquito netting were to be shipped overseas. There ought to be a railroad from Vera Cruz to the plateau. While pinning infinitesimal paper flags on a Mexican map of doubtful accuracy the excited monarch grew daily more prolific in hatching new ideas.

Jurien had meanwhile surrendered the supreme command to General Lorencez, who had brought the recruits. At the head of six thousand men Lorencez appeared before Puebla, May 4, 1862.

On the following day began the assault of the city. The French were defeated by General Zaragoza and his four thousand native volunteers. Though of no lasting consequence in the outcome of the struggle, a fine patriotic holiday—*El Cinco de Mayo*—was added to the Mexican calendar. The date also marked Eugénie's thirty-sixth birthday.

On May eighth the attack was resumed, this time under the French general, François Achille Bazaine and his experienced Foreign Legion. After a long and terrible siege Puebla capitulated to a vastly superior force, and the way to Mexico City lay open. President Juárez, after issuing a manifesto in which he promised to return victoriously, abandoned the capital and fled northward with his generals Porfirio Díaz and Juan José de la Garza.

On June eleventh the French general, Elie Fréderic Forey, officially occupied Mexico City where, with that courtesy which the vanquished races judiciously accord the victor, he was welcomed with a symphony of church-bells and a shower of magnolia blooms. The Conservative Party, largely responsible for this joyful reception (which inspired Forey to report to his emperor that the Mexicans were "avid for order, justice, and true liberty"), communicated at once with the émigrés in Paris and inquired about the progress—if any—that had been made in regard to a prince.

In France people embraced one another on the streets. Parisian silversmiths were busily inscribing medals wherewith Napoleon would decorate his brave cohorts. But Eugénie did not celebrate. She was at the bedside of her young son, who had suffered a serious intestinal disturbance. Easter Sunday of that year (it fell on April twentieth) the Empress had received a hundred-thousand-dollar egg from her husband, and Loulou had eaten the decalcomanias off it.

Across the seas, where a reply from the émigrés was awaited with impatience, a junta composed of thirty-five members of the monarchist group had been formed. These in turn created another junta with the title of *La Regencia*. The latter was headed by the ex-Minister of Mexico in Paris, Juan Nepomuceno Almonte, the "little colonel" whose father had died for the Republic in her struggle against Spain.

Chapter 5

Up to now, it must be admitted, the émigrés in Paris had not done very well. Despite a second drafting of the eloquent memorandum composed by Gutiérrez de Estrada, in which it was stated that "Mexico must perish if her savior does not soon appear," no scion of European royalty seemed to covet the vacant throne in the Valley of Forty Volcanoes. Three German princes who had been approached declined on the grounds that they could not renounce their Protestant faith. An elderly Duke of Modena did not believe his health would stand the strain.

The suggestion of Modena, however, led to another possibility. If there were no candidates in Italy, how about Austria? Those Hapsburgs were so quixotic. One could always count on a variety of debonair and idle Archdukes. Besides, here was Napoleon's chance to restore himself effectively in the graces of the sullen Franz Joseph. . . . The defeat at Magenta, which had cost Austria two of her loveliest provinces and launched a fashion shade in Paris commemorating the sad bloodshed, had left a deep scar on the escutcheon of her dynasty. That scar had festered. . . . Then there was the humiliation suffered by the former Viceroy of Lombardy and Venice, Archduke Maximilian, whom Napoleon's political chess game had temporarily forced into the ranks of the unemployed. What, by the way, had happened to that agreeable young man?

The question was uttered over after-dinner coffee at the Tuileries. José Hidalgo, the only guest present, shrugged cautious shoulders while the Emperor repeated the words to his wife. Eugénie rose and settled down by her sewing table near an open window.

"Even if we knew where he is," she said thoughtfully, "the Archduke Maximilian would not be interested."

"Oh, no. He would never listen," Hidalgo chorused, "not he. . . ."

Napoleon seldom contradicted his wife. His many infidelities burdened him with a perennially guilty conscience which led him to avoid domestic friction whenever possible. Differences of opinion, experience had taught him, were too easily steered into personal territory where the husband with bachelor habits had no ground to stand on. Consequently the Emperor of the French lighted another of his innumerable cigarettes and added his mite to the prevailing opinion about the Archduke. "No," he declared heartily, "he would not be interested."

There was an interval of silence during which the Empress fell into a sort of trance. Then, as if impelled by oracular vapors, she gasped suddenly: "Wait—I have a premonition that he can be reasoned with!"

An irresistible fascination seems to emanate from even the most casual boast of clairvoyance. Human beings who are equipped to know better never fail to toy with this informal substitute for logic. In the case of the Emperor and the scheming émigré this was particularly true, since both had reached the end of their combined ingenuity. If proposals at the Hofburg met with a rebuff, rather than admit England or Russia into the breach Napoleon would quash the Mexican bubble altogether. Eugénie's very feminine speculation struck just the right note of hope; if a woman's intuition augured well, two Latin gentlemen were bound by unwritten laws of gallantry to stand by her.

"In that case," Hidalgo rallied with an enterprising gleam in his eye, "let us send Gutiérrez de Estrada to Vienna. He talks very well."

"It will take some talking," Napoleon reflected sheepishly, "to win again the confidence of that proud young Austrian Kaiser. But let Monsieur Estrada try."

"France offers a magnanimous atonement for whatever wrongs the Hapsburgs may hold against us," added Eugénie.

Hidalgo jotted down a catchword or two from the imperial vocabulary and bowed himself out of the room. Three days later the Yucatecan lawyer Estrada was on his way to Vienna bearing a secret portfolio. In Paris, meanwhile, diplomatic wheels did not stand idle. Prince Richard Metternich, son of the great

Chancellor and lately appointed Austrian Ambassador to France, was approached by Eugénie herself and asked for his opinion on the Mexican venture. The tall bewhiskered statesman, who had an ugly wife and was very popular with the ladies, vouchsafed a blunt and discouraging answer. "What a lot of cannon shots will be necessary," he commented, "to set up an emperor in a foreign land, and what a lot more to maintain him there!"

This verdict being wholly unsatisfactory, a network of hopeful inquiry was spread out to include Austrian representatives abroad. Count Crivelli, the Viennese Ambassador in Madrid, modestly refrained from expressing his own views but offered those of the Spanish Minister-President, Calderón Collantes, instead.

"I feel absolutely certain," the latter was quoted as saying, "that it would be impossible to found anything durable in Mexico." Crivelli appended a postscript in his own handwriting to the effect that he was tempted to share these views.

But by far the most forceful protest came from a man who at the time was naturally better versed in American politics than all the chancelleries of Europe combined. He was Ritter von Hülsemann, Austrian Minister at Washington. Watching the course of the Civil War at close range Hülsemann foresaw its probable outcome. Discounting this, he foresaw another eventuality. Even if, as Napoleon continued to hope, the South were to prevail against the North, the leaders of the Confederacy would be thunderstruck at the French Emperor's duplicity in furthering his own advancement in Mexico. Before the outbreak of hostilities Napoleonic agents had visited Charleston and pledged France's approval of a "marriage with Central America," that will-o'-the-wisp cherished by the seceding states. To find themselves scotched as soon as they sought their reward for doing Napoleon the favor of breaking up the North American Union, was bound to bring trouble. Who else, if not France's tool on the throne of Mexico, would be the victim of their honest vengeance?

Ritter von Hülsemann did not mince words. "It would be unpardonable for the name and person of the Archduke, our Emperor's brother, to become entangled in this dangerous affair and exposed to its inevitable failure. And moreover, it is unthinkable that the fate of his Serene Highness, our Prince, should depend entirely upon the good or ill will of a randomly picked French bodyguard."

His Serene Highness, while such wise and timely warnings scurried back and forth in diplomatic pouches, sat in the music-room at Miramar playing the pipe organ. Life, with no care for the morrow and likewise no duty, continued to pall. Horticulture and counterpoint had become the Archduke's latest hobbies while Carlotta, recently returned from a brief sojourn at the Empress Elisabeth's villa near Funchal, nursed literary aspirations. Scarcely more than twenty years old, she had already produced two volumes entitled *A Winter on the Island of Madeira* and *Souvenirs of a Voyage on Board "La Fantasie."* The first book was a record of actual events in the tropic retreat where her sister-in-law sought respite from the interminable quarrels with the Dowager Sophie over Elisabeth's children. In "La Fantasie" Carlotta wove for herself largely a pattern of her own imaginings, a subtle armor against her own ennui.

She was busy at her small writing table, a piece once owned by Marie Antoinette, when the forensic Estrada arrived at Miramar for an interview with Maximilian. At the Hofburg in Vienna the Mexican's proposal had met with a surprisingly cordial reception. The fact that Napoleon III stood behind this proposal in the attitude of a condescending benefactor did not escape Franz Joseph. But the latter suffered from a gnawing realization that during his short rule the Hapsburg patrimony had lost power and prestige. The thought that through his brother Maxl the loss of Northern Italy could be made up carried implications that must not be despised. As a result, the young sovereign swallowed his pride and—to make the draught less bitter—interpreted Napoleon's offer as nothing less than recognition of a Hapsburg's fitness to govern.

This point having been conceded by Estrada, Franz Joseph brightened. It was now possible for Vienna to assume an attitude of condescension. The Archduke, Estrada was told, no longer resided in the Danube capital but led a life of ease at his pleasure palace near Trieste. While the imperial family would place no obstacle in Maximilian's way, the latter was by no means obliged to seek advancement outside the boundaries of his fatherland and must be persuaded to make his own decisions.

Heartened by the Hofburg's ill-concealed enthusiasm, the Mexican promoter now tackled the "Dreamer of Caserta"—(at Caserta, Garibaldi's stronghold in Campania Felix, Maximilian once had said farewell to Italy). With mellifluous diction Gutiérrez de Estrada broke once more into his oft-repeated metaphors about the "budding plant entitled to a place in the sun. . . . Do you, Prince, deign to become Mexico's redeemer? Lend her the support of your great fatherland, to which my ruined country once belonged as one of the fairest jewels in the crown of Charles the Fifth!"

Strangely these words recalled others spoken by Maximilian himself after his visit to the cathedral at Granada in Spain where he beheld the royal insignia of Ferdinand the Catholic. The diary *Aus Meinem Leben* records the Archduke's emotion. "With pride and a sad yearning I touched the golden coronet and the once mighty sword. What a bold dream for a descendant of the Spanish Hapsburgs to wield the latter in order to win back the former!"

The stage seemed to have been set by a strategic and invisible scenarist, for at no time in their lives could the Archduke and his wife have been more susceptible to the blandishments of flattery and the call of adventure. Due to their isolation they had lost track of world affairs to such a degree that it was impossible for them to distinguish between pleasant fantasy and more painful truth. The rosy binoculars through which Estrada bade them look at the beckoning overseas empire captured their imagination. Like fascinated children they listened while their gesticulating guest talked endlessly on. So beguiled were they by the Mexican's flow of language that the latter grew inflamed at his own eloquence and exclaimed:

"This day, like my wedding-day, I shall remember as one of the happiest in my life!"

Something about that maudlin exaggeration prompted Maximilian in turn to strike a pose. Up to this moment his blue eyes, round and astonished, had sparkled with animation. But suddenly it came to him that such a display of pleasure was not becoming to a man of his station. Drawing up to his full height he now frowned and cloaked his enthusiasm under a mantle of classic dignity.

The proposition, he remarked gravely, held certain attractions. But there would have to be guaranties of personal safety, the support of at least two naval powers—England and Spain, to be explicit—and some sort of document expressing the desire of a representative majority of the Mexican nation. For, as he put it, "a Hapsburg never usurps a throne."

Estrada, who was endowed with much sentiment but no political acumen, put these things down in a little notebook and observed with satisfaction that the above conditions would be promptly fulfilled. His satisfaction, however, suffered a considerable setback at the Tuileries where, a short time later, the contents of the little notebook had to be disgorged. Napoleon and Eugénie listened attentively to the report and entered into lively discussion.

"Exactly what does the Archduke mean by guaranties of safety?" L'Empereur wished to know.

Estrada shrugged polite shoulders and searched for the proper word. "A substantial bodyguard, no doubt," he suggested, "as well as pecuniary aid, since the prince can not be asked to risk his own fortune——"

"When they come for money and troops," Eugénie broke in violently, "I could scream!"

Napoleon toyed with his cigarette. "But I have twenty thousand marines and again as many fusiliers in Mexico already," he said, tapping ash into a tray.

"It is for the crossing," Estrada interpolated. "The Archduke would not undertake the voyage alone."

The Emperor paused to consider. "Even so," he announced, with a furtive glance at his wife, "her Majesty is right. France sponsors the idea and offers every moral support, but further legions—that will be difficult."

"And money?" the Mexican persisted hopefully.

"Ah—money there is none except by making use of the customary channels—a loan, señor."

The interview was concluded. Gutiérrez de Estrada retired to his hotel and a favorite occupation, the composition of interminable letters. He bombarded Miramar with a cyclone of missives punctuated with "Alas!" and rich in persuasive exhortations.

The Archduke Maxl was somewhat taken aback. With the impetuosity of youth he had already made plans; a conference with his brother was to take place within the next few days. It would have been most gratifying to inform Franz Joseph in the course of that conference of Maximilian's departure in a cloud of imperial glory all his own. With two important requisites—financial and military—failing from the outset, the cloud of glory darkened rapidly into a fog.

Maximilian frowned and threatened to withdraw from the enterprise. At this Estrada, far less happy than on his wedding-day, plunged into another orgy of correspondence while Carlotta likewise rose to the occasion. For the first time in her life the powerful fires of personal ambition stirred within her breast. For the first time her little hand touched history.

She wrote a detailed account of the situation to her father in Brussels. Complete confidence existed between King Leopold and his daughter ever since the death of Queen Louise Marie when Princess Charlotte had been only ten years old. To her father the young wife of Miramar could now confess that she had long ago discovered in her husband an amateurish lack of initiative. And, she added, if Maxl himself had not the fortitude to seize that which his uncertain heart was craving, they must combine to help him.

King Leopold gave the matter his full attention. Ripe in years, he had known the Bonapartes for a long time and heartily mistrusted them. If his children joined in the overseas venture—and the energetic Coburg was in favor of their doing so—steps must be taken for their protection.

As a younger man King Leopold had once been offered simultaneously the thrones of Belgium and Greece. Upon very little provocation he was wont to describe his astuteness in managing that affair.

"Without money," he wrote to his son-in-law, "your participation in the Mexican scheme is impossible. Why, in 1830 each of the three powers, England, France and Russia, offered me a guaranty of twenty million francs. They did this with extreme reluctance and only because I forced them to it by declaring that I wanted no crown."

Maximilian was impressed. "In regard to military support," the royal counselor went on, "even if you were to provide your own Austrian suite, the Emperor Napoleon is quite capable of recalling his troops from Mexico if anything goes wrong, in order to exonerate himself. Therefore you ought to have something definite in writing, a document as binding as a treaty. Insist upon having clear stipulations in reference to the period during which French forces will remain in the country—the longer the better. Remember, they constitute your main support! The Foreign Legion is of course excellent but care should be exercised in recruiting and selecting volunteers for it, lest too much riffraff be included. To sum up, it is folly to let yourself be confounded by polite phrases. One must guard against illusions. Besides, no one can be expected to do the impossible. This is all the more vital since all blame for a failure (due to inadequate resources) will fall upon the one who undertakes the enterprise. . . . Without money, without some sort of contract, I would not budge. They are in your power—you are not yet in theirs. The whole thing is of the utmost importance to the Emperor Napoleon, for he has got himself into it, whereas you are still free from any entanglement. . . . Heaven protect you. Always, my dear son, your faithful father,

"LEOPOLD."

With such pragmatical directions to follow Maximilian found it easier to take up the fencing match with Paris. A few months of argument now ensued and in the end the French Government made several concessions. A gunboat manned by conscripts from Marseilles was tentatively appointed to accompany Maximilian (who should, however, travel on a vessel supplied by the Emperor Franz Joseph). Financial guaranties would be extracted, not from France or any other European power, but from Mexico herself, since the entire expedition was being undertaken for that country's own good.

So far Napoleon and his advisers had been able to formulate more or less expedient principles without consulting either the rattled émigrés (who were busy quarreling among themselves over questions of priority) or their partisans across the Atlantic. But now a ticklish problem came up. It was the matter of procuring a written invitation signed by a representative majority of the Mexican people.

A message was sent to Almonte, head of the Regency in Mexico City, urging him to stir up the Conservatives into a consolidated effort. Almonte appealed to General Forey who in turn convoked a Junta Superior or Supreme Council composed of thirty-five members chosen from a total of two hundred and fifteen found fit and willing to serve. To this group the French commander submitted a Proclamation of the Empire, the authorship of which—owing to his moderate degree of literacy—had caused him no little effort.

The document, which was signed on July 11, 1863, and submitted to Maximilian early in October of the same year, consisted of four short clauses. It ran as follows:

"1. The Mexican Nation adopts as its form of government a moderate hereditary monarchy under a Catholic Prince.
"2. The Sovereign will take the title of Emperor of Mexico.
"3. The Imperial Crown of Mexico is offered to His Imperial and Royal Highness Fernando Maximiliano, Archduke of Austria, for himself and his descendants.
"4. If, owing to circumstances impossible to be foreseen, Fernando Maximiliano should decline the throne offered to him, the Mexican Nation will appeal to the wisdom of His Majesty Napoleon, Emperor of the French, begging him to designate some other Catholic Prince."

Two hundred signatories were drummed together to append their names to this "spontaneous call." A commission was next appointed to visit the candidate at Miramar. It comprised eight members, two of whom were expatriates living in France. Their names were listed in the proclamation drafts as:

José María Gutiérrez de Estrada
José Manuel Hidalgo
Tomás Morphy
General Adrian Woll
Ignacio Aguilar
Joaquín Velásquez de León
Francisco Miranda
Antonio Escandón

A scribe, Ángel Iglesias, served as secretary and general handyman to the group.

The patriots planned to start out from Vera Cruz and various parts of Europe for a preliminary meeting in Paris. At a word from the Archduke Maximilian they would then hasten to Trieste and with due ceremony offer him the crown.

In the process of getting started, however, numerous persons of uncertain credentials joined the deputation. At the Paris headquarters their number grew to alarming size, putting a strain on the commission's budget. Differences of opinion cropped up, obfuscating the issue in hand. Several months were thus spent in vociferous and satisfying debate which caused Señor Miranda to remark that Mexico had now so many saviors—it hardly seemed fair to expose a helpless stranger to their combined antics.

The Mexican adventure grew daily more confused.

Chapter 6

At Miramar the Archduke Maximilian was pondering over a new morsel of advice from his father-in-law. King Leopold recommended unflinching tenacity. "Don't hesitate to take a firm stand," wrote the Coburg parent, "and force them to put everything down on paper. Stubbornness pays. During my Belgian campaigns, when the army left me flat, I captured a bridge in the vicinity of Malmis by the simple expedient of sitting on it."

Exhilarated by these words Maximilian awaited Napoleon's next move. It came within a fortnight. A special envoy from the French Court, Monsieur d'Herbet, arrived with a bulging briefcase from which he drew a long memorandum. Before this impressive document was unfurled the envoy discoursed with gravity upon his sovereign's sincerity of purpose and pointed out that here was the Seal of France and here L'Empereur's own signature. As for the text, Maximilian would see for himself that his demands had received the most magnanimous consideration.

Dazzled by Herbet's phraseology the Archduke picked up the memorandum. It consisted of eighteen articles setting forth the conditions whereby France planned to insure Maximilian's future on the throne of Mexico. Unfortunately the latter's excitement at the mere sight of so many closely written pages dimmed his perceptions while skimming through the contents. To be sure, the outstanding points were all in the happy Archduke's favor:

"Article 1. Those French troops which are at present in Mexico will be reduced as soon as possible to a corps of twenty-five thousand men, including the Foreign Legion. This corps will remain in Mexico for the purpose of guarding the interests which motivated intervention and shall be subject to the following regulations.

"Article 2. All French troops shall evacuate Mexico gradually and at such intervals as will permit His Majesty, the Emperor of Mexico, to organize the forces necessary for their replacement.

"Article 3. The Foreign Legion in the service of France, and comprising eight thousand men, shall nevertheless continue service in Mexico for another six years, even after all other French forces have been recalled. . . ."

At first glance these stipulations seemed too good to be true. The clause about the Foreign Legion, Napoleon's crack troops, was especially gratifying. Six years would seem, on the surface, more than ample time for Maximilian to establish his authority in Mexico and to win the confidence as well as allegiance of his new subjects.

So much for the military end. The economic portion of the memorandum, composed by the French Minister of Finance, Monsieur Achille Fould, was more ominous in portent. According to its terms Mexico must foot the bill of the expedition's back expenditures—a total of two hundred and seventy million francs—which France judged to have been her outlay since first her uninvited warships had steamed into the harbor of Vera Cruz.

This was an innovation in the realm of war indemnities. Most conquered nations were made responsible for wreckage done by combined fighting parties. But as yet no government in the world had been asked to pay for the mobilization of an enemy and the transportation of the latter's troops. The demand appeared all the more bizarre since no armistice between the warring parties had as yet been declared.

As a matter of fact, France was by no means in control of Mexico. Her forces held the capital and a portion of the Atlantic coast. But Juárez was still President and nine-tenths of the population had rallied to his side. Despite recurring skirmishes between Bazaine's sharpshooters and the Indian's guerrilla bands native opposition could not be crushed. Juarista volunteers continued to spring up like mushrooms, now at San Luis Potosí, now in Oaxaca where the fiery Porfirio Díaz held an invincible stronghold, or at Paso del Norte (Ciudad Juárez) where the Republic ultimately was reborn.

But Achille Fould was the son of a Jewish banker and, while he knew how to compute a profitable interest rate, his knowledge of geography remained elemental. To him the whole overseas panorama was a delightful conglomeration of gold and silver nuggets, oil-fields, dying natives and abandoned treasure. It was as simple as that. France had only to help herself. Accordingly he wallowed cheerfully in ever new computations. . . .

French liners and packet boats stopped at Vera Cruz every two months with mail and provisions for the brave zouaves. Very well. "The expense for the said service, fixed at the sum of four hundred thousand francs per voyage (going and returning) shall be paid by Mexico."

Furthermore, after July, 1864, at which date the Legion would be left in complete command, the Mexican Government must pay one thousand francs per annum to each French soldier *"pour dépense de solde, nourriture et entretien. . . ."* It is to be assumed that *"entretien"* in this case did not mean "entertainment or pleasurable conversation," as Pierre Athanase Larousse—the lexicographer—allows in his list of synonyms, but the more prosaic "upkeep, maintenance."

There was a great deal more to Minister Fould's multiplication table, such as "surplus-of-the-war expenses" which amounted to an additional twenty-five million francs, and indemnities to French subjects residing in Mexico for the wrongs suffered by them—which wrongs had been the original excuse for the friendly expedition.

Lastly, the genius of the financier threw a somersault. Monsieur Fould remembered the Jecker bonds! "Seventy-five million francs," he added with a flourish, "in liquidation of the loan of three million francs incurred by the bankrupt Miramón."

Knowing little about Mexico and rather less about money, the Archduke ignored these tedious figures and turned back the pages for a second reading of the passage concerning troops. It was a very pleasant passage and he nodded to Monsieur Herbet and said so.

The Envoy agreed happily and informed Maximilian that several secret clauses had not yet been included in the present draft.

These concerned the Archduke's salary as Emperor of Mexico, a matter which it was thought prudent to conceal from Maximilian's future subjects, lest they deem their monarch an expensive fixture. The monthly allowance agreed upon amounted to one hundred and twenty-five thousand pesos for the new Emperor, while his consort drew sixteen thousand six hundred and sixty-six pesos and a precise fraction which would bring the couple's income to a sum total of one million seven hundred thousand pesos annually. . . .

This was really delightful. The Archduke Maxl felt impelled to clap Monsieur Herbet's shoulder-blades with gusto. He handed back the Frenchman's memorandum without further perusal and headed for his wife's boudoir.

"As soon as the second draft is made," he called back from the Gothic stairway, "I shall be ready to sign."

In the upper hallway, where a painting by Portaels glowed richly in the vanishing sunlight, he paused. The picture showed Carlotta robed in gorgeous Milanese costume. On her oval face lingered that dreamy Mona Lisa smile which always brought back to him the ecstasy of their Italian honeymoon.

"Carla," he cried suddenly, "we are rich! They are giving us a throne and a fortune as well!"

Through the open door of a small dressing-room where Countess Paula Kollonitz, the lady-in-waiting, arranged her mistress's hair, he shouted the details. Carlotta paled and flushed again with excitement. This was indeed good news! As a cadet son of a great house poor Maxl had enjoyed a far from lavish appanage. Miramar had been built with money advanced by Franz Joseph after King Leopold had refused to provide his daughter with a dowry. In her heart Carlotta had never ceased to feel humiliated by her father's shabby behavior.

But now, with such astounding figures as her darling Maxl stammered through the plush portières of her boudoir, they could—well—thumb their noses at grumpy old Papa, the Hofburg and the world at large. Not that she didn't love Papa. He was precious, and she was of course devoted to him, but on the occasion of her marriage he did behave badly.

"I must write a letter to Franzi," the Archduke's voice now trailed off in the direction of his own rooms. "Join me as soon as you can. We should send a courier before going down to dinner."

She was in complete accord with this. Dismissing Countess Kollonitz, she finished her toilet in haste and presently tiptoed to her husband's writing-table where she peered over his shoulder, pressing her head close to his. At sight of his beautiful calligraphy and the even more beautiful message of wealth and success which it conveyed, she bubbled over with jubilation.

"Oh, that sweet Napoleon," she cried, "that excellent Eugénie!"

At dinner that night the master and mistress of Miramar radiated happiness. Table conversation, in which the French Envoy took his customary active part, sparkled with wit and sanguine prophecy.

Chapter 7

The post carried Maximilian's report to Vienna and the Emperor Franz Joseph's reply came by return pouch. Its tenor was slightly disappointing. "Yes, yes," wrote the Austrian monarch, "those sums are colossal, but what about the support of Spain and England? From your letter I can see that you did not insist strictly upon the guaranty of the three powers, particularly Great Britain. I must remind you most urgently of this condition as originally stipulated. You can not be dependent upon France alone."

From King Leopold, to whom a message had likewise been dispatched, came objections of a different sort. "If French troops remain stationed in Mexico for the best part of a decade," the strategist from Brussels wished to know, "who will become Commander-in-Chief? I do not see it clearly stated in your personal report to me whether or not the Emperor of Mexico is to be supreme war-lord in his own dominions."

Maximilian himself did not know the answer to this. The draft composed by Monsieur Fould contained several paragraphs on the subject but they were ambiguous and difficult to interpret. Article 5, for instance, provided that "in garrisons composed of both French and Mexican troops, or in expeditionary forces so composed, the French officer is always to have the command." This would appear to leave the Emperor of Mexico without practical authority except perhaps "in cases where native imperialist troops operate alone." It was a foggy issue and Maximilian did not understand it very well. To tell the truth, he hadn't the faintest recollection of having read Article 5.

It seemed as if these irritating objections from his nearest kin now loosed upon the Archduke new avalanches of dismal prognostication. From the most unexpected quarters came unsolicited notes of warning. A total stranger, Baron Emil von Richthofen, who was Prussian Minister in Hamburg and had formerly lived in Mexico, declared that "nothing could be done with that country by Europe." A person of still less renown, the United States Consul at Trieste, Richard Hildreth, spoke a small piece. "I know," he asserted emphatically, "that the Mexicans have a desperate and innate antipathy for kings and aristocrats. Allow me to add that anyone aspiring to the throne of Mexico, if he really attains it, will have to be extraordinarily lucky to escape with his life."

England, in particular, raised her voice in earnest protest. Lord Palmerston called Mexico a "witches' cauldron." He saw no future whatever for that country's "effete and mongrel population." The former *Chargé d'Affaires* in Mexico, Sir Charles Wyke, who happened to be taking the cure at Karlsbad, hoped the Archduke would not "poke his head into such a hornets' nest. Maximilian must have been deceived in regard to Mexican sentiments, for the monarchist party exists, politically speaking, only where it is supported by French bayonets, which may be the case on the direct line from the coast to the capital, but nowhere in the interior of Mexico."

Even obscure and impecunious Italian poets who caught wind of the affair wrote doggerels advising all pretenders to "renounce the rotten throne of the Montezumas." Their foolscap offerings peeped impudently from the mass of unread missives which the valet Sebastian Scherzenlechner dropped into a drawer of the Archduke's desk; here they were doomed to oblivion. It so happened that Maximilian complained, now and then, of headaches caused by eyestrain. Of late, the valet had been entrusted with secretarial duties, since the Miramar budget did not allow for a complete staff of princely attendants. Among Scherzenlechner's daily tasks was that of sorting his master's mail and reading aloud such reports as Maximilian, who tired easily, was in the habit of brushing aside. It was naturally in the servant's interest to remove from the Archduke's ken all unfavorable and discouraging information concerning the Mexican situation. If the dream of empire materialized, Scherzenlechner could reasonably expect further promotion, since the Archduke was known to show the utmost loyalty to subordinates.

In Paris similar tactics were pursued. At the New Year's Day reception, 1864, the Empress Eugénie was drawn into a sobering conversation with William Lewis Dayton, the American Minister. "Madame," said the latter, "the war in my country is fast drawing to a close and the North is going to win. France must abandon her project or there is trouble ahead for the Austrian."

The Empress changed color. Her face twitched excitedly as she answered: "Permit me to assure you that if Mexico were not so distant, and my son not a mere baby, I myself would place him at the head of the French army, in order to write with his sword one of the most shining pages in the history of this century."

"Madame," the American finished with equanimity, "you had better thank God that Mexico is so far away, and that your son is still swinging a toy saber."

Eugénie turned from him, gelid with rage. She made a mental note that neither the Minister nor his daughter would receive another invitation to appear at Court. As for the obnoxious warning, she must dismiss it instantly from her thoughts, and take care that no hint of it should reach that vacillating Archduke. A cheerful flow of correspondence must be kept up between the Tuileries and Miramar. The prize, a transatlantic empire for France, was worth the gamble.

In Vienna they were playing ostrich too. Up to now, the Hofburg had maintained a strictly passive attitude, even though the entire Hapsburg clan was inwardly consumed with anxiety lest the Mexican venture fall through. Ostensibly Franz Joseph found fault with the proceedings, urging more securities and pledges. Maximilian must not allow himself to be made into "a satrap of France." At the same time, the Hofburg was ready to bolster up the Archduke's courage, in the event that no further pledges were forthcoming. The Austrian frigate *Novara* had been overhauled in all secrecy and put in readiness for Maxl's long journey, since it was quite evident that England and Spain did not intend to proffer a flotilla. King Leopold's repeated jaunts to London had netted the observation: "Victoria seems anxious to see me. The weather has been vile!" but no boats.

The ticklish question of a bodyguard was being settled under cover. Since Napoleon had not made any clear promises on this point, Franz Joseph was recruiting throughout his provinces for a volunteer corps which might be called upon to accompany the Archduke to Mexico. Trained officers from the General Staff, "artillery with competent gunners, and pontoon-trains" were included in the plans, and each man was promised the same rank in the Austrian army (in the event of a forcible return) as he had occupied before leaving it. Letters were written to Brussels, requesting a thousand soldiers for especial protection of the Empress of Mexico, who was a Belgian national.

Besides this the family coffers at the Hofburg had been opened and a fund laid aside, amounting to two hundred thousand gulden. This sum was to be placed at Maximilian's disposal in the event that his promised grandiose salary from overseas was for any reason slow in arriving. After the Archduke had once ascended the throne of Mexico his regular allowance of one hundred thousand gulden would revert to the Austrian Crown and serve to pay up the mortgage on Castle Miramar.

In all these things Franz Joseph quietly prepared for any emergency which might arise to confuse his brother and deflect him from the glorious opportunity that lay ahead. Whether his motives were dynastic or personal, Franz Joseph favored the experiment and firmly believed in its success. He bethought himself of many helpful little details and, to complete his efforts, he capped them with an afterthought. This assumed the guise of a most original gift which arrived at Miramar on a crisp spring morning in 1864. Boxed by the Austrian Court Jeweler and created after a special design, it was found to be a diamond-studded scarf-pin embellished with the presumable imperial arms of a new Mexico. With the bauble came a demand for Maximilian's renunciation of his rights to the Austrian throne.

This was a severe blow. Placed face to face with such an alternative, Maximilian realized that his consideration of the Mexican Crown was in reality a *faute de mieux,* or hobby, desired only because it might fill the emptiness of his existence. To relinquish in its favor the sacred rights of Hapsburg succession—Austria's little Crown Prince Rudolf was six years old and might well require a regent before his majority—this was more than he had bargained for. Again, to the consternation of every one concerned, the Archduke refused.

The news reached Paris, where Herbet was soundly upbraided for not having once and for all committed Maximilian by obtaining the latter's signature on Monsieur Fould's preliminary draft. A revised and much embellished copy was hurriedly drawn up and a date set for a convention at Trieste. Meanwhile, Eugénie herself came to the front by hitting upon a most presuasive measure.

She commissioned a military tailor in Paris to create an elaborate parade uniform of a supposed Mexican field marshal. This, together with a handsome supply of stationery bearing the Hapsburg crest superimposed upon an Aztec eagle, was now shipped promptly to Miramar in token of her Majesty's friendship and esteem.

Carlotta, hardly less chagrined than the Empress of the French, made a hasty trip to Brussels for a consultation with her father. Anxiety filled her heart for she, whose mother had been a mere queen, "was wild to be an empress." What did Papa think of Maxl's new objection? Had he heard that the Archduke's feelings were hurt and that he intended to move to Rome as a private citizen?

King Leopold, it appeared, was au courant with the whole affair. He had confidential agents in Vienna who, when there was nothing else to report, sent on the imperial menu. On the subject of Maximilian's renunciation the Coburg temper flared up. It was wicked of Franz Joseph to trap his brother at the last moment with a matter which should have been decided upon before the Mexican negotiations had actually opened. Besides, where his own purse was not involved, Leopold believed implicitly in clamoring for one's patrimony. After all, Carlotta and her unborn children had a claim to Maximilian's inheritance, and renunciation meant that these descendants of the Coburg line would be deprived of their just rights.

"What are we to do?" the Archduchess asked.

"Be firm. Don't give up an inch."

"But Franzi will not relent—and we are in his power, since, as head of the family, he must give his consent before Maxl can accept the crown of Mexico. Should we forego this crown?"

King Leopold shook his head with still greater vehemence. "No, under no circumstances! You must never lose your great prospects in the New World."

"Well, then——" Carlotta saw that it was not easy for her father to find a way out of this labyrinth of paradoxes.

"Temporize," he said at last, with a resentful groan, "and demand some assurance that, in the event of a—fiasco—overseas, you will be reinstated and invested with your former rank and privileges."

Ignoring her father's involuntary admission that the Mexican adventure could conceivably end in failure, Carlotta committed his words to memory and returned to Miramar greatly heartened. She found her unhappy spouse browsing through a variety of painful missives, all of which were designed to stir him out of his dudgeon. Foremost among them was the Hapsburg Family Pact which listed the terms of Maximilian's renunciation and bore Franz Joseph's meticulous autograph. In addition to this there was a letter from the Austrian Emperor which began: *"Mein lieber Herr Bruder, Erzherzog Ferdinand Max!"* Under this solemn address of "Sir, my dear brother, Archduke Ferdinand Max" the reasons for the Hofburg's attitude were made clear. Historic precedents were quoted, among them Louis XIV's grandson, Philip, Duke of Anjou, who had been forced to renounce "all the rights of a French prince, rights of succession and regency, as well as appanage" before he became King Philip V of Spain.

The argument sounded reasonable. Franz Joseph claimed that he had been prompted by the interests of Maximilian as well as by those of Austria. "In the event of my death during Rudolf's minority," he wrote, "how would you perform the functions of a regent from Mexico? Had you intended abdicating the Mexican throne? If so, would you not in the meantime have become a total stranger to conditions in Austria?—Your duty lies in the direction of your new subjects to whom you must prove your love by renouncing all personal rights and devoting yourself henceforward to Mexico alone."

Couched in such felicitous terms the demands of Vienna seemed rather less grim. Carlotta felt certain that King Leopold's clause about future reinstatement could be wedged in.

But far more cutting than the dialectics of nervous relatives was a long harangue in Napoleon's almost illegible scrawl. It had been brought to Miramar by the latter's aide-de-camp and inspector-general of artillery, General Charles Auguste de Frossard, and was dated March 28, 1864.

> "Your Imperial Highness [wrote L'Empereur] has assumed responsibilities which you are no longer free to drop. Indeed, what would you think of me if—after your Imperial Highness reached Mexico—I were to declare abruptly that I can no longer keep the pledges to which I have put my own signature! . . . No, it is impossible for you to turn back on your plan of going to Mexico, or to admit before the whole world that you have allowed family interests to nullify all the hopes which France and Mexico have reposed in you. It is in your own interest as well as that of your kinsmen that these obligations be carried through as arranged, for the honor of the House of Hapsburg is at stake. . . . I plead your forgiveness for these apparently brutal words, but the circumstances are so stressing that I am forced to speak plainly."

Bonaparte shrewdness had inspired these lines, for Napoleon was well aware of the Archduke's subconscious reaction to an "ethical" challenge. Honor was Maximilian's most vulnerable spot.

In reality, despite the above recriminations, the French Emperor knew that his candidate was not yet bound by even oral agreements. But he felt that there would be no harm in a bold attempt to shake Maximilian's poise. One could always take a Hapsburg by his pride. A blunt accusation and the threat of certain scandal would bring the recalcitrant young man to terms.

General Frossard had instructions to assume his most martial mien while visiting at Miramar. If possible he was not to leave again without having extracted from Maximilian the long awaited answer for the stranded Mexican delegates who roosted in Paris cafés while awaiting the call of their sworn Emperor.

Frossard rather overplayed his part, strutting through the halls of Miramar with the airs of a prefect of police. His attitude so incensed Carlotta that she came to her beloved Maxl's defense, breaking into a conversation between the two men.

"We know perfectly well, General," she snapped, "that in going to Mexico we are performing a neat service for the Emperor Napoleon."

The Frenchman eyed her coldly. "A service," he replied, "which, I believe, is mutual——"

Carlotta flinched, for she perceived in his voice a galling lack of deference. "Perhaps so, Monsieur," she retaliated, "but you will grant that there is a discrepancy in values."

"And Madame the Archduchess wishes to say by that——"

Carlotta's next words came tremulously. "We may forfeit our health and our lives in that far land," she murmured; "surely this outweighs the paper exertions of your master!"

The duel of words ended there, with little gained, since nothing was more remote from Carlotta's mind than to strengthen her husband's present dislike for the Mexican candidature. Her tiff with the general was on personal grounds; she had to put the soldier in his place.

After the sparring was over it became necessary to solicit Frossard's aid in applying a kindly subtle pressure upon the Archduke. With feminine elasticity Carlotta smoothed her feathers and this time cajoled the corrected Frenchman into dropping his militant manner. Peaceful disquisitions ensued and by the end of the week Napoleon received a telegram in which Maximilian pledged himself to relent as far as his dignity would permit, while a separate courier carried the clause proposed by King Leopold to Vienna. If the former elicited joyful encomiums the latter brought only half-hearted cheers. Franz Joseph composed a reply to the effect that a place would most certainly be made for the Archduke and his wife, in the event of a miscarriage overseas. "A place" was not what Maximilian had asked for. A second note from Vienna modified the text of the first by the addition of agreeable predicates, while yet a third added that the Emperor of Mexico and his dependents would "at all times find a warm reception in the bosom of the family, with due regard for their former rank." But the rights of succession and inheritance received no specific mention.

Frossard continued at Miramar, interpreting—with Carlotta's able assistance—each new message from the Hofburg. Franz Joseph's cryptic phraseology did not strike them as cryptic at all! The French officer and the Belgian princess felt that the three autographed notes supplemented one another and completely covered Maximilian's demands. With considerable effort on his own part the Archduke allowed himself to be convinced. General Frossard departed for Paris with Maximilian's invitation to the Mexican commission.

CHAPTER 8

THE whole project which had languished for so many months was now imbued with a fresh glow of vitality. The émigrés and members of Forey's deputation gave up their constant bickerings and united once more under a common banner. Estrada brushed up on his Proclamation-of-the-Empire speech while sundry clerics rehearsed the ritual of administering an oath of allegiance.

At Carlotta's instigation a teacher of Spanish was promptly summoned to Miramar and Maximilian's library began suddenly to abound in grandiloquent treatises and starkly biased histories of colonial life. Judging from the authors who cluttered his bookshelves, the Archduke's information on the American scene in its fullest continental sense must have been a spurious mixture of Jules Verne, Karl May and James Fenimore Cooper, with a romantic dash of Don Quixote added for good measure.

The date for the arrival of the Mexican deputation at Miramar had been set for the early part of April. This left a brief span of time for a series of conciliatory visits to be made by Maximilian and Carlotta about the capitals of Europe, particularly in those countries where explanations were in order. Spain had at first been discounted. "No ships, no visit!" wrote Eugénie in regard to a call at Madrid. But in the end it was thought prudent to show civility to Queen Isabella. An exchange of courtesies with this Bourbon lady brought to light that the Queen of Spain held a definite grudge against the estranged colonies for not having offered the crown of Mexico to her daughter. She was readily consoled, however, by vague promises of a probable transoceanic marriage after the little girl grew up.

In London Queen Victoria, though pleased by the niceties of Viennese etiquette, was not amused. Sir Charles Wyke, back in his homeland, continued to make biting commentary. Being told that a deputation of Mexicans was even now en route to Miramar, there to represent the majority of their countrymen, the cynical

Briton declared: "Yes, some of them bring a majority vote from places inhabited by two Indians and a monkey." Nor was Lord Palmerston more cheering. In self-defense Maximilian pointed out that several Bourbon princes were eager to seize the Mexican Crown if he declined it. Perhaps the Queen's government preferred such an alternative. At this the gaunt Premier mellowed and broke into his roaring laugh. "A Bourbon," he shouted, "there's not one of them worth a fig!" And now Victoria too joined in the mirth, a thing quite rare in these days of her widowhood. True, she did not crow as she had done in her youth, when Mr. Creevey was moved to write in his diary: "A more homely being than our little Vic you never beheld. She laughs in real earnest, opening her mouth as wide as it can go, and showing not very pretty gums. She eats quite as heartily as she laughs; I think I may say she gobbles." But the Widow of Windsor's chuckle vouchsafed goodwill (if not a naval escort) to the Archduke, for she thought him a "genteel and likable young man."

Carlotta in turn won the Queen's heart anew by her tactfulness and charm. As far back as 1856, while still a young girl at Laeken, she had incurred Victoria's displeasure by not accepting King Pedro V of Portugal for a husband. The British sovereign had written copious letters to her uncle, King Leopold, insisting that "for Portugal an amiable, well-educated queen would be an immense blessing, for there never has been one." Elsewhere she had added: "I am sure you would be more likely to secure Charlotte's happiness if you gave her to Pedro, than to one of those innumerable Archdukes or to Prince George of Saxony." And, as an afterthought: "Pedro should, however, be written to. . . ."

But Carlotta had married one of those innumerable Archdukes and his delightful manners pacified the thwarted matchmaker of yore. In fact, had it not been for Parliament, Victoria was at the point of weakening and giving the "dear young people" a frigate. Experience with her Lords and Commons alone deterred her.

Before leaving England the future Emperor and Empress of Mexico had another somewhat poignant call to make. At Claremont, where the youthful Leopold had lived with his first bride

Princess Charlotte in the shadow of an English throne, now dwelled in exile the widowed Queen of France, Marie Amélie, and her daughter Clémentine, who had a very long Bourbon nose and suffered from insomnia. The relict of poor Louis Philippe was in a state of confusion over her grandchildren's adventurous schemes. Her knowledge of geography was dim, but she was familiar with the conduct of republican mobs—"horrible creatures, with cruel, fiendish faces"—storming a royal palace.

"They will murder you!" she repeated over and over, raising a bony finger in warning. The Princess Clémentine, who was very devout, clicked her rosary in time to the ominous words. With more haste than courtesy the Archduke and his wife took their leave.

Paris was next on their schedule. At St. Cloud Napoleon III graciously descended to the sixth step of the royal stairs (in 1856 he remained stonily at the top) and embraced his prospective cousin-in-ermine. Beside him stood Eugénie, radiant with satisfaction. She at once presented Maximilian with a gold medallion of the Madonna, murmuring: "It will bring you luck, Monsieur." For Carlotta there were a Spanish mantilla and one of those sandalwood fans with gold and silver filigree which Eugénie was in the habit of ordering in Madrid from her sister Paca . . . *"ten la bondad de comprarme dos abanicos escarlatas. Que sean los más bonitos que puedas descubrir y si ningunos te satisfacen búscalos hasta Cádiz. . . ."*

Such postscripts to Eugénie's letters were invariably written in Spanish, since only in her mother-tongue could the Empress prevail upon her sister that she must "search as far as Cádiz for the most beautiful scarlet fans with long staves and the most elegant panels. . . ."

Apart from these minor attentions Napoleon himself had prepared a more lavish gift. The firm of Christofle in Paris had been commissioned to engrave a silver tea and coffee set with the initials M.I.M. (Maximilian I, of Mexico) and a jewel-studded crown. A part of this set was designed for *petit déjeuner* or intimate and individual use, while the remaining portion followed the traditional banquet requirements. Queen Victoria, whose tastes ran to solid sterling, would have sniffed disdainfully at the modest silver content of French Christofle plate. Her Prime Minister would gleefully have drawn a caustic parallel between the spurious preciosity of Napoleon's offering and the dubious worth of the empire that went with it.

But the Archduke and his wife were dazzled by the flattery that enveloped them. As they drove through Paris streets people cheered. Carlotta was especially remembered because of her French mother, Louise Marie, who in her day had been as pious as her surviving sister Clémentine. "*Bonne chance, Madame l'Archiduchesse d'Autriche!*" cried the inflammable Parisians. To what extent such acclamations were spontaneous or prearranged can not be determined. It is a well established fact that no European monarch ever depends upon voluntary outbursts of homage from his people. They are apt to be embarrassing. When royalty goes visiting abroad professional cheer leaders are everywhere set in motion.

Thus an ovation had been planned to take place at the opera. But the affair was canceled at the last minute when news arrived from Munich that the King of Bavaria, Maximilian II (of the House of Wittelsbach to which Napoleon the Great had been so friendly), passed suddenly away. The Dowager Archduchess Sophie in Vienna was a Wittelsbach, as well as Empress Elisabeth, Franz Joseph's consort. It was therefore unseemly to engage in further festivities.

Instead, a few business matters were happily wound up. On March 18, 1864, Napoleon III had written to the timorous Archduke: "I urge you to count upon my everlasting friendship. You may rest assured that my support will not fail you in the accomplishment of the feat you are so courageously undertaking." To these pledges were now added the specific stipulations in regard to French troops and guaranties of safety drawn up in the revised memorandum of Messieurs Herbet and Fould. The Seal of France as well as L'Empereur's signature were appended to this new document, leaving a space for Maximilian's name (to be filled in after the formal acceptance of the Mexican Crown at Miramar). A witness to these proceedings was General Count Auguste Charles de Flahault de la Billarderie, one-time lover of careless Hortense, and father of Morny who possessed most of the Jecker bonds. This old martial figure and the suave shadow of his bastard son were as much a part of the Second French Empire as the Bonaparte goatee.

While the men were thus attending to affairs of state, Eugénie and Carlotta visited the more fashionable churches of Paris and prayed for the good of humanity in general and that of France and Mexico in particular. They went about heavily veiled, while the staunch Señor Hidalgo accompanied them. In his diary he noted that at St. Sulpice the Empress Eugénie fell into such a trance of religious fervor that, pushing her way through a crowd of nondescript worshipers, she reached the crucifix and kissed it "although a huge negro servant in livery had just finished doing so before her."

But at last the pleasant Paris days came to an end and the royalties parted with tenderest embraces. The trail led northward again, toward Belgium, where King Leopold awaited his children. Once more the streets of Brussels were festooned in honor of illustrious company, and at Laeken paternal eyes beamed.

Yes, King Leopold was pleased with his little Charlotte. Bursting with pride the old monarch dwelled fondly on the theme of Coburg prowess, admitting that Maximilian shared in this prowess, as it were, by proxy. Carlotta's two brothers, the Duke of Brabant and the Count of Flanders, hovered over their sister with unaccustomed gallantry. The older (later Léopold II of Cléo de Mérode escapades) saw fit to congratulate Maximilian in an address wherein he topped his rhapsodic felicitations with a characteristic personal note:

"The Hapsburgs, when joined with the Coburgs," he declared, "find ever new opportunities to indulge their legitimate passion for doing good to the most different peoples!" Cléopold, whose famous mistress earned him that nickname, was obviously content.

Carlotta appreciated the sentiment but marveled at the point of view. It was becoming quite clear that her family looked upon the Mexican project in terms of nothing but Belgian aggrandizement. The Coburg destiny became the subject of every conversation; it flavored opera, badminton and the soup. After the solitude of Miramar, where Carlotta had learned to dissect boredom until she almost loved its morbid languor, the vibrant atmosphere of Laeken seemed too stifling to bear. She welcomed Maximilian's suggestion that they continue on their journey.

It had been decided in private conclave that little time was to be lost in Germany where a grim gigantic figure loomed over Prussia. Otto Eduard Leopold, Prinz von Bismarck-Schönhausen, was putting the Teutonic household in order and planning great things for his country. The Catholic dynasty of Hapsburg did not figure favorably in these plans and Napoleonic chess games overseas were frowned upon. Obviously the thing to do was to tiptoe through the Reich and make for Miramar as soon as possible. Vienna had been scratched from the itinerary after a telegraphic message had reached the travelers on the Belgian border, announcing that the Mexican deputation was already assembling at Trieste. A dispatch from the Hofburg further assured Maximilian that the Emperor Franz Joseph and his younger brothers would set out in company of other members of the Court, hoping to reach Miramar in time for the convention. The stage was set and the curtain ready to go up. . . .

Chapter 9

The crystal chandeliers were gleaming in the marble ballroom of Miramar where no one ever danced. Under a gold-embroidered silken canopy the Archduke and his wife sat on gilded chairs and bowed to the strange guests whom the master of ceremonies, Marquis Corio, was ushering into their presence. Through tall arched windows a flaming sunset trembled over a turquoise sea. It was a late Sunday afternoon in April.

Maximilian had dressed in his most impressive uniform, that of an Austrian vice-admiral. He wore the orders of the Golden Fleece (granted exclusively to royalty and highest nobility) and the Grand Cross of Saint Stephen. Carlotta looked ravishing in a robe of crimson velvet. It was a color she did not usually enjoy wearing despite the vivid contrast it lent to her dark hair. Great quantities of Brussels lace inherited from her mother had been used for trimming bodice and skirt. Besides the archducal coronet she wore a necklace and bracelets of diamonds and the Black Ribbon of the Order of Malta.

Many friends had come from Austria, among them all of Maximilian's former instructors. There were the old tutor Count Heinrich and his son, Count Karl Bombelles; Prince Eszterházy who taught Hungarian at Court; Count von Schneider (mathematics); Baron de Binther (diplomacy); Pater Meyer (religion); and Vice-Admiral Zerman (naval tactics and Italian). Among them stood also Stefan Herzfeld, the young ensign who had shared Maxl's early days aboard a man-of-war.

In another group could be seen Napoleon's aide-de-camp, General Frossard, and the special French Envoy, Monsieur Herbet. They talked in low whispers with Belgium's Minister to Austria, Monsieur Monier, who had entered with the captain of the French gunboat *Themis*.

The Archduke was unaware of their presence. His blue eyes seemed fixed on far horizons and his full lips were pressed together in a straight line as if to force a determination which he did not feel. Carlotta knew that his thoughts were removed from this assembly where he would be offered an imperial crown; they were with his three brothers who had come to say farewell and had departed on the same day for Vienna. To the last Franz Joseph had upheld the dignity of his house by refusing to take more than a passive part in the proceedings. None of the Mexican delegates should catch sight of the Emperor of Austria, lest it be said that he negotiated a deal for his relative like any bourgeois tradesman.

Only yesterday, in a private room adjoining the great hall, the brothers had spoken to one another for the last time.

"You will bring honor to our house," Franz Joseph had said gravely, "and restore the luster which under my unlucky star was lost."

"I shall bring you no shame," was the simple reply.

"Mama and Sisi are waiting for you at home. Sisi couldn't come because of her rheumatism."

"What—at her age?" Both brothers seemed grateful for small talk.

Franz Joseph smiled. "Oh, yes, it's because she never stays indoors. Count Grünne asked her if the malady ran in her family, and she told him no, just in her legs."

There was a pause. Then the Emperor added: "Papa will be down from the Hradschin when you come to say good-by."

"That may be impossible. The Emperor Napoleon has fixed our sailing date for to-morrow."

"Max——"

Overcome with forgotten tenderness Franz Joseph clasped his brother's hand. Both men embraced in silence. The only audible noise in the room was the faint rustling of paper in the Emperor's breast pocket. It contained Maximilian's renunciation and signature. Franz Joseph could feel the words burning above his heart.

"Dynastic law compels us, Max, to do inhuman things." He turned quickly to go.

The younger brothers, Karl and Ludwig, saw no reason for such grief. The Archdukes Rainer, Salvator, Joseph, all cousins, joined in a chorus of congratulations. They raved. In their bleak aristocratic childhood they had all devoured the *Leatherstocking Tales,* and Maxl's good fortune was regarded by them with frankly envious eyes. With but a word of encouragement they would, each and every one of them, have packed up a rucksack and followed Vasco da Gama around the world. . . .

But duty squelched their glowing fantasies. The young men had been trotted back to Viennese barracks, drills and the amenities of Frau Sacher's famous restaurant. The Archduke Maximilian stood alone before his fate. Not quite alone, for beside him was Carlotta, devoted, vibrant, happy. She embodied the courage and assurance which he, the irresolute dreamer, lacked. Hers was the nature of a positivist. The Coburgs were all practical souls, untroubled by doubts. Through Maximilian's veins coursed the blood of older and more experienced races which rendered him more sensitive to light and shadow, to premonitions of failure and success.

It was Carlotta's smiling composure which turned the Miramar convention into a memorable event. The delegates from overseas were charmed by her elegance and poise. She was surrounded by ladies of title: the Marquise de Ville, the two Countesses Zichy (sisters) from Hungary, the Countess Paula Kollonitz, and Princess Pauline Metternich-Sándor whom Paris society called *"ce remuant petit monstre"* because of her clever and devastating tongue. The very sound of these distinguished names was pleasing to Latin émigrés who longed to breathe the air of Courts.

Following the Marquis Corio's painstaking directions the deputation had assembled in a semicircle about the great baldachin. Señor José María Gutiérrez de Estrada stepped forward and read the proclamation of the Regents of Mexico. Immediately behind him waited two notable orators, the prominent lawyer Pablo Martínez del Río and his colleague Francisco de Paul Arangoiz y Berzabal. As soon as their turn came a contest of admirable speeches ensued. With verbal blandishments as charming as they were unconstitutional the gentlemen whose tongues wagged so well explained to Maximilian that they represented the "overwhelming majority" of their countrymen. If in reality they scarcely represented one-tenth—and their deliberations or conclusions in no way proved binding for the unwitting balance of the Mexican nation—the Archduke had no way of either guessing or knowing the truth. The members of the deputation were themselves intoxicated by their own eloquence and, being misinformed by General Forey in regard to true conditions overseas, acted in perfect good faith.

To the final offer of the diadem of Mexico Maximilian made answer in moved and solemn phrases. "It can only be flattering to our house," he said, "that at the first mention of the word 'monarchy' the eyes of your countrymen were at once turned to the race of Charles V. I am ready to accept the throne, supported by the acquiescence of the high chief of my family and confiding in the protection of the Almighty."

On hearing these words Estrada knelt down before the Archduke and paid homage to him as the new sovereign. The president of the deputation raised Maximilian's hand above the heads of the assembly and cried enthusiastically: *"Viva Su Majestad Fernando Maximiliano, Emperador de Méjico!"* He then moved on to the Archduchess and repeating the gesture proclaimed her Empress of Mexico.

Throughout the room the salute was repeated while the delegates and attendants bowed in profound reverence. And as the venerable Abbot of Lacroma administered the oath of allegiance to Maximilian an almost atavistic belief in the divine right of kings surged in the latter's breast. How else, if not through predestination, could such things happen? Obeying this mystic credo he reverently placed a long white hand upon the Book of the Gospels which was presented to him by Dr. Ignacio Montes de Oca, a Mexican priest. The Empress, drunk with similar emotions, followed his example and repeated the vows spoken for her by Father Tomás Gómez of the Spanish Order of San Francisco. The organ in the palace chapel rang forth a majestic Te Deum and the entire company filed through the marble corridors in elaborate procession.

The ceremony over, Monsieur Herbet presented his documents for Maximilian's signature. The "Convention of Miramar," dated

April 10, 1864, became effective. The remainder of the evening was spent in acquainting the new sovereigns with some of their tentative officials. Señor Joaquín Velásquez de León was put forth as Minister of State, General Woll as aide-de-camp, Señor Ángel Iglesias as Secretary of the Cabinet.

The Empress meanwhile exercised her small and recently acquired Spanish vocabulary. In signing the pledge of allegiance she used for the first time the Spanish spelling of her name: Carlota.

That night the delegates stretched out luxuriously upon brocade-covered beds in the well appointed guest rooms of Miramar. For the first time the passages and stairways echoed forth a veritable Babel of voices while the deputation, penniless for the most part, reveled in the comforts of home. Count Émile de Kératry, who kept track of all expenses for which France could later make Mexico responsible, made a quaint notation on the margin of his accounts. "We paid for the apparel of the notables who went to Miramar," wrote the conscientious Frenchman, "as well as the flowers which were thrown under the feet of Forey's troops upon their entry into Mexico City (July, 1863)."

If the deputation slept well in its sheets the same could not be said for the newly proclaimed Emperor. On reaching his rooms Maximilian fell into a state of nervous despair. The full import of his momentous action loomed suddenly before him and he shuddered at the irrevocable step he had taken. The confusing foreign sounds that filled his quiet villa were but a symbol of greater perplexities to come—would he, an alien by birth and upbringing, be capable of meeting them? All at once the thought of exchanging the idle calm of his Adriatic retreat for the mingled joys of governing an unknown people appalled him. He developed a headache and rang for his physician, Doctor Jilek.

"They expect me to leave to-morrow," he complained. "Carla hasn't begun packing, and besides, one can't tear away from Europe as abruptly as that!"

The doctor spoke placating words and took his master's temperature. Maximilian was running a high fever. Defense mechanisms, destined to become fashionable in a psychoanalytic future, seemed to be at work. When spiritual distress becomes acute the body obligingly furnishes symptoms whereon may be pinned an excuse. The celebrated Jenny Lind always developed a spontaneous bonafide head cold when overcome by sudden stage fright. This physiological phenomenon has since become every singer's standard alibi.

Alarmed by the state of the Emperor's nerves Doctor Jilek feared a breakdown. Exercising his professional authority, he ordered a postponement of the trip. Since Maximilian's dejection lingered, the date of departure was twice shifted, being set for the twelfth and again for the fourteenth of April. The thirteenth had been discounted because of its sinister portent.

During all this time the Empress Carlota presided over banquets and receptions held for the special envoys who arrived daily with felicitations from Paris, Rome, Brussels, London and Madrid. There was a telegram from Napoleon:

> "I send congratulations to Your Majesty and adjure you, with all my heart, to rely upon my friendship and support."

Maximilian drafted a melancholy response in which he referred to his malaise "following a chill caused by the advent of His Majesty the Emperor of Austria, my brother." In glancing over this epistle Carlota did not approve of its implications and quickly composed one better. The chill was not mentioned.

And now the fateful hour was at hand. The morning of April 14, 1864, dawned gloriously over Trieste. Togged in their best finery the townspeople had gathered in a thick crowd along the flower-strewn Molo which stretched far out into the harbor. Representatives from Milan, Venice and the Istrian cities brought eloquent salutations to their former Viceroy, while the Burgomaster of Trieste in full regalia delivered himself of a touching farewell address. A copy of the latter was signed by approximately ten thousand burghers and presented to Maximilian in token of affection. It now appeared that every one had loved the gentle Archduke and that no one liked to see him go.

Among the last-minute telegrams was one from the Dowager

Sophie in Vienna. "Farewell . . . Papa's blessings and mine, our thoughts and tears accompany you. May God shield and guide you. Again, farewell from your native haunts where, perhaps, we shall meet no more. . . . We bless you now and forever from our aching hearts."

Maximilian was intensely moved, though hardly to a point where "with streaming eyes and convulsively heaving bosom, no word could pass his lips," as Mr. Percy F. Martin quotes an anonymous scribe of the age. Those were days when eyes must stream and bosoms heave for purely rhetorical purposes. Far more credible is the statement made by an eyewitness, the Countess Melanie Zichy. According to the latter's report the Empress of Mexico noticed her husband's suspiciously moist glance and whispered to her companions:

"Look at my poor Maxl! How sad he is——"

As for Carlota herself, no parting grief dimmed her joyous anticipation of the future. She had thoroughly enjoyed the hectic bustle of the past few weeks. With immense relish she had assisted her household staff in the sorting of trunks and boxes for the great voyage. Now she stood smiling in her straw bonnet, taffeta costume and lace mitts, poised on the brink of adventure.

It was a radiant day in April, the same date on which—more than a century and a half ago—the Bourbon Philip had made his entry into Madrid after being called to the throne of Spain. The analogy, already employed with such success in gaining Maximilian's renunciation of his Hapsburg rights, was complete.

Beside the embarcation steps a slender passenger launch rocked softly against the stone pediments. Tall and straight, its eight pairs of oars rose into the air, held by a crew at rigid attention. Out in the harbor, white and agleam, the *Novara* had weighed anchor. Beside her another Austrian gunboat, the *Bellona,* thundered forth salutes which were answered by the French frigate *Themis.* The imperial yacht *Phantasie* and six cruisers decked with pennants stood by to escort the outgoing ships for an hour. Fore and aft, on all the decks, bluejackets presented arms.

A fanfare of trumpets announced the moment of departure.

The municipal band of Trieste played the stirring Austrian anthem:

"Gott erhalte, Gott beschütze
Unsern Kaiser, unser Reich!"

With heads uncovered the crowd began to sing. At the end of the first stanza there was a hush, for the brasses now blared forth the unfamiliar measure of a newly composed Mexican national air.

The royal couple stepped into the launch. In the distance, from the topgallantmast of the corvette *Novara,* fluttered the imperial standard of cabalistic, inscrutable Mexico. . . .

III
THE PLAY

III

THE PLAY

Chapter 1

Count Giovanni Maria Mastai Ferretti from Sinigaglia—the ancient Sena Gallia in the Italian province of Ancona—thoroughly enjoyed his occupation. He was Pope Pius IX and in this venerable capacity he shuffled through the Quirinal in softly padded slippers pursuing the multifarious interests of heaven upon earth.

Posterity accords him an ample niche in the hall of the immortals mainly because of two magnificent gestures executed during his long reign. Cheered by the comforts of spiritual and temporal power he arose one day from his pontific breakfast of hot chocolate and buttercakes to proclaim the infallibility of Popes, present and future, "when on the subject of faith or morals they issue decrees ex cathedra to the universal Church." And again, after the summer palace of the Quirinal was unceremoniously coveted and seized by the King of Italy for royal residence, his Holiness refused all proposals of accommodation elsewhere and retired in splendid wrath to the Vatican where he declared himself a permanent prisoner. The obligation to nurse this grievance was bequeathed to his successors.

But on a fair spring morning in 1864—April eighteenth, to be exact—this energetic gentleman had not as yet adorned his biography with either of the above-named feats. Instead, he had for many months been busy brooding over the calamities that were befalling his faithful flocks in one of those preposterous Latin-American republics. The so-called reform laws advanced by that infidel Juárez caused no end of mortification to the Holy See. Archbishop Labastida of Mexico City had taxed the Supreme Pontiff's patience as well as his supply of sherry while reciting once again the woeful story of an ignominious and unepiscopal chase through the more unsuitable sections of a wicked town.

The Holy Father, who in days to come was so erroneously to deem himself incapable of error, became incensed. Putting a strain on his imagination he concentrated fearfully on proper punitive measures wherewith to daunt that distant Antichrist, only to wind up with his most conventional expedient—the discharge of a snorting papal bull. But Juárez, the Indian, jeered at the ferocity of this parchment monster which reminded him of the pasty complexions of well-fed clerics. Paying no heed to edict or anathema he continued to relieve church coffers of their bounty.

It was this circumstance which forced the cause of God to join that of Napoleon and to work henceforth toward the establishment of a monarchy in Mexico. To be sure, the new régime must be headed by a prince "belonging to a strictly Catholic dynasty" who would immediately annul the onerous Juárez decrees and restore the rich monastic properties to their rightful owners. The candidature of Maximilian of Austria admirably suited the expectations of the Holy See.

Cannon boomed from the forts of Cività Vecchia, the ancient Roman port, as the imperial flotilla bore Mexico's Emperor through the Tyrrhenian waters. They were French cannon. After aiding Mazzini and Cavour in ousting the Hapsburgs from the regions of the Po, France had neglected to remove her own troops from Italy. She left them there until the war of 1870, when there was need of them to fight the bad Bismarck in the North.

Hearing the harbor salutes Pope Pius made ready to receive his august visitors. The sumptuous Palazzo Marescotti had been prepared in advance and here Maximilian and Carlota took up their lodgings for the brief period of their stay. A papal audience was granted immediately and the former Archduke, still weighted down by his inexplicable depression, asked for the blessing of the Church. Pius IX dispensed this freely, interspersing indirect morsels of advice as he did so. There was always reason to suspect Napoleon of—well—caprice, and the Holy Father must look to the interests of his flock. Before administering holy communion to the kneeling Emperor he warned: "Although the rights of nations are great and must be respected, those of religion are much greater and holier."

Maximilian, aware of a subtle pressure which was designed to extract unfair concessions from him, compromised. "While honestly endeavoring to fulfil my Christian duties," he replied, "I have been called to rule a state whose interests I must primarily protect." With this the benediction was resumed, a trifle frostily, and after the customary ceremonies of leave-taking the imperial party once more put to sea.

In passing, a stop was made at Naples to greet Italy's royal family. Victor Emmanuel II, whose oiled moustachios reached behind his ears, had recently won the admiration of England's youthful Prince of Wales. During a visit at Windsor the lusty Italian King had boasted that he could sever an ox's head with one stroke of the sword. Such prowess captivated the future Edward VII. However, Vittorio Emmanuele, the Sardinian monarch, had made a more astounding boast to Britain's Queen. One day, after appraising Victoria's well-stocked nursery, he drew from a coat pocket a photograph of his children. The maternal Queen doted on the little ones and expressed her admiration.

"Oh," was the modestly immodest reply, "this is nothing at all; you should see my other family!"

At which the good Queen gave a piping little gasp and froze into austerity. As for Bertie, on future trips to the Continent he was forbidden to accept the depraved monarch's repeated invitations. Bertie always regretted this. He wondered ever after whether Victor Emmanuel, like the Shah of Persia, slaughtered beasts in the middle of the drawing-room floor and wiped his sword on the window draperies as was the case when the Oriental potentate visited European Courts. New rugs and upholstery had to be ordered for literally dozens of palaces after the touring Shah decided to clear out.

The Emperor Maximilian was troubled by no such vagaries. In showing courtesy to the brawny Victor Emmanuel he disarmed a former foe, for it had been the present King of Italy who with the aid of Garibaldi drove the Austrian Viceroy from his throne at Milan. And so the Neapolitan sojourn ended satisfactorily for all concerned. The King, whose profuse and fondly cherished goatee made him look like a rough replica of Napoleon III, found

Carlota enchanting and lost no time in telling her so. As for Maximilian's opportunities in the New World, the Italian had no words to express his genuine envy.

Again the travelers returned on deck and the blue panorama of Naples vanished in the distance. Corsica, the cradle of the Buonapartes, and wild Sardinia stretched out to starboard, and presently the brown coast of Spain came into view. Málaga, the Empress Eugénie's home town, lay smiling in the sunshine while straight ahead the massive Rock of Gibraltar proclaimed proud Albion's strength. As the ships entered the Straits a surprise awaited them. From all the British forts and anchored battleships cannon thundered forth their salutes to the imperial party. Queen Victoria, regretting her default in not cooperating with the Mexican expedition, was making amends. Albion's pride could show good manners. The fleet had orders to accord full honors to Maximilian and to respect his standard as soon as it approached British waters.

Spain and Portugal entered into the spirit of the thing and likewise touched off some nitro-glycerine when the *Novara* hove into sight flying her new colors. It was all in the best tradition and Maximilian took a vast delight in the proceedings. He quite misinterpreted the kindly action of his wife's royal relative and felt that the British booms promised even better things to come. While Victoria's guns conveyed veiled apologies for a government which intended to remain aloof, he told himself that now at last England had joined his cause.

To strengthen this erroneous impression, there was a tea party at the house of General Codrington, who commanded the naval fort. Within sight of the famous Rock the Englishman's daughter poured, and the guests enjoyed their last taste of hospitality on European soil. But the conversation veered discreetly away from political matters and remained frothy in character. It was perfectly clear that the agreeable din about Gibraltar, while very martial in tone, by no means contributed to the safety of the Mexican venture.

And now the incredible moment was at hand. They, an emperor and empress of the unknown, were gliding out toward the shoreless wastes of mid-ocean. They had taken that one small footstep—from a continent to a gangplank—a trifling, tiny interval like millions of other footsteps and yet so utterly unlike them that hardened globe-trotters pause for an instant of appalling vertigo before taking it. The *Novara* nosed ahead through foaming white breakers into the roar of the great Atlantic.

The lighthouse beacon at Cape St. Vincent grew faint and as it vanished the Hapsburg mood changed. Maximilian's melancholy returned. He found himself—in every sense of the word—at sea. For days he fought regret and a Sibylline sense of evil. Locked in his cabin he wrote ineffectual nostalgic stanzas which, incidentally, were to remain his last lyric efforts. Gradually, however, the tang of the salt air lured him from his retreat. He wondered about the other travelers, the Empress, her ladies, the secretary-valet Sebastian Scherzenlechner, the Mexican gentlemen. Probably bad sailors, all of them. Emerging from his seclusion he appeared on deck and studied the situation. Just as he had suspected, the Countesses Zichy and Kollonitz lay moaning behind steamer rugs while Herr Scherzenlechner meandered along the companionway with a face the color of fresh Gorgonzola. It reminded Maximilian of the little village by that name, near Milan, where during happy viceregal days the gluttonous manservant had gorged himself on the famous cheese.

Carlota, on the other hand, showed no signs of weakness. With never-ending curiosity she had roamed over the length of the ship. Her favorite occupation seemed to be the absorbed study of lacy patterns formed by the spume of spent waves before they rose again to be tossed over new brinks. So fascinated was she by this eternal play of the sea that at sight of her husband she took his hand and drew him at once to the railing. Her eyes were shining. He looked up from them to the vast horizon and was suddenly heartened by its promise.

Why did it all seem somehow unreal—like a dream of adventure—a play of fancy? Carlota pressed against him and whispered softly: "There is nothing to fear, Maxl!" The facile Viennese dialect sounded strange so far from home, but it had a good sound. And she was right, his brave Carla. Why should they be afraid? Were they not seeking the legendary dominions of his own illustrious forebears, Ferdinand and Isabella? Were they not retracing gloriously the path once taken by Cortés under that Hapsburg whose realm knew not the sunset—the Fleming Charles the Fifth? . . .

The rest of the voyage was profitably spent in preparation for the life that lay ahead. The Spanish tutor again took up his duties and Emperor and Empress memorized irregular verbs. As the *Novara* rocked past the Canary Islands a covey of small fishing smacks surrounded her.

"Skirting her flanks in gibbering flocks,
Gypsy traders from all the docks. . . ."

Doing their own haggling in snatches of the native tongue, the imperial pupils were able to make a number of useless purchases. It was a triumphant day.

Somewhere below the Tropic of Cancer Maximilian drew up a plan for his Cabinet, which he wished divided into a civil and a military secretariat immediately responsible to the Crown. To Scherzenlechner's vast disappointment the Belgian Félix Eloin, whom King Leopold had confidentially attached to Maximilian's suite, received the enviable post of a councilor of state. This gave rise to a feeling of latent rivalry between the former valet and the civil engineer Eloin, a phenomenon which was to recur with greater frequency in the Emperor's further appointments.

On the subject of a personal bodyguard Maximilian had devised a memorandum and submitted it to the French Government shortly before sailing arrangements were completed. "As ruler of Mexico," it ran, "I ought to command an armed force of my own which would enable me to exact respect from a nation possibly less prone than any other to accept authority without military backing. It would therefore be advisable to take with me a detachment of troops recruited in Europe but wearing the Mexican cockade and carrying Mexico's flag. In time these men will ask to be relieved. There will be vacancies which should gradually be filled by Mexicans, establishing the nucleus of a native army." In compliance with this request the *Themis* now followed in the *Novara's* wake, bearing her cargo of recruits. From the captain's bridge of his own vessel the Emperor regarded the daily drill exercises through a pair of monogrammed opera-glasses and transmitted orders to the *Themis* with the aid of a semaphorist.

He hoped to make an impressive entry into his new realm. For the purpose of training his retinue in the unfamiliar ways of an imperial Court he began to jot down points in etiquette and ceremonial which he remembered from Vienna. Presently the notations grew and expanded until there were more than six hundred closely written pages, with sketches and illustrations showing the pattern to be followed by his resplendent Court. The pleasure-loving Mexicans should not be disappointed in their monarch; every Sunday morning after mass the Emperor would grant audience to all subjects who wished to see him. The classic austerity of European absolutism should be tempered by most liberal reforms so that the glory of the throne might shine upon the great and the humble alike.

It was very upsetting that in the midst of such utopian preparations Maximilian should come upon a missive which the cautious Scherzenlechner had failed to extricate from the last minute conglomeration of mail. As the final pouch was brought on board at Gibraltar the secretary had inspected it with haste and sorted what looked like a batch of innocuous congratulatory messages. In the course of the voyage these messages were read. Among them waited a grim anonymous threat. Judging from the dialect used it seemed to come from an Austrian anarchist residing in the New World. Profoundly shocked, Maximilian meditated over its import.

> "The rumor goes that Mexico has been proclaimed an empire with your person at its head, a sample of impudence typical of Louis Napoleon. It so happens that I have a gun and a good aim. I pledge my honor that as soon as you reach American shores in the rôle of usurper you shall have proof of this. Don't worry, no tyrant escapes me. . . ."

The words stunned him. Here was something that had never occurred to him. He had a personal enemy! To the popular Archduke Maxl whom every one liked the realization came as a painful blow. He cut short his treatise on etiquette, which needed cutting anyway, and retired once more to solitary ruminations in his cabin.

Quite soberly he examined his conscience. Was he coming to Mexico for the sole purpose of liberating a war-torn people from the curse of self-destruction? Was he bent upon bringing happiness to a nation he did not know and very likely would never understand? Humble and honest with himself the Emperor wrote down an answer to his own questionnaire:

> "In all circumstances of my life I shall be only too happy to make every sacrifice, no matter how great, for Austria and the future of my house. Throughout the centuries every dynasty in Europe has adhered to the prudent practice of appointing cadet sons to conspicuous posts where they might further the interests of their mother country. This policy has been known to embrace diplomatic and political as well as commercial fields. . . . Owing to the accelerated pressure of modern conditions the power of our family has diminished. While the adaptable Coburgs take throne after throne, our ancient house has in recent times forfeited two sovereignties (the province of Tuscany in 1859, and the seat of Austria-Este in Modena during 1860). In view of these misfortunes I have become convinced that it is the sacred duty and desire of every Hapsburg to wipe out this stain. I cannot but believe that a good impression will be made upon the world, and especially upon our weakened Austria, if the Mexican enterprise attains success."

Having eased his mind with this piece of self-revelation he filed the statement among his private papers and returned on deck. It was the ninth of May and the island of Martinique had just been sighted.

On the twelfth the ships reached Jamaica where Queen Victoria's kindness again warmed the travelers' hearts. They were greeted by Admiral Sir James Hope and taken ashore at Port Royal by the military governor, General Ashmore. There was much tea-drinking after which the civil governor, Mr. Edward John Eyre of "Gordon Riots" fame, arranged a sightseeing trip.

While the royal party sampled its first coconuts in the shade of waving palms the United States Minister to Mexico was reading a terse code message from his government ordering him to pack his grip.

A few days later the approaching Emperor of Mexico met the departing American representative out at sea, off Habana, and there was no greeting.

Chapter 2

On May twenty-eighth, after six weeks of untroubled sailing, the ships dropped anchor at Vera Cruz. The travelers set foot upon a sun-baked alien land. There was no one to meet them, despite previous instructions from Paris ordering an official reception and a banquet.

Appalled by this impasse the Emperor and Empress returned on deck for their evening meal. While they were listlessly pecking at their monotonous nautical diet of potted meats the report was brought that General Almonte had just scampered into town. With true Latin irresponsibility the President of the Regency had forgotten the exact date of Maximilian's proposed arrival and, not wishing to expose himself to the ravages of yellow fever, had stopped to enjoy the ozone up-country at Orizaba.

The French Rear-Admiral Bosse and an aide-de-camp, both of them in a very bad temper, now rowed ashore and exchanged angry words with the lackadaisical Almonte. At this a belated salvo of salutes burst forth from the fortress of San Juan de Ulúa while a few shrill *"vivas"* broke the ominous stillness that hung suspended over the town. After that there was silence. The harbor presented an unchanging and desolate spectacle, for the population of Vera Cruz remained cold and would not acknowledge the presence of an emperor. The zouaves who heralded his coming had not been forgotten.

That night brave dreams began their battle with reality. The Belgian princess tasted fear.

At dawn the imperial party landed once again and without further ado made for the little railroad station. Their passage through the deserted streets was hailed by the unfamiliar croak of zopilotes, hideous vultures circling from time immemorial above the dank tropical beach. Like Gothic gargoyles these gloomy members of the Andean condor species squatted on the cornices of buildings or poised themselves, with a macabre sense of line, upon fluted columns of organ cactus. They gathered one by one on the cross of a near-by church until the holy symbol loomed as a black outline against the morning sky. With primordial patience the huge birds sat, waiting for carrion.

The Empress gasped in sudden dismay. Turning to the French commander of the port, she asked whether the repulsive scavengers were hard to destroy.

"Madame," was the reply, "they are protected by law, because the carelessness and indifference of the inhabitants to sanitary matters makes them a necessity."

He made an encompassing gesture toward the surrounding swamps from which a meridional sun distilled a slow deadly poison. "An evil place for Europeans," he added with detachment, "there's a graveyard full of them over yonder."

The tiny train chugged through the dreary flatlands toward the slowly rising plateau. After a few hours of travel La Soledad was reached. A little over two years ago England, Spain and France had come to differences on this spot, causing the former two powers to retreat from Mexico while the Empress Eugénie wrote to Miramar: "Here we are, thanks be to God, without allies!" And now, in 1864, the master and mistress of Miramar sat in the untidy inn of the place called Solitude, and again a messenger from Juárez appeared from the interior. Clutched in his hand he held a grimy note. Maximilian gulped his lukewarm coffee and rose to decipher the scrawled message from the Zapotec patriot.

> "It is given a man, sir [he read with Almonte's aid], to attack the rights of others, seize their goods, assault the lives of those who defend their nationality, make of their virtues crimes, and one's own vices a virtue, but there is one thing beyond the reach of such perversity—the tremendous judgment of history."

Again Maximilian stood aghast. He had no way of knowing that while he studied the compass in mid-ocean the brutal Bazaine "whipped men and women publicly in the patios of university buildings and archbishoprics of Mexico City" in order to convince a stubborn nation of the benevolence of its invader. . . . The awful truth began to dawn. He, the Emperor, was being foisted upon a land that quite possibly did not want him. He was coming as an enemy! But this was not what Maximilian had meant when he declared himself willing to bring every sacrifice for the glory of Austria. One did not come by glory in such a way. To a prince who wore a jeweled sword for purely decorative reasons, the fierce accusations made by Juárez were appalling to a profound degree. He felt a little sick at the whole affair.

But what was there to do? Matters had gone this far with the eyes of all Europe fixed upon the Mexican experiment. To turn back at this point would bring down upon his name the scorn and derision of the whole world. It was impossible to admit defeat without making at least one desperate dash for victory. . . . In 1519 Cortés, the Conquistador, had experienced a similar access of funk but had whipped up the courage of his men by secretly burning his ships and sinking them off La Villa Rica de la Vera Cruz. . . . The Emperor Maximilian was morally obliged to do the same. Turning his back upon the things that lay behind he pressed on toward the midlands. The capital of the ancient Montezumas must be his goal.

The train climbed bravely upward over serpentine tracks until it reached Tomalto where the railroad came to an end. The royal party scrambled out once more and prepared to continue the journey by diligence. Maximilian had brought his own carriage, a ponderous and ornate vehicle built by an English firm and transported as far as Tomalto on a freight car. Mule teams were now chartered for this elaborate contraption and harnessed, first two abreast, then four, and then again two, while a skilled native driver was entrusted with the confusion of reins. Slowly the coach was set in motion, rumbling precariously up-hill, while the imperial suite of more than one hundred persons followed by stage.

> "A Mexican diligence is a most wondrous vehicle [wrote Princess Agnes Salm-Salm many years later], only surpassed by the wondrous roads. . . . The coachman keeps up a perpetual conversation with his mules, which he calls by their names,

animating them by all kinds of extraordinary sounds. His eloquence alone, however, would scarcely succeed in persuading them to do their duty, if not supported by an assistant, a boy as active as a monkey. The latter runs along the road collecting stones with which he clambers up beside his chief for the purpose of peppering the recalcitrant beasts with emergency volleys."

The roads were so atrocious that during the rainy season it became a difficult task to send a mail-coach from capital to coast without mishap. The contractors used to promise a bonus of one hundred pesos to every driver who managed the trip for a month on end without upsetting his load. Since the company was founded this premium never had needed to be paid.

Another hazard which lent an undeniable flavor to the enterprise was the traditional chance of encounter with masked robbers. The latter, frequently in league with rich rancheros of the region, indulged in the harmless sport of undressing travelers and snatching from them whatever baubles appealed to their vandal tastes. These holdups took place according to ritual. At sight of a band of swaggering bandits, elegantly dressed and mounted on splendid horses, the diligence came to a quick halt. After an exchange of courtesies the ruffians went about their business while the coachman and his aide sat meekly on their perch, their eyes fixed straight ahead. The sounds which emanated from the interior of the conveyance disclosed the course of operations so that even the imperturbable mules were able to gauge the exact moment when they might resume their gentle trot. A roar of ribald laughter and a cloud of yellow dust marked the close of the ordeal—and disconcerted travelers were free to use their smelling salts.

The imperial caravan was protected against such calamities, for General Almonte had provided a mounted escort. A young colonel, Don Miguel López, was to watch over the Emperor's personal safety. He rode beside Maximilian's carriage. But even a mounted guard could not offset the perils of the road-bed. On the banks of the River Chiquihuite, which was swollen by recent cloudbursts, a wheel of the Emperor's calash splintered into bits.

"Toward seven o'clock that night [wrote Carlota to the Empress Eugénie] we were stuck in a dense forest and not until two in the morning did we reach Córdoba, entering the town in a republican stage-coach. The journey has supplied me with ineradicable recollections. . . . The Mexicans kept apologizing for the roads—we had lumbered through half a dozen ravines by that time, some of them hemmed in by rocks several meters in length. Of course we insisted that we didn't mind in the least, but as a matter of fact it was all beyond words. We needed every ounce of nerve and good humor to pull us through without damage to life or limb. . . . However, let me assure you that the roads are the only detail which I have found rather worse than I anticipated."

Her gallant spirit would not acknowledge the immensity of their disappointment.

Not far from the scene thus described a second mishap overtook the party. It was in a spot designated with Indian felicity as the *Sal si puedes* (Get out if you can) Gully.

"Between La Cañada and Palmar [Carlota's narrative continued] one large barouche that followed us upset with six gentlemen in it. Our Minister-President of the Empire, Señor Velásquez de León, was at the bottom of the spill and had to climb out through a window. All this happened merely because it had been raining for about a quarter of an hour. . . . Your Majesty will realize that a trip through this country is no trifling matter, yet we were not the least bit tired."

Orizaba, with its snow-capped volcano which on clear days could be seen from the Gulf, was approached at ten on the following morning. From here the journey across the high mountain passes offered terrific hardships for the road now ascended abruptly toward the plateau of Anáhuac.

The *Tierra Templada,* or temperate land, soon disclosed its profusion of colors and smells. Donkeys laden with vanilla trotted down from the slopes of Oaxaca, their furry hides perfumed by the precious spice. After stretches of almost impenetrable jungle, with lianas and giant orchids entwined among the treetops, there followed vast geometrically laid out maguey plantations. Here and there the century-plant (Agave Americana, known in Europe as aloë) had burst into bloom, its tall-stemmed flower rising up into the air like a slender palm tree.

Cockatoos and gaudily plumed parrots, among them the exquisite quetzal, screamed from thatched roofs in remote villages surrounded by living enclosures of cactus. Prickly pears of succulent ripeness tempted the diligence drivers. The pebble boys gave the mules a rest and descended to browse among the fair wild delicacies.

Mexico's strange and quite peculiar face was revealed to the awed peregrines. Nowhere on earth, Carlota felt, could nature have composed a more harmonious landscape. Everything seemed to belong—the limpid air with its purple hues, the savage flora, the sickening sweetness of unfamiliar scents. Thick-walled adobe huts, some of them whitewashed with lime, stood out vividly against this background. Indians in peaked hats and hand-made sandals unconsciously assumed the plastic serenity of mural paintings. Their brown figures clad in white cotton and wrapped in bright red blankets made vivid al fresco silhouettes upon a scene already riotous with color. Little girls, miniature replicas of their mothers, moved softly in long pink skirts and fringed *rebozo* shawls of Virgin Mary blue—the blue of Raphael, and Correggio, and Leonardo da Vinci—under a sky of sapphire richness. Beside them ran barefoot urchins in rain capes made of dried rushes which stood off in all directions like the quills of a porcupine. Here and there a woman swept invisible dust from the well-stamped earth of her door-step with the single leaf of a giant palm. . . .

The former Archduke and his bride from Laeken were spellbound. They felt impelled to show some sign of benevolence toward these new and exotic subjects but were deterred from their purpose by a dismal French warning. The scourge of the black pox was a frequent visitor in this pastoral region.

Silently the travelers pressed on, listening with alarm to the wild beating of their hearts. Languid dark eyes peered after them, marveling at the strange caravan of Rhenish and Bohemian noblemen, Hungarian hussars, French lancers and Viennese flunkeys.

Night came and under its dark curtain the scenery changed anew. The plateau of Puebla was in sight with its bare stretches of volcanic lava over which the Spaniards had carved a path three hundred years before. That ancient *Camino Real* had long ceased to be a King's Highway. Its prodigious humps and crevices bore witness to a stoical and democratic disdain for hardships. However, the imperial bones endured even this test without flinching. More than that, toward noon the high cordillera known as *Las Cumbres* had to be crossed on horseback. Weary and aching, the travelers ensconced themselves on improvised saddles while the lightened vehicles followed gingerly behind. It was the seventh of June and the Empress Carlota's birthday. She was twenty-four years old.

La Puebla de los Ángeles, where the greatest battle in Mexican history had been fought more than a year ago, was a strong French garrison. Fanatical Conservatives from Mexico City had gathered here under foreign protection to prepare a reception for the Emperor. Decked with flowers and imperial bunting these ardent royalists galloped to the city gates to meet the astonished arrivals who by this time no longer knew what to expect. There were cheers of *"Viva Napoleón! Viva el Emperador Maximiliano!"* which brought tears to Carlota's eyes. It was the first sign of welcome and she described it faithfully in her long letter to Paris:

> "The governor of Puebla and General Brincourt came out to meet us at Puente Colorado. I can not praise Brincourt enough to your Majesties; of all the capable officers here, he is, to my mind, the most remarkable in courage, energy and tact, for he understands and humors the Mexicans better than anybody. I believe he will render distinguished services to our cause."

Her gratitude did not consist of words alone. Brincourt and the Puebla reception committee were the first to receive the Grand Cross of the Order of Guadalupe in April of the following year, after this decoration—which had been founded by Iturbide—was revived by the Emperor Maximilian.

Carlota's pen described the last lap of the journey. "Leaving Puebla we continued to Cholula and attended mass on the *teocalli* in the chapel dedicated to the Virgin of *Los Remedios*. There is something quite touching about this shrine on a pyramid where human sacrifice once took place. . . . The surrounding valley reminds me so much of Lombardy; this holds true of Mexico City as well—its location is enchanting. The officers who were with us during the Italian campaign agree about the resemblance. This makes us really happy for we imagine ourselves to be in Europe."

After Puebla and Cholula the road narrowed and led still higher toward the region of fir and pine. From mountaintops thickly covered with cedars the strangers now beheld Anáhuac, the ancient Aztec realm. One of the finest panoramas in the world, it stretched before their fascinated gaze like an immense magic carpet.

In the distance shone the eternal snows of Popocatepetl and Ixtaccihuatl, the Smoking Mountain and the White Woman. Mythology described the former as a jealous lover watching over his frozen mate.

At their feet the bright waters of Lake Texcoco reflected a purple and topaz sky, giving to the valley its name Anáhuac—Near the Waters. For many years preceding the Spanish Conquest the rich city of Texcoco, populous seat of Tezcucan kings, rivaled Tenochtitlán in social and political importance. The entire province was a literary center. Here the erudite Netzahualcoyotl, who was called the Tezcucan Solomon, lived and wrote the odes of his halcyon days. And here the invading Spaniards launched their brigantines (built in Tlaxcala and brought hither in sections) against the island stronghold of Montezuma.

The stupendous view fired Maximilian's imagination. Already he was beginning to grasp that life in Mexico was an everlasting paradox, a contradiction between the tragic and the sublime. Everything in this land seemed to be violent, remote, breathlessly exciting. Violent were the contrasts of color and landscape, violent the climatic changes and the pressure on the membrane of human ears as men climbed or dropped two thousand feet per hour.

The royal caravan paused on the summits to wipe bleeding noses and calm pumping hearts that fought against the altitude. Languidly the march was resumed toward Guadalupe, the last stop before entering the capital.

In Guadalupe the ceremonies of Cholula were to be repeated, for the Emperor wished to hear mass before the miraculous image of that name. While still at Miramar Maximilian and Carlota had familiarized themselves with the legends and traditions of their distant empire. This enabled them to honor customs that were sacred.

The shrine of Nuestra Señora de Guadalupe, three miles from Mexico City, had long been to Mexicans what the Ganges was to the Hindus, Mecca to the Mohammedans, and Nikko to the Japanese. Like most Mexican churches, the Catholic basilica rose above the ruins of a pagan temple to some Aztec deity (in this case Tonantzín, protectress of the Totonaqui Indians, and goddess of the Earth and Corn).

The name Guadalupe was derived from the town of Cuautlálpam which to Spanish ears recalled a famous sanctuary in Estremadura. The original Virgin so baptized was treasured by the rich Geronimite monks in Spain, concerning whom the proverb ran:

"Quien es conde y desea ser duque
Métase fraile en Guadalupe. . . ."

("He who is count and would be duke
Should take his vows at Guadalupe. . . .")

The Mexican namesake of this much exploited lady had a quaint history. On the morning of Saturday, December 9, 1531, (ten years and four months after the fall of Tenochtitlán), an Indian of low birth, one Cuautlatohua, who had been converted and given the Christian names of Juan Diego, was walking from his native town of Cuautitlán to Tlaltelolco, there to pray and learn his catechism.

The road led over a barren hill known as the Tepeyac, on which grew no leafy vegetation save cactus and the eerie shapes of yucca palms. The latter, especially on moonlit nights, resembled human forms marching hand in hand—and in assorted sizes—across the wilderness.

Now poor Juan Diego was fifty-eight years old and given to pulque bibbing, for his uncle Juan Bernardino owned a juicy little maguey patch. At any rate, during this pilgrimage the pious Indian suddenly became aware of a purling, plashing, sibilant music which increased in volume until his ears fairly rang with bombilation. He raised heavy lids from eyes that swam in happy moisture and endeavored to detect the source of such sweet tones, but as he did so a magnificent rainbow blinded him. Bare rocks took on the prismatic tints of opal, sapphire and burnished gold, until Juan Diego felt dizzy with wonderment. And now, in the center of all this effulgence, he beheld a beauteous female apparition who called to him *"Hijo mío!"* (my son), and introduced herself as the Mother of God.

"I should like," the lovely lady said, not without verve, "a church to be built on this spot, so that all who pray here may be blessed."

At this Juan Diego fell to his knees and made a noble effort to kiss the hem of her garment. But the heavenly visitor had fled. There remained only the echo of her command.

Juan Diego scrambled back to his feet and ran to the Bishop, Fray de Zumárraga, to whom he related his experience. The Bishop was skeptical. He sent the Indian on his way. Again and again the apparition now began to haunt Juan Diego, giving him the same order which —since he was not an architect—he could not fulfil.

After his fourth encounter with the celestial vision Juan Diego decided to avoid the Tepeyac by taking a little path that led around the hill. He was on his way to his uncle who lay ill of a fever called *cocolixtle* when, on the twelfth of December, the Virgin came strolling down the hill with the unmistakable design of intercepting him. The whole thing had become rather awkward and Juan Diego now bent quickly over a near-by well (thereafter called Pocito de Guadalupe) pretending to drink. But the Virgin called to him and asked about that church.

The Indian wept and explained that no one would believe him unless he brought a sign. At this the Madonna bade him cull roses from the crest of the barren Tepeyac and wrap them in his blanket. Juan Diego obeyed. Climbing to the top of the hill he felt himself enveloped in a deliciously perfumed breeze while with trembling hands he plucked great blooms from the cactus thicket.

Burdened with the blossoms which he had tied up in his *tilma,* or mantle, he again visited the Bishop who, meanwhile, had thought the matter over. It was not at all a bad idea, Zumárraga reflected, for Mexico to have a local patroness. He accepted the Indian's *tilma* with the aromatic flowers and retired to his oratory where he remained cloistered in episcopal secrecy.

A few days later the story of the miracle was made public with the added embellishment of an almost life-sized likeness of the apparition painted in oils on Juan Diego's rough blanket. How the image got there constitutes a pleasant mystery, but ecclesiastic records explain that the flowers in dropping from the folds revealed the divine form.

Certainly one can not but admire the positive genius of Zumárraga in disclosing the Virgin, not in the guise of a Spanish woman, but attired like an Indian princess and bearing a decided resemblance to the goddess Tonantzín, thus striking native credulity at its roots. A wave of apostolic piety hereafter overtook the semi-pagan land. Jealous friars evangelizing the provinces of the interior soon discovered another Juan Diego at Tlaxcala whose *ayate,* or knapsack, bore a picture of the Holy Mother of Ocotlán. In the solemn words of Princess Agnes Salm-Salm, this portrait was also painted "probably by some angel."

Maximilian and Carlota had the wisdom not to quibble over matters of faith. They appealed to the susceptibility of a devout nation by worshiping at its most cherished sanctuary. Upon first seeing the brown features of La Guadalupana the Empress was puzzled, but she remembered presently that the blessed lady was known for her idiosyncrasies, appearing to the Germans with blonde Gretchen tresses and in Africa as a negress. Religion bowed to the mandates of ethnology.

The service in the basilica was short. After its close the royal party emerged from the incense-laden darkness to find a large crowd gathered in the public square. Innumerable carriages with elegantly dressed Mexican ladies, escorted by *caballeros* (gentlemen-on-horseback) in European apparel, had come from Mexico City to meet the Emperor and Empress.

In a compact little group just beyond the temple doors stood General Bazaine and the French Minister Marquis de Montholon, as well as the Austrian *Chargé d'Affaires* and his staff. Intimidating all citizens of the capital who held opposing views, the friends and relatives of the Paris émigrés had united with the French authorities to proclaim the Empire.

In triumphal procession, marked by deceptive outbursts of enthusiasm, the cortège now moved over the ancient causeway flanked by a double row of *chopos* (black poplars) and *álamos* (white poplars) which led to the Plaza Mayor in Mexico City.

Chapter 3

On June 12, 1864, Maximilian and Carlota entered their capital after what seemed to them an interminable trek. Weary, yet pleasantly surprised, they found a cheering populace assembled before the great cathedral where without further delay a preliminary coronation took place. Since no one in Mexico had the remotest knowledge of royal insignia and trappings a second ceremony was to follow as soon as a crown, scepter and ermine train could be provided. Iturbide's mercurial reign had not lasted long enough for such symbolic adjuncts, whereas the vesture of the Montezumas defied memory.

However the occasion was not lacking in solemnity. At the steps of the high altar Maximilian took the oath of fealty. Toward the close of this act all the cathedral bells rang out in chorus while the imperial couple walked slowly toward the Zócalo, as the Plaza Mayor is now called, and entered the Palacio Nacional.

This rambling two-storied structure with its enormous portals and eleven hundred windows was not unlike an army barrack. It had fallen into decay since the departure of the last viceroys and showed signs of recent hurried repairs. The apartments assigned to Maximilian and his young wife resembled nothing so much as a suite of third-rate European hotel rooms. To complete the picture, the establishment was alive with vermin. The imperial couple were routed during the first night by presumably Jacobin bugs and obliged to take refuge on a billiard table.

Some days later the Court made a speedy change of quarters by moving to Chapultepec, the summer castle on the outskirts of the city. It had been built in the years 1783 to 1785 (under the forty-eighth and forty-ninth Viceroys, Don Matías and Don Bernardo de Gálvez) on a rock of basalt and porphyry overlooking the capital and the valley of volcanoes. This spot of enchantment, the original site of Montezuma's legendary palace, at last offered adequate shelter.

But here, too, a number of improvements became necessary. Like most antiquated residences in Europe the castle of Chapultepec lacked certain details of plumbing. Royalty everywhere was accustomed to odious makeshifts in this respect. The old Hofburg in Vienna boasted no bathtubs. Until the arrival of the rebel Elisabeth, who at once ordered modern equipment from England, ablutions took place each morning in a portable zinc pan, with attendants laving the imperial forms. Ample Maria Theresia had got along quite happily in her basin.

Conditions were not very different in the aristocratic residences of Berlin. Here discreet cabinets were installed in the walls and hidden behind embroidered screens. Members of the Court made use of them unconcernedly while peruked sentries patrolled the length of the passages.

But France capped all for nonchalance. The château of Versailles lacked all sanitary trimmings save the crockery which recent generations have consigned to nurseries. All the most renowned manufactories of faïence and majolica did a thriving business with the articles in question, embellishing them with initials, crests, mottoes and various quaint conceits. Some had clocks, while others were equipped with music boxes. Despite such refinements, however, it is a well-known fact that from the days of the great *Roi Soleil* up to the last unhappy Bourbon, visiting diplomats avoided calling at the world's most famous palace during the morning hours, for at this time the royal chambermaids were busy emptying a diversity of vessels from the upper balconies to the flower-beds below.

But the site where Aztec princes had built was endowed with natural advantages. Montezuma's crystal pool glistened among the tall cypresses overhung with Spanish moss, while an aqueduct nine hundred and four arches long carried water from hidden springs down to the city.

Maximilian's creative urge gained new impetus. He dreamed of Roman baths and a second Miramar. A well-known architect, Rodríguez Arangoitia, was commissioned to renovate the buildings and terraces and to decorate them in the Tuscan style.

The tangled forest at the rear of the castle was cleared, handsome roadways were cut through it, and an eucalyptus-bordered avenue laid out from the palace gates to the cathedral. Over this boulevard, called the Promenade of Carlota and later changed to El Paseo de la Reforma, the Emperor and Empress rode in their carriage *à la Douamont* with a team of "six buff-colored mules with zebra hoofs, two of them harnessed to the shaft and the other four in a row forming the lead, an outrider in rich silver-gallooned Mexican accouterments, and the whole turn-out racing madly along with the swiftness of an arrow."

To Carlota fell the joys of interior decorating. With great zest she took up the planning of her new abode. Awed by the thousand-year-old *ahuehuete* trees under which the last Montezuma had walked, she devised for her intimate use a small enclosed garden in the upper patio of the castle. Surrounded by a graceful loggia which overlooked the resplendent city, a replica of the Pincian Garden at Rome began to take shape.

While the imperial tenants were thus engrossed in getting settled Mexican society found itself in a sort of flutter. The belles and grandames of democracy quivered with delightful uncertainty, for the Empress would soon be choosing her court of honor. Behind latticed windows ambitious females bestirred themselves practising curtsies. Languid limbs ached from such unaccustomed exercise but eligibility to high places loomed as a reward. Twenty matrons attained their hearts' desire. The Señoras bore names still renowned in the Mexico of to-day:

Luz Blanco de Robles
Soledad Vivanco de Cervantes
Guadalupe Cervantes de Morán
Manuela de Plaizora
Dolores Peña del Hidalgo y Terán
Dolores Quesada de Almonte
Ana Rosa de Rincón-Gallardo
María Barrio de Campero
Francisca Escandón y Landa
Rosa Obregón de Uraza
María Muñoz de Peraz
Carolina Barrón de Escandón

Dolores Germandín de Elgüero
Rocha de Robles
Luz Robles de Bringas
Josefa Cardeña de Salas-Varela
Luisa Quejano de Rincón-Gallardo
Concepción Lizardi del Valle
Manuela Gutiérrez-Estrada del Barrio
Otea de Sánchez-Navarro

All these ladies were married. They resided in their own houses and took up their duties at Court in relays. These duties were simple enough. Carlota longed to perfect her knowledge of Spanish and to this end a reading circle was established. Legends, customs and traditions of the land were discussed in her presence while with that ever facile pen of hers she took down notes. Her love of music recaptured the inspiration once known at Milan. Concha Méndez, the Cuban nightingale, was at the Teatro Imperial singing a new habanera called *La Paloma*. . . .

<table>
<tr><td>"Cuando salí de la Habana,
Válgame Dios—
Nadie me ha visto salir
Si no fui yo.
Y una linda huachinanga
Allá voy yo,
Que se vino tras de mi—
Que sí señor!</td><td>("One day, in God's name,
I left Habana—
No one could have seen me go,
Unless it be myself.
Yet, as I wandered along,
A lovely girl from Huachinango
Came after me—
Indeed, sir!</td></tr>
<tr><td>"Si a tu ventana llega,
Ay, una paloma—
Trátala con cariño,
Que es mi persona.
Cuéntale tus amores,
Bien de mi vida;
Corónala de flores,
Que es cosa mía.</td><td>"If at your window there should arrive
A dove—
Treat it tenderly,
For it is my person.
Tell it about your love,
My life's enchantment;
Crown it with flowers,
For it is a part of me.</td></tr>
<tr><td>"Ay, chinita que sí,</td><td>"Oh, chinita, say yes,</td></tr>
</table>

Ay, que dame tu amor—	Say you give me your love—
Ay—que vente conmigo chinita	Oh, come with me, chinita,
Adonde vivo yo!"	To the place where I live.")

The song of *The Dove* became Carlota's favorite. She hummed it constantly, and in a moment of ecstatic rapture she sent one of her jeweled bracelets to the Creole singer.

Countess Kollonitz, who had accompanied the Empress from Miramar in the privileged rôle of a confidante, did not entirely approve of her new associates. She found the Mexican ladies a trifle dowdy in their striped and polka-dotted finery. The Señoras had discarded native shawls and mantillas in favor of European bonnets and furbelows which in most cases did not constitute a change for the better. Paula von Kollonitz sniffed with a superior air. Her sniffing was fiercely resented. By November of the same year Carlota found it advisable to ship the offending damsel back to Trieste. Manuela del Barrio was promoted to the rank of a marquesa and lady-in-waiting extraordinary, while another de Estrada was added to complete the original twenty.

The departure of Countess Kollonitz was soon followed by that of Countess Melanie Zichy and several other noblewomen who had attached themselves to the Court in unofficial capacities. Carlota was left with her new companions, with whom, on such brief acquaintance, she could have but little in common.

The Latin ladies, whose life was composed of fiestas and siestas, abhorred exercise. The Empress, a splendid horsewoman, rode alone through the forest of Chapultepec on a brightly caparisoned mule (horses were scarce) and, meeting glances of disapproval from repressed dowagers, soon learned to curtail and finally give up this sport. Patiently she studied the novel pattern after which she must fashion her day. She who had the true Nordic's passion for sunshine discovered the shade-loving ways of tropical matrons longing for a lotus skin. In Mexico City no self-respecting woman rose before the middle of the forenoon and, since after the midday meal the entire population adjourned for its daily doze, the feminine world was seldom in its stays before five o'clock.

Evening brought these rare nightblooms to light. Pale oval faces of orchid delicacy smiled over fans of ivory and lace, and, after a dozen years of continued hothouse slumber, folded up behind rolls of double chin.

Carlota looked to her husband for companionship. But Maximilian's time was taken up during those early months with a multitude of cares. In accordance with Clause 17 of the Miramar Convention—"The French Government pledges itself to liberate all Mexican prisoners of war at the moment when the Emperor of Mexico enters his domains"—the prisons had been emptied on Maximilian's arrival. Fiery republicans, tasting freedom once again, had lost no time in joining their scattered partisans to north and south. Bazaine and his cruel henchman Colonel Dupin tore after them and launched a new season of guerrilla warfare against the invincible cohorts of Juárez.

The Emperor had lost his last illusion concerning a pacified Mexico which unanimously clamored for him. Leaving Carlota at Chapultepec he set out on a tour of the surrounding provinces in order to ascertain with his own eyes the exact status of the monarchist party.

It was a bold and brave gesture which won Maximilian sympathies in quarters fundamentally hostile. Ignoring the discomforts of the rainy season the monarch remained for days in the saddle. He stopped at Cuernavaca, Morelia and León. Everywhere he spoke haltingly in his newly acquired Spanish to dark masses of silent Indians.

On September sixteenth, the national holiday, he reached the town of Dolores where in 1810 the priest Miguel Hidalgo y Costilla had proclaimed the first defiant cry for independence. Shortly before midnight cannons boomed and bells began to peal in memory of that moment long ago when Hidalgo uttered the *Grito:*

"Long live the Americas and death to bad government!"

Hatred for the Spaniards (who wore the traditional *cachucha* or Basque *béret*) caused a later substitution of the words "Death to the bonnet-wearers [*gachupines*]!"

Maximilian knew the patriotic significance of the occasion.

Bracing himself against every danger, he assumed an intrepid and magnificent pose of outward calm. He chose a climax for his most daring appeal. From the balcony of the Cura Hidalgo's house he made a speech. Talking was difficult indeed, since at any moment a murderous missile might have been hurled through the darkness, yet talk he did. What his true emotions must have been is revealed in a letter to his brother Karl, dated September 21, 1864, which contains a gem of understatement. "You can't imagine," confided Maxl, "how embarrassed I was. . . ."

As it happened the address was received with frenetic ovations and a genuine display of enthusiasm. At sight of this blond giant with his smiling blue eyes and his easy scorn of cowardice the candid citizenry of Dolores felt utterly disarmed. It was impossible to resist such a combination of virtues as were displayed by this prince who bore a likeness to the fabled fair-haired god Quetzalcoatl.

While a chorus of *"Vivas!"* filled the air Maximilian dreamed of advancing as far as Monterrey on the wings of oratory. But his Pegasus was turned southward within the next twenty-four hours. While galloping along the highway the Emperor was caught in a rainstorm and drenched. He sneezed. By evening a feverish cold set in and Scherzenlechner, the lackey who had become a coddled courtier, was able to dissuade his master from further hardships. To the craven Sebastian all contact with the copper-colored race (*"la race cuivrée"*) was distasteful in the extreme. As private secretary to an emperor he hankered after pomp and circumstance, not feats of heroism. Bundling up to his ears against the innumerable germs with which he felt the atmosphere to be saturated, Sebastian led the way back to the capital.

A stop was made at Toluca de Lerdo, nine hundred feet above Mexico City and nearly nine thousand feet above sea-level. Here Maximilian paused to admire the frozen peak of Xinantecatl, "The Naked Man," also called El Nevado de Toluca. A lake of potable water filled its now inactive crater.

More and more the raw beauties of this land captured the monarch's fancy. He reached Chapultepec with chattering teeth and a fantastic vision of empire. . . .

Chapter 4

Carlota received him with the news that Rome had sent a nuncio. Monsignor Meglia was here to settle the Church question. Maximilian, as a sincere apostolic monarch, would be expected to make amends for the many wrongs committed by the infidel Juárez.

Lest any doubts on the matter existed the Vatican had chosen to submit an outline of its demands. It was an unequivocal outline, requesting:

"1. Annulment of the Reform Laws.
"2. Ratification of the Catholic faith, to the exclusion of all other creeds, as the basic principle of the Mexican Empire.
"3. Complete freedom for the clergy in the exercise of ecclesiastical functions.
"4. Restoration of convents and monastic orders.
"5. Subordination of private and public instruction to religious authority.
"6. Removal of all restrictions which tend to keep the Church dependent upon the State."

The Emperor frowned. This was absurd. Only a short while ago he had expounded to the Archduke Karl those new ideas of liberalism with which the New World had inspired him.

> "This continent is very progressive in a political sense [he had written], more so by far than European states with their exaggerated self-esteem. What we know in the Old World as mandarinism, with all its ridiculous bathos, is utterly incongruous here. All the stilted trumpery with which we so stupidly encumber ourselves in Europe, and shall continue encumbering ourselves for centuries, has been discarded over here. . . ."

Yet there was "mandarinism" of the most retrogressive sort in this attempt on the part of the Vatican to throttle a struggling nation with the weight of its medieval despotism. Maximilian believed himself a sincere Christian. But he felt that the Church problem demanded a judicious as well as a Catholic solution.

Monsignor Meglia raised disapproving eyebrows. "His Holiness, Pio Nono," he sputtered, "has instructed me to relinquish not one iota of that which is asked."

The Emperor's lips compressed, growing a trifle white at the corners. There was a prolonged scratching of pen on paper which resulted in a counter-proposal of nine subheads, most of which were diametrically opposed to the Pope's desires. With Maximilian's instructions in the pocket of his cassock the nuncio departed.

He went straightway to Archbishop Labastida, who had recently returned to Mexico and avidly pursued his lost riches. Together the two clerics reviewed the situation. They grew incensed. While proclaiming the Catholic faith as the State religion, Maximilian nevertheless intended to grant freedom of worship to all creeds. The Church's feudal holdings, nationalized by Juárez, he would not restore. Instead he proposed to conclude a concordat whereby the State would assume responsibility for the salaries of the clergy.

Labastida groaned. Neither he nor his frocked colleagues could survive—in the style to which they had been accustomed—if they accepted a picayune "salary" from a temporal government. Besides, it was revolting even to think about. Did not such action degrade the Church to serfdom under a civil power? The holy men retired into acrimonious silence.

Several days passed. The Emperor waited for an answer. Since none was forthcoming he sent his Minister of Justice, Pedro Escudero, to confer with the recalcitrant nuncio. The conference was declined on the grounds that pontifical orders admitted no parleys.

At this the Emperor's temper flared up. He let it be known that as a modern and enlightened sovereign, which he wished to be, it might become necessary to get along without the Roman Curia.

Carlota, though a devout Catholic, supported her husband. In the presence of Marshal Bazaine she exclaimed, violent with indignation: "The only thing to do is to throw that nuncio out of the window!" To Empress Eugénie she wrote on the same day:

> "You must admit that to expect this country—burning with resentment against theocracies—to return the enormous holdings of the clergy would be not only blind and irrational, but silly beyond compare."

Monsignor Meglia meanwhile accumulated his share of venom. With the aid of his tonsured brethren he composed a biting letter to Maximilian in which he heaped criticism upon the latter's mundane and wicked axioms. The missive was delivered at the imperial chancellery where Escudero inadvertently opened it. Finding fault with Monsignor's epistolary style (almost every word violated diplomatic form) the Minister of Justice took a liberty. He sent the letter back.

The situation was bound to become acute. Since recriminations had already been exchanged Maximilian did not trust himself in another interview with the ecclesiastics. Yet he was not willing to force a breach. Seeking one more amicable approach he induced Carlota to visit the nuncio and to negotiate an acceptable truce. It was the Christmas season, he reflected—a propitious time beyond doubt.

The interview took place on December twenty-third. For two whole hours Carlota stood her ground, but to no effect. She described the duel of wits to Eugénie:

> "Everything slid off that man as from polished marble. . . . I offered all conceivable arguments in every possible shade of tone, grave, gay, menacing, even oracular, for I felt that much was at stake. Serious differences, perhaps even a rupture with the Holy See, would be so harmful to the cause of religion! It was useless. He brushed my premises aside like so much rubbish and offered nothing in their place. In fact, he seemed to feel quite at home in the nebula he spun about his person. . . ."

Maximilian saw the futility of further parley. But he did not capitulate. Instead, on January seventh of the new year, he passed an edict forbidding papal bulls to be published in Mexico without imperial sanction. This was the first step in the inevitable rift with Rome.

The nuncio and the clerical party, many members of which were Conservatives who helped establish the Empire, met the challenge with acerbity. Mexico City was in an uproar. Public opinion wavered between the opposing camps only to lean, eventually, toward that which was more familiar—the dominance of the priests. A large portion of the aristocracy, though monarchistic in sentiment, was too bigoted to second any action against the Church.

The royal couple spent an unpleasant week.

> "How I wish it were over [wrote Carlota]! The bishops formulate petitions (which are at least politely worded). The nuncio indulges in testy notes, while society ladies pout. In short, the most childish passions are let loose. Newspapers are at swords' points. Radicals and Liberals proclaim aloud that the doctrines of Juárez have triumphed. Our own Conservatives, on the other hand, regard themselves as retainers of the Pope and behave like dolts—excuse my language—to whom religion is synonymous with tithes and the power to hold property. Of course we know well enough that behind all the antics of the nuncio, who is a mere puppet, stands the shadow of Monsignor Labastida. I am so familiar with this fellow's bad Italian that I recognize it in every one of the nuncio's tirades."

It was the beginning of an unfortunate and long-drawn-out conflict between the Emperor and his own supporters. Even the Paris émigrés, who lately were drifting back to their homeland in growing detachments, gave themselves over to conflicting emotions. One and all, they had clamored for a monarchy because in so doing they hoped to recover the decorum and godliness of another day. That a scion of Europe's oldest dynasty should become infected with progressive ideas was unthinkable. It was dangerous. Maximilian underestimated the influence of even a dispossessed clergy.

Some of the prominent families who had gone out to Guadalupe to welcome the Emperor and his consort now locked themselves up in their stone mansions and refused to appear at Court. Contact with Carlota's ladies-in-waiting became a trifle stilted. "One hardly ever catches sight of them," wrote Maximilian to his brother. But he quickly added that this was due to the "great seriousness of the Mexican character, a trait I admire and which, thank God, insures me plenty of time for my real work."

Even so, while Carlota's ladies did not get in the way or interfere with his work, the Emperor grew at times wistful. There were bleak passages in his letters. "Things are very quiet at Chapultepec and we lead a most retired life. Our routine is even simpler than at Miramar. We seldom give dinner parties, eating most of our meals alone, and in the evenings we see nobody at all. . . ." Lest this be misconstrued, however, he finished on a thin note of defiance. "The so-called delights of European society, the elaborate soirées and gossip conventions, tea-parties, etc., of stuffy memory, are still unknown here—and we are going to be careful not to introduce them."

This was an empty threat, for presently, unable to endure the uncomfortable tension, both Emperor and Empress made a new bid for popularity by throwing open the gates of their castle for a series of well devised gala receptions. The latter were imbued with a richness and opulence calculated to beguile the Latin love of splendor. The plan was intelligently conceived. It worked. Sulking aristocrats blinked at crested invitations and felt themselves galvanized into action. It would pay to go, if only to notice who besides oneself had been asked.

The first of these palace functions took place in January, the month which marked the fatal débâcle with the nuncio. By special proclamation the Order of the Mexican Eagle—"the highest of all ranks, and having for its Grand Master the reigning sovereign"—was created, and Maximilian let it be known that certain deserving supporters of the Empire would be decorated on this occasion. [illegible] the *caballeros* were alert. Many believed themselves not only called but chosen. Bishops and sacristans were shelved along with their grievances, while ambitious politicians inspected the new bauble on display—under glass—in an anteroom of the palace. It represented a spread eagle holding a serpent in its beak and bearing above its head the imperial crown, together with the transverse swords of equality and justice. A blue silk ribbon bore the words: *"Equidad en la Justicia* [Equality in Justice]." . . . The order comprised six classes—to be awarded within the following limits: two hundred officers, one hundred commanders, fifty grand officers, twenty-five grand cross, twelve grand cross-with-collar, and no restriction upon the number of knights.

Carlota, too, sponsored an order instituted especially for ladies. In honor of her patron saint, San Carlos Borromeo, the decoration received the name *Orden Imperial de San Carlos* and it consisted of two classes—the grand cross and the small cross. These were to be conferred twice annually, on the Saint's day, November fourth, and on Carlota's birthday, June seventh. Great discretion was exercised in an effort to limit the members who might thereby be distinguished, but jealousy broke out among the ladies and they raised an astonishing clamor. There was nothing for it but to bestow the emblem freely and without restraint.

Two military orders were also revived, the European *Pour le Mérite* in gold, silver and bronze, and President Santa Ana's Cross of Constancy (*La Cruz de la Constancia*) created in 1841 and confirmed by Maximilian on April 10, 1865. And lastly, since every one seemed highly pleased with the proceedings, Iturbide's Order of Guadalupe was polished up to a new brightness. Five classes were established, five hundred officers, two hundred commanders, one hundred grand officers, thirty grand cross, and an unlimited number of knights.

But medals and patents of nobility were only the preliminary blandishments with which Emperor and Empress now wooed their subjects. Wining and dining in a manner hitherto unknown among Creole societies followed each act of investiture. A battery of precious liquids from the imperial cellars was lined up before defenseless though fervent victims. From fifteen to twenty different wines and liqueurs were sampled over gleaming banquet tables. The finest Hungarian labels, both white and red, alternated with vintages from the Rhine and Rhone. Maximilian's baggage train from overseas included the costly seals of Prince Metternich, Veuve Clicquot and Roederer.

As for the banquets themselves, they were not to be equaled in the Mexico of another hundred years. Beginning at three-thirty in the afternoon, these state dinners lasted no less than three hours; and generally an hour or so was spent in polite conversation over the inevitable demitasse. People who attended court parties took leave of their kin as if they were embarking on some distant trip.

Invitations were sent separately by both sovereigns. Maximilian's card ran as follows:

De Orden del Emperador, la Secretaría de las Ceremonias tiene el honor de invitar al
Señor ....
....
á comer con Su Majestad en el Palacio Imperial de México, el......................*de 186*. .*á las*............................*de la tarde.*
Traje:
Para los Señores de mañana
Para las Señoras..............

Measuring six by four inches, approximately, Carlota's invitations resembled the above with the exception that full dress was understood. The engraving ran thus:

El Gran Chambelán de la Emperatriz tiene la honra de invitar de orden de Su Majestad al
Señor ....
.....................*y Señora*...........
para la tertulia que tendrá lugar en el Palacio de México el . . . *de* . . . . . *de 186* . . *á las ocho de la noche.*

The imperial menus were imposing. On March 29, 1865, a state dinner was offered to Bazaine in honor of the latter's elevation to the rank of Grand Marshal of France, an appointment granted by Napoleon on November fifth of the previous year. With the aid of a nervous kitchen staff the Magyar cook Tüdös devised a delectable feast immortalized by the court printer.

À Mexique, 29 Mars 1865

MENU DU DINER DU GRAND MARÉCHAL DE FRANCE

Potage Brunoise
" Tapioca

RELEVÉS

Bouchées aux huîtres
Poisson aux fines herbes
Filet braisé, sauce Richelieu.

ENTRÉES

Côtelettes jardinière
Vol-au-vent financière
Saumon à la Tartare
Cailles Périgueux.

PUNCH À LA ROMAINE

Rôts
Dinde au cresson
Selle d'agneau.

ENTREMETS

Pois à la francaise
Asperges hollandaise
Gelée au marasquin

Gâteau d'abricots
Pudding diplomate
Glace à la vanille

2 Pièces montées.

Menus for more ordinary occasions were couched in Spanish, although the proportions showed little change. The following recalls a bite of supper provided at one of the Empress's musical soirées:

COMIDA DEL DÍA 27 DE ABRIL DE 1865

Sopa al estilo Sévigné
Las croquetas á la Mazarin
Las riselas con ostiones
Los lomos á la parisienne
Las truchas á la genovesa
Las costillas jardinera.

Los patés con aceituna
Los filetes de gallinas á la Tolosa
Los pasteles de Strasburgo
Los chícharos á la francesa
Los coliflores á la francesa

ASADOS

Los pollos con trufas
Las godornices con trufas

ENSALADAS
POSTRES

Pudín de sago
Croquetas de arroz
Crema de todas las frutas
Conserva de peras
Queso y mantequilla
Helados de fresas y leche
Frutas y Pasteles.

A marginal note on the joys of the table is given by the Emperor in a letter to Vienna. "Due to special efforts, our cuisine ranks among the best in existence anywhere, as does the imperial cellar. The diplomats gulp and guzzle so strenuously that after dinner they can do nothing but lisp inarticulate nonsense."

The musical aftermath to these Sybaritic pastimes attracted the ladies who sat in picturesque array about their hostess, nibbling chocolate bonbons from dainty individual tongs. Occasionally the munching ceased as one of the Señoras relaxed in beatific slumber to the strains of Verdi and that famous Strauss who, back in Vienna, afforded a soothing obbligato to the Countess Gaby Dietrichstein's happy dozing. Since most of the musicians had come from Europe in the Emperor's entourage the programs followed a characteristic cliché currently stylish in Paris, London, Berlin. Only upon rare provocation did the orchestra contend with the intricacies of Spanish rhythm or Creole syncopation. The concert following Carlota's supper of April twenty-seventh provided one essay of this sort, a Cuban habanera, bravely attacked and meekly surrendered for the more lucid measures of a Germanic Euterpe. In translating the Herr Kapellmeister's notations into Spanish, the imported court printer's linguistic acumen struck a snag. The "Overture" of *Orpheus* became that subject's "Aperture," to wit:

PROGRAMA

del día 27 de abril de 1865

N. 1. Marcha, por .... Sauerthal
N. 2. Orpheus (Abertura), por .... Offenbach
N. 3. Cellonen (Valso), por .... Strauss
N. 4. Un Ballo di Maschera (Cuadrilla), por . Verdi
N. 5. Waldröslein (Mazurka), por .... Fahrbach
N. 6. La Zingara (Divertissement), por ..... Balfé
N. 7. La Campana (Habanera), por .... Delgado
N. 8. Demclirer (Polka), por .... Strauss
N. 9. Laxenburger (Schottisch), por .... Kaulich
N. 10. Marcha, por .... Sauerthal

"Valso," as an approximation to the correct *"vals,"* did very well. Mexican society, the most courteous in the world, remained graciously unaware. In fact, to save the foreigners from all embarrassment in this respect, native gentlemen and ladies gravely imitated errors and employed them in conversation thereafter, a practise adhered to by their descendants to-day.

Whenever an ambulant Italian opera troupe chanced through Mexico City the Court rejoiced. Messengers were sent to rout the Thespians from their sordid lodgings for a command performance at Chapultepec. Imperial largesse took the place of meager road earnings, and the salons of the castle resounded with the unstinted efforts of grateful talent. No bonbons were served on these occasions. The ambitious selections of one such soirée have been preserved:

PROGRAMA DEL CONCIERTO

del día 5 de mayo de 1865

Primera Parte

1. *"Serenata de Fausto"—Gounod—Cantada por el Sr. Biachi.*
2. *"Mon Fils, Romanza del Profeta"—Meyerbeer—Cantada por la Srita. Sulzer.*
3. *"La Donna é Mobile"—Verdi—Cantada por el Sr. Mazzolenni.*
4. *"Fantasía Brillante" para el Violin, (dedicada a Su Majestad el Rey Leopoldo de Bélgica y ejecutada por su compositor el Sr. Jehin-Prume, con acompañamiento de la Orquesta.)*
5. *"Terceto de los Lombardos"—Verdi—Cantada por la Srita. Ortolani y los Sres. Mazzolenni y Biachi.*

Segunda Parte

6. *"Aria del Barbero de Sevilla"—Rossini—Cantada por el Sr. Orlandini.*
7. *"Recuerdos de Chateaubriand"—Quidant—Ejecutado en el Piano por el Sr. León.*
8. *"Aria de la Traviata"—Verdi—Cantada por la Srita. Ortolani.*
9. *"Brindis de Lucrecia"—Donizetti—Cantada por la Srita. Sulzer.*
10. *"Élégie," compuesta para el Violin por Ernst y ejecutada por el Sr. Jehin-Prume con acompañamiento de Piano.*

11. "Cuarteto de Rigoletto"—Verdi—Cantada por las Sritas. Ortolani y Sulzer y los Sres. Mazzolenni y Orlandini.

However, not all of the Empress's receptions were of so serious a character. She arranged for an intimate ball once a week after the custom of the French Court.

"I have decided to give some evening parties exactly like your Majesty's [she wrote to Eugénie], and people seem to like my Monday affairs. The guests put on their best finery and really look presentable. There are many types of beauty hereabouts, suggestive of your Majesty's homeland. One Spanish lady, the wife of a doctor named Solis, is exquisite; at the masked reception of the Bourse quite recently she had powdered her hair and woven a poppy-colored ribbon about it. The effect was dashing—a perfect Sappho of the classic age. Another handsome woman is Madame Sánchez-Navarro, one of my attendant ladies. Hers is the face of a Murillo Madonna, with the black brows and long eyelashes of an Oriental. To offset so much dark beauty she wears a string of enormous pearls from the Pacific Ocean (which reminds me that I must have some fished for in the spring—that seems to be the proper season). . . . In regard to our own appearance, we have made it a point to dress in Mexican fashion. On horseback I wear a sombrero. Our menu becomes daily more native in flavor, we have a carriage drawn by mules with tinkling bells on their harness, we use no wraps other than *sarapes,* and I go to mass in a lace mantilla. In short, as far as harmless externals go we have adopted indigenous tastes to such an extent as to startle even the Mexicans themselves. You see, it is not reforms that shock men, but the manner in which they are introduced. . . . My soirées end after one o'clock. Next Monday will be the sixth. I usually whirl through several quadrilles, one of these with General d'Héril-lier. (In time I hope to invite all the French officers, even the paymasters who, we have been told, are very anxious to dance.) At the finish there is a loud cornet signal, whereupon we all start into a *galop* which goes so fast that somebody always ends by falling down."

The nuncio and his wailing bishops had been forgotten.

CHAPTER 5

KING LEOPOLD asked a question.

"What has become of the military command? Remember the First Napoleon's adage that God is always on the side of the heavy artillery!"

It was a pertinent query. For some time past Maximilian had endeavored to confer with Marshal Bazaine about the matter. But Bazaine seemed to have an obsession for eluding the Emperor with ever new excuses. When more commonplace alibis failed the wily soldier would suddenly leave Mexico City on some fresh expedition against Juarista bands roaming at large.

Maximilian temporized. As a Hapsburg he was not cut out for strife. There always stirred within him an instinctive urge to placate people and to turn to life's more pleasant things. What if the greatest soldier in history, the unforgettable Bonaparte, had given bold impersonations of Cæsar, Alexander and Charlemagne—was not his life-story caked over with blood? Literature provided the most fitting epitaph for the colossal conqueror.

"Dieu était ennuyé avec lui," wrote Victor Hugo in his best allegorical vein, "God was bored with him. . . ."

No cannier explanation could be found anywhere for the downfall of earth's mighty. Napoleon I, shorn of glory and prowling over his dismal island prison trapping birds or wrangling with a boorish jailer who refused him obeisance, presented a picture which seemed hardly worth emulating. No, Maximilian was not impressed by the example of the Corsican. And so, for the time being and despite his father-in-law's advice, he left the heavy artillery to Bazaine, who seemed very attached to it.

A quarrel over military precedence would have been especially indelicate at this time, for the elderly Frenchman had just entered upon a romantic interlude. At fifty-four the marshal contemplated marriage to a shy Mexican girl of seventeen. According to Carlota the future bride was "a true Spanish beauty in miniature, with the most perfect grace of manner." Of Bazaine she said other things. Her usual tolerance exploded after watching the infatuated marshal dance the habanera at one of her parties. "He reminds me of a huge, lazy fly, gloating over that child-like fiancée of his. . . ." And again: "I sense Bazaine's character. Why do men of his type look so demoniacal when they are in love?"

Maximilian admitted the Frenchman's ungainliness without holding it against him. In fact, the sons of *La Patrie* had grown touchy of late and required handling with a silken glove. Napoleon III complained that important offices in Maximilian's Cabinet were filled by too many Mexicans while his own worthy subjects had been discriminated against. This was true. Maximilian was planning a Mexican Empire for the Mexicans. He believed that they had given him coronation in their sacred cathedral for no other purpose.

King Leopold applauded from Brussels. "You have acted wisely," wrote the Coburg sage, "in surrounding yourself from the outset with committees composed of natives; it is the only way to prevent the Mexicans from feeling that you underrate them."

But such measures were a decided damper on French imperialism. Napoleon seriously considered enlarging his expeditionary force. Eugénie supported him vigorously.

"Those *pantalons-rouges* [red trousers] you are planning to send will do more toward permanent colonization than all the correspondence in the world."

Napoleon nodded. "I had marines in mind," he said, "they wear blue ones, dear."

The new troops arrived in Mexico soon after, and with them came a startling request. According to an "agreement" made by the French Minister, Marquis de Montholon, and a member of the late Regency, Señor Luis de Arroyo, the immensely rich mineral province of Sonora (comprising 198,496 square kilometers) was to be ceded to France. Would Maximilian ratify this agreement? It is recorded to the latter's credit that he would do nothing of the sort. The aforesaid Señor Arroyo happened to have moved to parts unknown and could not be questioned in regard to his remarkable dealings in real estate. In any event, Maximilian emphatically denied his consent to such spoliation. The tension between Paris and Chapultepec grew. The task of appeasing two widely divergent factions—his French sponsors on the one hand and his uncertain Mexican subjects on the other—assumed still larger proportions before Maximilian's eyes.

At any rate, Bazaine's marriage would offer an opportunity for certain conciliatory gestures. In deference to Napoleon's wishes the event was celebrated with great pomp at Chapultepec Castle where the French commander was accorded the highest honors. The new *"maréchale,"* Josefa Peña y Azcárate de Bazaine, and her mother, a widow of obscure family, sat beside the Empress throughout a special reception following the religious ceremony. "I need not mention the fact," wrote Maximilian (making a special point of mentioning the fact), "that we have donated the handsomest palace in Mexico to the marshal on the occasion of his wedding." The letter, addressing Napoleon as "Sir, my brother," was dated May 26, 1865,—the date on which the last Confederate forces under the command of General Kirby Smith surrendered to a victorious North, somewhere on a dreary Texas plain. The American Civil War was entering its last stage.

At first this portentous event did not make nearly so great an impression south of the Río Grande y Bravo as the fact that the Emperor of Mexico had given away a sumptuous colonial mansion to a detested French minion. Juarista spies, honeycombing their way through the capital, had waited for just such an opportunity as this to raise a great scandal. The Hapsburg usurper was robbing the country of its art treasures! Now what had the blind Conservative Party to say for itself?

The clergy joined in the refrain. Forgetting that Benito Juárez had dispossessed the Church, the vindictive army of priests turned rabidly republican. A flood of anonymous pamphlets spread over the city, besmirching Maximilian's character. The Empress Carlota's parties were held up as ribald orgies which drained the nation's treasury.

At first the authorities were helpless to determine the authorship of the pamphlets. One evening, early in June, a dark figure was discovered prowling along the Corredor de la Vitrina at

Chapultepec and the mystery was solved. Nabbing the culprit by his floating cassock the Guardia Palatina led him into the Emperor's presence. Maximilian gazed upon the guileless face of a French abbé named Alleau. This must surely be a mistake. But careful exploration of the cleric's undergarments revealed that it was not. A complete outline was found, in code, which defined a systematic scheme of propaganda against the Empire. There were also letters from that masterful demagogue, Señor Gutiérrez de Estrada, who in an access of religious fanaticism had taken up the banner of the Pope abroad and was inciting the Catholics of Europe against his former protégé. Maximilian's face changed color. Perhaps his father-in-law had been right after all.

"Beware of harsh measures," King Leopold had written after Carlota's bout with the nuncio, "the Blacks may become dangerous."

But the warning had been ignored and here was Rome's revenge. A still greater shock now awaited Maximilian. Just before turning the abbé loose, since diplomacy demanded indulgence toward a subject of France, the holy man's breviary underwent inspection. A scrap of folded paper came to light. It contained an ugly piece of libel, smeared over with penciled corrections, to the effect that the Empress Carlota had become a pleasure-mad creature because of her secret sorrow at being childless. The reason for this frustration, so the abbé's jottings explained with some detail, was to be found in the Emperor's dissipated youth; while an admiral in the Austrian Navy, the Archduke Ferdinand Maximilian had caught a disease in a Brazilian bagnio. Although checked, the virus had permanently destroyed all hope of begetting children.

It was a vicious act of perfidy which, regardless of political considerations, demanded punishment. The priest, unmasked as an *agent provocateur,* was held for trial. At this the French Minister Marquis de Montholon entered a formal protest asserting that a son of *La Patrie* could not be prosecuted in foreign law courts. Angry words followed. Maximilian reported the affair in a letter to Napoleon and the case was finally turned over to France. The abbé was allowed to leave Mexico unmolested. Montholon had won the day.

He was to lose something in turn. Maximilian never trusted him again and thereafter referred to Montholon as a "low, wretched character with the bad manners of a former consul versed in petty intrigue." The Emperor refused, furthermore, to receive the French *Chargé d'Affaires* in private audience, which crippled the business of diplomacy. In the end Montholon was forced to tender his resignation. He was removed to a minor post in Washington while Monsieur Alphonse Dano was appointed as his successor.

The flurry of opprobrious innuendo against the imperial government now subsided but Maximilian was left in a state of uneasiness. He had been accused of spendthrift, prodigal excesses. His wife's innocent social pastimes had been termed dissolute and wanton. What could this mean? Where had they trespassed? Was there a foundation for such charges?

Suddenly, with a sinking feeling, he realized that he had as yet made no effort to study his country's finances. The condition of Mexico's treasury had not troubled him. The vast salary which had been promised at Miramar would surely cover all expenditures hitherto made, including the spectacular wedding-gift to Bazaine. A conference with Jakob von Kuhacsevich, who had served as Maximilian's purser at Trieste, would clear up the whole matter and prove that neither the Emperor nor his consort could have been exceeding the ample limits of their respective allowances.

After supper that evening he summoned the old treasurer. The latter found his master pacing back and forth like a sentinel across the northern terrace.

"I am taking my exercise, Kuhacs."

"That is excellent, your Majesty."

"Yes, I am sure. But you shall take it with me for your sins——"

"Very good, your Majesty."

Shaking his forlorn gray locks the Hungarian shuffled into a trot beside his beloved sovereign. This big, overgrown Maxl, he reflected, was a *charmeur*. He would have done so well in the fine royal palace at Budapest! Instead, here they all were, in this incredible land with its extraordinary and terrifying anticlimaxes.

For the space of an hour the two men walked and their interview proved to be just that—a terrifying anticlimax. Maximilian, believing his income safely in the hands of Kuhacsevich, discovered now that neither the celebrated deputation of the Regency nor the French authorities in control up to the moment of his accession had advanced a single copper of the one hundred and twenty-five thousand pesos promised as the monthly imperial stipend. Kuhacsevich in turn, unwilling to overstep his bounds, had tactfully awaited the moment when Maximilian would turn over to his trust the funds which he naturally supposed in his master's possession. That this transfer did not heretofore take place the old purser cheerfully ascribed to the fact that travel expenses and other obligations had demanded earlier liquidation.

"But how can we have got this far without money?" Maximilian exclaimed in consternation.

"There were the two hundred thousand gulden advanced by your Majesty's family. From this sum I have covered all outlays that reached my department."

"And there is nothing left?"

Kuhacsevich faltered miserably. "A mere fraction. The household, retinue, secretaries, lackeys, all have demanded their regular pay. At Miramar we were never behind in such matters. I did not know, I could not tell——" The old man broke down and wept. Maximilian clasped his trembling shoulders.

"It's not your fault, Kuhacs," he said gently, "I've made a horrible mistake."

Throughout that night the Emperor sat at his desk. Gathered about him, with lines of worry written over their faces, were the motley members of his Cabinet. Though the hour was unpropitious and certainly inconvenient for business of such a nature, Maximilian would not relax until each man had rendered full account of his financial entanglements. From Almonte, who had played so important a part in the Regency, he demanded an exact reckoning of that body's neglected obligations. The information thus gleaned proved staggering. In actual figures it filled countless sheets of note-paper.

The first rays of dawn found the Emperor still lost in a maze of figures. In view of the fact that one of the ostensible causes of Napoleon's intervention was the Juárez moratorium repudiating Mexico's foreign debts (because of her inability to pay them), it was all the more shocking to discover the expenses incurred by France for Mexico in bringing Maximilian and his suite across the seas. To be sure, the French Government had not put forth a single sou. The Mexican treasury had been bled for all the sums here quoted:

1. Given to various persons to induce Maximilian to come	$104,902.32
2. Furniture and improvements at Palacio Nacional in Mexico City (despite which the Emperor and Empress were unable to sleep there!)	101,011.83
3. Furniture and art objects for Chapultepec	15,210.50
4. Reception at Vera Cruz (which never took place) and Mexico City	115,348.41
Total	$336,473.06

In addition to this, Mexico had the privilege of supporting the entire French army of occupation, at the rate of one thousand francs a man per annum, not mentioning the fancy salaries of Bazaine, Douay, d'Hérillier, and a vast coterie of minor officers.

With dreadful clarity Maximilian saw the dawn of retribution for not having gone into these matters more thoroughly at Trieste. Words and phrases he had glossed over superficially without grasping their meaning now returned to etch themselves into his consciousness. Article 9, the most preposterous of Monsieur Achille Fould's eighteen clauses known as the Convention of Miramar, danced before his burning eyes:

> "The outlays incurred by the French expedition to Mexico, and charged to the Mexican Government, have been fixed at the sum of two hundred and seventy million francs for the entire duration of said expedition up to July 1, 1864. This sum is to bear an interest rate of 3% per annum."

A colossal fortune to be paid to France for alleged sacrifices in connection with a campaign which had been promoted from start to finish for her own advantage! It was insane. He, Maximilian, must have been mad or struck insensible to have allowed such a thing to happen. But it had happened. A French inspector of finance was even now on his way to Mexico, instructed by his government to press for payment of the first instalments on these sums. Monsieur Bonnefond would arrive at Vera Cruz with the next packet boat. Upon his landing the nightmare would begin.

Groaning in impotent despair the Emperor buried his face in his hands.

CHAPTER 6

CARLOTA walked with her ladies in the flowered patio atop the palace of Chapultepec. With nimble steps she circled the tiled fountain and returned to the trellis against which delicate colibris quivered as if suspended in mid-air. She was taking the walk which in all Spanish countries is taken *para hacer la digestión*—to make the digestion. It was eight o'clock in the evening and the Empress had supped alone. She had not seen her husband since yesterday, when he had locked himself up with his ministers. Work was killing poor Maxl; she must persuade him to let her share some of his tasks, such as the interminable audiences to newly accredited diplomats. Foreign representatives were arriving constantly, which proved that Maximilian's government was recognized abroad. England had recently sent Sir Peter Campbell-Scarlett, while from Austria came Count Guido Thun, and from Prussia Baron von Magnus. Like Eugénie, who acted as regent during Napoleon's recurring holiday trips, Carlota wished to make herself useful. There burned within her an urge to live intensely, creatively, a fact for which beyond doubt a latent maternal instinct could be made responsible.

The Empress walked, rapt in that abstract concentration which so easily could be interpreted as haughtiness. Silent footmen cleared a sandalwood table in the loggia, bearing away candelabra, and épergnes filled with spiced fruits. In departing, the flickering candles cast an oblique glow upon the silverware that bore an imperial crest.

Beyond the loggia a gallant moon rode through the skies. Its radiance played on the crowns of Montezuma's giant cypresses which brushed the castle on the crag. It filled the sheltered patio with daytime brightness.

"The birds are fooled by it," thought Carlota.

Two gorgeous macaws preened their tinted feathers and swayed toward her as she passed. They chortled with a soft exultance, cocking wise heads the better to listen to the patter of the Empress's small feet. Rocking to and fro in a transport of rhythm, they danced on their perches to that patter.

"Those divine creatures," thought Carlota.

Moonlight lying like snow on the forest, and Aztec *guacamayas* dancing in her garden. . . .

She was beginning to get used to it. She was beginning to love this Mexico with its violence, its color, its deep underlying peace. Pagan and Biblical, Oriental and Homeric Mexico! One day she would go beyond loving, one day she would come to understand it. Poets and dreamers went in search for such a place as this; a place where one walked under tulip trees, and where cities could be recognized by flower odors—the strong clove of Xochimilco's carnation pinks, the heliotrope of Tacubaya, and the jasmin of distant Monterrey.

In her correspondence, of late, she had identified herself with this land of her adoption. She spoke of Mexican affairs as "our affairs," in contrast to those of Europe, although she herself may not have been conscious of this change.

Maximilian followed her example. In a letter to his former physician at Miramar, Doctor Jilek, he admitted an attack of *Meerweh* (nostalgia for the sea) but added: "We live here in a free land among free people and under enlightened principles such as you at home can not even dream about. No longer do I feel shackled by fetters, for here one is allowed to express oneself and to pursue high ideals. Although Mexico is backward in certain respects, lacking material wealth and development, in social questions—which to my mind are paramount—we are far ahead of Europe, and more specifically of Austria. Ours is a healthy democracy, free from the rabid and fantastic quality of that prevailing in Europe, yet imbued with a force of conviction such as you will not attain without a struggle lasting fifty years. . . . Moreover, European ideas in regard to this country are for the most part mistaken. Europeans can not and will not grasp true conditions out here; they are too proud to admit that we Americans have left them far behind in the things that really count."

Carlota, describing a tour of inspection through the paper factory and cotton mill of Tlálpam, informed Eugénie: "These places are managed by two Spaniards from Asturias and Castilla la Vieja respectively. Your Majesty would have enjoyed hearing them speak with that pure and correct accent which we Mexicans do not have, but which is much nicer."

Her sensitive ear for languages was one of Carlota's great gifts. She was articulate with that *Sprachgefühl,* a feeling for diction, which freed her from inhibitions and rendered her capable of repeating strange sounds. Talent and opportunity combined to make her a natural linguist.

She made full use of these advantages, especially in her correspondence. Her flair for writing was in itself unusual. Without those letters which she penned so faithfully it would be difficult to recapture the chimera of her existence. By comparison the Empress Eugénie's replies were flat and lifeless. To be sure, Carlota wrote under the compelling stimulus of travel in remote places, while her friend was forced to draw material from the commonplace experiences of the stay-at-home. Furthermore, the Empress of France was discontented and barely on speaking terms with her husband, while Carlota felt herself a woman loved.

Both sovereigns engaged in many courtesies on paper. At times their adherence to punctilio, while improving their style, obscured its meaning. The use of titles in preference to names led to entanglements which in turn needed explaining, thus from Carlota's pen: "The Emperor—our Emperor—has been indisposed, though not seriously." Again, when letters assumed the proportions of a Dumas serial she apologized: "I am telling your Majesty all this for I realize what pleasure you take in descriptions. Madame Almonte and I often declare how delighted we should be if the Empress Eugénie could come for a visit, and then we start deploring the ocean and the immensity of space."

There was in Eugénie an early weariness, a disenchantment. But Carlota wrote of her life like one who could not bear to miss a moment of it. An inexorable law of compensation was illustrated by these two women. The Empress of France had moved from the glitter of a sophisticated youth toward the chill of a premature twilight, while Carlota had stepped from pale and cloistered girlhood to the very brink of romance. Beauty, poignant and intoxicating, wove its spell about the little girl from Laeken.

She had a preference for marine colors, ranging from faint lime through lilac to deepest purple. But most of all she loved clear azure, and the billows of her crinoline shone like blue crystal when she drove from the heights of an Aztec palace hill to the portals of a Spanish cathedral. And her story is the story of a phantom crown. . . .

At least, so it seemed to Maximilian as he came upon her suddenly in the moonlight that bathed the world in silver. "She is an empress in a dream," he murmured to himself, "and I must rouse her before it is too late."

She had heard him coming up the stone stairs with slow unnatural steps. Dismissing her ladies-in-waiting she turned to meet him.

"What is it, my heart? You look so white——"

He took both her hands and kissed them. "I am tired, Carla. Tired and fed up with everything!"

"Work?" she asked sympathetically.

His nod was absent-minded. "There's a chasm that grows deeper and deeper; I haven't the power to bridge it——"

"Of course not. You are overtaxing yourself and I won't let you keep on. The new Spanish Minister, Marqués de la Ribera, called this afternoon to present his credentials, but I sent him away. He looked a bit *ofendido,* too." She broke into her quick laugh as she recalled the proud diplomat's indignation. Being a true Castilian hidalgo (*hijo-de-algo,* a son of something), the good marqués was not in the habit of standing before closed doors.

Maximilian leaned against the balustrade, his hands gripping the stone. "I must talk to you, Carla," he said, and there was a gravity in his tone that startled her.

She listened very quietly to the words that followed. Her eyelids closed as the voice beside her went on, humbly, incisively, laying bare their absurd mistakes. At last the outpour of self-accusation ceased and only the splash of a near-by fountain filled the stillness. Somewhere a cricket chirped shrilly and subsided again. Crickets were queer—how could anything so small make so much noise? . . .

Carlota turned to her husband and faced him. "You are not at fault," she said firmly, "whatever happens. It was I who said at Miramar—'Good, let us go!'—and I will help you now."

He pressed her to him. "But what are we going to do? Nothing will make the slightest dent in those figures."

"You can give back your salary. I shall get along without an allowance from the Mexican treasury."

Maximilian forced an ironic smile. "I forgot to tell you that we have so far been using Franzi's money. There is nothing to return——"

This was a blow she had not expected. The vast sums involved in French claims and indemnities had at times haunted her consciousness like some dread specter, although their very enormity seemed to preclude actual danger. The extortionate terms surrounding the Jecker loan had been the talk of Europe, but no one took them seriously. People everywhere believed that France, having made a profitable investment which gave her a foothold in Mexico, would be more than satisfied with this political gain. Certainly the Emperor Napoleon professed an abstract concern over the welfare of the Latin-American nations.

There was nothing abstract, however, about Maximilian's salary. And as for that relatively small sum—Carlota's allowance—if this could not be paid, then Mexico must indeed be in a sorry strait.

The Empress brooded. "I have it," she exclaimed presently, "we must cut down expenses. You can discharge the great Moo and I will see what may be done about my Señoras."

"The great Moo," as Scherzenlechner had come to be known because of his bloated self-esteem, was something of a nuisance. His bovine presence never failed to create discord, especially among the native members of the Emperor's following. There were those who wondered what Maximilian saw in the insolent former valet who aspired to the highest offices. In this matter of selecting competent advisers, royalty has ever notoriously sinned against royalty. Particularly was this true of the Hapsburgs, who reacted at once to a favorable exterior regardless of the rascality it might conceal. Writing to his wife at Budapest, Count Julius Andrássy described Franz Joseph's Cabinet members: *"Der grösste Fehler der Minister des Kaisers ist, dass sie Esel sind.* [The greatest fault of the Emperor's ministers lies in the fact that they are asses.]"

Even so, Franz Joseph had lucid moments when—unlike Maximilian—he was able to recognize a rogue at sight. One of the Hofburg secretaries, although commendable for his orthography, was a shameless liar. Franz Weckerle, the amanuensis in question, was asked by his Majesty to report on the weather.

"Majestät, es regnet [it is raining]," was the reply.

Franz Joseph went to the window and looked out. With a twinkle in his eye he turned to the secretary. "You have made a mistake, Weckerle. It really *is* raining."

But in far-off Mexico all perspicacity seemed to have been lacking, for Scherzenlechner had succeeded in bullying everybody, including his master. Maximilian now actually brightened at the unexpected excuse for discharging the lackey in a tactful manner. As it happened, Scherzenlechner did not merit such gracious treatment. When told that his services could no longer be afforded the erstwhile manservant tore off his insignia and decorations, shouting that he would never wear them again. Maximilian's offer to secure for him a post at the Hofburg in Vienna was rejected with the same vehemence. Sebastian wanted nothing unless the stain upon his imaginary escutcheon was wiped out.

"Der grosse Muh ist fort [The great Moo is gone]!" wrote Frau von Kuhacsevich to Frau von Radonetz whose husband was Prefect of Miramar. "It is the greatest blessing for the Emperor; he admits it himself. Whether things can still be straightened out with the government, nobody knows."

The matter of the Señoras was less simple. To be sure, the ladies-in-waiting held purely honorary positions and received no pay. Their removal could hardly affect the nation's treasury. But by reducing personnel at Court the outlay for ceremonials decreased perceptibly, and certainly the confectioner's bill would be cut in half. So, with the utmost delicacy, Carlota eliminated six of the less formidable dowagers—limiting her personal attendants to fourteen (the queens of Spain had sixty!). Objections from the offended aristocracy were met with a demure reference to the clerical party which had accused the Empress of extravagance.

To royalty the practise of economy must be a novel and unattractive experience, but Maximilian and Carlota were now consumed with a zeal for reform. Court balls and banquets, scheduled to celebrate their first anniversary upon the throne of Mexico, were canceled. A portion of the silver hollow-ware was left to tarnish in velvet-lined boxes; only the *petit déjeuner* set remained in use.

Outside the palace equally significant changes took place. Parades in gala uniform became taboo and Maximilian's plan to import horses on a large scale had to be dropped. Only the Emperor himself and the officers' corps continued to ride thoroughbreds. Furthermore, a curb was put on Bazaine, "the big spender"—(*le grand dépenseur*)—whose spasmodic military expeditions drew incalculable sums from the national purse. Henceforth Maximilian himself wished to direct all operations against the rebel Juárez and, if possible, engage in negotiations for a truce.

In all things the imperial couple bowed to necessity and, in an effort to set a proper example, even decried their former habits as foolish. The new order was wholesome and "so democratic." Emperor and Empress applauded the return to a simple life quite as if no one had ever promised them an annual income of fifteen hundred thousand and two hundred thousand pesos respectively.

Only one trifling matter remained unchanged—the tenor of their letters to Europe. No one abroad must have a chance to ridicule the Mexican venture or point with scorn at its grotesque outcome. Carlota continued to pen glowing accounts to Laeken, Paris, Vienna. Unsparing with adjectives, she described her "feast-day promenades, in shawls of rich lace and with hair dressed in the Mailand fashion (heavy knots on either ear, or loosely curled beneath a diadem of gold leaf)." She exaggerated bravely, brazenly. Everything in Mexico exceeded their most daring hopes, in fact, they were sitting in the proverbial lap of luxury. If disappointment, nay, utter failure lay ahead, Carlota could not bring herself to admit it.

Maximilian's letters to his mother and brothers were no less misleading. He boasted about his vast palaces, assuring Franz Joseph (to the latter's great irritation) that they were more imposing than the Hofburg or Schönbrunn. He described the Pompeian delights of *El Jardín de la Borda,* a pleasure estate in tropical Cuernavaca, and of his *Buen Retiro* at Orizaba "where the enthusiastic inhabitants have decided on their own initiative to build a villa for us in one of the fairest settings of this paradise."

On the subject of female pulchritude he waxed especially eloquent. "Mexican ladies are the loveliest I have ever seen, even in Andalucía." The younger Archdukes back in Austria were surprised to learn that the chorus of the Viennese opera could not compete with Latin charm. Furthermore, as if all this were not enough, Maxl's steed was a rare white Arab unsurpassed by the finest Lipizza stud. His private railroad coach appeared to be a florid affair worthy of Rubens (who had decorated the coronation carriage of the Hapsburgs). And if Maximilian must cut short the rich flow of his epistles it was because he found himself submerged in the authorship of a code on social precedence modeled after the liberal Messidor. "This strikes me as the most rational improvement, for Spanish etiquette has become outmoded. The whole matter will be published in an official gazette which is to appear daily." In truth, the imperial pen was busy. It produced seven volumes of statutes for the regulation of court ceremonial. The sonorous title of this opus, composed by the exalted author himself, contained only two idiomatic errors and one capricious omission of a capital letter: *"Reglamento Provisional por el Servicio y ceremonial del Corte."*

By thus fixing the exact privileges of rank in accordance with the degree involved, Maximilian hoped to banish those constant quarrels over priority which constitute the favorite sport of every royal entourage. For, unlike that chief of the Scottish clan who yelled "Where the MacGregor sits, that is the head of the table!" the average court darling lost his appetite or ran a temperature over some slip in the order of place-cards. Such vexations had their counterparts in history. There was the medieval tiff between the Archbishop of York and the Archbishop of Canterbury during a church council, when, since neither would surrender the seat of honor, both took turns settling down on each other's lap. A more enlightened and democratic future was to witness the Alice Longworth—Dolly Gann deadlock in the Washington of 1929.

With dissension banished from their drawing-rooms the imperial couple now concentrated on some means of demonstrating their adherence to Catholicism despite the hostile attitude of the clergy. What could be more convincing than the annual observance of Holy Thursday with the Washing of Beggars' Feet? This ritual, commemorating Christ's ministrations to the Apostles, had been traditionally re-enacted by all the popes as well as those sovereigns who enjoyed the papal attributes of Most Christian, Most Faithful, Most Catholic and Most Apostolic Majesties. These were in the order named the rulers of France, Portugal, Spain and Austria-Hungary, at whose Courts the ceremony of the Lavation was held according to prescribed form.

Once a year during Holy Week twelve poor men and as many ragged shrews were gathered up from city slums and spirited to the palace. Here they were scrubbed, clothed and abundantly perfumed before being led into the royal presence. Under the watchful eyes of the papal nuncio, a cardinal, an archbishop and the grandees of the realm, silver basins were next placed under the right foot of each beggar. Hereupon the sovereign, girded in a spotless apron, performed lightly with a decanter of blessed water and a fresh linen towel, after which he bowed and perfunctorily kissed the mendicant's metatarsus. It was a joyless business, but Jesus had done it, so it could be done. Maximilian found it helpful to remember the fact.

While this went on, the prelates, their acolytes and a choir chanted the corresponding Gospel of Saint John and the wretched men (as well as their female counterparts whom the royal spouse attended) felt exceedingly uncomfortable.

Ablutions now being completed, the awed beggars were directed to a magnificent banquet table where, on gold and silver dishes, a repast of twenty-five separate courses was spread out before them and served by the sovereigns in person. However, since the lowly guests were far too embarrassed to eat, it was customary for them to leave all the food untouched and to carry it away later in large baskets. Once outside the palace gates these baskets brought a handsome profit, since their contents could be sold at retail to a waiting crowd of middle-class citizens eager to purchase even the driest *queso de bola* (Edam cheese) if only it came from the royal pantry. Nor did the authorities interfere with such lively sales. It was deemed perfectly proper for any pauper who did not wish to gorge himself on the supply in his basket to change this into hard cash.

Maximilian and Carlota obeyed church traditions to the letter. With commendable zeal they introduced Rome's most stringent customs into Mexico, shirking no abasements. Their sincerity could not be doubted.

Politically, too, they meant to turn over a new leaf. If the Empire lacked resources something must be done to remedy this need. On paper, Maximilian allowed his imagination to weave palmy speculations of conquest. He recalled Napoleon's dream of enlarging Mexican territory down to the borders of Panamá, thus dividing the American continent into three major units, the Anglo-Saxon Republic to the north, the Mexican Empire, and that of Brazil. In this connection he strongly advised his youngest brother, Archduke Ludwig, who was undoubtedly leading a frivolous existence in Vienna, that Dom Pedro II of Brazil had two marriageable daughters. Here, if anywhere, opportunity knocked for Ludwig. But that odd young man proved impervious to feminine allure, especially at such long distance, and seemed loath to abandon his appanaged leisure. To Franz Joseph's profound chagrin, the Brazilian princesses found other husbands. The elder, Isabella, married the Count of Eu, while the younger, Leopoldine, became the bride of Prince August of Saxe-Coburg-Gotha-Koháry (the Hungarian Coburgs, now the dynasty of Bulgaria).

Other flights of Maximilian's fancy miscarried like the Brazilian marriages. The construction of a large navy and the founding of a monastery in the Holy Land were mere illusions wherein the harassed monarch sought escape from an all too painful reality. But the vicissitudes of his reign had just begun. Heretofore his troubles had sprung from religion, the deficit and questions of internal policy. Now there approached the harbingers of danger from without. Disjointed at first, yet growing daily more emphatic, reports drifted southward across the Río Grande that the American Civil War was definitely over. Banquo's ghost, in the shape of the detestable Monroe Doctrine, would soon be haunting the feast.

A minor calculation made by that authority on American affairs, the Emperor Napoleon III, had gone wrong. . . .

IV
THE CURTAIN

IV

THE CURTAIN

Chapter 1

At Belair, Maryland, thirty miles from Baltimore, the half-mad English actor, Junius Brutus Booth, drilled Shakespeare into the resisting skulls of his young offspring. The elder boy, Edwin Thomas, learned with considerable ease and, after his father's death, filled the latter's pending engagement as Richard III. A tour of the country followed. Loyal audiences everywhere approved the continuity of a famous name and so, in 1864, the year of Maximilian's arrival in Mexico, Edwin Booth played Hamlet to packed houses for one hundred consecutive nights in the city of New York.

It was not so with his younger brother. John Wilkes, named after the famous statesman and maternal ancestor, did not learn well. True, he appeared in *Julius Cæsar,* attuned to its keynote:

> "... poor Brutus, with himself at war,
> Forgets the shows of love to other men."

But he felt overshadowed by Edwin's greatness. Even before hostilities broke out between the franchised North and the slave-holding South, John left the stage and enlisted with the Virginia militia. What, after all, was grease paint? He would be a hero in the flesh! He would earn nobler laurels than those won behind footlights. He would die for a victorious South.

And then there had been no victorious South. Not only this; he, John Wilkes Booth, lost his enthusiasm for soldiery long before a climax was reached in the fray. When the Confederate armies disbanded he was nowhere among them. He had returned to provincial boards and was back where he started, plodding along in the shadow of his brother's glory. It was unbearable. He began to dramatize his own failure in less personal terms, by sorrowing over the defeat of his military comrades. He joined a secret group of conspirators who were going to Washington with vague plans of vengeance. Nights of fasting and inflammatory discussion crystallized these plans. There stood a man before the public eye who symbolized the struggle in which the South had been humbled.

> "Let's be sacrificers, but not butchers, Caius.
> We all stand up against the spirit of Cæsar;
> And in the spirit of men there is no blood:
> O that we then could come by Cæsar's spirit,
> And not dismember Cæsar! But, alas,
> Cæsar must bleed for it! And, gentle friends,
> Let's kill him boldly, but not wrathfully;
> Let's carve him as a dish fit for the gods,
> Not hew him as a carcass fit for hounds:
> And let our hearts, as subtle masters do,
> Stir up their servants to an act of rage,
> And after seem to chide 'em. This shall make
> Our purpose necessary and not envious:
> Which so appearing to the common eyes,
> We shall be call'd purgers, not murderers."

On April 14, 1865 (the anniversary of the *Novara's* sailing from Miramar), President Abraham Lincoln and his guests attended a performance at Ford's Theater. In the course of the evening the actor Booth was able to conceal himself in the presidential box where, at close range, he fired a revolver. The bullet entered Lincoln's neck, causing death early the next morning. John Wilkes Booth escaped but broke his leg in the attempt and was found hiding in the Virginia hills a short time later. Refusing surrender, he fell before the volleys of his pursuers on April twenty-sixth, without impressing an outraged world with his interpretation of the deed.

The tragic news caused apprehension in many quarters. The gaunt American President was known for his benevolence, but what about his successors? Secretary of State William Henry Seward, stabbed at his residence on the same night of the assassination, bristled with aggressive policies. Vice-President Andrew Johnson, Lincoln's automatic successor, rose to power on a wave of blustering nationalism. Nothing seemed to weaken the Colossus of the North. On the contrary, the War of the Secession had imbued the Union with a new realization of power which might well be used against her neighbors. Having crushed insurrection at home, the United States appeared eager to accept any challenge. Latin America took notice.

In a public address just before his end Abraham Lincoln had said: "I do not know what the nation wants. All I know is that there will be no more wars under my presidency." Imperial Mexico had drawn great comfort from these words, for Maximilian hoped in time to win Lincoln's sympathy.

But death had changed all that. After President Johnson's investiture a confidential messenger, Don Mariano Degollado, left Mexico City with a letter of condolence from Maximilian and a proposal for a conference between the two governments. Washington officials remained aloof. Señor Degollado returned with his letter and the information that, as far as the United States were concerned, Benito Juárez was still President of Mexico. In fact, raised eyebrows were turned in the direction of Chapultepec, and an inquiry might soon be forthcoming.

Maximilian grew anxious. For some time past he had hoped to place a diplomatic representative in the neighboring republic, only to be told that Matías Romero, the minister appointed by Juárez, still held office. The Hapsburg intruder had no chance of a hearing.

Politically the Mexican picture now underwent a slight change. After the close of the American Civil War restless Yankee elements began to look about for further adventure. Countless filibusters drifted toward Paso del Norte, on the border, to join the rebel camp and take up arms against the Austrian usurper. Aided by this unexpected influx of war material Juárez was able to launch a fresh campaign. Like a plague of locusts new hordes of guerrillas sprang up throughout the country. At Chihuahua, Monterrey, Torreón and Saltillo the imperial garrisons saw themselves surrounded by growing bands of marauding Juaristas. Inexplicably, the Indian patriot's forces cropped up on the highway to Vera Cruz within a few miles from Mexico City.

Carlota found things very exciting. She wrote:

"Life here seems quite like the Middle Ages. One moment we are gay, comfortable and serene, only to realize that at any minute a band of guerrilleros may fall upon us. Cannon have been installed up here (at Chapultepec) and a system of signals was worked out to keep us in communication with the city. Even so we are constantly on the *qui-vive*. . . . Two nights ago I jumped out of bed on hearing artillery fire. It turned out to be a boisterous celebration in honor of the Virgin of Tacubaya, as if God had picked four o'clock in the morning for the Annunciation! But I suppose people here try to allow for the difference of time between Mexico and Jerusalem. They celebrate all religious occasions at night amid explosions of firecrackers and a din that seems to rip the earth asunder. Daytime festivals are less violent."

Both Emperor and Empress were of course puzzled by the renewed impetus with which Juárez now attacked them. In another letter to Eugénie, Carlota ventured a shrewd enough analysis:

"Your Majesty must consider that no one can foresee whence guerrilla bands may spring up. Theirs is a kind of spontaneous generation. As I understand the matter, a man leaves his village with a horse, a weapon and the firm determination to acquire riches by any means except work. He has plenty of audacity and a certain disregard for his own safety. If he gets shot it won't matter, for life is dull anyway and the only thing he cares about is lucrative adventure. Such a fellow as this has little trouble recruiting others of the same kidney. (We have here a shifting population with just the right propensities.) They plunder the first hacienda they come to; this achievement constitutes their baptism into the bandit profession. Newspapers make the most of it and lend importance to the band by reporting all its escapades in a given region. The robbers grow bolder and next hold up a stage-coach, carrying off a few rich people who can be held for ransom, and retreating over unknown trails across the sierras into some remote district. Here another band, and sometimes a third, can be found in hiding. Likely as not they all merge, swelling in number from a handful to several thousand."

While this description did justice to the more normal phases of banditry, the Empress's report failed to recognize the special factor in the present crisis. Neither she nor Maximilian could know that contraband arms and ammunitions were being smuggled across the frontier at Brownsville by United States citizens who had a knack for business, as well as a burning interest in the welfare of republics. In New Orleans a society known as the "D. M. D." (Defenders of the Monroe Doctrine) had been formed for the express purpose of supporting Juárez. In open violation of professed American neutrality, members of this organization marshaled men and funds to rebel headquarters.

New York harbored a similar group called the "Mexican Patriots" who were busy floating a loan for the Indian chieftain. In an effort to obtain subscriptions these stout souls offered Lower California as security, Upper California and one-half of Mexico's original territory having already passed under the ample folds of the Stars and Stripes in 1846. In the face of such competition Maximilian, whose shibboleth was money, saw his own prospects dwindling.

To add to the predicament, his Majesty's forces had lately shown signs of terror. Bazaine, whose mind dwelled on the joys of a belated honeymoon, blundered clumsily through every encounter. This was not entirely the fat marshal's fault. No European could hope to master the intricacies of guerrilla warfare; even the black Chasseurs d'Afrique, accustomed to desert fighting, were baffled by the surprise tactics of the enemy. Appearing in small ragged detachments the Juaristas lured their prey into a cunning trap, only to fall upon the foreigners from ambushed hide-outs. At a great sacrifice of young Belgian volunteers, Bazaine occupied and evacuated one spot fourteen times before comprehending the futility of his efforts. In the end he began to withdraw from the northern provinces, establishing his headquarters at San Luis Potosí. From here he sent a distressing report to Paris.

Napoleon III was smoking an incredible number of cigarettes. He always did this when he was nervous. The cause for the present seizure had been a visit from Mr. John Bigelow, newly appointed American Minister to France, who had come to deliver a message from Secretary Seward at Washington. The message consisted of a single question, courteous but categorical. What, Mr. Seward wished to know, was the French *tricolore* doing in Mexico?

L'Empereur cleared his throat. He regarded his finger-nails, becoming quite absorbed in their high polish. Monsieur Disdéri, the court photographer, provided a welcome interruption at this point by announcing a sitting of his Majesty with the Prince Imperial, beside a bust of Napoleon I and a portrait of the Duke of Reichstadt (Napoleon II). The composition was to be entitled *Quatre Napoléons*. It was grandiose! Mr. Bigelow began to cough.

Ah, to be sure, that splendid Monsieur Seward of the glorious *Etats Unis*—he had a question?

"What," said Mr. Bigelow, "is the French *tricolore* doing in Mexico?"

But of course. It was a simple matter which his Majesty would explain at once. There were monetary obligations incurred by past Mexican administrations. In an effort to protect its own interests the French Government had sent a commission—partly military in character—to investigate this matter of the debt. A purely temporary arrangement, it would be concluded in no time.

"When?" asked Mr. Bigelow.

"As a matter of fact," L'Empereur remembered, "just about now."

"What of this Archduke Maximilian who has placed himself upon the throne of Mexico?" the American inquired further.

Oh, he was an Austrian. Mr. Seward would do well to confer

with the Emperor Franz Joseph's representative in Washington, Baron von Wydenbruck. And now, if this was all, Napoleon III wished to be excused for he had some letters to write.

This was perfectly true. The post departed that same day from the Tuileries with stringent orders for Marshal Bazaine to evacuate Mexico as fast as possible. In a more detailed memorandum which followed this first message the marshal was instructed to use tact and discretion. Maximilian was not to learn of Napoleon's plans until the last minute, when objections could be disregarded on the grounds that they had come too late.

Bazaine embraced the idea whole-heartedly. He began to call in French troops from all distant outposts, leaving Hungarian cavalry and Austrian *Jäger* regiments guarding the towns he abandoned. Simultaneously he encouraged the recruiting of native brigades, a matter in which heretofore he had opposed Maximilian's wishes, since the imperial forces were to remain predominantly French.

It was this ostensibly generous move which first aroused suspicion in the capital. A rumor sprang up that at its last session the French Chamber of Deputies had voted down all further appropriations for the support of the Legion in Mexico. Bazaine's sudden eagerness to drill Indians, whom he despised, lent credence to the story.

Carlota was the first to do something about it. She hurried to her writing-table and scribbled a note to her good sister Eugénie, asking for a denial of the reports. "We hear whisperings, Madame, that in France a strong wind has started blowing toward economies in the military budget. I implore you not to forget that we resemble the ivy. Although we expect to become sturdy trees, for the time being we must have a trunk to cling to."

Even as this letter made its way across the ocean the signs became clearer. Straggling detachments of fugitives arrived in Mexico City with tales of horror. Due to Bazaine's contradictory tactics the imperial troops were everywhere outnumbered by Juaristas who slaughtered all prisoners and subjected native captives to particular tortures. Maximilian winced. He grieved for the beardless youths who had followed him so enthusiastically overseas, but even more poignant was his sorrow for Indian martyrs to his cause. The Europeans, foolhardy spirits for the most part, had after all set out in search of a thrill. Well, they were getting it. But Indians, stoical, bewildered, fighting for a cause they did not understand . . .

Of late he had taken a profound liking to them, their anxious eyes, their philosophic gestures, their genteel speech. He rather envied them that indifference to clocks and calendars which culminated in a sublime Aztec inertia and formed an everlasting barrier against the neuroticism of Nordic cultures.

In time Maximilian had hoped to do something for this vast backbone of his empire. Among his papers were numerous drafts proposing reforms which would restore the race of Montezuma to its former eminence. By what a gaping margin he had missed his goal! Taxes and contributions bled the country dry in order to meet the monthly interest on the foreign debt; even the customs officials at Vera Cruz were French, lest any source of revenue be overlooked.

And now that the legionaries (who had lived off the fat of the land) sought cover, an exhausted native population was expected to defend the monarchic principle. It didn't make sense. Napoleon could not possibly approve the dispositions which his self-willed marshal was enforcing. At the risk of causing Bazaine's downfall, the French Government must be informed of true conditions.

The time for optimistic trumpery was past. Maximilian wrote to the Emperor Napoleon in dead earnest:

> "I am frankly telling your Majesty that this situation has become very difficult for me. As a loyal friend I may add that trouble lies in store for both of us; for you because the glorious name of France will be exposed to ridicule, for me because all my plans (which are primarily yours) can not be carried into effect. Amid such military and material disorder the noble idea of a regenerated Mexico must fail; with such a drain on the finances, and the consequent perennial deficit, I can not govern. With a people whose faith in me has been shaken, since French protection proved so fickle, I can achieve no

lasting results. What native followers I have are well aware that the guerrillas hang or shoot without mercy every individual who sympathizes with the Empire. It is not to be wondered at if people are careful not to declare themselves in favor of a government which is quite obviously incapable of defending its own subjects."

Carlota joined in these entreaties, disclosing a few facts which heretofore she had lightly glossed over:

"It must be admitted that in this country everything must be started all over again from the very beginning, for there is nothing but nature in either the physical or the abstract sense. I am reminded of the Mexican railway; civilization seems to have begun at several points, but intermediate stages and the most important connections are still missing. There is a need for education in the very fundamentals of living. Fortunately one finds a general docility among natives, a docility which has enabled Mexicans to endure the most barbarous and criminal oppression. Because of this we are reconciled to our task and shall consecrate ourselves to duty in the full knowledge of what we are doing. Personally, I have been shocked by nothing but the country roads. All the rest struck me as an improvement on what we actually expected. . . . Adieu, Madame and good sister. Our affairs will work out nicely, if only your Majesties continue to grant us your support."

Such outright appeals to their honor could not but touch Napoleon and Eugénie. But sentiment in Europe had changed. The French middle classes were tired of subscribing to government loans which in the end served only to enrich a handful of greedy bankers. Moreover, the Mexican campaign was beginning to accrue a list of casualties. Widows and orphans of fallen soldiers demanded compensation.

In the Low Countries public opinion was aroused by a suspicion that Bazaine sacrificed Belgian battalions in preference to those of his own nationality. Mynheer Vleeschouwer, an incensed tribune, published a protest in *Het Nederduitsche Bond* of June 14,

1865, which contained the following paragraph: "The French Emperor cannot tolerate freedom or independence anywhere. His aim is to strangle liberty even beyond the oceans. He has sent an army to crush the Mexican people, imposing an emperor by force. Mexico languishes to-day under the yoke of foreign domination and Belgium is expected to go to war for the simple reason that our Princess is married to the despot who rules that land."

Such criticism could not fail to reach Napoleon's ear. It rendered his position exceedingly uncomfortable. Unpopular in his own country and sneered at abroad, *Moustachu* found it difficult to extricate himself from the meshes in which he had become entangled. Maximilian believed it a simple matter for a man to keep his word. This was apparent throughout his letters; their hidden reproaches cut Napoleon to the quick. In desperation Napoleon therefore temporized. He resolved to postpone the evacuation until the following spring. Perhaps the thing could be done by degrees, so as to be less noticeable.

At any rate, L'Empereur spent a night and a day engrossed in a reply which would pour balm over Maximilian's alarms and prevent an immediate panic. He likewise instructed Bazaine to move slowly, drawing his legions toward the coast where they could in time be absorbed by Europe-bound steamers. Meanwhile the recruiting of native troops must continue and, if volunteers were not forthcoming, General Forey's courts martial must be revived.

Bazaine understood. He put in an appearance at Chapultepec and explained that the new French policy was directed toward Maximilian's own good. There was no idea of leaving him in the lurch. Whatever had made his Majesty think of that? But, if a well-meant piece of advice might be allowed, Maximilian's government lacked the proper severity. The Foreign Legion might remain in Mexico through several decades, yet no national army would form if one did not exert oneself.

"What is it you mean?" asked Maximilian.

"Conscription, your Majesty."

"By force?"

Bazaine smiled. "Certainly. No nation in the world can depend upon volunteers in time of war. Private citizens lack the necessary enthusiasm to die."

"In that case I don't see what I am to do with subjects who are not even of my own race. I can't compel them to fight for me——"

"Why not? Your Majesty has the power to issue decrees. I have here a copy of the manifesto promulgated before your Majesty's arrival on these shores. It bears proof that Forey and myself did not take Mexico City with silk gloves."

Bazaine drew from his pocket a soiled scroll of parchment. The Emperor bent over it, scanning the grim text.

"I see," he said slowly, "severity means hangings."

"For traitors, deserters and every captive enemy—Juárez is doing no less, your Majesty. This is only a copy of a similar decree he passed four years ago."

Maximilian bit his lip. "Juárez can afford such things. He is their countryman. But I would never be forgiven."

With a shrug of shoulders Bazaine turned to go. His expression showed plainly that he did not think much of this Hapsburg who repudiated the absolutism which had made his forebears great. What were monarchies coming to if a sovereign refused to recognize his power over life and death? In another century not a throne would be left, and nations would bow before the tyranny of the masses.

The marshal, who was a disciplinarian at heart, shuddered.

But Maximilian wrote in his diary: "One can do everything with bayonets, except sit on them."

Chapter 2

Although the interview with the French commander did not sway Maximilian in the direction of more aggressive policies, it restored a measure of calm in royalist circles. Napoleon III had reiterated his pledge to stand by the Mexican Empire. Did this not prove once again what gossip was worth? Maximilian was determined to apprehend the scandalmonger who had cast such unworthy reflections upon the integrity of his good friend, the Emperor of France. A sort of example ought to be set. The culprit in question would be banished to an unpleasant life in some remote province.

For the rest, the Court resumed its accustomed routine under the new ægis of economy. Parties and dances having ceased, Carlota spent more time over her diaries. She did not know that as "foot-notes to history" her jottings would acquire inestimable value. She merely obeyed an impulse to communicate her thoughts. She wrote with that quick spontaneity which Léon Daudet attributes to the talented feminine pen.

The question of Catholicism troubled her. She was baffled to find that the orthodox faith she had known in Europe had nothing in common with the archaic preachments of Labastida and his ilk. Until the reform laws of Juárez broke the spell, religious matters in Mexico had been governed by sixteenth-century formalism. Learned ecclesiastics collected tithes, blessed their flocks and published dissertations on astral topics such as the question whether God had large hands and feet, or, if He sat on a cloud, where did He sit when it rained?

As for the lower clergy, they were steeped in a confused mysticism. On excursions to Uruápam or the enchanted Tzintzuntzan Carlota encountered village priests who topped their vestments with feathers and other heathenish accessories. The spiritual level thereby disclosed struck her as untenable. Here was a crying need for enlightenment.

"We are trying," she wrote her brother, the Duke of Brabant, "to make this a Catholic nation, for it never has been converted to Christian beliefs as we know them."

Her statement did not lack truth. For three centuries Spanish Jesuits, Franciscans and Dominicans had preached the Gospel to a heathen people gifted with an extravagant imagination. All that the friars taught delighted the native children; they embraced each symbol, every fetish of the Roman Church, and merely added these to prehistoric cults of their own. Behind each quaint madonna, each saintly apostle, lurked the spook of an Aztec god or demon—as the case might be. To this day the Virgin of Guadalupe, brown patroness of the Indians, enjoys a higher rating in the hearts of pious devotees than the bearded and venerable Jehovah himself. "It is," the pensive peón will readily admit, "because she understands us."

Carlota had not been transplanted long enough to know that precisely therein lay the strength of Rome. Due to the constant menace of volcanoes, earthquakes, hurricanes and other elemental violence, there is a natural religiosity among tropic peoples which was quickly recognized by early evangelists. In Mexico the story of Nazareth was so well told by those first heroic monks that priests became thereafter almost unessential.

Mexican churches are never empty; people linger in them regardless of the fact that no service happens to be going on. They love the saints. These darlings of their imagination take part in town and village life; in sunny weather they are wheeled outdoors to enjoy the warming rays. The Virgin of the Conquest, *La Conquistadora,* has charge of rain. When begged to do so, she supplies it copiously, sometimes so copiously that it ruins crops, whereupon she is marched about the countryside and soundly scolded: *"Mira lo que tu hijo ha hecho!* [Look what your son has done!]" Faith is the very substance of indigenous thought. . . .

"Wide swing cathedral doors.
El Cristo Rey, beyond the chancel rail,
Looks out upon the plaza where his flock
Raise up a wild, enthusiastic cry,

And incense pours
From out the church. With lurid, fiery trail
The rockets soar and burst; firecrackers shock
The adobe houses clustering nearby.
The crowd adores.

"Yes, Mexico,
Your people, old and infinitely wise,
Have learned what Nordic minds were never taught.
Worship is joyous; dull morality
May come and go,
But pagan beauty under pagan skies
Has naught to do with stodgy ethic thought—
It lives throughout this earth's eternity
For man to know.

"And, Roman creed,
There's tribute even in the errant soul
That knows not your protection. You have wrought
A wondrous thing among your votaries.
In giving heed
To those whose vibrant Aztec gods you stole
And fusing them with deities you brought
From oversea, you managed to appease
A warlike breed."

No, Carlota could not bring herself to accept this blend of orthodoxy and heathenism. The candor with which Mexican ladies translated the rigors of Lent into a convenient period for complexion bleaching, nettled her. While expiating their sins by foregoing the customary pleasures of the table, devout penitents sucked a daily egg through a carefully made opening at one end of the shell. After forty days of this there were many delicate shells which could be tinted, stuffed with confetti, and used as *cascarones* (toy bombs) at the first dance after Easter. Such ribald antics would have been inconceivable at Laeken. Carlota could not refrain from denouncing a delinquent clergy for permitting them anywhere else.

Her criticism was ill-advised, for Maximilian had already discovered that his position suffered from lack of ecclesiastic approbation. He regretted the break with the Holy See and was casting about for an opportunity to reopen negotiations with the Vatican. Profoundly tolerant at heart, he did not make the Church responsible for the follies of those who served it. Besides, he well understood even Napoleon's aversion to equal freedom for all creeds—Protestantism opened one of the channels through which the Anglo-Saxon invasion gained peaceful access. But Maximilian had a prophetic suspicion that in a not distant future the tides of commerce would sweep aside such petty barriers, causing Latins and Nordics to fuse their mutual interests, despite all efforts at racial isolation.

Though he did not intend, in the main, to alter his stand on the religious question, he felt that a revision of the entire matter would be of some value. Perhaps if his ideas were couched in more amiable terms the Pope would allow himself to be placated. A new concordat with Rome would certainly create a better feeling throughout Mexico; it might even help in establishing the native army on which Bazaine put such emphasis.

Of late there had appeared in capital circles a certain Father Augustus Fischer whom Señora de Sánchez-Navarro favored in the confessional. Subsequent investigation disclosed that this pious gentleman of Teutonic origin had been a Texas farmer who, endowed with gifts not appreciated by the Lutheran Church, had turned Jesuit. For years he had served as chaplain to the Bishop of Durango. He spoke English and Spanish fluently and had almost forgotten his German when Maximilian's arrival in Mexico caused him to brush up on that tongue. With imperial favors to cozen, the good padre bade his episcopal master good-by, packed his knapsack, and repaired to the capital.

He was prepossessing in appearance. Persuasive of speech (he had won many a damsel's secular devotion), Father Fischer had no trouble in becoming society's bosom friend. But he wanted more. Madame Navarro talked to her husband who in turn introduced the holy brother at Court.

Maximilian was agreeably surprised. Due to enforced economies the Emperor had discharged innumerable members of his suite and was now surrounded almost entirely by Mexicans. To discover in Fischer a man who not only spoke Maximilian's tongue, but knew Mexican conditions inside-out, seemed too good to be true. Carlota also rejoiced, although she perceived in the Jesuit that same mixture of civilized and barbarian traits which so dismayed her.

The moment being propitious, Father Fischer was at once consulted on the subject of a new concordat. Would the Church, Maximilian inquired, be willing to reconsider the entire ecclesiastical problem? The Jesuit brooded over the matter and replied in the affirmative. He made a number of suggestions and finished by offering to go to Europe himself for an audience with the Pope. Decidedly, he avowed, a settlement with the clergy would win for the Empire all the sympathies it lacked in the remoter districts where loyalty and superstition went hand in hand.

The Emperor was delighted. The chancelleries set to work at once, drawing up the terms of an agreement whereby certain restitutions of property were to be made, and offering an unbiased consideration of further wishes expressed by the Curia. But on one point Maximilian remained adamant. There was to be no barrier to creeds, regardless of their nature. He would be sponsor to pantheist and atheist alike. Father Fischer frowned. It did not look well for the second concordat. But he yearned for travel and the sailing date had been set. Toward the middle of September of 1865, the tonsured minister-without-portfolio breezed across the Atlantic.

Before his departure, Fischer unwittingly shot a poisoned arrow into the domestic idyl of Chapultepec. The scurrilous reports concerning the Emperor's sexual impotence had, in certain circles, undergone a change. Slander was now directed against the Empress. Her apparent sterility was discussed with nonchalance by monarchists and reactionaries alike. How could a hereditary dynasty hope to establish itself if its most symbolic support, the heir to the throne, was lacking? Maximilian must realize that a ruler's easiest hold upon popular favor lay in the royal nursery. The proletarian masses never fail to grow maudlin at sight of a chosen infant. Even the rabid revolutionary guard who jammed himself into the carriage of Louis XVI and Marie Antoinette after the unsuccessful flight to Varennes marveled at the little Dauphin passing water into an appropriate receptacle, emblazoned with the lilies of France, and supported at a helpful angle by the child's father. This gentle ministration so impressed the hardened Jacobin (who, presumably, believed royalty immune to a simple human urge) that he relaxed his brutal grip upon the travelers and eased their return journey to Paris as much as possible. The competent manipulation of his small son's chamber pot almost, though not quite, saved the King's life. Too many members of the Commune were absent during that touching scene.

Father Fischer, in shrewdly analyzing Maximilian's situation from this angle, meant well. He suggested that in the tenth year of a childless marriage it was time to take measures of one sort or another. Since the escapades of his own dissipated youth contrasted badly with his present frocked state, the prudent Augustus advised a conventional solution rather than one of more libertine implications. As a matter of fact, he had something quite definite in mind.

At the old Palacio Iturbide in Mexico City lived the sorry remnant of Mexico's Second Empire. The Emperor Don Agustín de Iturbide had left three sons—Agustín, Ángel, and Cosme—and a daughter, Josefa, who lived in comparative penury in their father's abandoned mansion on the Avenida San Francisco opposite the House of Tiles (*La Casa de los Azulejos*). Josefa was a spinster devoted to fine embroideries for the altar of the near-by Franciscan church. Spanish tradition had laid out the pattern for a vestal life, although there were those who rebelled against it....

> "Old maids dress the saints!
> So the proverb goes.
> And every one knows
> That Josephine
> Should long be coiffing Saint Catherine,
> But there she walks
> Flaunting ripe charms,
> Causing alarms
> To pious folk—

Since who can say
But that some fine day
The saints go in tatters
For all that it matters
To Josephine,
And those of her ilk
Who believe that silk
Should console live virgins
For minor burdens."

Agustín seemed likewise to be destined for celibacy. But Ángel and Cosme were married, the former to an American known as Doña Alice, and the latter to the Creole Doña Sabina. Sabina's child, Salvador, was a lad of school age. Alice also had a son, two years old, named after his imperial grandfather.

Ever since Maximilian's accession the Iturbide clan, though not to the purple born, used the dynastic "we." In the opinion of its members, the various classes into which Mexican society was divided really began where the Hapsburgs and the Iturbides left off. To be sure, at Chapultepec this little idiosyncrasy was not known, since the descendants of the self-styled Emperor Agustín had not as yet appeared at Court. The state of their finances—and wardrobes—rendered this effort prohibitive. But so trifling a detail as their postponed presentation did not daunt the erstwhile royal family. In their dusty sitting-rooms they discoursed upon poor Carlota's difficulties with those ambitious females who made up her entourage, "vulgar social climbers, all of them." As for Fernando (the use of Maximilian's first name emphasized a non-existing intimacy), he would do very well in time, provided . . . Ah, and here was the rub! The Iturbides were in their third generation, whereas Maximilian had no issue. Daily the Empress drove past under the balconies of the Iturbide house on her way to the cathedral, yet the binoculars of Josefa and her brothers detected no change in her figure.

And then, one morning, while delivering a richly orphreyed chasuble to the sacristan of Churubusco Convent for the abbot's use during Holy Week, Josefa had heard about Father Fischer. The latter's recent promotion to the rank of Court Confessor had made a stir in ecclesiastical circles. It now made a stir in the Iturbide household. On certain days the new padre officiated at the cathedral. The Iturbide ladies reviewed their sins and determined to win his special brand of absolution at the earliest opportunity. Josefa, whose repertoire was thin, went first. With a fringed shawl wrapped about her spare frame she lingered near the *Altar del Perdón,* hoping to catch a glimpse of the friar who would hear her venial iniquities. Luck was with her, for Father Augustus prayed in the wing known as *El Sagrario Metropolitano* before entering the confessional. She caught a clear view of his profile as he passed. He wore a stole with the imperial cipher embroidered at one end. Josefa's eyes fastened upon it. She felt that the letters enhanced the padre's not inconsiderable charm.

"Misereatur tui omnipotens Deus, et dimissis peccatis tuis perducat te ad vitam aeternam. Amen."

His Latin was beautiful. It inspired Josefa to an exhaustive inspection of the darker corners of her soul. She confessed and invited the padre to tea.

At the Iturbide mansion, a few days later, the desired meeting took place. The tea was weak, but the conversation that went with it lacked no vigor. Father Fischer was allowed to study the two small boys, Salvador and Agustín, the grandsons of an emperor. . . . He went away with an idea.

At Chapultepec Maximilian listened to a strange proposal. Realizing the importance of such a step for the future of the Empire, the Iturbide family offered one of its members for adoption as a crown prince. Maximilian was free to choose between the children, whose relatives asked nothing in return. Nothing, that is, beyond a pension suited to their rightful station.

The Emperor was taken aback, yet on further reflection the scheme did not displease him. In his present precarious position the advent of a royal baby would have been a true blessing, since even the savage Juaristas might have been moved to sympathy for a child of the realm. Failing such a token, why not then make use of this substitute? Who but the offspring of a former ruler would qualify for the place of an adopted heir apparent? Besides, Maximilian was fond of children and felt keenly the lack of family ties. In letters from Vienna his mother, the Archduchess Sophie, described rollicking times spent with Franz Joseph's children Rudolf and Gisela, and their fat cousins Otto and Franz Ferdinand. The latter belonged to the Archduke Karl, Maxl's younger brother. Another generation was growing up at the Hofburg while Chapultepec concealed its secret sorrow.

With a degree of misgiving he spoke to Carlota. She paled, a deep wound gnawing within her. She had always hoped. But this, the very word—adoption—gave shape to her humiliation. It stamped it as irrevocable. It brought an admission that now hope must cease, that the world deemed her unfit for motherhood.

She grieved bitterly and fought for two nights and two days with her spirit. Then she herself went to the Iturbide house and looked at the boys. She picked the younger, because he was so white and fair. And to her husband she said: "Take this one, he is so little. But if you want one of your own send me away. I will love you from afar."

He took her hand and held it. "I will have none, Carla, if not from you."

And so the Iturbide plan was realized. By special decree the Emperor conferred upon the two children the hereditary title of prince, but only Agustín was formally adopted. In return for an annuity of one hundred and fifty thousand pesos (to be paid by Maximilian in regular instalments, from funds which he hoped one day to raise through the civil lists) the relatives of the little crown prince agreed to travel in Europe for a few years. This would make it easier for the child to assimilate his new environment. Maximilian was justified in specifying such an arrangement, since the boy must hereafter be reared as a Hapsburg and not as an Iturbide. Furthermore, no insidious form of nepotism needed to be feared if the heir to the throne forgot his earlier connections and learned of them only after a strong attachment to his foster parents had been established.

The terms were accepted enthusiastically by the entire Iturbide clan, with the exception of the little boy's mother, who did not want to be separated from her child. At this the Emperor and Empress relinquished the plan, since the adoption lost all significance if Agustín did not belong to them wholly. Josefa and her brothers saw themselves doomed to a drab existence in place of the French spa they had already picked for their holiday.

In a body they descended upon Alice de Iturbide and reasoned with her. What kind of mother was she, after all, if she stood deliberately in the way of her son's success? Could she not have other children and give this one to her country? Ángel, her husband, seemed to think so. As for making a decent living, Ángel wasn't so good at that; whereas they might all bask in the Emperor's generosity, with never another worry until their dying days.

Alice reconsidered. Maximilian and Carlota were likewise to make a concession if she relented. Once a year she must be allowed to visit Agustín, even if her identity must remain hidden. The condition was accepted. As a further consolation Maximilian offered to engage the child's aunt, Josefa, as royal governess with the temporary title of princess (to be relinquished at her death). This was too much for the lady in question. Doña Josefa moved to Chapultepec in a flurry of ostrich feathers and impromptu majesty. She slipped into her rôle of an Imperial Highness with never a qualm wasted on the pleasure resorts of France.

The Iturbide family sailed for Europe on October 2, 1865.

Chapter 3

Secretary Seward wrote another note to the American Minister in Paris:

"Our Government is astonished and distressed at the announcement, now made for the first time, that the promised withdrawal of French troops from Mexico, which ought to have taken place in November (this month), has been put off by the Emperor. You will inform the Emperor's Government that the President desires and sincerely hopes that the evacuation of Mexico will be accomplished in conformity with the existing arrangement. . . . Instructions will be sent to the military forces of the United States, which are placed in a spot of observation, and are waiting the special orders of the President; this will be done with the confidence that the telegraph or the courier will bring us intelligence of a satisfactory resolution on the part of the Emperor in reply to this note. You will assure the French Government that the United States, in wishing to free Mexico, have nothing so much at heart as preserving peace and friendship with France."

Consternation reigned at the Tuileries when this dispatch was made known. Napoleon recognized that the position of the two nations had become inverted; the United States now gave orders. Frenchmen everywhere resented Yankee interference, regardless of their private views on the Mexican venture. Paris newspapers carried flaming editorials: "The United States tracked French policy step by step; never before has the French Government been subjected to such dictatorship. During America's civil strife France spoke boldly to Ambassador Dayton—'Do you want peace or war?'—To-day our foothold in Mexico is challenged by Washington and the Emperor Maximilian will fall because our Government allows its conduct to be dictated by American arrogance."

Much oratory was devoted to the matter but in the end Napoleon was obliged to declare his hand. He did so in a veiled manner, indicating that France did not possess a sufficient number of transports to permit complete evacuation at a given date. Bazaine, however, would receive new instructions in regard to the embarcation of troops. Mr. Seward growled irritably and once more allowed the matter to rest.

In Mexico unpleasant rumors revived. The legions were seen concentrating along the coast, while to the north fresh garrisons fell daily before the onslaught of Juaristas. Only one explanation seemed possible. The diplomatic pouch carried long polemics from Carlota to her "friend and sister" Eugénie, polemics in which a note of worry mingled with a new emotion, bitterness.

> "It is all very well for the English Parliament to declare that Mexico ought to get along without help from anybody. In spite of this advice we are here confronted with realities. This country can not become civilized unless one is absolute master of it. To gain control one must have big battalions; there is no arguing against them. Any authority which can not be enforced has a doubtful value, like funds which fluctuate. Ours have been declining steadily which explains our desperate need of troops. The Austrians and the Belgians, you must know, are nice in time of peace, but when storms break there is really nothing like the red-trousers. If your Majesty will allow me to say just what is in my mind, I believe it impossible to weather these present crises unless our army is strengthened. The troops are far too scattered and instead of recalling any there ought to be an increase. I beg you to consider, moreover, that your interests can not profit if ours suffer. . . .
> P.S. We are wrong in thinking that this country is eager for regeneration. Everybody makes a great noise about the idea, both in books and speeches, but in reality they love chaos simply because it is old and ugly. They revel in it because it is so old that it has become national."

She was beginning to lose that unfailing optimism which had formerly characterized her. Tension and incessant worry drained her vitality. "I am growing old," she said once, after the stigma of barrenness was fixed upon her through the little Iturbide's adoption. "It's not the years, but something inside me. I am worn with anxiety."

Her portraits captured this change of mood. The pictures of her youth showed a gay challenging Charlotte who longed to exchange dull virtue for a thrill. In Venice and Milan the Vice-Regent Carlotta glowed in bridal ecstasy. The painter Portaels used his richest colors to immortalize the radiance that was about her. Again, at Eugénie's behest, Winterhalter's brush showed Carlota in Mexican coronation robes, a vision of ethereal loveliness not unlike that artist's conceptions of the Empress Elisabeth, Eugénie herself, and even Queen Victoria in a remote and unlikely past.

On this subject of royal portraiture contradictory opinions prevail. In oil or gouache the Empress Eugénie seems to have been extraordinarily handsome. Then there are photographs which show her to have looked rather like a fishwife. This is true of so many reputed belles of the past that posterity is forced to conclude that photographers were not very clever—and painters much too clever.

At any rate, to Winterhalter all noble ladies looked equally ravishing. He refused to see their bad points. It was left for the uncompromising candor of the camera lens to reveal that Elisabeth's eyes were narrow, Eugénie's nose was of an uncomely longitude, and Disraeli's "Faerie Queene" had squirrel teeth.

During the early Mexico days an unknown Spanish artist portrayed Carlota at her best, proud, confident, serene, in a turquoise blue crinoline, with the Cross of Malta on her left shoulder and a diadem of blossoms above her high brow. But her next picture, a daguerreotype made by Le Graive, when she was at the age of twenty-six, disclosed that inner change which the Empress herself confessed. A face with a disdainful frown, eyes that burned darkly behind drooping lids, a sullen mouth—this was the Carlota who had grown aware.

She suffered recurring attacks of migraine at this time and did not sleep well. Her shapely shoulders lost some of their delectable plumpness so admired in that day of the "feather-bed woman."

With horror she discovered in her mirror an unmistakable expanse of collar-bone marring the smoothness of her fine throat. Thereafter she would wear no more décolletage.

Maximilian saw the slow wilting of her beauty. He grew apprehensive and proposed moving to Cuernavaca, away from the extreme altitude of Mexico City. In the tropical gardens of their country estate the pother of politics could be forgotten.

The plan was carried out promptly. Princess Josefa and little Iturbide accompanied the Empress while Maximilian remained behind to wind up his most pressing affairs. Another and more trenchant appeal must be sent to Europe. The Emperor addressed himself to Major Loysel, discarding all pretense:

> "It must be divulged without reservations that our military position is now at its worst. I entreat you to inform the French General Staff of this fact, stressing the seriousness of our plight."

Carlota strolled listlessly under mango and pomegranate trees that circled the Borda pools, when a message came from Brussels, reporting her father's last illness. For years King Leopold had been a martyr to his gall bladder. On November 12, 1865, already failing in health, he had confided to his son-in-law a final bit of counsel: "Success is the only thing that counts in America. Everything else is poetic twaddle and a waste of money. God bless you, my boy, for I am unable to write more——"

Maximilian lost no time in sending his Belgian secretary to Laeken to be at the old King's side. Eloin had always enjoyed Leopold's confidence. Besides, it was necessary to guard Carlota's interests in the event of tragic developments, for her brothers had lately turned against the Mexican entanglement. Secretary Eloin arrived in time to win for his Empress a small patrimony but no battalions. On December tenth Belgium mourned its first Coburg ruler and Léopold II ascended the throne, his canny eye fixed on Africa. The Mexican recruiting offices in Brussels were padlocked.

Quite apart from his wife's sorrow Maximilian was to sustain a double blow from this loss. Coming out of a land that was puny and eager for recognition, the Belgian volunteers had been the Empire's most daring supporters. Whenever Bazaine's legions wavered and took to their heels the brawny Flemings and Walloons plunged headlong into the thick of battle. Their gallantry was matched only by the Hungarian Honvéd Hussars who made up Maximilian's bodyguard. Furthermore, in the person of his father-in-law, the Emperor of Mexico had had a loyal champion who was respected and feared for his political cunning. Léopold II had inherited this cunning but he did not intend to employ it in behalf of his sister's blundering husband.

The Mexican situation now ceased to be critical; it became desperate. For the first time Maximilian began to consider Marshal Bazaine's plan to levy native troops by force. A tentative transcript of Forey's courts martial had already been drafted at Bazaine's headquarters in expectation of a change in the imperial viewpoint. Having learned from unofficial sources that Juárez frequently crossed the United States line for the purpose of negotiating with secret agents, the French commander now indulged in a piece of strategy. He prefaced the decree with a manifesto to the nation:

"Mexicans!

"The cause which Don Benito Juárez upheld with such constancy and valor has succumbed both to the national will and to those very laws invoked by the rebel chieftain in support of his titles. To-day even the banner under which that cause degenerated has been abandoned by its leader who has left the fatherland.

"The National Government has long shown indulgence and clemency to those recreants who ignored true facts as well as their chance to join the majority of the Nation in a return to duty. Even so the Government has achieved its purpose; honest men have rallied to our flag and accepted the just and liberal principles of our policy. Disorder is maintained by only a few brigands misled by unpatriotic passions and supported by a demoralized rabble, as well as that unbridled soldiery constituting the sad dregs in all civil strife.

"From now on the struggle will continue merely between the honest men of the Nation and those hordes of criminals and bandits. Indulgence must cease, lest it encourage the desperadoes who burn villages, rob and murder peace-loving citizens, persecute the aged, and violate defenseless women.

"The Government, strong in its power, will henceforth show itself inflexible in punishment, for such are the demands made by the precepts of civilization, the rights of humanity, and every moral canon.

"Mexico, October 2, 1865."

The above pronouncement was carefully worded. It dismissed the entire revolutionary party as non-existent and implied that the Empire had but one enemy—lawlessness. By spreading the fallacious report that Juárez had fled across the border, never to return, Marshal Bazaine meant to hoodwink public opinion. He was also bent upon mitigating the shock which was sure to be caused by the sequel to his excellent manifesto. This sequel, submitted to the Emperor for approval, conformed to Forey's pattern and was couched in that martinet's terms. Bazaine would see that it was published in the official newspaper, *Diario del Imperio,* on October third. The text ran as follows:

"We, MAXIMILIAN, Emperor of Mexico, by the advice of our Ministerial Council and our Council of State, do decree that:

"Article 1. All persons who are members of armed bands or societies not authorized by law, whether or not of a political nature, and regardless of size, organization, character or denomination of the groups in question, shall be tried by a military court and, if found guilty of merely such membership, shall be condemned to capital punishment and executed within twenty-four hours after passing of sentence."

In all, there were fifteen paragraphs of equally stringent character making up the dangerous edict. Maximilian rejected it at sight. But behind Bazaine stood the members of the imperial

Cabinet, demanding a decisive move on the part of the sovereign. Maximilian reconsidered. He studied the clause which specified the raising of a native defense:

"Article 9. All male citizens between the ages of eighteen and fifty-five, free from physical disability, are expected to come to the defense of any town threatened by hostile bands; any one refusing to obey when called to arms shall be punished by a fine of from five to two hundred pesos, or fifteen days to four months of imprisonment. If the authorities deem it necessary to punish an entire community for not having defended itself, a fine ranging from two hundred to two thousand pesos may be imposed, to be paid jointly by all who being aware of this decree disregarded it."

Then there was a paragraph concerning a popular form of crime:

"Article 12. Kidnappers will be judged and sentenced in accordance with Article 1 (court martial), regardless of the manner and circumstance governing each case of kidnapping."

But as a conciliatory measure Article 14 promised "full amnesty to all who have belonged or still belong to armed guerrilla bands but prefer surrender to the imperial cause."

Here was something more in keeping with Maximilian's rather skittish tactics. One ought to stress that point about amnesty. In fact, one must subscribe to it. With some degree of relief he nodded his approval and next turned to inspect the list of signatories who advocated publication of the courts martial. It was composed of the Empire's leading figures:

José Vicente Ramírez, Minister of Foreign Affairs (*Negocios Extranjeros*)
Juan de Dios Peza, Minister of War (*Guerra*)
Luis Robles Pezuela, Minister of Improvement (*Fomento*)

Pedro Escudero, Minister of Justice (*Justicia*)
José María Esteva, Minister of the Interior (*Gobernación*)
Manuel Siliceo, Minister of Education (*Instrucción Pública y Cultos*)
Francisco de Paul César, Secretary of the Treasury (*Hacienda*)

Allowing himself to be coerced by this impressive alignment of names, the Emperor put his seal to the fatal edict. Proclamation followed, and in its wake there came a series of persecutions unlike anything hitherto witnessed. Almost at once the discovery was made that Don Benito, far from retreating into voluntary exile, was very much at hand. With renewed ferocity the conflict was resumed.

Meanwhile the "Black Decree" roused the country to indignation. When two popular republican heroes, Generals Arteaga and Salazar, were executed by over-zealous imperialist soldiers, even lukewarm citizens turned in droves to the Juarista camp. In the end, although Bazaine and the entire ministry had promulgated the edict and demanded its enforcement, Maximilian alone bore the full brunt of public wrath.

In vain did the Emperor now point out what every one knew, namely that Juárez himself resorted to measures of far greater cruelty. The Indian patriot was a son of the land, for whom Mexicans could die without shame. Maximilian found that despite his own wide-brimmed sombrero, his *charro* costume, and his ironic jibes at "senile Europe" he remained a foreigner still.

Bazaine's janissaries tried to help. Bullying the rural population, they drummed together a regiment of native *Cazadores* which might correspond to the Austrian *Jäger*. But Maximilian took no comfort in recruiting among men who regarded him as a tyrant. He was confounded by the paradox of his own position and yearned for respite.

Cuernavaca. Pleasaunce. A haven of peace and tranquillity where scenes of domestic joy awaited him! Cuernavaca became his escape. Here the child Agustín sailed little boats between the water-lilies while Carlota, restored by sunshine and rest, sat on the edge of the pool, watching his sturdy figure stamping up and down the flagged pathway. Occasionally the boy stopped to regard her. He was a mischievous and hale youngster whose brief English vocabulary mingled in droll fashion with the Spanish of his present life. "*Mucho* fish!" he cried pointing out marine specimens that floated about among his sailboats. Again, with an ecstatic shout of "*Mamá* Carlota" he tumbled into her lap, pressing dirty fists into the silken folds of a regal dress. She held him close to her heart, this son who was not hers, and as her face pressed against his damp yellow curls she forgot the nightmare that was gathering about them.

It was Maximilian who broke to her gently the news of her father's death. She took it quietly, donning heavy mourning in respect for the man who had filled her motherless childhood with its only sustaining affection. But because of the boy playing in her garden she returned to bright colors as soon as the prescribed period *de rigueur* was past. The ladies of her suite were shocked at this manifestation of a callous nature.

"Es fría," they whispered among themselves, "she is cold."

For the rest, she had grown skeptical in regard to the political outlook. She no longer believed in the utopia described in her earlier letters.

"It is our mission," she now declared, "with mild and cautious methods to lure to Mexico an influx of immigrants who can absorb the old population, for the existing elements are hopeless and nothing whatever can be done with them. I would say quite openly, if I were not afraid some one might repeat it here, that I rely upon colonization. Europe alone can properly people this Empire."

On learning of the unrest that followed the notorious decree of October third, her cynicism grew. Reports came from Mexico City that Labastida and the sulking ecclesiastical party were stirring again, happy to find a new ground upon which to attack the Emperor. By daily post Maximilian attempted to refute accusations which stamped him as a bloodthirsty monster. He was forced to issue pardons by the score, thereby admitting the indefensible severity of the courts martial and laying himself open to ridicule.

Carlota's self-control reached its limit. She wrote to the Empress Eugénie in terms more caustic than any she had ever used:

"Unquestionably this country has a character all its own. The talkative Gutiérrez was quite right about that too, except that he approved, and we don't. We fail to see anything of real worth and are determined to bring about a change. The broad masses here are outrageously dull and ignorant, a state which the *licenciado* class [intelligentsia] will certainly do nothing to correct. This explains how the clergy could get its stranglehold over the common people; no one has bothered to educate the poor, they are left in their stupor, and because they are left in it the Church has gained control. . . . I am prompted to remark, at this point, that your Majesty has surely read Marie Antoinette's charming letters edited by that Monsieur d'Hunolstein? The implication is of course that everything will some day come to light, whether one becomes famous or not. You never can tell what will happen, and when uncharitable judgments (such as these) find expression it is not at all desirable—*enfin,* your Majesty must know what I am driving at. In order to make quite certain that the Mexicans will not discover what I am saying about them, at least not until a new nation is formed which will agree with me, I urge upon your Majesty to destroy all my letters. They are, after all, just conversations; once the ideas are voiced, my purpose has been accomplished. In complying with my request your Majesty will do me a service which I shall appreciate deeply."

Needless to say, Eugénie did not perform this service. Few people do. Their treachery is a boon to biographers.

But the tenor of Carlota's writings no longer amused the French sovereign. In fact, with the arrival of each mail packet from overseas the tension at the Tuileries grew. Always a reluctant correspondent, Eugénie put away her ink-well.

The Empresses exchanged no more letters.

Chapter 4

Since Maximilian's hegira to the New World the European scene had altered considerably. This fact must be recalled in order to understand the wary spirit which now animated Paris, and more specifically the household of Napoleon III.

As early as 1863, while the Mexican negotiations were in progress at Miramar, France and Austria had nursed a common preoccupation. It concerned the gigantic shadow of Bismarck which loomed with daily increasing menace just across the Prussian borders.

Franz Joseph in particular was beset with an anxiety which perhaps diminished his interest as well as active participation in his brother's Mexican expedition. For a long time the Danube monarchy had cherished a fond vision—to see the Germanic nations united under one symbol, the ancient scepter of the Holy Roman Empire. This ambition was both logical and justifiable but, in the light of modern trends, impractical. The state of Prussia, being Protestant and the most progressive of the German Confederacy, saw in a return to feudal Hapsburg rule a useless, if sentimental, retrogression. Bismarck, who regarded Austrians as genial models of incompetence, performed the delicate operation through which the young dynasty of Hohenzollern (High-Tax-Collectors) superseded that of the legendary Habichtsburg (contracted to Habsburg, Hapsburg, Castle-of-the-Hawks) in leadership and power.

He accomplished this task in the most convenient manner possible. Since the dark Middle Ages, Germany and the tiny kingdom of Denmark quarreled over the border region known as Schleswig-Holstein. At different periods in the world's history these two provinces belonged now to the one, now to the other of the opposing factions. There being an equal percentage of Danes and Germans in the territory it was not possible to decide by plebiscite whose authority was the more valid. Besides, such a solution would have removed from the European map one of the most popular war hazards, vying with Alsace-Lorraine and Poland as a succulent bone of contention.

But in 1864, shortly after the turn of the year, King Christian IX of Denmark (to whom Johann Strauss once dedicated a waltz) was credited with causing some trouble. For no good reason save the "natural folly of kings," this royal cavalier embarked upon a policy of harassing stolid Germans who dwelled in the Nordic duchies. Bismarck took notice and rejoiced in the opportunity thus presented to him. He called upon the *Bund* to defend its brethren and invited Austria to join the fray. Franz Joseph, flattered by this honor, sent the pick of his military side-show. It was a comfortable little war. Its details faded away in a confusion of diplomatic palaver, so that in the end Lord Palmerston boiled the matter down to a neat after-dinner speech.

"Only three persons," said England's Prime Minister, "really understood the war of Schleswig-Holstein: the Prince Consort, who is dead; a German professor, who has gone mad; and I, who have forgotten all about it." (The German professor being Nietzsche.)

When the shooting was over, Prussia picked the plums of her reward by incorporating the duchies once more under her own banner. The Austrian troops were politely sent back to their Emperor.

It seemed a trifle nonchalant. Franz Joseph believed that Austria deserved more than a breezy dismissal for her services. The Danube regiments had been fed during the campaign by Prussian commissaries, but they had done their own bleeding. Where were the spoils of war?

Again Bismarck struck while the iron was hot. This was just what he wanted—to pick a quarrel with Austria. Evasive, condescending, challenging notes went back and forth between Berlin and Vienna. Franz Joseph, unaware of the far-sighted Junker's goal, parried strenuously, hoping to preserve a precarious peace.

The rest of Europe looked on with mild concern. Dissension in one's neighbor's yard is always interesting and sometimes salutary, especially when backward obligations can be cast to the winds while that neighbor is too busy to assert a claim. Napoleon III had long dreaded an appeal from the Hofburg urging him to keep his word and stand by Maximilian. With Austria on the verge of a new conflict, this appeal would never come; L'Empereur could afford to ignore the predicament of a Hapsburg in distant Mexico.

On the subject of Maximilian's fate only one thought ruled Paris. France must abandon as soon as possible that maze of disillusions and bitter sacrifices known as the Mexican Empire. Even now Napoleon tarried over the task of notifying Maximilian that the game was up, but the red-trousers continued to drift stealthily down to Vera Cruz and into the bowels of nameless schooners which spirited them homeward.

Curiously, there came at this time a lull in the thick of Mexico's storms. A sabbatical calm descended upon Chapultepec due to the caprice of a date on the calendar. November thirtieth had marked the expiration of the Juárez presidency. With the end of the legal term at hand the Indian patriot would be obliged to retire and, if no fresh election had taken place, the head of the Supreme Court—Don Jesús Gonzales Ortega—automatically became *Presidente Provisional de México.*

It was the middle of December when this little matter was pointed out to Juárez. Due to the political situation there had of course been no elections and Señor Ortega began preening for his high office as first gentleman of the land. He sent a dispatch to Paso del Norte inquiring how soon Benito Juárez intended to surrender the presidential chair.

Impassive and stony of countenance, the Indian was nevertheless moved to smile. It was a quaint dispatch and one that deserved a fulsome reply. On the back of Ortega's letter the words were scrawled: *"Todavía no, amigo!"* (Not yet, my friend!) By his favorite lieutenant, Porfirio Díaz, Juárez conveyed this message to his would-be successor.

Ortega meanwhile had drawn about his insignificant person a considerable flock of adherents to whom, in accordance with the principles of democracy, he promised agreeable advancements under his administration. These political barnacles clung to him now and urged resistance against the brash dictatorship of Juárez. Such promptings seldom fall upon deaf ears. For Maximilian, resting in the sunshine of Cuernavaca, the year 1865 ended with an uproarious hullabaloo in the enemy camp. While the glorious Republic settled its difficulties in the traditional manner, with the armies of two presidents chasing one another up and down the banks of the Río Grande, the Empire settled back to catch its breath.

Maximilian, ever prone to delude himself, believed his troubles to be over. Of late he had begun to lose faith in the divine right of kings, but it was patent now that a benevolent Deity watched over him. If this was so, the time had come to take up the interests of peace: Mexico needed schools, art galleries, cultural expansion. Let the reactionaries mow each other down,—he would profit by their mistakes and strengthen his own position while the insurrection collapsed in its suicidal strife.

It was pleasant to banish the nightmare of battle. With his ministers, who had goaded him to sign the obnoxious decree, Maximilian henceforth communicated only by letter. He wanted every suggestion, however trivial its nature, to be put on paper in black and white—lest he be accused again of plotting despotic measures. Long ago King Leopold had introduced this custom at Brussels. "In a constitutional monarchy," the wise Coburg had declared, "one must never assume a responsibility alone." Maximilian concurred.

Now he felt better. He could go about collecting pictures for the gallery he planned to set up in the Palacio Nacional. During his early excursions about the environs of Mexico City he had come upon neglected works of art that rotted away in old churches and colonial palaces. At Coyoacán, in the house of Cortés, there were seven portraits of the first viceroys. There must be more. A complete pictorial history of Mexico's rulers, from Montezuma to the present day, would eventually hang in the vast salons of the palace on the cathedral square, for future generations to enjoy. In addition to this, Maximilian requested that Montezuma's scepter and other regalia be returned to Mexico from Vienna, where they had been taken by the Spanish Hapsburgs during the days of the Conquest. Franz Joseph surrendered these valuable relics, retaining only the mantle embroidered with *quetzal* feathers and precious stones which would not withstand another journey without undergoing irreparable damage.

Besides the gallery, Maximilian wished to found an academy of sciences and a school for Indian painters who had a special gift for murals. The art of heroic painting was dying out in Europe; Italy alone prized her frescoes. But here in the New World primary colors dominated everything. Stalwart, robust patterns confronted the eye. It was impossible not to grow visionary, not to predict that on this soil art would one day be reborn in strength and splendor.

For the present, however, even the lowly grade schools needed reform. Youngsters learned with their ears and memories alone. They acquired the short Spanish alphabet by means of salty jingles:

"San Isidro labrador,	(Saint Isidore, gardener and huckster,
Quita el agua y pon el sol!"	Take away rain; give us sun!)

—And the letter, dear children, is I—

or else,

"San Serafín del Monte,	(Saint Serafin of the Mountain,
San Serafín cortés!"	Polite Saint Serafin!)

—The next letter? It must be S—

Since picturesqueness is seldom practical, Maximilian meant to change all that. He hoped to attract pedagogues and teachers from other parts of the world, inducing them to adopt Mexico as their homeland and to propound grammar lessons with less rhyme but more reason. He would inspire, build, restore. The Third Empire must become Mexico's Golden Age.

So the Emperor dreamed. And while he ran his fingers over dusty canvases to test their authenticity, Juárez finished off Ortega and his partisans. The republican front was once more united, with its guns pointed toward Chapultepec.

This time the emergency was acute for it coincided, early in February of 1866, with Napoleon's unequivocal announcement that Bazaine and his troops would be withdrawn. At "Our Nest" in Biarritz the French Emperor had finally summoned the necessary courage to wash his hands of Mexico. He made an effort to sweeten the pill by suggesting that Maximilian might call upon Vienna for support; surely Austria would be willing to succor, albeit single-handed, a scion of her ruling house. Napoleon was confident of that. He finished with a belated expression of condolence on the occasion of King Leopold's death.

Maximilian received this message at Cuernavaca where he lay swinging in a hammock, with little Iturbide riding on his stomach. He put the child down and read. A bluish vein rose on his temple, while a feeling of nausea caused him to grip a chair for support.

It was a stinging blow. He had never believed that this could happen. Never. "Your Imperial Highness," the Emperor of France had written once, very long ago, "has assumed responsibilities which you are no longer free to drop. Indeed, what would you think of me if—after your Imperial Highness reached Mexico—I were to declare abruptly that I can no longer keep the pledges to which I have put my own signature!"

It was impossible. Things like this simply couldn't happen. A man did not write two such letters. But he had written them and the impossible had happened.

Carla must be told and they must face the worst together. Like a pair of sleepwalkers the royal dupes stared at the scrap of paper that sealed their fate, but neither comprehended its meaning. Neither accepted the full import of its treachery. In 1861 they in the Tuileries had plotted Maximilian's rise; were they now plotting his ruin? If so, two languages were spoken in that palace.

A night of mental torture brought more clarity. With the dawn of a new day Maximilian found it possible to strike a disdainful attitude. He sat down at his desk and on February 18, 1866, worded a reply:

"Sir, my brother,

"In your Majesty's opinion pressing circumstances warrant

the breach of solemn treaties which you signed with me hardly two years ago, and you inform me of this change with a blandness which can not but do you credit. . . . I have been too much your friend to wish misfortune upon the Bonaparte dynasty, either directly or indirectly. For this reason I propose, with a zeal equal to your own, that you immediately withdraw your armies from the American Continent. There is no need for stretching the procedure out over a period of time. As for myself, guided by my honor as a Hapsburg, I shall try to make arrangements with my fellow-countrymen in a decent manner, placing my life and services at the disposal of my new subjects.

"MAXIMILIAN."

In a postscript Carlota's gratitude was expressed for the message of condolence. The advice concerning help from hapless Austria was dubbed extremely "bright," like all that sprang from Napoleon's "lofty intelligence."

The irony of these words brought burning blushes to the rouged cheeks of *Moustachu*. In his private study at St. Cloud the Emperor Napoleon cursed the moment when a Spanish wife had lured him into that tragic labyrinth across the sea.

At Rome there were curses too. Father Augustus Fischer, who had come to conquer the Pope, found himself smartly rebuked and ejected from the Vatican. It appeared that the Holy Father was well informed on all points concerning the handsome cleric's past.

Quite apart from this, the terms of the second concordat infuriated the Holy See. After all the crimes that had been committed against the Church, restitution of properties was not yet in sight and Maximilian still persisted in granting freedom to all creeds. It was sacrilegious, no less, to expect a truce with Rome! The Curia had already discharged that rusty blunderbuss, its bull of excommunication, against Juárez and the whole French army. Maximilian would be similarly castigated. That was Pio Nono's answer. Crestfallen and much sobered, Father Fischer embarked again for the Americas. His vast self-esteem had suffered a severe jolt.

It was the truce with the Vatican upon which the Emperor

of Mexico had placed his last hopes. True, he had written at once to Vienna and to Carlota's older brother at Brussels, reporting Napoleon's knavery and pleading for aid. Belgium had refused outright, but Franz Joseph promised to send recruits to Trieste where a Mexican vessel might pick them up. This was something, of course, but not nearly enough. An Austrian regiment could be no more than a drop of oil on a sea of trouble. Peace with the Church, on the other hand, would have won for the Empire a host of adherents whose opposition up to this point had been no more than a gesture. Certainly the clerical party had nothing to gain from Juárez and could not sincerely have joined his ranks. To all concerned the concordat appeared as the only solution. But Father Fischer's return brought complete disillusion on this score and devout Mexicans remained hostile.

Maximilian with his dwindling forces stood alone. He looked them over—a bevy of homesick Honvéd Hussars, swagger courtiers and a personal physician who feared the worst in regard to his master's liver. How oddly clashed their Danubian names against the liquid vocals of Latin and Indian speech: Colonel von Khevenhüller, Colonel von Kodolitch, Count Hadik, Baron Czismandia, Count Károlyi, Doctor Basch. Strangers all, in a land that would remain forever incomprehensible to them. It was their lot to count the days of the dying Empire.

He knew when he was beaten. He saw no further reason for attempting the impossible. Sir Peter Campbell-Scarlett of the British Legation in Mexico City counseled abdication, urging Maximilian to retire as soon as possible to the safety of his Adriatic villa at Miramar. The Prussian Minister, Baron von Magnus, advocated the same. In his own heart Maximilian knew that these men were right.

Once, in 1859, when revolt swept over Italy, he had written from Milan to his mother:

> "Although I am expecting many taunts and insults, I shall quietly stick to my post. It is not my habit to turn my back on danger. Two reasons govern my actions—one is the trust vested in my person and not to be shaken off at the first crisis,

the other involves a natural reluctance to obey the rash promptings of fright and nerves. Whether or not I shall want to continue here when order is restored and all dangers are over, is another matter. While there is a fire I shall stand by to the last moment, even though flames surround me; but after that, if the reins of mediocrity are to guide the chariot of state let another nag be harnessed to it."

In Mexico he had stood, surrounded by flames, as long as prudence allowed. To sacrifice the lives of faithful followers, to endanger Carlota's security and that of the child they had taken to themselves would be folly indeed. He decided to abdicate.

But he had not reckoned with the pride that stirred in his Coburg Empress. "Abdication," she stormed, "is tantamount to proclaiming oneself incompetent. Such a thing is admissible only in old men or idiots but never in a prince thirty-four years of age. Our most sacred possession is our sovereignty!" Truly dynastic sentiments were these, assured, defiant and totally impractical.

To Carlota's eloquence was added that of Father Fischer. Although his efforts at the Vatican met with failure the busy Jesuit had paid a hasty visit to Vienna and talked with the Archduchess Sophie. The possibility of a Mexican fiasco had figured in their discussion and at one point the Dowager Archduchess was heard to exclaim: "My poor Maxl—how it will gall him to reappear in Europe as a failure!"

Fischer had no difficulty in distorting these words of the hardy kingmaker. He admonished Maximilian that at the Hofburg sentiment was in favor of tenacity. "One must bury oneself with the ashes of Mexico rather than admit defeat."

Once again the Hapsburg prince felt the challenge on that most sensitive issue, his honor. He dreaded nothing so much as ridicule. Very well, if a man could not turn his back on useless danger without becoming a comic character, he would stay. He would see things through to the bitter end. Henceforth the monarch wavered no more. He faced the future with a constrained sort of bravado.

In refusing to surrender crown and scepter Carlota had obeyed something stronger than caprice. She had been the first Coburg to attain imperial glory, a fact which never left her consciousness. Maximilian, having been born *"kaiserlich,"* made less of this distinction and sometimes completely forgot about it. But Carlota remembered. She knew that one did not cast aside the highest earthly rank. One died with it.

This does not mean that she was thinking of death, for at no time did the idea enter her young head that—in the event of a catastrophe—there might conceivably be anything but a throne to lose. Her irrepressible spirit had revived in the sheltered hush of Cuernavaca and she was ready once again to slip into the caress of an imperial mantle.

The new crisis perplexed her. She wondered whether Napoleon would have abandoned them if Maximilian's cause had been better represented in France. Eloin, Hidalgo and that bigoted Gutiérrez-Estrada, what men were they? No more than sycophants, hired underlings. She came to a housewifely conclusion:

"Things don't get done properly unless you have a hand in them yourself."

And now the realization came upon her like a flash—it was up to her to save the Empire. She, Carlota, must take a momentous step. She must cross the Atlantic alone and compel the French sovereigns to keep their pledge.

"I'll go to Europe for an army corps," she cried impetuously, "I'll force my way into the presence of Emperors and Popes. I'll scream the truth into their faces and win you the concordat, or stalk from door to door as a ragged beggar and as thundering justice!"

Her voice broke at a shrill pitch. She paused, clasping her throat breathlessly and waiting for approval. Maximilian demurred. The thought of hiding behind a woman's skirts was distasteful to him. Also this was midsummer, an evil time for any one to travel down through the fever zone, let alone this frail and delicately nurtured Carla. Finally, apart from such considerations, there was the small item of money. With a growing paucity in coin of the realm, the treasury had been emptied of all save the "Inundation Tax" (a thirty-thousand-peso fund set aside for welfare work in time of floods). Carlota was not daunted by this impediment. The flood moneys could be annexed and replaced as soon as her share in King Leopold's fortune had been paid out.

After convincing an apprehensive Court that this was the only thing to do, the Empress went ahead with her plans. She wished to be accompanied by a retinue of persons who would sufficiently impress the household at St. Cloud. Accordingly Maximilian appointed the following staff:

Don Martín Castillo (*Chargé d'Affaires*)
Conde del Valle (Grand Chamberlain)
Marqués Neri del Barrio (Junior Chamberlain)
Marquesa Neri del Barrio (Lady-in-Waiting)
Graf Karl Bombelles (Commandant of Palatine Guards at Chapultepec)
Herr von Kuhacsevich (Treasurer of Miramar and Chapultepec)
Frau von Kuhacsevich (Lady of the Bedchamber)
Señor Montalba Poliakowitz (Secretary)
Fräulein Mathilde Doblinger (Maid)

It was not until some weeks later that Maximilian's secretary, José Luis Blasio, joined the party abroad. The Mexican successor to Eloin was to keep Carlota posted on the latest developments overseas and to report back to Maximilian the exact progress of her mission.

Meanwhile it would seem that Carlota's decision to travel in state was not a happy one. Just as the imperial couple's enthusiastic letters of an earlier day made their subsequent cries for help so pathetically unconvincing, the current purpose of attracting attention by means of an elaborate royal suite can be put down as childish. Yet Carlota felt instinctively that she must keep up appearances and present a bold front. If her morale broke down and she arrived at the French Court in the humble guise of a petitioner they would feel no compunction about sending her away, forgetting only too readily that she was the daughter of a king and the consort of an emperor.

"Think you I am no stronger than my sex,
Being so father'd and so husbanded?"

No, she dared not invite contempt. They who were guilty of perjury would take advantage of a blush.

And so the Empress made ready. The villa at Cuernavaca was closed and Princess Josefa had been installed at Chapultepec as sole guardian over the boy Agustín. In the long corridors of the castle Carlota's trunks stood about, their contents sprinkled with lavender and dried heliotrope. Daily the laundress, Adelaida Cruz, added another layer of freshly ironed lace or batiste.

It was the twenty-first of June, 1866, and in far-away Bohemia—at Zwickau and Oswiecim—Austria and Prussia exchanged declarations of war.

Chapter 5

News traveled slowly. They did not know in Mexico until much later that Franz Joseph's gold and white cavalry stormed northward toward Olmütz and Sadowa where, on July second, Hapsburg's pride was crushed. Nor that at Königgrätz on July third, the remaining gaily costumed Danube armies ran with poised bayonets headlong into a barrage of Prussian gun-fire. Even the volunteers who were to gather at Trieste for Maximilian were swallowed in this holocaust. Bismarck dictated his peace after a struggle lasting not quite two weeks.

On July sixth a special Te Deum was sung in a Spanish cathedral for the Empress of Mexico whose date of departure had been set for the ninth. Shortly before dawn Maximilian escorted his wife as far as Ayotla, a village lying two kilometers from the capital. Here they parted. The last moments were an ordeal. Returning alone to Chapultepec the Emperor poured out his grief in a letter to Vienna. "Dearest and best of Mothers," he wrote, "Carla is hurrying to Europe on a secret mission. . . . Words can not picture what it costs me to part from her, but great sacrifices must be made for great ends. I am praying that God will watch over her and bring us together again!"

The travelers meanwhile rolled along toward Puebla where the Empress was put up for the night in the house of the Marquesa de Guadalupe. At ten the following morning the journey proceeded in more leisurely fashion to Orizaba, while the third day ended at Córdoba in the midst of torrential rains. More than forty hours were employed in traversing, at a snail's pace, a distance generally covered in fifteen. This was due to the fact that royalty is hampered by ceremonial (blue blood will not, as a rule, rise early) and also to Carlota's squeamishness in regard to the roads. Conditions had not improved since the day when the Empress first crossed the cordillera, for she wrote to her favorite palace lady, Josefa Salas-Varela, "You've no idea of the state these highways are in. Near Córdoba the carriage of my gentlemen was again upset. My coachman assures me that it was only through the help of the Virgin that I was not upset. I suppose he meant the Guadalupe one. . . . Good-by, dear Pepita, my heart remains in Mexico. Write to me and believe in the affection of your CARLOTA."

More serious calamity befell near Paso del Macho. Here the imperial caravan was trapped by a band of insurgents who with a wild cry of *"Adiós, Mamá Carlota!"* snatched the mule teams and made off with them into the wilderness. Drenched by another downpour the travelers continued on foot through jungle thicket until the French railroad was reached. From here scouts with fresh beasts were sent after the luggage while the Empress and her dripping retinue waited.

At last, on July thirteenth, Carlota arrived in Vera Cruz where the commander of the port, Captain Cloué, led her to the embarcation docks. Here she stiffened with surprise. The launch which awaited the Empress of Mexico flew the French *tricolore* and the only available mail steamer in the harbor was called *L'Impératrice Eugénie!* Carlota broke into a fit of rage. She would not enter the launch unless the Mexican colors were hoisted. Before this could be done the consent of the Prefect General, Monsieur Marin, had to be obtained, which in turn caused needless delay.

The packet boat anchored in the roads had been holding back steam in order to accommodate the imperial party; but at length, the sailing hour being long overdue, a siren was sounded. This completely disrupted Carlota's composure. To be tooted at by a French fog-horn was the last indignity. She boarded the ship in blazing anger and made a silent passage over an ocean that shared her wrath. For the first time in her life she was violently seasick. The ladies and gentlemen of her suite found their mistress a high-strung and irritable traveling companion.

A stop was made at La Habana where the Spanish authorities and the fleet accorded the Mexican sovereign a fitting welcome. Carlota felt momentarily soothed and she finished her chat with Pepita. "Only a few words before the boat leaves. I am quite well despite a day of *mal de mer*. The heat here is intense and the voyage a long one; it is only out of pure patriotism that one can accept these hardships with any degree of forbearance. . . . I did not go ashore, since the Emperor would not have wished it, but the principal personages of the town visited me. There is a very polite bishop. Most of the dignitaries had walking-sticks which reminded me of Mexico and pleased me. The head of the *Real Audiencia Española,* whose very aspect recalled to me the colonial history of our country, sports a tortoise-shell cane which, judging from its exquisite carving, must be from Yucatán." The vexations of Vera Cruz and the danger encountered before Paso del Macho were not mentioned. Obstacles existed in order to be overcome.

After the West Indies had been left behind the steamer nosed toward mid-ocean. Due to long practise in the transportation of troops French navigation had improved and the trip to Europe now required a scant three weeks. On August fourth the moorings of Saint Nazaire were reached and Carlota disembarked. She dispatched a telegram to Napoleon and set out at once for Paris. Late the following day L'Empereur's reply was handed to her en route through the town of Nantes.

"St. Cloud, August 5, 1866. 4:40 P.M.

"Your Majesty's wire has just reached me. Since I returned from Vichy quite ill, I am obliged to stay in bed and therefore can not see you. But if, as I assume, your Majesty will first visit Belgium, I shall find time to recover. NAPOLEON."

She had no trouble deciphering this conundrum. It spelled out "Not at Home" and clearly endeavored to push Carlota off on her royal relations. Her presence in France was decidedly not welcome. For weeks the government offices on the Quai d'Orsay had ordered Paris newspapers to denounce as "arrant calumny" a current rumor, spread by returning soldiers, that the Empress Charlotte had left Mexico. Without official confirmation from Chapultepec such an eventuality must not be allowed to prey upon public sympathies.

Now that the truth could no longer be withheld Napoleon found himself in a state of acute discomfort occasioned by more than physical infirmities. To be sure, he had not been well of late. *L'amour* had become his Nemesis. Incontinent love-affairs wasted his strength; he was scarcely able to walk or eat and had lost all capacity for sleep. The waters of Vichy again and again became the Pool of Bethesda where he would, but could not, wash his body clean.

But there were other matters quite as depressing as his carnal ills. Eugénie was arguing again. This time her speculations concerned Germany, where with manifest accuracy she foresaw the rise of Bismarck's Reich and the attendant danger to France. During the recent hostilities between Austria and Prussia she had urged that Franz Joseph be helped, lest Austria's humiliation lead to that of France, when the victorious Junker turned his steps westward across the Rhine. With dreary insistence she quoted Marshal Randon, Napoleon's Minister of War: "It is the French Empire, and not the Austrian, that was defeated at Sadowa!" Yes, Bismarck must be crushed now, upon any pretext, before he built a Germany which would be too much for the Bonapartes.

But Eugénie had been wrong about Mexico and now Napoleon would no longer listen to her. He sent her about her business, rejecting female interference in government problems. She was left to quarrel with the court dressmaker, Charles Frederick Worth, who wished her to discard "that monstrosity—the crinoline" once devised to satisfy her vanity. Napoleon, for his part, strutted about, happy to have put his wife in her place. Nothing could have been more inopportune at a time like this than the telegram from Saint Nazaire.

Still unwilling to permit Eugénie a hand in the matter, he determined to handle things himself. But a warning from the Prefect of Nantes that the Empress of Mexico had continued on her way to Paris despite L'Empereur's message revealed to him the limitations of his genius. A trifle embarrassed, he now turned to his mate. The Spaniard reflected briefly and came to his rescue. To begin with, the unexpected visitors must be disconcerted by finding no welcoming committee at the Gare. It would be easy to explain, in a subsequent torrent of apologies, that the reception party had gone to the wrong station. The "mistake," however politely cleared up, would have served its purpose as a decided damper. Before those Mexicans recovered from the shock time would have been gained for devising further tactics.

On August ninth Carlota arrived and was indeed disconcerted. She regarded the absence of court carriages and attendants as an intentional slight and, for a moment, did not know which way to turn. As a princess of royal blood she had naturally counted on lodging at one of the French châteaux; it was an unwritten law among ruling families that visiting "cousins" must be treated as equals, especially so when they were of sovereign rank. What, then, did one do in the present dreadful predicament? Did an empress wander about an unhospitable city searching for a rooming house? Could she suffer the humiliation of disclosing her identity at a fashionable hotel?

Old Kuhacsevich at length made the only possible decision. There was an obscure hostelry which he remembered having patronized in his youth. It bore the persuasive title of "Le Grand Hotel" and thither the daughter of King Leopold betook herself in a hired cab. She locked herself up in her room and wept angry tears. Late that evening the reception committee which had meanwhile scoured the streets of Paris in a fruitless search finally appeared and presented its glib apologies. Napoleon's chief aide-de-camp, General Waubert de Genlis, had been too well instructed by his sovereigns, for he blurted out a maladroit question:

"How long does your Majesty plan to stay in France?"

Carlota paled. She said nothing. At this point Count Cossé-Brissac, a favorite at St. Cloud, leaped into the breach by announcing that the Empress Eugénie would make a personal call at two o'clock the following afternoon, provided such a visit was agreeable to her Majesty, the Empress of Mexico. Not a word about an immediate change of quarters to some more fitting abode. Not a hint about a carriage and pair to be placed at Carlota's disposal for the duration of her visit. It was certain now that a hard task awaited her.

"Yes," she said quietly, "two o'clock will be quite agreeable."

On August tenth, at the appointed hour, Eugénie arrived in the company of her chum, the Countess of Montebello (née Princess Essling), and the First Lady-in-Waiting, Madame Carette (née Bouvet). All three ladies were elegantly attired. Eugénie bubbled over with joy at seeing her dear Charlotte and promptly launched a catalogue of questions in regard to life in Mexico.

"Countess Melanie Zichy came through here, some time ago, on her way to Vienna. She told us about a charming national dance called *El Jarabe!*"

Carlota nodded. It was a quaint little affair. And how was the Emperor Napoleon? When would it be possible for her to see him?

"But Louis is still unwell," said Eugénie. Her voice acquired a little edge and now Carlota slowly perceived the change in what she had supposed to be a lifelong friendship.

"Even so," she insisted, "I have come a long way. Perhaps he will not refuse a brief audience."

Eugénie shook her head. She had come to forestall Carlota's arrival at St. Cloud, and to ward off any possible petitions which the distraught woman might present. The Empress of France stood her ground.

"In that case," Carlota announced calmly, "I am going to see him to-morrow, *et je ferai irruption* [I shall break in]!"

It was Eugénie's turn to pale. She reflected quickly that the Empress of Mexico could not very well be refused admittance at the palace gates. Since a gleam of unmistakable determination sparkled in the Coburg eyes, there was nothing for it but to arrange the distasteful meeting. Passing off Carlota's threat as a saucy witticism, Eugénie hastily agreed that a visit could of course be arranged. A court carriage would come for Carlota three days hence and convey her to the summer residence of St. Cloud. A hidden touch of spite had caused the Spaniard to select the thirteenth day of the month, hoping thereby to stir up latent inhibitions in her rival's breast. And now, with tender embraces and sundry graceful tears, the Empress of the French rippled down the narrow hotel stairs, satisfied that—in part, at least—she had achieved a diplomatic victory. During the three days that followed she would have time to drill into the skull of her poor Louis all the correct answers, and, if necessary, a few incorrect ones. . . .

For Carlota it was an unbearable ordeal of waiting. Although her sanguine temperament would tolerate no cowardice, the slow idle hours in Paris began to conjure up before her mind strange dangers to her beloved Maxl's cause. Dimly she sensed that precious time was being wasted—days, even minutes, which could never be recovered. She spent every moment at her desk, reviewing with Señor Castillo every detail of her Mexican report, and writing to Maximilian during the remaining hours.

At last the eventful morning was at hand. Accompanied by her chamberlain, Count del Valle, and Maximilian's trusted *Chargé d'Affaires,* Don Martín Castillo, Carlota entered the waiting carriage. The drive to St. Cloud, some eight miles west of Paris, led through beauteous suburbs. Beyond the town itself the castle lay hidden in a vast wood, but although the gentlemen of her suite pointed out innumerable scenic splendors the Empress of Mexico took no notice. She sat for the space of an hour, brooding in the depths of the closed carriage. A pall of late summer heat hung over the countryside.

In St. Cloud, at the foot of the grand staircase, the little Prince Imperial greeted the visitors. He was ten years old and very serious for his age. He wore the gold chain of the Mexican Eagle on his collar; it was a gift from Maximilian. Carlota noted it at once and her hopes rose. She kissed the lad and asked him to lead her into his father's presence. Loulou smiled and with touching gravity took her hand.

The audience was held in a somber reception-room on the ground floor. To Carlota's great disappointment she did not find Napoleon alone. Very erect and forbidding the Empress Eugénie stood in front of her husband, flanked by Court Librarian Prosper Mérimée and Foreign Minister Drouyn de Lhuys. Behind this human bulwark, and on either side of the monarch's chair, Minister of Finance Achille Fould and Minister of War Marshal Randon were stationed like sentinels prepared for an attack. Napoleon sat snugly in their midst with a furtive eye cocked in the direction of his visitor.

The scene struck Carlota as comical and she smiled, but lack of response extinguished her mirth. She was at a loss for a proper course of action. Would no one speak? Would they send her away? Still, there was Loulou, wearing Maximilian's decoration in her honor. She must not quaver then, while addressing her words to Napoleon directly.

"Sire," she began, bending sidewise to get a better view of him, "I am representing a cause which is yours no less than it is our own."

A polite cough issued from the enclosure, followed by the Emperor's reply. Carlota learned that the leading members of the French Ministry were here assembled to discuss the Mexican situation, if possible, for the last time. Napoleon pointed to Monsieur Drouyn de Lhuys who immediately took the conversation in hand. In what manner, this gentleman inquired, could France be of service?

Carlota ordered Castillo to empty his brief-case upon a table, spreading out the exact accounts which had been drawn up at Chapultepec for this purpose. Every expenditure, every economy made during Maximilian's short and hapless reign, was quoted in detail. The insolvency of the Mexican exchequer was laid bare and the military problem reviewed. People in Europe had no inkling of the monstrous facts which had been concealed from Maximilian in order to lure him to the Mexican throne. If he were now abandoned in that vortex the entire French expedition would go down in history as a criminal waste of lives and money.

At the mention of money Monsieur Fould rose to the occasion, countering with strong arguments to the effect that Mexico was excessively slow in paying her monthly interest on the loans. Lately, in fact, there had been no payments at all.

"Before we wind up that Mexican business, Madame," he announced curtly, "France will be out a round three hundred million francs for her trouble."

Carlota flushed. "That may be what your bankers have extracted from the French public, but where is the balance between those figures and the sum actually forwarded to us? Do you think we don't know whose pockets are stuffed with gold while Mexico must foot the bill?"

Fould had recourse to veiled invective. He accused Maximilian's associates of sharp practise and fraud, indicating that no control had been exercised over them from above. Oh, it was appalling, this battle of words and figures. She would never make them see while they battered down her reasoning with their cool sophistries.

She turned to Napoleon who sat meekly in his chair. His eyes bulged with alarm and something told her that his heart went out in sympathy to her. Throwing back the mantilla that drooped over her face she leaned across the table.

"Sire," she pleaded, "you have not answered me."

"Madame, I am afraid I can not," he mumbled, but she interrupted him as soon as she caught the negative note. One must prevent an outspoken refusal; one must spar for time. Panic overcame her momentarily. Then she remembered the letters in her hand-bag, Napoleon's own signature under those flaming words: "I urge you to count upon my everlasting friendship. You may rest assured that my support will not fail you in the accomplishment of the feat which you are so courageously undertaking."

She would expose him. She would shame him for breaking his word. But no, she could not do that; she could not so disgrace an Emperor of France before his own ministers. Did she after all know what overwhelming compulsion governed Napoleon's actions? Might there not be some extenuating circumstance which would explain his apparent turpitude?

"I've had an angry letter from the Emperor Maximilian," he was saying in a tone at once defensive and placating, "but I am not offended. On the contrary, I can understand what he must be going through since my decision was announced to him."

"That is kind of your Majesty," Carlota breathed, and now she believed that if it were humanly possible this gentle little man would help.

But Eugénie did not like the tenor of the present conversation and, employing a woman's expedient, she teetered gracefully against a chair, pretending to swoon. Her technique proved bad, since Carlota was not fooled, but it succeeded in breaking up the meeting.

There was a moment of embarrassment. The letters, thought Carlota swiftly, now was the time for the letters! Yet, was it? Napoleon had hurried to the side of his wife, whose eyes remained resolutely shut despite an unpleasant dousing of cold water from a large cut-glass decanter. L'Empereur's cheeks had turned a deep cinnabar. No, Carlota must not strip him of his honor, she must not humble him here in his own palace.

"Thank you, gentlemen," she said vaguely to the room at large and turned to go. Although she may have expected it, no effort was made to stop her.

From her hotel that night she wrote to Maximilian. "What has struck me most forcibly," she confided, "is the fact that I know more about China than these people here do about Mexico, yet they are responsible for one of the most serious crises in which the French flag has ever been embroiled." Nor could she refrain from indulging in a feline critique: "I noticed that the Empress has lost much in looks and youthfulness since that day when we last saw her. Amid all their pomposity Napoleon and his wife are unable to cope with real issues and it is my conviction that they will not last much longer. The throne of France ages those who occupy it, casting them off before their time. History shows that this nation, like the fickle goddess of fortune, always smiles on new faces. . . ."

Elsewhere in Paris there was equally engrossing correspondence. Prosper Mérimée, who raised gossip to the pinnacle of literary satire, was writing to his friend, Sir Anthony Panizzi, Italian librarian at the British Museum. Referring to Carlota's visit he mused: "They will give her a dinner, no doubt, but I don't think she will get money or soldiers. It wouldn't surprise me if Maximilian abdicated within a few months, after which there would be a republic or, what is more likely, a state of anarchy. This, to my mind, will be followed by lynch law on the part of the Yankees who are hoping to introduce Anglo-Saxon colonization."

In the meantime the Austrian Ambassador, Prince Metternich, had been summoned to the Grand Hotel where Carlota unburdened her plight. His Excellency listened with the utmost patience but was forced to admit that Austria's defeat at the hands of Prussia had completely undermined Maximilian's prestige with the Bonapartes. Even so, a second audience at St. Cloud—and preferably a private one—was advisable.

Carlota agreed. A happy thought had occurred to her. August fifteenth, Napoleon's name-day, was at hand. This date, honoring Louis IX, holy Crusader King of France, was celebrated throughout Spanish countries as *La Fiesta de San Luis Rey*. (In more recent years it was found that the good St. Louis conflicted with the proper Ascension of Mary and so his day was advanced to August twenty-fifth.)

Now what could be more natural than a note of respect, bearing salutations to his Majesty and dropping a hint in regard to another audience? Carlota penned her greeting and sent it by messenger on the morning of the fifteenth. Concealing her purpose in amiable invocations for Napoleon's welfare, she begged him to see her alone. She had not long to wait. An innocuous and airy reply thanked her for her kind solicitude but his Majesty refrained from alluding to a rendezvous. Instead, Eugénie added a postscript. Poor Louis, its text disclosed, lay supine—the imperial ague having taken a turn for the worse. The Empress of Mexico would do well not to press her suit further.

But they didn't know the Empress of Mexico! Upon reading the above lines Carlota arranged her mantilla. Without uttering a word she rushed through the festive Paris streets accompanied by a single lady-in-waiting, Señora del Barrio. Shortly before eleven o'clock she stood at the portals of St. Cloud demanding admission.

The palace was thrown into confusion. Napoleon, who had just finished dressing for a cheerful jaunt in the Bois, scuttled back to his bedroom, there to assume the air and appurtenances of invalidism, while Eugénie, still in her boudoir, was notified by a page that her consort had urgent need of her.

All this time Carlota had been left alone in the great hall below, but she was not easily thwarted. Familiar with the interior of many royal residences, she ran up-stairs and espied the Emperor's quarters before any one could stop her. With her firm little fists she knocked on the door to his chamber. In the face of such determination Napoleon and Eugénie were forced to admit her to an adjoining study where, with the greatest coolness possible, they granted audience to the staunch daughter of a notably staunch king.

To-day Carlota did not implore; she demanded. From her bulging reticule she drew forth letters which bore the imperial signatures of France, letters which urged and encouraged the Mexican expedition, promising every conceivable assistance during its experimental stages. Napoleon chose to hide behind the loophole of a definition; he declared Maximilian's affairs to be past such a point.

"But the Treaty of Miramar," she insisted, "wherein your Majesty guarantees that the Foreign Legion shall remain in Mexico six years after all other troops have been recalled——"

Napoleon shrugged helpless shoulders. "Madame, I am in a very ticklish position. America threatens me through that unpleasant Monsieur Seward, and my own subjects refuse their support unless I keep peace with Washington. Madame had better not indulge in futile illusions."

"Your Majesty," cried Carlota indignantly, "is seriously compromised in this affair, and should not indulge in any either."

Napoleon's face wore a drawn and miserable look. He glanced at his wife, as if in desperation, before beginning again: "Once and for all time, Madame, let me state that you can not hope——"

But Carlota interrupted him quickly and began talking before he could utter the fatal—and final—word. Reaching for a last straw she persuaded Napoleon to confer once more with his ministers and reserve his answer for another meeting.

In an adjacent chamber, meanwhile, a French and a Mexican lady-in-waiting were conveying to each other by means of eloquent gestures the peculiarities of their respective mistresses. It developed in the course of the curious dialogue that the Empress of Mexico was fond of drinking *naranjada,* especially on a sultry day. Eagerly the French *dame de la cour,* Madame Carette, took advantage of this disclosure and interrupted the heated interview in the Emperor's rooms by sending in a footman with some freshly prepared orangeade.

Due to the overwrought condition of her nerves, as well as her outraged pride, Carlota recoiled from the proffered beverage which she thought was intended as a crafty sign of dismissal. Even as she did so a dark suspicion sprang up in her mind. For the first time she felt a sensation of physical danger. Not only was Maximilian's cause lost, but they were going to poison her! Overcome with terror she fled from the palace.

Late that same afternoon the first telegraphic message from Mexico arrived in Paris over the newly laid transatlantic cable. It was from the Emperor Maximilian, who by this courtesy hoped to propitiate the French sovereigns and dispose them more kindly toward his wife. The missive doing honor to Napoleon's name-day read:

"Chapultepec, August 15, 1866.

"Availing myself of the most glorious scientific triumph of our era, I am sending your Majesty my sincerest congratulations.

"MAXIMILIAN"

Only a few years earlier, over a cable that broke under the strain, the United States and Ireland had exchanged a note of whimsy:

"Europe and America are united by telegraph. Glory to God in the highest, on earth peace, and good will among men."

Chapter 6

Carlota returned to the Grand Hotel where her worried retinue awaited her. She spoke to no one and retired promptly to her room where she dropped exhausted upon a *chaise-longue* and fell into a deep slumber.

At six o'clock in the evening Señora del Barrio entered with a cup of *yerba buena* (peppermint) tea and inquired about her mistress's wants. Carlota seemed refreshed and rather calm; she asked that secretary Montalba Poliakowitz bring her writing materials.

For a while she dictated an outline of the day's events, but this soon tired her and she dismissed the secretary. Her mind was troubled by the thought of what Maximilian might do if he knew how badly they had treated her. In an access of fury he might leave Mexico and join her, but she was not yet ready to give up. Perhaps it would be better to hold back ugly details and to write an intimate letter which would keep Maxl informed on the most essential points without unduly alarming him.

Summoning all her strength she sat down to this task. In her slightly imperfect German she tried to conceal the hopelessness of the situation. No one must know that her own courage was breaking; she would prevaricate again, as she had prevaricated in her early correspondence with Eugénie.

For the second time that day she wrote the date, August 15, 1866.

"Dearly beloved Treasure!

"Before all else I am in excellent health and let your heart be at ease about this point. Next, it is my conviction that something can be accomplished here since there is an interest in our cause, but among those higher up disinclination and helplessness are great and I know through a positive source, Metternich, that during the past two years the Emperor Napoleon has been sinking physically and mentally. The Empress is not capable of managing the affair—she constitutes no barrier against the ministers and does more damage than good. They have grown old, and both are childish. They burst into tears occasionally, but I don't know if that will lead to anything. I made every conceivable effort and submitted our ultimatum to the Emperor at once. After that I had to start working for those 500,000 piastres which I hoped to send back with the ship, but I soon realized that this was not feasible. Still, it was my duty to try.

"Just the same, I have not yet played all my cards against the Emperor Napoleon. I visited him only twice and the second time I brought him excerpts from his own promises in order to rankle him secretly. He talked a great deal about Mexico, and yet they seem to have forgotten all about the subject long ago. Incidentally, he cried more the second time than the first. If things succeed here they will certainly do the same in Rome and Washington.

"This letter is disjointed because Poliakowitz is about to go out. All day long I have people around me who take all my time.

"I am clinging to you from the depths of my soul.

"CHARLOTTE"

When she had finished, the cheer she simulated went out of her. She fell to brooding, and now her mind was tortured with visions of her adored husband's very real peril. Like the blows of an unseen hammer the realization beat upon her consciousness—not power and glory, but life itself was at stake!

Slowly the days dragged on but there was no news from St. Cloud. Had they forgotten her? If so, she must plot another attack.

The eighteenth of August was Franz Joseph's birthday. Early in the forenoon of that significant date the French Minister-President Monsieur Eugène Rouher visited the Grand Hotel and paid his respects to Carlota. After a few embarrassed phrases he inquired whether the Empress of Mexico had read the last issue of *Le Moniteur*.

"No," Carlota replied, "why?"

Rouher squirmed a little before quoting the press announcement that Napoleon had gone off on a vacation.

This was an evasion she could hardly have foreseen, but Carlota retained her poise. Not a trace of agitation could be detected in her voice as she countered:

"Then he will come to see me, as is only due, immediately upon his return."

Rouher grew still more awkward. He had in his pocket, he observed, a written answer from the French Government in regard to the whole Mexican problem.

"Oh, but I wasn't negotiating with the French Government," she parried icily, "I have been dealing with the Emperor Napoleon. If I have received you, Monsieur, it is because you asked for an audience with me. But I regard your visit merely as a personal attention, nothing more."

"But your Majesty——" Rouher began again, unfolding his document.

Carlota brushed the paper aside. "I take my answers," she said haughtily, "from the man to whom I put my questions—from the Emperor himself."

Rouher was dismissed.

It was not long after the crestfallen gentleman's departure that a special messenger arrived from the Tuileries, Napoleon's town residence. Carlota was handed a small note from his Majesty. It appeared that the Emperor's journey had been of very short duration; in fact, there must have been an error in print. The imperial family had simply moved in from the country, so that there hadn't been any real journey at all. And now that this was quite clear the superlatively polite monarch wished to know at what time he might see her.

A meeting was arranged for the following afternoon. Carlota enjoyed a modest triumph.

On August nineteenth, at four o'clock, the Emperor's carriage stopped at the Grand Hotel and Napoleon III honored this undistinguished hostelry with his presence. Carlota awaited him with unconcealed emotion. Her nervousness was transmitted to Castillo, del Valle, and the remaining members of her suite, who stood at attention throughout the greeting on the stairs. During the private audience that followed the Emperor himself was not at ease. He had tried by various means to shift upon others the painful duty that now lay before him. He had come to make an end. His first words imparted the sad *fait accompli*—France's unconditional refusal.

Carlota felt the ground rocking under her feet. A wave of blood rushed to her head.

"We shall abdicate!" She threatened, with a last attempt at bravado.

But Napoleon called her bluff. "Abdicate, then," he said grimly and turned to go. He made a mental note that she must receive the refusal in writing.

This was enough. As she watched him endeavoring to wriggle out of her presence she despised him, but she despised herself even more. How could she ever, in accepting a throne from this upstart, have forgotten that the blood of three dynasties flowed in her veins?

"You charlatan," she gasped in a voice that was almost a whisper, "you hypocrite! What, after all, could I—a daughter of the race of Orléans—have expected from the word of a Bonaparte!"

Without casting another glance in his direction she called for her serving woman and gave immediate orders to pack. In the midst of an unparalleled disregard for his person the little Emperor took himself down-stairs.

For Carlota all was over. When Napoleon's *billet* arrived on the following morning, stamping her failure as irrevocable, she knew that in France she was an outcast. She spent another sleepless night and longed for the dawn, her whole being filled with a single purpose. She must leave Paris and hasten to Rome. The Holy Father would help.

At an inordinately early hour she was up and about her feverish tasks, when Doctor Bohuslavek entered an objection. He disapproved of a direct trip to Rome without first stopping at Miramar and waiting for instructions from Mexico. Besides, the Empress's neurotic state made an immediate delay imperative. By means of sleeping powders, administered surreptitiously, he was able to restore Carlota to a degree of composure. She rested a few days and even allowed herself to be lured on a shopping tour with her ladies. She bought a new hat. But her mind was not on fashions.

Somewhere in her childhood setting she had seen Albrecht Dürer's wood engravings of the Revelation of St. John. The Four Horsemen—War, Famine, Pestilence, Death—had frightened her from infancy. They haunted her now, and all of them looked very much like Napoleon.

She began to speak incoherently and to gesticulate as if in answer to some unseen presence. Unmistakable symptoms of derangement caused Bohuslavek to suspect something more than nervous exhaustion. He remembered that Carlota's mother, Belgium's "Holy Queen," had died of religious mania. Had the Empress of Mexico inherited the taint and was this the beginning of mental disintegration? It certainly seemed to be, for her waking hours were dominated by a fixed idea. Napoleon's iniquity must be exposed. She thought of the French Emperor as the symbol of all that was vile; in her scorn she reduced him to a mere pronoun to which, however, she accorded the formality of a capital letter. On August twenty-second her grief and rage found expression on paper. She wrote again to Maximilian, falling into French where German failed her.

"Darling: In the morning I am leaving for Miramar via Milan, which will prove to you that I have achieved exactly nothing. . . . But there remains the satisfaction of having defeated their arguments, torn down their dishonest pretexts, and in the end having won a moral victory for you. Nevertheless, He has turned against us, and no power on earth is of any avail, for He has Hell on his side and we have not. You must not believe that the opposition comes from outside, for He himself appoints legislative bodies to do his will; nor is this professed anxiety about the United States the real reason for his stubbornness. He wants to commit a long premeditated crime, not through fear or change of heart, or for any motive whatever, but only because He is the incarnation of villainy on earth and means to destroy what is good. It is because men do not see the perversity of his actions that they adore him.

"Up to the last I interrupted him *pour parer et ignorer le refus* [in order to parry and prevent his refusal], but it is obvious that He alone chooses to be unmerciful, for the least of his ministers would have softened. I can assure you of this much, that for me He is the Devil in person; at our last meeting his expression would have made your hair stand on end, and this ugliness was a reflection of his soul. . . . He has never loved you, for He is incapable of loving. Like a viper He fascinated you with tears that were as false as his words, and with deeds that were perfidy. You must be freed from his claws as soon as possible.

"Even while delivering his final no, by which He knew you would be ruined, his conduct was oily. A genteel Mephistopheles, He kissed my hand; but I can recognize pantomime, for I have seen through him twice. It still appalls me to realize that the world has never known and never will know his like, but *le règne touche à sa fin* [the reign touches its end] and soon we shall again be able to get our breath.

"You probably think I am exaggerating, but conditions here absolutely resemble the Apocalypse, with Babylon on the Seine fitting the picture; it makes hardened skeptics believe in God when they can see the Devil so close at hand. . . .

"As a direct result of my visit *le vin est dévoilé* [the wine has certainly been spilled] for humanity to judge and condemn. I got a peep at the records of the Finance Commission, another putrid affair from start to finish. Count de Germiny promised to pay the poor legations, which will be something at least—provided he does it; everything they tell you here is untrue. But you must not believe that I grovel before these people. I just tear off their masks and then thunder at them, without getting vulgar, to be sure. They have probably never in their lives been more mortified. . . .

"I can not understand their willingness to let you abdicate. It seems to me that you ought to hold on, because the day is coming when He will be dethroned and France as well as the whole of Europe will see that their interests are furthered by an empire in Mexico. The Old World is crumbling because He has his finger in every pie; you can smell him in the bloodshed of all the nations struggling for unity. He uses Prim and Bismarck as his agents and spreads a network of propaganda across the map, laughing at those whom He has victimized. There's no defying him except from the other side of the Atlantic.

"Austria is changing into a Magyar state and will soon collapse. In Italy they have a financial depression, while Spain is ablaze with unrest. You have nothing to hope for in this hemisphere where He would destroy you with his hate, for He can scarcely bring himself to utter your name. I advise you to dismiss his hirelings and to control your army without French interference, otherwise you will be lost. The whole military question proves this. If you can enlist native sympathy success is still possible, but never again put your trust in the French. If the truth about your situation were really known abroad, money would pour into your treasury from all sides, for even the French people are materially concerned in this matter in view of their foreign trade.

"I shall be overjoyed when you send for me. Don't plan to come to Europe yourself because He will crush you; He wants to own everything from the North Cape to Cape Matapan. Call me back after you have emancipated yourself from him in Mexico. It is quite apparent that my presence here has been the worst blow He has had in years. I must also add that many charming people are taking a real interest in me.

"I embrace you with all my heart. Always your faithful

"CHARLOTTE.

"P.S. Naturally I have not lived here in the style you expected. . . . But now I am receiving my inheritance and some very fine jewels, among them a magnificent Golden Fleece for you. . . ." (Presumably her father's decoration. Maximilian, of course, had one.)

This irrational piece of writing gave evidence that the Empress walked already on the brink of that darkness which was soon to enfold her forever. If her original plan to speed to Rome over the shortest route had been followed, Carlota's nerves would have snapped on the first day out of Paris. But she had given in to Bohuslavek and allowed herself to be convinced that a sojourn at Miramar would prepare her for a successful interview at the Vatican.

On August twenty-third the Mexican party finally got under way and left France, traveling through Aix-les-Bains, Hautecombe and the alpine pass of Mont Cenis. From here the Italian frontier could be sighted, causing Carlota to draw a deep breath of relief. She had escaped the poisoned atmosphere of Satan; "He" could harm her no more.

The shifting scenes served to distract her from her preoccupations. At Turin and in Milan she was met by old friends whose kind attentions warmed her heart. At times she almost, though not quite, forgot Napoleon and his villainy.

At Lake Como she occupied her father's villa and brought out her pen and ink. She wrote Maximilian a tender as well as a sensible letter:

"Villa d'Este, Lake Como. August 26, 1866.

"Dearly Beloved!

"Here in this land so full of memories belonging to the best years of our life, I think of you constantly and am impelled to send these lines on the heels of my Paris report. Everything here speaks of you; your Lake of Como, which you loved so much, stretches out before my eyes in blue serenity and it all looks the same—only you are over there, far, far away, and nearly ten years lie between then and now! Still, I remember things as if they had happened yesterday, and Nature bears witness to those bygone moments of untarnished joy rather than to pain and disappointment. Every name, every event emerges once more from some unused nook in my brain, and I rejoice again in our Lombardy as though we had never left it; in these two days I have relived two years which once were precious to us.

"If only you could be here to see the friendliness of these people. Early yesterday morning I went to mass before the tomb of San Carlo and also visited the cathedral which happened to be crowded. People surrounded me in a moment, but it was not from curiosity as much as because of an enduring affection which they still harbor. In my bedroom I came upon a youthful portrait of you, put there on purpose, no doubt; it was inscribed *Governatore Generale del Regno Lombardo-Veneto*. . . . And now I am hoping, dear treasure, that you will be pleased with me. I am doing my utmost for your cause. . . .

"The moon has just come up and I can hear singing; it is all so indescribably beautiful. Ever your CHARLOTTE."

While she was thus lost in reveries Bohuslavek communicated with Prefect Radonetz at Miramar, instructing him to prepare a reception for the Empress. In consequence of such forethought the travelers crossed from Venice toward the port of Trieste and met with a happy surprise. The Austrian fleet under command of Admiral Baron Wilhelm von Tegetthoff lay at anchor in the bay and fired a battery of salutes, while from the garlanded walls of the castle innumerable cheers rose up in greeting.

Carlota had come home.

On the landing pier she found Secretary Blasio, recently arrived from Mexico. He had brought the elder Iturbide boy from Paris for a holiday. The child beamed with anticipation and romped through the great mansion with an effervescence not unlike that of his small cousin at Cuernavaca. Carlota responded instantly to this stimulus. She discovered a loveliness about Miramar which she had never seen before. Her wounded spirit yearned for soothing flattery which the good people of Trieste were only too glad to shower upon her. With Frau von Radonetz she ran through the rooms of the palace, stopping at every window and staring out in wonderment at the gardens Maximilian had planted. His palm-trees, weeping willows and cedars had reached their full growth and for many surrounding miles the Adriatic shore borrowed their much-needed shade. All this was described in enthusiastic reports to Mexico.

"It will bring you satisfaction," wrote Carlota at Marie Antoinette's desk, "to hear that my Mexicans are enchanted with Miramar and that I myself am just beginning to appreciate it to the full. Like a child I am entranced by every trifle. In the dining-room I found the imperial crown surmounting a shield with the arms of Mexico. Your old Doctor Jilek, who feels very bitter and says he still objects to the expedition, has wreathed it with a mass of thorns."

The Adriatic sunshine seemed to restore Carlota both physically and mentally to perfect health. She wore her Paris hat and visited the Burgomaster of Trieste. In her free moments she reviewed her recent happy experiences in Italy. "Just think, the King made a special trip from Rovigo to Padua in order to greet me. While I sat in the Padua station, Victor Emmanuel settled down beside me and Cittadella (the senator Giorgio, Count Cittadella-Vigodarzere) remained outside, but I called him in and inquired about the welfare of the Venetians since our departure, whereupon he said emphatically '*C'e molto desordine* [there's much disorder].' Both spoke the language of the future and left me with a conviction that Italy is going to be a great power. I liked the King much better than I used to. Once he rolled his eyes like Jeanningros [a French colonel in the Mexican army]. He asked me to thank you for your courtesies toward him, and to tell you that he loves you because, as he put it, you have '*de si bonnes idées* [such good ideas].' He is a big-hearted man and he has an undying faith in Italy where, incidentally, he plays a far more important rôle than is supposed. I would say that he is one of the wisest sovereigns in Europe, for he is close to the people. . . ."

With remarkable accuracy she predicted coming events: "Europe is due for a series of convulsions which will last many years. Austria is going to lose all her lands. . . . But we, on the American continent, are in the prime of life and need only civilizing influences and strong men to attain a prosperity never known before. Somehow European matters strike me by contrast as mere toys. Everything is on such a small scale, but one does not perceive this until one has been away, as we have. The glory of the House of Hapsburg crossed the seas with the name of one of its last triumphs, Novara. Over here it has been sinking with the sun, but it will rise again on that other shore. Remember that the motto of your forefathers was *Plus Ultra.* Charles the Fifth led the way as you have followed. Do not regret this, for God's hand is over us as it was over him."

The leitmotif of her existence had returned. She reiterated it to herself and to those around her: "We must not lose hope!"

While she was thus beguiling herself with rainbow-hued fancies, conditions were less cheerful at the Tuileries, where the Emperor Napoleon gnawed the end of his penholder. He was engaged in composing a long-deferred reply to Maximilian's telegram of congratulation. The point that disturbed his Majesty was the question of tone. Did Maximilian know the details of his wife's Paris visit? If so, one must be cool. On the other hand, that poor lady had doubtless suffered a temporary derangement which—after passing over—might dim her memory and preclude an exact account of what had happened. In that case, one was fraternal. L'Empereur decided in favor of the latter. He stopped chewing and with a great flourish wrote:

"St. Cloud, August 29th, 1866.

"Sir, my brother—

"It gave us a vast pleasure to welcome the Empress Charlotte, although I found it painful not to be able to fulfil the requests which she addressed to me. It so happens that we are approaching a decisive moment with Mexico, and your Majesty will have to adopt some sort of heroic resolution since there is no time for further half-measures.

"Let me begin by informing your Majesty that I can not lend Mexico another silver *écu* or another man. This detail being disposed of, there remains the question of what your Majesty will do. Are you able to maintain yourself through your own resources or will you be forced to abdicate? In the former case I can arrange for my troops to remain with you until 1867, but in the latter I would have to take other steps. It seems to me that your Majesty ought to try a public appeal, explaining the noble ambition that first prompted you to accept the mandate offered by an impressive number of Mexican citizens; next you might announce that insurmountable obstacles now compel you to relinquish your post. If they allow this to happen you may still take advantage of the presence of the French army and propose an election of a new government.

"Your Majesty must understand how unpleasant it is for me to be going into such detail, but we can not afford to lull ourselves any longer with fallacies. It is essential that the Mexican problem, as far as it touches France, should finally be solved.

"In conclusion, I ask your Majesty to believe that I shall continue to cherish a feeling of deepest sympathy for you, and that I long to alleviate—as far as my power will permit—the grief which must assail you in these hours of trial.

"Permit me to repeat to your Majesty my assurance of high esteem and true friendship with which I remain,

"Your Majesty's good brother,

"NAPOLEON."

This letter should convince posterity that the Emperor of France by no means enjoyed playing the part of a scoundrel. Despite his actions, largely forced upon him by political trends over which he had no control, Napoleon's compassion went out to Maximilian. At that last meeting with Carlota dour words were spoken, yet he did not hold a hysterical woman responsible for the vituperations she had hurled against him. In fact, he knew he deserved them. But if she had slapped his face, Napoleon could not have changed his course of policy without endangering his own throne—a throne from which he was destined to tumble before long because he could not win the war of 1870. Carlota had been right; France was a hard taskmaster. Monarchs who did not bring her glory were cast upon the rubbish heap.

Napoleon's last effort in Maximilian's behalf, his advice to abdicate while abdication was possible, lacked no sincerity. But the Mexican Emperor had just received Carlota's latest dispatches from Miramar, in which she quoted the Garibaldians recklessly assuring her:

"L'Empereur Maximilien entrainera toute l'Europe avec lui! [The Emperor Maximilian will sweep all Europe with him!]"

He was stirred up by her new faith in his cause. Besides, Carlota's frantic report from Paris led him to mistrust Napoleon's motives, for it was obvious that Louis loved no one but himself.

The rhapsodies from Miramar continued: "If you triumph over circumstances, as I know you can, colonists will pour into Mexico from Europe and elsewhere. Yours will be the best empire in the world. Surely you are not tempted to trade a throne which dominates both oceans for your former location in Venice, where you commanded scarcely two million people bled white by taxation. I am only trying to give you a picture of the wretched conditions prevailing even in Italy, not to mention the rest of degenerate Europe."

Such words as these caused him to cling more doggedly to a post which he had long ago wished to abandon. Perhaps Carlota was right. Perhaps there was no place for him in the Old World. And was it not conceivable that France might be jealous of his fine empire, so that Napoleon's counsel amounted to just one more stroke of perfidy? Guileless by nature, Maximilian's temperament underwent a momentary change. He sent a wily reply:

"Chapultepec, October 8, 1866.

"To His Majesty the Emperor of the French.

"Sir, my brother—

"I shall take advantage of Commandant Loysel's imminent trip in order to thank your Majesty for the amiable message addressed to me from St. Cloud on August twenty-ninth last, which I read on the third of this month at Cuernavaca.

"It is my duty to convey gratitude to your Majesty and the Empress Eugénie for the manner in which you were good enough to welcome my wife. In a recent letter she described to me her emotions at the reception your Majesties accorded her.

"In regard to the political portion of your letter, my conscience stands in the way of a decisive reply. I am handicapped by my position which forces me to ponder seriously any step upon which would depend the fate of so many loyal adherents. But, whatever Providence may hold in store, your Majesty must be aware of my sentiments and the degree of my attachment. I ask your Majesty to impart a salutation to the Empress, and to be assured of that esteem and friendship with which I also am,

"Your Majesty's good brother,

"MAXIMILIAN."

It was the retort courteous. Crammed with dual meanings, it made a fitting link in this tragedy of errors, the end of which drew inexorably nearer.

CHAPTER 7

ON SEPTEMBER sixteenth, Mexico's national holiday, Miramar celebrated a fiesta. Fireworks, which had annoyed Carlota at Chapultepec, now gladdened her heart. She stood on the terrace by the sea watching the cascade of lights bursting across the horizon, and her thoughts were far away. Nostalgic memories began to envelop her as she followed the upward flight of glittering sparks but took no notice of their descent in darkness, and suddenly the symbolic play of fire stirred her to renewed action. Why was she tarrying here, forgetful of her mission? Why was she wasting time when Mexico's future lay in the balance? *Plus Ultra!* She must speed on, higher, higher, to the very court of the Infinite.

That same night she demanded to set out by boat for Venice. Only a warning that all ships reaching Italy were quarantined, due to an epidemic of cholera that raged in the Grecian islands, caused her to delay her purpose another twenty-four hours. Prefect Radonetz was added to the imperial suite as the party rolled out of Trieste by post-chaise on the morning of September eighteenth. Secretary Blasio and the bursar Kuhacsevich had been sent ahead to Rome where they were to find accommodations for the Empress and smooth out difficulties.

Carlota started on the journey in a happy, almost gay, frame of mind. But this condition did not endure, for as soon as she found herself upon the open road again her mind began to focus on the business ahead. She remembered the terrible days in Paris. Was it possible that failure awaited her for the second time? Slowly she mulled it all over and over in her brain, exhausting her energies with morbid anticipation. The fatigue of the trip did the rest. The Empress arrived at Botzen in a state of anxiety bordering upon collapse.

Castillo, who helped her from the carriage, noticed that she was trembling. On the threshold of a small inn he paused to regard her more closely.

"Your Majesty does not feel well?"

Carlota shook her head and now an expression of alarm spread over her face. "I have been poisoned," she declared with vehemence, "in heaven's name double your vigilance!" And, as Castillo tried to calm her, she finished abruptly: "I will not go to Rome; I am turning back."

This left her retinue in a quandary. What was to be done? Did the Empress mean what she was saying?

Carlota had grown impatient. "Back to Miramar," she cried petulantly, "do you hear?"

Yes, she meant it. A telegram was sent on to Blasio and Kuhacsevich who meanwhile must have reached Mantua. They were told to cancel all plans and return at once.

While this went on Carlota retired to a guest room where the innkeeper's wife served her a simple supper. She grew mellow again after appeasing her hunger, and now, before dropping into bed, she brought out from her hand-bag an unfinished note to Maximilian. Within a few days Blasio was leaving for Mexico where the Emperor had need of him. She must send more instructions to her lonely Maxl, lest he weaken.

> "The Mexicans loved you from the first, as an individual [she exhorted], their flag is your flag and you are the nation, or, as Juárez calls himself, *El Soberano*. You must proclaim to all Mexico that you are the Emperor; nobody has any real use for presidents. Nor can you as an emperor's son call yourself president, so don't encourage unnecessary elections. Make them bow to you. A republic is no more than Protestantism, namely *une marâtre* [a stepmother]; whereas the monarchy is mankind's haven. A monarch is a good shepherd, while presidents are mercenaries; that absolutely expresses the point. If you could get the Mexicans to see it this way all your troubles would be over, and we would receive help from all quarters. As for troops, you will need very few once the rebellion dies down; and then, there you will be, acclaimed before all the world by your own happy subjects. . . ."

As she wrote she became intoxicated with the easy flow of her pen. Like many imaginative persons she had the faculty of hypnotizing herself with words; she was held spellbound by her own excursions in composition. In fact, she perked up again. She wasn't poisoned at all! Mathilde must hurry and tell that poor Señor Castillo they were going on to Rome anyway. Counter-instructions were to be sent to Mantua that very night.

On the following day a special train carried the imperial party to the border, where the Austrian garrison made obeisance to the Empress of Mexico. Across the line the Italians took up the strain and fêted Carlota with music and parades, for despite previous political discord, the Lombardo-Venetians remembered Maximilian and his consort "as individuals," not as pawns in the game of statesmanship.

It gratified Carlota to know that her Maxl remained to date the only monarch against whom no personal enemy had actually raised his hand. Not long ago a young man cracked his walking-stick on Queen Victoria's head as that busy lady took the air in Hyde Park. Seven attempts were made on the British matriarch's life, almost as many on that of Napoleon III, two on Franz Joseph, and as for the Tsars of Russia—history lost count.

The royal progress through Italy was indeed a joyful one. Reception after reception met Carlota along her way. The authorities of Reggio had decked themselves in full dress for a luncheon served in her honor at the palazzo of the Cavaliere Ferrari-Corbelli. Farther on, in Bologna, the plumed Bersaglieri troops escorted her through their city and lastly, at Foligno just outside Rome, a colossal banquet awaited the travelers who by now were overfed and weary from loss of sleep. Shortly upon arriving, the Empress was seized with another attack of tremors, followed by violent palpitations of the heart. Señora del Barrio protested against further exertions for her mistress, whereupon the retinue did honor to the dinner but Carlota went to bed.

Late the next evening, in a sluicy downpour of rain, the Eternal City was reached and straightway the imperial party put up at another Grand Hotel. Beginning with the name of the hostelry, the Roman visit was destined to duplicate Carlota's Paris experience in more ways than one. There was the parallel of the go-between. Like Napoleon, Pope Pius IX heard of her arrival and tried to avoid a meeting with his fair petitioner by sending his representative, Cardinal Giacomo Antonelli, to deflect the lady from her course. At the same hour which Eugénie had chosen, the Cardinal (who held the offices of Minister-President and Minister for Foreign Affairs in the Papal States) ascended the hotel stairs with a flourish of skirts. He had come to pay Carlota an afternoon visit.

"I greeted him," wrote the Empress in her notes for that day, "on the upper landing of the stairs. In his red cassock and mantle he looked quite picturesque and imposing. A whole hour went by, during which he listed for me all my consort's sins against the Church, adding that there could never be any sort of concordat."

It was difficult to interrupt the capable Antonelli, for his vociferations were kept up regardless of whether inhalation or exhalation engaged his sturdy lungs. As a final parting gesture he played an ecclesiastic trump. He broke into Latin. Long after his Eminence had vanished, Carlota remained standing in the exact middle of the carpet, the canonical and historic papal *"Non possumus"* drumming in her ears.

And now hope was dying within her. She had no peace. Daily she wandered through Rome in the stifling heat, with Señora del Barrio trotting faithfully behind her. From the heights of the Pincio she would gaze down upon the panorama of the Tiber city, plotting always new methods whereby she might obtain entrance to the Vatican for a personal interview with the Pope. Bathed in perspiration both ladies would return to the hotel, there to receive callers from the local aristocracy and the diplomatic corps. Through these persons, as well as others who signed the visitors' book, the Empress constantly endeavored to further her plan. At length the Austrian Embassy interceded for her and on September twenty-seventh, at eleven o'clock in the morning, the Holy Father was prepared to grant an audience.

As long as he had relented, the Pope, like Napoleon, determined to do things right. He indulged in the grand gesture and placed at Carlota's disposal the state coach, drawn by four Spanish barbs, as well as an escort of his own cuirassiers. When the Empress arrived at the Vatican she found the Papal Guards (in their obsolete costumes, designed by Michelangelo) flanking the central staircase straight to the throne-room. The Holy Father, however, was not alone. High dignitaries surrounded his person so that the meeting was in no danger of becoming unofficial.

With almost superhuman effort Carlota forced her wits to meet this last challenge. She genuflected to kiss the Pope's foot, but he granted exemption by gently lifting her face to his ring. She waited for the benison, then, without flinching, broke the immense silence with her plea:

"I am not here, your Holiness, to beg for gold or soldiers. I can not even hope for the concordat, although it would win my husband all the adherents he lost in his own empire——"

She paused, gasping for breath. She was growing a trifle dizzy; the strain of picking each word with careful attention to its fitness, its shading, overtaxed her strength. She felt herself weakening. But no, it would pass over, it must pass over—there was so much more to say.

"I have come," she began again, "with one request. Your Holiness must reason with the Emperor Napoleon, commanding him to keep an honorable pledge. It is easy, it will cost your Holiness no more than the effort of writing a note——"

Again she stopped, and this time a gray pallor spread over her face. She looked as if she were about to faint. Pius IX, already much relieved by the discovery that no concessions would be demanded of the Holy See, decided to continue the audience privately so that he might be able to offer the Empress a chair. He motioned both their suites to withdraw, and himself led Carlota into an adjoining room.

This simple action, intended merely for her comfort since she looked so ill and unable to stay on her feet, completely unbalanced the afflicted woman. It was the first response she had encountered since the beginning of her long pilgrimage, and, although the Pope's solicitude concerned itself with her physical distress only, she quite misunderstood her position. At last, she reflected, here was protection. Here was the fair tribunal before which she could enumerate the many wrongs she had suffered; now she would find a just hearing. Seated upon a carved Dante chair she tried to assemble her thoughts but the growing disorder of her brain engulfed her. She could remember only one thing—the poison.

"Santissimo Padre," she cried, and her voice pierced the walls of the chamber, *"ho pàura*—I am afraid. . . ."

Before the Head of Christendom had quite recovered from this shock she rushed up to him, pointing behind her with a fluttering hand. *"Questo Luigi Napoleone e la sua Eugenia mi hanno invenènato*—they have poisoned me!" With a disdainful toss of her small head she spat out that name "Eugenia." And now, with these two ogres materializing so vividly before her eyes, she began to see others who were bent upon murdering her. Bohuslavek, the doctor, with his sleeping powders. Castillo and del Valle, hovering about her with a display of concern that was positively revolting. Ah, and that Doblinger woman who combed her hair—might not each pin be dipped in some lethal substance which would act slowly, insidiously? Those headaches, those splitting headaches that bothered her of late, they came from hairpins that had been tampered with! The Holy Father must order the arrest of her entire suite. No, not Señora del Barrio; there was a faithful soul. But the rest, she did not give a fig for them. They must be instantly punished.

Pio Nono found himself in a dire dilemma. Certainly in proposing a private interview he had anticipated nothing of this sort. Casting papal dignity to the four winds, he scampered from the room on noiseless slippers and summoned the imperial retinue. With graphic waving of arms he reported the scene that had just taken place and urged that the Empress's companions leave immediately for another hotel. Señora del Barrio, meanwhile, must endeavor to quiet her mistress and remove her from the Vatican.

Bohuslavek at first objected. Were they not all responsible to their master for the Empress's safety? It was treason to abandon her, ill as she was, in a strange city. But his Holiness remained firm. Carlota must somehow be convinced that her suite would spend the night in jail. The Pope had caught a desperate gleam in her eye; he was taking no chances. Sadly the little group left the Vatican, while Señora del Barrio accompanied his Holiness, who tiptoed back to the room where his visitor still sat alone upon a carved Dante chair.

Carlota had calmed down again. She had got her fears off her chest and now she felt much better. Happy that the Pope was ready to take up the feud with her enemies, she was perfectly willing to go away with dear del Barrio. But Pio Nono must promise to pay them a return visit. They would pour him a cup of that nice "muddled" chocolate, which they had brought from Mexico. It had cinnamon sprinkled over the top, and there was a clever way of beating it up with a twirling-stick. Wishing no argument, the Holy Father agreed without reservation to any and all plans. Under the stress of the moment his conscience would have licensed approval of every prank the Empress might suggest. What he chose to do after the irresponsible lady had left the shelter of his roof was quite another matter.

At the hotel that night Carlota's tranquil mood continued unchanged, so that Señora del Barrio felt safe in ordering dinner to be served in a secluded mezzanine parlor. But as soon as the clatter of dishes caught her attention the Empress began to sniff and peer about. Her suspicions had returned and, although she made no complaint, she refused to touch anything on the table. Once she caught sight of the waiter bearing a bowl of fruits and nuts. She summoned him to her side and carefully inspected his wares, poking and squeezing them with much ado. When she had made sure that peels and shells were truly intact she kept an orange and a few filberts. These she would eat in her room. The persecution mania that was fast possessing her did not lack a degree of consistent logic.

When bedtime came she refused to retire. Instead, she remained in a rocker on her balcony through half the night, reflecting that her tête-à-tête with the Pope had not lasted long enough. Her disclosures were not nearly ended. Despite the fact that in distant Mexico Pio Nono's intractability had enraged her, she now felt that he was her only prop, the only being worthy of her confidence. And there were staggering revelations she must yet make to him in regard to the cunning of her foes.

On the morrow, after the most perfunctory toilet, she sallied forth with her lone companion. A cab was hailed and by eight o'clock the two ladies had reached the famous Fountain of Trevi. Here Carlota, who had taken no liquid for days, cupped her hands and drank of the freshly spouting water. And now, pretending to follow an abrupt impulse which must have hovered clearly in her mind, she ordered the driver to head straight for the Vatican.

At the gates of the Pope's palace they did not recognize her and paid no attention to any demands for admission. It was Señora del Barrio who finally established a satisfactory identification whereupon Carlota was led into the Supreme Pontiff's presence. His Holiness had just sat down to breakfast when, pale as a ghost, yesterday's visitor stood again before him.

Even in the brief spell of a single night the Empress's malady had left dire traces on her face. Her fine eyes seemed to be falling back into their sockets. From these unsuspected depths the green-circled pupils borrowed a furtive and uncanny quality. Pio Nono shivered.

And now Carlota rushed forward, while a hectic flush colored her cheeks. She was about to recite a minute tabulation of crimes which her murderers were at this very moment plotting against her, when the delicate vapor of hot chocolate was wafted in her direction. She stopped in her tracks, searching the room. And now her eyes fell upon the Pope's breakfast tray and the steaming potion in his cup. A mound of whipped cream floated atop the succulent liquid.

It seemed to her that she had gone without food for days. Her throat was again parched with thirst. At sight of the Pope's appetizing pabulum she could not resist the pangs of hunger. She made a lunge for the tray and immersed three fingers of her right hand into the cup. . . . Her story, the vital mission she had crossed an ocean to perform, all was lost in a disjointed stammer of meaningless ejaculations. Only one thing was clear—she had been forced to starve herself, because she was so afraid.

At this point her powers of deduction leaped to a startling conclusion. Since there were dangers lurking everywhere she would stay at the Vatican, for here alone could she feel safe. The Pope, who meanwhile had endeavored to snatch a portion of his breakfast, choked on a piece of buttercake.

"Madame," he expostulated, "that is impossible! Madame must leave the Vatican at this moment for it is the hour of my official audiences."

When it became clear to her that she was retarding the papal business, Carlota promptly suggested that a guide might show her about the establishment while his Holiness was occupied. There was nothing for it but to leave her in charge of Colonel Bossi, of the Vatican *gendarmerie,* in whose obliging company she inspected the gardens and the library. While she was outdoors another fountain caught her eye and she asked for a glass. After drinking from it she slipped the glass into her hand-bag and would not release it again.

Toward noon the Holy Father made inquiries and learned to his acute dismay that she was still there. Cardinal Antonelli was ordered to join Bossi throughout luncheon, which was served to the visitors in a private room. Carlota behaved her best. She was docile, witty, even a little gay—but she insisted upon eating from the same plate as her lady-in-waiting. After the brief repast she agreed to take a nap.

It was now mid-afternoon and the Pope's embarrassment grew, for the Empress showed no inclination to return to her hotel. Overtures were made in this direction but Carlota declared that murderers were lying in wait for her behind every door; she would be in mortal danger if they forced her to spend the night elsewhere. Why not, she suggested slyly, let her have one of the reading-rooms just off the library? Her pontifical host shook his head in protest. She pleaded. She cajoled. And finally, as darkness came, she wept bitterly, for great fears were upon her.

"I can sleep on the pavement in the corridor," she wailed, "if you have no other room!"

In the face of her anguish they desisted. The papal housekeeper, Monsignor Bartolommeo Pacca, set up two cots and lighted a pair of candelabra. Señora del Barrio took her unhappy mistress by the hand. Like a child, Carlota allowed herself to be undressed and put to bed. She fell instantly asleep, for she was worn out by her many experiences. But the lady-in-waiting did not lie down. She sat up all through that night beside her loved mistress, watching wide-eyed, and thinking sad Mexican thoughts.

Officially, this was the first and only time in recorded history that a woman slept in the abode of St. Peter's Vicar.

Chapter 8

When Carlota awoke she stared timidly at her surroundings. On learning where she was her meek and grateful attitude at once returned, for she promptly recalled that an evil fate was dogging her footsteps. Perhaps, if she behaved very sweetly and caused no one the slightest bother, they might let her remain indefinitely under this holy roof. There was always the chance, though, that they might not. In that case she had better make her will, for out in the world she was sure to be poisoned shortly, oh, very shortly. One must prepare for the end. Could some one fetch her paper and ink? Some one did.

In a few moments she drew up her testament, leaving all her property and jewels to Maximilian, and setting aside small mementoes for her brothers as well as the faithful del Barrio. She finished with a note to her husband:

"Rome, October 1st, 1866.

"My dearest Treasure!

"I am saying good-by, for God may soon call me to him. But first I must thank you for the joy you always gave to me. May you be blessed with eternal happiness. Your devoted,

"Charlotte."

When this task was completed and the Empress had partaken of a meager breakfast, the Pope's household wrestled once more with the problem of her removal from the Vatican. At the slightest hint in this respect she grew unresponsive and refused to stir. In desperation his Holiness had a telegram sent to Brussels, informing the King of Belgium of his sister's unfortunate condition. While waiting for a reply the resourceful Cardinal Antonelli proposed to take Carlota for a morning ride in one of the papal barouches. But she saw through his ruse and flatly turned down the offer.

No sooner had she rejected this stratagem, which would most certainly have ended with her being deposited on the threshold of her hotel, than a more workable solution presented itself. Monsignor Pacca was on delightful speaking terms with the Mother Superior of the near-by Convent of St. Vincent where, not infrequently, he gleaned advice on questions of gastronomy. An invitation might be obtained for Carlota to visit the pious sisters and the model orphanage over which they held sway. The suggestion was followed with alacrity and by noon the good prioress arrived in a decrepit conventual hack. She was a dimpled rosy creature who instantly won the confidence of both Empress and lady-in-waiting. A bit cramped for space, the three women soon rumbled back over the cobbled streets for an inspection tour of the children's home.

During the trip Carlota veiled her face with a scarf, to prevent any one from recognizing her.

The afternoon at the nunnery passed off without mishap until a lay sister persuaded her Majesty to investigate the scullery regions. In the kitchen a toothsome *ragout* simmered in its juices. The hospitable cook offered the Empress a small serving. Carlota's nostrils quivered and she accepted the dish, but before tasting its contents her glance fastened upon a speck of lint lodged between the prongs of her fork. Blood left her cheeks.

"The knife and fork were not polished," she carped, "there is poison on them!" Before the cowled assembly she dropped to her knees and prayed a *Salve Regina* because her enemies had once more been foiled.

Still her reason wandered. She stood up again and let her eyes scan the stove, fixing this time upon a kettle of boiling soup. Hunger gnawed at her vitals, for in her absorption with formulating a testament she had eaten almost nothing that morning. The broth bubbled merrily, and it looked so harmless. Before any one could guess what she might be about, the Empress had plunged her hand into the pot and was fishing for a joint of meat. Her fingers were shriveled by the scalding, and as they led her to the infirmary where the raw wound was bandaged she fainted with pain.

While she lay insensible some one hit upon the idea of hurrying her back to the hotel. She was lifted into a cab, but at the moment of starting she regained consciousness and screamed for help. With difficulty the carriage doors were clapped shut. After a wild race through Rome the hotel was reached, but here Carlota would not get out. In full sight of a gaping crowd of onlookers two porters had to grip her wrists and propel the Empress across the sidewalk.

And now she remained locked in her room with no one but Señora del Barrio in attendance. All meals were prepared under her own supervision, with her companion tasting each dish before Carlota would consent to eat. Soon even this precaution did not satisfy her. A kitten was obtained and the Empress watched it lap up milk and nibble at viands. Once the milk soured, due to the summer heat, and the animal spurned it. Thereafter all liquids were banished from Carlota's menu. Instead, there were tiring excursions on foot or by cab to a different public fountain every day. Here, with the tumbler she had filched from the Vatican, the Empress of Mexico quenched her thirst.

Meanwhile, although she did not know it, her entire retinue had returned to the hotel and was watching over her with growing despair. It was decided among the gentlemen that Doctor Bohuslavek must speed overseas and inform Maximilian of his wife's illness. Doctor Jilek at Miramar had already been notified and a famous nerve specialist from Vienna was on his way to Trieste. Carlota's younger brother, the Count of Flanders, announced his arrival for the seventh of October.

Two days before that date the Pope gave way to a merciful impulse. On hearing the details of the convent visit he signed the concordat, a draft of which Carlota had presented to him on her first appearance at the Vatican. His Holiness also wrote a note; it disclosed that Pio Nono was an observing man.

"*Maestà:*

"I am returning the document your Majesty submitted, and shall be delighted to have you keep that glass. In my daily prayers I beg that God may restore your peace of mind and free you of those suspicions which cause you such wretchedness. I bless you with all my heart. "PIUS IX."

She had attained that which she had promised her adored Maxl. But it came too late. Her mind, once brilliant and enviable, was now a total blank.

With the arrival of the Count of Flanders a necessary change was made. Señora del Barrio, on the verge of a nervous collapse due to the prolonged strain, was put to bed for a few days in an adjoining room. While the lady-in-waiting captured some much-needed sleep, the Belgian prince made a pretense at keeping house for his sister. He hovered over the little spirit-stove, "cooking" a variety of masterpieces which were smuggled to him in their finished state from the hotel kitchens below stairs. He performed other small services, such as brushing the Empress's hair, and buying a quaint silver heart with a special inscription on it: *"A Maria Santissima, in riconoscenza di esser stata liberata da un pericolo di vita il 28. 7tbre, 1866.* [To Mary Most Holy, in acknowledgment of having been saved from deadly peril on September 28, 1866.] *Carlotta, Imperatrice del Messico."*—Italian Virgins were addressed in Italian.

Although it made him feel a trifle conspicuous to do so, Philip of Flanders carried the trinket to the Church of San Carlo, where he hung it as a votive offering on the nearest peg.

A few days later, after Señora del Barrio had recovered her strength, they removed Carlota to Miramar by way of Ancona.

It was November. The leaves had fallen and her heart was heavy with foreboding. The beauty of that marble villa had taken on a bleak austere accent which increased the sadness that filled Carlota's being. She wandered aimlessly about, but she did not recognize the once familiar place. Professor Riedel, the alienist from Vienna, shook his head, and with the new year Carlota returned to Laeken—the home of her childhood—after a brief reign of only eighteen months. She was twenty-seven, and they had pronounced her incurably insane.

At the German spa of Heiligenberg a fourteen-year-old girl kept an inconsequential diary. On the thirty-first of October, 1866,

Marie zu Erbach-Schönberg, Princess of Battenberg, used three exclamation points. "Mama read to me out of the newspapers details of the sad condition of the unfortunate Empress Charlotte of Mexico. Poor woman!—Poor Emperor Max! How bitterly they must regret ever having accepted the throne offered them by Napoleon!"

V
THE EPILOGUE

V

THE EPILOGUE

Chapter 1

Marshal Bazaine would have been out of Mexico long ago, but he was trying to sell his house. It was the handsome *Palacio Buena Vista,* situated along the *Calle del Puente de Alvarado,* which he had received from the Emperor Maximilian as a wedding-present.

Most of the French troops had sailed, and those that remained behind did so because of loyalty to Maximilian's cause rather than to that of their own government. In fact, as the twilight of his fantastic reign drew ever nearer, the Emperor of Mexico saw himself surrounded by a small group of men—heterogeneous in origin—who clung to him although he could not pay them, and whose sole purpose in life seemed to consist of foolhardy attempts to guard his safety while jeopardizing their own.

But these were not Bazaine's reasons for staying on. Early in the year 1867 the marshal and his wife, who had recently given birth to a little Bazaine, sat at the semicircular windows of their mansion waiting for a purchaser. The building known as *La Casa de Media Luna* (the House of the Half-Moon) was much admired because of its elegance and originality, but no one came to buy it. When at last Bazaine could stay no longer the great double portals were closed and shutters put up. People scorned the place. No one would live there. In modern times a cigarette factory moved in and is doing a thriving business.

As far as the marshal was concerned, he would have waited indefinitely for a sale. But the United States Government at Washington became daily more disagreeable, watching his every move and inquiring testily as to the French commander's reasons for not joining his homeward-bound legions. The confinement of his spouse and a series of lesser alibis having outgrown their force, the old soldier finally wound up his affairs. On March 12, 1867, Bazaine took sail, his ears having been lashed to a bright crimson by the parting words of the Mexican Councilor, Don Alejandro Arango y Escandón:

"Go then, Marshal, leave Mexico with your army; but carry with you the bitter conviction that you have done little for religion, less for the Mexicans, and nothing, absolutely nothing for the honor of the French."

Captain J. J. Kendall (late of H. B. M. 44th and 60th regiments), an English soldier of fortune who served Maximilian for a time, contributed a personal opinion to the London papers:

> "I cannot but condemn [wrote Her Britannic Majesty's subject] the conduct of Marshal Bazaine during the latter portion of his sojourn in Mexico. He doubtless had instructions to do all he could to induce the Emperor Maximilian to abdicate, but he overstepped all bounds, not only of diplomacy and of the laws of nations, but also of honour on the part of an officer and a gentleman, to say nothing of the dignity of a Marshal of France. . . . Several pieces of cannon that he could not take with him were spiked at the gates of Mexico City; an immense quantity of surplus small arms and ammunition was thrown into the Viga Canal. On the morning before he left the city he is reported to have gone to the Emperor and to have demanded some paltry sum due for the lodging money of his officers, threatening (if immediate payment were not made) to sell by public auction all cannon belonging to the Mexican army then in the city."

Whatever the nature of Bazaine's last business transactions, misfortune overtook the departing Frenchman on the road to Vera Cruz. A roving Juarista band explored his baggage and made off with a chest of solid gold bars which doubtless had been destined to assuage the rigors of a rainy day. Though always an excellent provider, the marshal was never able to repair this loss. He ended his career in France with no more than an honest citizen's umbrella.

Having prevailed against Napoleon III up to this point, the authorities at Washington now turned to the problem of evicting Maximilian from Mexico. In various states of the Union excitable orators wrestled with the matter. Mr. Samuel S. Cox, a representative from Ohio, advocated action: "We ought to be prepared not only to say, but to make it effectual, that no crown shall be established on this continent."

In Paris, although the Mexican bubble had been at last forsaken, the attitude of Mr. Seward and his associates continued to arouse indignation. Even if it had been propitious to recall the Foreign Legion from the American continent, this was no reason for approving the dictatorial policy of the United States. The Yankees were trying to lord it over the entire Latin race. Baron Jérôme David, an influential deputy, addressed the Corps Législatif in Paris during the summer of 1866. He voiced a scathing indictment of Uncle Sam. The words employed by David found many an echo in the Spanish-American countries of that day:

> "By what right and for what purpose do the United States interfere in the affairs of Mexico? The population of Mexico is composed of Creoles, half-breeds and Indians. There is no kind of analogy or relation between the Mexican (Spanish-American) race and the Anglo-American. Manners, temperament, language, religion,—all differ, all are in opposition and contrast. Is it to be expected that the one must conform to a type of government which happens to suit the other?—There is much talk of the Monroe Doctrine. Since when has a 'doctrine,' enunciated in a message to one nation, assumed the category of a 'law' for foreign nations? The Monroe Doctrine happens to be a paragraph in a political speech, foisted upon Latin America without a 'by your leave.' We could understand the United States becoming alarmed over an aggressive neighbor, or one jeopardizing the institutions of the Union. But simply because the government at Washington happens to be republican in form, it cannot be contended that monarchies have no place in the New World."

Still, no matter how rational the speaker's colleagues deemed his argument, the Gallic *tricolore* had folded up before the menacing blasts occasioned by the Stars and Stripes. Despite the proud adage that "France is not in the habit of marching, except to her own tune," the red-trousers trotted obediently back to their ships. Nor had the authorities at Washington the slightest doubt that the Emperor Maximilian could be persuaded to do likewise, as indeed he might have, if the United States had chosen to deal with him personally.

But north of the Río Grande, Imperial Mexico was being severely ignored. The prevailing attitude was one of spinosity which characterized even American representatives abroad, as is evidenced in a letter from Mr. James E. Harvey, United States Envoy at Lisbon. On March 30, 1866, this diplomat wrote to his home office:

> "I have the honor to transmit a translation of an address delivered by the so-called Minister of Mexico (representing a person styling himself MAXIMILIAN THE FIRST, and claiming to be the ruler of that country), on presenting his letters of credence in that capacity near this Court, and the reply of his Most Faithful Majesty to the same, as a part of the current history of the times, and not because either the ceremonial or the occasion has the smallest importance in my estimation. . . . I shall not hesitate to decline all official intercourse with the person in question, as I did with his predecessor who came here from Madrid during the past year to establish diplomatic relations with Portugal."

Similarly, when Secretary Seward of the State Department had something to say about Maximilian he referred to the Hapsburg scion as "that Austrian fellow." If there were messages or demands to be addressed to Chapultepec, the American Minister in Paris, Mr. Bigelow, was instructed to convey them to the French Foreign Minister, Drouyn de Lhuys, who relayed the whole business to the "alleged Emperor of Mexico." For Mr. Seward could not bring himself to acknowledge Maximilian's very presence on the American continent as anything but an act of intrusion, and he would not communicate with the "usurper" directly from Washington.

It was only natural that any information on United States policy, if it reached Chapultepec at all, lost emphasis in transit, quite apart from the fact that Maximilian could not grow seriously concerned over the cavils of a stranger who did not even accord him the courtesy of an address. When an occasional truculent ultimatum from Mr. Seward confronted him (after a journey across the globe) the Emperor merely thought it an odd thing and placed it neatly upon a shelf.

Up to now the powers at Washington had remained undecided as to a proper point of attack. The Monroe Doctrine alone did not appear, even to its sponsors, a sufficient pretext for going to war against Maximilian. Its main premise was directed against further conquest in the Western Hemisphere on the part of European potentates. Napoleon III had violated this premise, but Maximilian had not come as a conqueror. Since the removal of French troops, moreover, Maximilian's presence in Mexico could no longer be construed as European aggression. The Mexican Emperor held office by virtue of an election on the part of a native monarchist group; he had not imposed himself upon the people.

It was a trifling incident which ultimately gave Mr. Seward an advantage. In October of 1866 an American reporter was able, for the first time, to get hold of the Iturbide affair, which up to now had never been used as "copy." The relatives of little Agustín lived comfortably on the French Riviera and never mentioned their agreement with Maximilian. But as soon as it had become generally known that Napoleon was withdrawing his forces from overseas, Alice de Iturbide began to worry about her child. She wrote a letter to Maximilian asking for her son's restitution, and at the same time appealed to Washington for aid in revoking the terms of the adoption. A newshawk carried the tale to his editor, who exploited it with true journalistic gusto. It made a perfect sob story. The picture of a young mother (an American by birth!) robbed of her infant son—who now languished in the clutches of a foreign tyrant—this proved too much for the tender sensibilities of a reading public. Countless enraged letters poured into the Department of State, demanding action.

Mr. Seward was delighted. He harangued Mr. Bigelow across

the ocean, who harangued Monsieur Drouyn de Lhuys across the Seine, who——

But Maximilian had just been told in a cable from Miramar that Carlota was desperately ill. The exact nature of her malady was not divulged, since Blasio and Bohuslavek were already en route with oral reports.

"Who is this Professor Riedel?" the Emperor asked his substitute physician, Dr. Samuel Basch.

"Oh," the latter replied innocently, "he runs the lunatic asylum in Vienna."

It was only now that Maximilian understood. The blow numbed him. Nothing in all his life was ever to strike him more deeply. Nothing would ever matter so much as this. His mind went empty of all but a single thought—he must go to her. At once. Not another day in this land of shattered dreams, not another hour of struggle for a realm that crumbled in his grasp. . . .

"It is two o'clock," the voice of Doctor Basch was admonishing gently. "Your Majesty ought to lie down before the fever attack——"

Fever? Yes, of course, he was having malaria these days. He must pamper himself and take his powders like every European in these latitudes, while Carla sank into darkness somewhere beyond his reach.

"No, Basch," he said after a pause, "I'm afraid I can't wait for the fever."

"But your Majesty——"

The doctor's distress was genuine.

"It's all right," Maximilian answered a mute question, "you see, I must go away. She—I can't leave her like that——"

Basch saw. He listened to his master who talked on, as if to himself, in a heartbreaking monotone.

"Carla needs me. Mexico doesn't. Mexico never needed me. I will give it all back to them, the throne, the crown, the boy. And I will go back to Miramar where—if we had known what we know now—we two would have been content."

It was the eighteenth of October, three days after the date on which Carlota had intended to sail for Mexico. Now he must go and find her in a borderland from which there was no return.

That night he gave orders for departure, as soon as possible, on the Austrian corvette *Dandolo* which lay at anchor in the harbor of Vera Cruz. He drew up a parting message to his ministry, and another to his military staff, in which he renounced all further attempts at domination. The courts martial, the fighting, the political persecutions, all must stop; the "Black Decree," actually discarded long ago, was officially revoked on October 21, 1866, by a *de facto* annulment.

On October twentieth, Maximilian wrote a letter to Alice de Iturbide, assuring her that her son would leave Mexico at once with his aunt, the ex-Princess Josefa. (Since the Iturbides themselves, and not the Emperor, wished to break the terms of a strictly legal adoption, Maximilian requested that they drop their titles.) Josefa, who was enraged at her Yankee relative, relinquished her borrowed tiaras and her train in a torrent of abuse. She kissed the Emperor's hand, wept copious tears, and bundled up the little Iturbide, who wondered what all the fuss was about.

"Qué pasa?" he asked in an imperious tone. "What's the matter?"

Maximilian stroked his fair head. "Nothing, my child," he said, and there was a note of relief in his voice, "you are just being saved from calamity."

"Is that all?" commented Agustín, who was accustomed to adult rhetoric which he did not understand.

The Emperor smiled. "Yes, that is all." He stooped to tuck the little man's sailor bib into his coat. "And now I am quite sure you won't catch it."

The boy threw his arms around Maximilian's neck. "I never do," he said gravely. Their mysterious dialogue ended, as usual, in perfect understanding—while a puzzled Aunt Josefa stood by, shaking her head at such unadulterated nonsense.

And so the little Iturbide left Chapultepec and the shadow of a throne. He was taken to Europe where he lived in France for a while, and later in Hungary. He forgot both the Spanish and English of his early childhood, for he spent most of his life in Magyar boarding schools. And after that, he married a Baroness

Mikosch, without ever again achieving the importance he once enjoyed—however briefly—as a possible *casus belli*. . . . In far-off Washington, Mr. Seward's righteous ire had been forced to subside within itself. The steam of his fury was spent in vain, when the Emperor of Mexico made not the slightest effort to do battle with an American mother for the custody of her innocent babe.

Chapter 2

Father Augustus Fischer was upset. The complete dissolution of the imperial household was not at all to his liking. He remonstrated with Maximilian and termed the latter's decision to leave Mexico both foolish and undignified. More than that, it was a shade dishonorable for the Emperor to abandon his followers at the precise moment when they needed him most. To be sure, they all felt for him in his sorrow. But personal feelings must not outweigh duty.

"My followers?" asked Maximilian bitterly. "Who are they?"

Fischer began to enumerate. "Prince Karl zu Khevenhüller, your Majesty, who is supporting troops out of his own pocket; Alfons von Kodolitch, who——"

"You are beginning the wrong way," Maximilian interrupted, "by mentioning the foreign elements first. I will listen, if you can show me the other side of the slate."

He went on with his preparations, ordering chests and crates for his personal effects, correspondence and secret archives, to be sent ahead to Vera Cruz. Stefan Herzfeld, Maximilian's confidant since the days of the latter's apprenticeship in the Austrian Navy, supported the Emperor in his decision to leave and urged still greater haste:

"*Fort, fort aus diesem Land, wo sich in einigen Wochen der blutigste Bürgerkrieg abspielen wird!* [Away, away from this land, where in a few weeks the bloodiest civil war will break out!]"

Maximilian was ready. He had instructed Colonel von Kodolitch to sell the Austrian cannon (which were the Emperor's private property), and to give the money to disabled officers and men of the corps. Within the month all European troops were to leave Mexico. And now Maximilian himself, shaking with fever, set out for the coast. The captain of the *Dandolo* had coaled his ship and waited at the quay for his exalted passenger. But the imperial party never reached Vera Cruz, for at Orizaba a great surprise awaited them. Father Fischer had done some nimble thinking. Making use of his countless connections in the capital, he had assembled as many Mexican royalists as the shortness of time permitted and, by dangling future emoluments before their visionary eyes, had persuaded them to follow him to Orizaba. Since all this had taken place a few days before the monarch's departure, the resourceful Jesuit was able to rehearse a breathtaking demonstration in behalf of the Empire.

The actual performance went off with a spontaneity for which the versatile stage-manager has never received quite his due. Toward evening, as Maximilian approached the town, fireworks and patriotic cheers greeted him. A stream of boisterous people filled the streets, crying: *"Viva Maximiliano! Viva el Emperador de México!"*

In their midst the agile Father Augustus darted here and there, modestly effacing himself. At last the Emperor spotted him.

"What's all this?" he asked gruffly. "Who are these persons?"

The Jesuit bowed. "Your Majesty wished to see the other side of the slate," he said in an almost apologetic tone.

Maximilian was touched. He was flattered. Never since his arrival in Mexico had he met with so overwhelming a reception.

"Now," Father Fischer asked, "will your Majesty run away? Is there still reason to say that the Mexicans do not want you—that they do not need you?"

Herzfeld stepped between his sovereign and the priest. "Be firm, Sire, do not let yourself be swayed. The storm is breaking on all sides. The Yankees are invading the country."

These were the wrong tactics. Maximilian always bridled at the merest suggestion that he feared danger. "Father Fischer is right," he said, "it must not be trumpeted around the world that I have run away."

"But her Majesty, the Empress!" cried Herzfeld desperately.

It was too late. Herzfeld should have thought of Carlota before he thought of storms and Yankees. Maximilian was already busy trying to prove that whatever foolishness a Hapsburg was capable of, he would never be afraid. It was this that Fischer had counted on. From the beginning the priest had never spoken of the Emperor's departure, but always of his "flight." The very repetition of that word had come to confuse Maximilian, so that he himself wondered whether cowardice and not Carlota's need could have been responsible for his sudden decision to leave his post. Certainly her illness had nothing to do with his present change of mind. Already resolving to turn back, he raised a half-hearted objection to the effect that his baggage van might in the meantime have reached the *Dandolo.* But Father Fischer had an answer for everything.

"Herzfeld, here, seems anxious to go," he suggested, "why not send him ahead with the boxes?"

The officer snarled an oath, but Fischer went on unperturbed. "There is no thought of abandoning the journey altogether. The matter will merely be postponed, that is all. As soon as Mexican conditions improve, your Majesty will naturally hasten to the Empress's side."

That settled it. The idea that his presence on these shores was of such momentous importance, and that a trip to Europe remained still in the offing, eased Maximilian's conscience. After all, Carlota was in the best of care. She had probably improved since that dreadful cable, and anyway, he would soon be receiving more detailed news. Perhaps he had better stay and hold the Empire together, at least until the arrival of Blasio and Bohuslavek.

While these deliberations went on two Mexican gentlemen approached. Teodosio Lares, a member of Maximilian's Cabinet, delivered himself of a passionate speech. He made reference to the Emperor's pledge, on Independence Day, from the balcony of the priest Hidalgo's house. He reached back to a more remote past and recalled the oath sworn at Miramar, adding that a horrible fate awaited Maximilian's followers at the hands of Juárez, if the Empire were allowed to collapse. And lastly he had recourse to the fusty formula concerning a Hapsburg's indifference to danger. "What," he cried dramatically, "will be the judgment of the world and of future historians, if this classic dictum is rendered untrue!"

Don Luis Arroyo, the second suppliant, lamented in the same

key: "It will spell disaster for our people, if your Majesty's decision to go is final."

And while Arroyo paused for breath, Father Fischer broke into the refrain: "Did not the Empress sacrifice her health, as she would even yet offer her life, for this cause? How much more are we then entitled to ask of a brave woman's husband!"

But there was no need for such a climax. The imperial landau had already been turned over to Herzfeld who, willy-nilly, was pushed off to Vera Cruz. Maximilian planned to wait for the return of both vehicle and armed escort, basking meanwhile in the balmy climate of Orizaba. To fill in the time a champagne supper was arranged by Lares, Arroyo and Fischer, in celebration of the Emperor's victory over himself and, be it added, over his better judgment.

It chanced that at this period the British Minister, Sir Peter Campbell-Scarlett, was enjoying the rose gardens of Orizaba and a welcome change of altitude. As soon as the vacationing Englishman learned of Maximilian's arrival he strolled over to the imperial villa for a chat. A warm friendship existed between the two men. Maximilian admired England and frequently expressed the opinion that the British intelligence service was the best in the world. He now rejoiced in so splendid an opportunity to confer with Sir Peter on his present predicament.

Surprisingly enough, the Briton favored Maximilian's return to the capital. Although heretofore Campbell-Scarlett advised abdication, he had lately altered his views. As far as he could see, the French Intervention had never ceased to irritate the Mexicans, but with the retreat of Napoleon's forces the whole tableau was changed. A popular inquiry might disclose that monarchy, under some benevolent despot, was still the desired form of government. At any rate, there ought to be a vote.

Maximilian was soothed. He recovered his poise. And when he was permitted a glimpse at a note marked "Private," which had been addressed by Sir Peter to Father Fischer, his confidence took another leap. "It is quite certain," wrote his Excellency, "that after the departure of the French a strong party will rally round the imperial flag, in order to save Mexico from civil war and its consequences. For this reason I now consider abdication to be both premature and unnecessarily precipitate."

The scales of destiny received a final tip. How fortunate that Herzfeld, who feared for the master, had been banished. As the corvette *Dandolo* drifted beyond the horizon the Emperor Maximilian rolled back to his capital in style.

From now on things began to happen at an accelerated pace. Chapultepec looked bare and dismantled, for its furnishings had been stored and most of Carlota's dainty bric-à-brac was gone. Maximilian shunned the castle and accepted instead the hospitality of a Swiss immigrant who owned an estate on the outskirts of the city. Here, on the Hacienda de la Teja, he took stock of his financial and military resources. Money being scarce, the first of these points was quickly dismissed as negligible. But the second had possibilities. As yet the Emperor could count on his four loyal *M*'s, the Mexican generals Miguel Miramón (former president), Leonardo Márquez, Ramón Méndez and the Indian Tomás Mejía. Each of these had a variable following of his own.

Among the Europeans who placed their swords and pocketbooks at Maximilian's disposal were Colonel Prince von Khevenhüller with his regiment of hussars, Lieutenant-Colonel Baron Hammerstein with an infantry corps, and Count Edmund Wyckenburg with the Austrian *Jäger* (mounted police). In addition there were stray detachments of French volunteers who disapproved of Bazaine's conduct and had banded together in support of the Empire. Altogether the survey disclosed that Maximilian had at his command a total of sixteen thousand men. The constantly increasing Juarista forces amounted to sixty thousand.

Geographically, the Emperor was at a still greater disadvantage. Aided by American capital as well as freebooters who drifted across the Río Grande, Juárez had conquered the entire north of Mexico down to San Luis Potosí. In the latter city he established his headquarters. This left Maximilian in control of only four strategic spots, Mexico City, Puebla, Vera Cruz and Querétaro—virtually the same narrow sector he had found when first he arrived in the country.

On realizing what odds were against him the Emperor saw also the futility of aggression on his part. He decided to end the uneven contest by offering Juárez a truce. He proposed interrupting hostilities long enough for a special election to take place throughout the nation. If, he averred, the Mexican people voted in favor of a republican administration there remained no excuse for further bloodshed. Automatically the imperial government would accept this judgment and dissolve, while he, Maximilian, returned in dignity to his former home across the seas. But if, on the other hand, Mexico longed for the Empire, the Juaristas ought to make the best of it. The Emperor would honor his foes by admitting their leaders to a congress. In this manner the monarchist principle would blend with liberalism in its ideal sense, and the patriot Juárez would still have a hand in the management of his country.

Needless to say, the offer was received with a sneer. Benito Juárez seized the messenger, Antonio García, as an easy hostage and, for the rest, announced that Mexico's ills must be cured "by the sword, and only by the sword." To back up his words he ordered his men to march on Querétaro, the Empire's weakest citadel.

This action forced Maximilian's unwilling hand. If the war would be fought to a finish it was high time for him to lay out a plan of campaign. First of all the imperialist camp had better move to Querétaro and prepare for an attack. Next, it was necessary to quell small rivalries which sprang up among his native generals, each of whom wished to be commander-in-chief of something. To eliminate friction, Maximilian appointed Márquez chief of staff, while Miramón was given sole power over the infantry, Mejía the cavalry, and Méndez the raw levies. Lest any one of the good *M*'s be tempted to lord it over the other the Emperor himself assumed the supreme command of all troops.

To avoid resentments on another score it was also decided that the foreign regiments were to remain behind in Mexico City during Maximilian's absence, in order to prove that the monarch had the fullest confidence in the mettle of his Mexicans. This was an unfortunate choice. Even if the capital were to need an armed defense, Querétaro was at the moment in far greater danger, and the hour hardly called for a *beau geste*. Since he was already outnumbered by the foe, Maximilian could not now afford to split his forces. Besides, in cutting himself off from the Europeans he relinquished an advantage of which, to date, he had made little use. If they did not shine in guerrilla tussles, the foreign troops were nevertheless thoroughly conversant with the technique of defending a city under siege; Querétaro was their big chance to show what superior generalship and a knowledge of tactics could accomplish. Without eclipsing the personal virtues of the *M*'s, Khevenhüller and Hammerstein were highly specialized strategists, and strategy—if anything—was the Emperor's last gamble. But he did not take it.

Juárez, meanwhile, lost no time in organizing his motley columns. He marshaled his best generals, Mariano Escobedo, Porfirio Díaz, Corona Régules and Vicente Riva Palacio, to close in from the north, south, southwest and west, respectively. To all appearances the four men were heading straight for Querétaro. But one of them, Porfirio Díaz, had his eye on Puebla and Mexico City. As soon as Maximilian evacuated the capital the Indian from Oaxaca planned to fall upon both those garrisons, blocking the Emperor's retreat.

On February 10, 1867, a vanguard of cheering royalists loaded the Empire in its wagons and departed. Maximilian was to follow within forty-eight hours, convoyed by fifteen hundred fusiliers and eighteen cannon. But at the appointed time the usual hitch occurred; the treasury lacked money sufficient for one week's provisions. It became necessary to trade the imperial silverware (which had not yet been shipped to Europe) for comestibles and cash. This was done after some difficulty and at last, on the morning of the thirteenth, the nervous monarch was able to set out. As the caravan started over the causeway toward Tlalnepantla and Lechería, the Emperor's secretary Blasio (recently returned from Europe) became aware of a poignant coincidence. Carlota had sailed from Mexico on the thirteenth day of the month, and her pilgrimage ended in failure. Did better luck await them now? He confided vague tremors to Basch, the only foreigner who—since he was not a military man—trudged quietly beside him.

Querétaro, then a town of thirty thousand souls, lies one hundred and sixty-seven miles north of Mexico City in a valley fringed by low hills. Its original name was Taxco—a Tarascan Indian word meaning ball-court. In the days of the Conquest the Castilian Don Fernando de Tapia had advanced upon this Taxco with a band of mail-clad *caballeros*. The Otomí chieftain who ruled over the region had already learned that Indian bows and arrows were of no avail against the strange garb of the white men. He therefore proposed a fist-fight, pointing out that any other method of snatching his estates was unfair. The Spaniards—always susceptible to good oratory—agreed. They put down their armor and, on the morning of July 25, 1531, the boxing match began. Thousands of Spaniards on the one hand, and hordes of furious Indians on the other, waged what was perhaps the greatest battle of fisticuffs on record. It lasted till sundown. The white men won, whereupon the Indians, proving themselves good losers, spent the night dancing in honor of their new sovereign—Charles V—in distant Madrid.

That sovereign's descendant, the Emperor Maximilian, now traversed this very territory in forced marches. It required almost six days to cover the short distance from the capital, due to constant skirmishes with Juarista outposts. At every turn in the road there seemed to be terrorists lying in wait for the imperial party, so that literally every one, including the Emperor, was forced to keep a hand on the trigger of his gun throughout the journey.

It was during one of these encounters that Maximilian discovered a personal friend among his dusky followers. Prince Felix zu Salm-Salm, a former German officer who had served as a colonel in the American Civil War, had managed to continue his adventurous career in Mexico, where he passionately embraced the imperialist cause. Despite Maximilian's order that no Europeans were to join him at Querétaro the youngish aristocrat had attached himself to the rear of the column. In a moment of danger he had reached the Emperor's side. Crouching in the dust with Maximilian, while both held their muskets in readiness, the prince had suddenly whispered something in German.

"*Majestät sind nicht allein.* [Your Majesty is not alone]."

The Emperor, disconcerted at first, threatened to leave the disobedient fellow behind. But in reality he was delighted to unburden his misgivings to a soldier who spoke his own tongue. He pressed Salm's shoulder and was about to thank him when a bulky figure rolled between them. Under a crushed French *képi* they discovered the red grinning face of Doctor Basch.

"Zum Teufel nochmal——" said Maximilian. ("What the devil——")

"Querétaro won't be so bad, your Majesty," answered Basch, kicking at the mud on his boot, "Khevenhüller will bring the hussars *sobald die Sache ernst wird* [as soon as things get serious]."

Things were serious now. Desperately serious. But the three who had chosen the dirt road to Querétaro talked one another into a swaggering nonchalance. Between random tiffs with ambushed Juaristas the Emperor drew from his pocket a letter from his mother, the Archduchess Sophie. It was dated January 9, 1867, and reported a rumor current in Europe concerning the Empress Carlota's illness.

According to this, the French Government had spread the story that Carlota had lost her reason, in order to alarm Maximilian and cause him to abdicate. The Hofburg, apparently not in touch with Professor Riedel, fumed at this new perfidy on the part of Napoleon.

> "We absolutely sanction your decision to remain in Mexico [wrote the aged Sophie] despite your natural urge to join Charlotte. Remember that one must shun any suspicion of having been driven out by intrigue. Gustaf von Sachsen-Weimar came to dinner yesterday, and when I greeted him he exclaimed with an earnestness which touched me : 'I confess to your Imperial Highness that I find Kaiser Max quite splendid. It is my firm conviction that he will hold his ground. In fact, my friends have started betting on it, and I am wagering a neat sum that he will still be in Mexico at the end of May.' "

The letter went on with a description of the holidays spent in the family circle:

"On December twenty-sixth Papa and I had our four grandchildren and their parents over to see the Christmas tree. Gisela and Rudolf adore spending Christmas with their small cousins of whom they are both enormously fond; they were all very sweet and showed one another the toys they had brought along from their own trees. The Emperor, who can be so charming with small children, stuffed fat Otto into a Dutch sled and pulled him all over the place, after which Rudolf got a chance to give the others a ride. But Franzi [the three-year-old Archduke Franz Ferdinand, one day to be assassinated at Sarajevo] picked himself the better part; he climbed up on the sofa and settled down beside your sister-in-law, Sisi, with whom he babbled at great length. Beauty seems to be a magnet attracting small boys no less than grown men, whereas little girls, I notice, show more indifference toward it.... On the Sunday following, the Emperor and Karl brought their children again for luncheon, and just as we were sitting down the big clock struck—the one in the hall, with your works from Olmütz. It seemed for a moment as though your voice, and not the chime, sounded among us from afar. Tears welled up in my eyes. The Emperor saw them, I believe, and must have known the cause, for he quickly turned the other way and engaged somebody in conversation. . . . Yet despite my own weakness, I hope you will maintain yourself in Mexico as long as this is compatible with your honor. Farewell, my Maxl. We all embrace you and from the depths of our hearts wish you luck in the New Year. MAMA."

Banal words, exchanged so indiscriminately the world over. Yet they filled Maximilian's being with a glow. For his soul was far away, and his eyes beheld that Viennese gathering instead of the blue hills that encircled the trap of Querétaro which was slowly coming into view.

Chapter 3

THEY entered the town on February nineteenth. The advance troops, numbering about nine thousand, welcomed the Emperor with jubilation and offered him his choice of the four highest hillocks that overlooked the citadel. One might make a bivouac on the Sangremal, the Cerro de las Campanas, the Cerro de la Cruz, or San Gregorio.

While Maximilian studied the topography preparatory to making a selection, the Juarista General Escobedo conferred with his spies. Now was the moment to strike. From opposite ends the rebel bands began to close in, seizing one bank of the swift Querétaro River and blocking the main highway. By the time the imperialists had picked a satisfactory mountain view they found themselves confronted with a cordon of enemy rangers, leering savagely and spitting fire from good Gringo guns.

Hurriedly the Emperor descended, surrendering the panorama for the more protected confines of the Convento de la Cruz. Here, in an abandoned monastic garden, a council of war was held. The generals and Salm proposed an immediate sortie, forcing a battle before additional rebel troops arrived. The Emperor's physician, Samuel Basch, believed in remedies rather than risks.

"The hussars, your Majesty," he said significantly.

Maximilian brightened. Of course, there lay the solution. By leaving the foreign regiments behind him he had given proof of his faith in the brave Mexican *M*'s. But now, seeing themselves overwhelmingly outnumbered, Miramón, Mejía, Méndez and Márquez would not object to a little assistance. It was immediately decided to dispatch several messengers to Mexico City for aid. Late at night the imperial scouts were sent through the enemy lines.

For a few days a vast stillness hung over the conventual headquarters of the Emperor. Every one hoped the Juaristas would not attack. A week passed so quietly that at last curiosity drove the imperalists from their retreat. They trudged up-hill once more to survey the terrain. Yes, the cordon of leering faces was still there and, as the Hapsburg epaulettes came into view, the crack of muskets cut the air. It was identically the same scene witnessed a short while ago, except for those lifeless figures which hung by the feet from a lasso. They were strung up on trees, at intervals, all around the besieged town. Their skulls were shattered. It was easy to see that not a single messenger had reached the hussars in Mexico City.

Now Prince Felix could no longer control himself. One did not stand by in idleness, allowing the Emperor's person to be fired upon. Besides, here was the opportunity to make a surprise attack, before the encamped rebels could scramble for their cannon. He cried out a signal. Bugles sounded over the hills and the imperial columns descended upon the Escobedo flank with drawn bayonets. So sudden was their onslaught that the Juarista general and his astonished cohorts took to their heels with heavy losses. At the close of the skirmish Salm found himself credited with a personal triumph, for he had dragged back, single-handed, a pair of enemy artillery pieces. His prowess was offset, however, by Corona's capture of the San Gregorio ridge where, despite Escobedo's defeat, the insurgents were able to hold their positions.

One thing had been gained by Salm's burst of temper; the road to the capital lay open. After duly appraising this fact it was decided in the imperial camp that General Márquez must go back to Mexico City. Maximilian wrote a note to Father Fischer at Chapultepec, explaining that the general would replace the foreign commanders who, in turn, were to hasten to Querétaro as soon as possible. Besides this, Márquez would keep an eye on the *alten Weiber* "old women" (the Emperor's ministers), who doubtless were up to some mischief after being without supervision for so long.

> "It is of course possible [the letter continued] that Mexico City may also be attacked. But in this event, since there is such a reduced garrison, I instructed Márquez to take care of you and the two palace guards, Karl Schaffer and Rudolf Günner. He assures me that he will place you with himself in the center of his troops."

After accounting thus for the longevity of generals, the Emperor asked whether any of his personal belongings had been forgotten at Chapultepec. If so, the Austrian or the British Legation was to take charge of them. This referred in particular to the library which Maximilian prized. However, should there be the slightest chance for Fischer to slip into Querétaro, nothing would be more welcome than "something to read, my field glasses, some sheet music and the burgundy."

> "God be with you [closed this very civilized epistle]. Despite all manner of tribulations, we manage to keep up our spirits. What worries me most is the conduct of those feeble old wigs in the capital, who are probably engaged in open treason out of sheer funk and inanity. . . . But let us hope that we may meet again in happier circumstances."

Maximilian spoke English with some fluency and generally used this language when corresponding with Fischer.

As for the accusation of treason, the Emperor pointed especially to his Minister of Finance, who withheld certain funds accruing through the civil lists. Supplies and ammunition were running low at Querétaro, yet no convoy with new provisions from Mexico City loomed in sight, although orders had been given for several such convoys to follow the imperial caravan.

Surrounded by a mounted escort, Márquez was able to make his sortie during the night of March twenty-third. He rode at full gallop toward the capital, when frightened villagers along the way warned him that Porfirio Díaz had reached the gates of Puebla. Entering Mexico City on the twenty-seventh, Márquez communicated at once with Khevenhüller and Kodolitch, who set out with him for the City of the Angels. It was too late. La Puebla de los Ángeles capitulated on April fourth, the imperialist General Noriega (who defended the citadel) having had no hint that help was on the way. As the Hungarian cavalry thundered into view, a tattered white flag was waving from the tiled dome of the cathedral and Porfirio Díaz, in full possession of the town, was making ready for his march on Mexico City.

Knowing well that the banner of truce had not been raised in their behalf, the imperialists hastened to retrace their steps. Márquez, leading a detachment of artillery, turned back on the main road while the cavalry scattered through open fields. But they had been sighted from the flat roofs of Puebla and the chase was on. Pressing his tired men relentlessly forward, Díaz caught up with Márquez on April tenth. A frantic skirmish ensued, during which the panic-stricken gunners cut their horses' traces, leaving cannon and commander to their respective fates. The road to Chapultepec was clear, and Díaz lost no time in following it.

Maximilian waited at Querétaro. Soon after the departure of Márquez fresh reenforcements had bolstered up the rebel ranks so that the town was again surrounded, this time by a human wall forty thousand strong. The water supply had been cut off and, lest the besieged forces (which had dwindled to four thousand) make use of the river, the corpses from the battle-fields were sent floating down-stream. Food was becoming so scarce that the Emperor himself submitted to a limited daily ration, doled out by the nuns of a neighboring convent. Bread had to be baked by these pious sisters from the flour destined for the Host. Broiled mule and horse meat became a coveted luxury.

In a measure corresponding to their growing hardships, grave signs of disintegration now appeared among the soldiery. At first it was possible to stem the tide of discontent by granting decorations and honorary titles to hungry men who demanded their pay; barefoot Knights of Guadalupe and an assortment of dukes in sandals or rough ponchos abounded in the inner citadel. But Maximilian could not hand out baronetcies indefinitely. The democratic prodigality with which he distributed privileges soon palled, for men do not enjoy being equal. With titles available for the asking, the premium on beans and corn meal grew. Soon there were outbreaks of mutiny. Ringleaders had to be arrested and punished, although Maximilian permitted no court martial.

Since the long siege kept artisans and farmers from their work the suffering became general. The sight of innocent townspeople sharing his own misery caused the Emperor particular distress.

He appeared daily among them, his cheeks brightly tinted by the fever, his eyes hollow from the ravages of dysentery. Patiently they listened to his words which, with the coming of each dawn, assumed ever new guises of assurance.

"To-morrow, at the latest, the hussars will be here."

Women sat idly in the plaza. There was no maize to grind on stone *metates,* and clothes could not be washed on the sunny banks of a river that bore the dead. With their brood of little ones clustered about them they sat in that deep meditative stupor so characteristic of the race. *El indio triste* (the sad Indian)—thus the soul of a people had long been epitomized. For Aztec sadness is the Greek melancholia, a strong and pensive gloom. . . .

Late in April the news arrived that Puebla was lost and Márquez had been beaten. A charcoal pedler who had come over the mountains on foot and crept miraculously through the enemy lines brought a detailed report from the capital. He carried, concealed in the peaked recess of his hat, two sticky bits of paper. One of these, almost illegible from much handling, listed the names of twelve French officers who had deserted the imperial cause by offering their services to the Liberals. Their proposals were refused by Porfirio Díaz as well as Mariano Escobedo with the scathing words: "The struggle can be fought out by ourselves without accepting services of people who in the face of their suffering comrades can make such an infamous offer."

On the second slip of paper Maximilian read a stirring protestation of loyalty from the remaining French volunteers, many of whom fell before Puebla. The text ran as follows:

> "Since those officers (who throughout the siege offered no help) are French, and since your Majesty might believe that they justly interpret our sentiments, we hasten, Sire, to reject all participation in this unspeakable act, which has aroused our indignation."

Many signatures honored this document which Maximilian placed in his breast pocket, murmuring: "I can only say that the Foreign Legion has been heroic."

The list containing the names of the deserters was burned over a sputtering tallow candle. Porfirio Díaz alone kept a record of these gentlemen, two of whom were of decidedly Teutonic origin. Their names survived, properly catalogued as to rank:

Capitaine Ernest de Rozeville
Capitaine Charles Schmidt
Capitaine Henri Morel
Capitaine Xavier Gaulfrèrons
Lieutenant Jean Ricot
Lieutenant Félix Kieffers
Lieutenant Émile Tronin
Lieutenant Théodore Héraud
Lieutenant Émile Péjun
Lieutenant Victor Nomel
Lieutenant Paul Guyon
Sous-lieutenant (Ensign) Eugène Bailly

While countless sons of France bled unsung for the dying Empire, these twelve drifted safely down to Vera Cruz, where they were lucky enough to catch a boat. Favored by benevolent winds, they were wafted back to a world of comfort and—to doubtful immortality.

At Querétaro puzzled Indians continued to shamble about the main square, but Maximilian no longer talked to them. He locked himself up these days with a young colonel, Don Miguel López, who offered the Emperor some advice.

López was a striking example of a certain Hispano-American type. He was handsome, polished, vain and passionately fond of life. During the early days after Maximilian's arrival on Mexican shores, López had escorted the imperial caravan over the mountain wilderness that led to the capital. Prancing on his mount beside the Empress's carriage window, he had done his utmost to display all the dash of his horsemanship for Carlota's particular delectation. They installed him as an ornament at Chapultepec.

But the days of pomp and glory had vanished, and López followed Maximilian to Querétaro. He did this, not because of any strong political convictions, but because he was a born courtier.

Nothing made him happier than to spin about the sovereign and sun himself in the royal presence.

Still, a fly swam in his ointment. López did not want to die, and the siege of Querétaro was beginning to look like a race with death. The dapper officer began to reconsider his position; everybody's position. He rationalized. In the end he arrived at a shocking but perfectly sensible conclusion. Seeking a private interview with Maximilian, he expressed himself vigorously on several issues which did not strictly pertain to a courtier's province. The present deadlock, López opined, was both hopeless and absurd. Further resistance would neither restore the Empire nor save a town already stalked by starvation and plague.

"And what do you propose for me to do?" asked the monarch in despair.

"I think," said López quickly, "that I would negotiate with the enemy."

Maximilian was taken aback. "But my honor as a Hapsburg and a sovereign—have you thought of that?"

"Life is very precious," López sighed, "and there are several thousand families in this city who do not understand about your Majesty's honor."

As usual, Maximilian was able to see the other side of every argument. Throughout his life he seemed to be dogged by this chameleon-like faculty of sympathizing with the other fellow's point of view. He admitted to himself at this moment that the inhabitants of Querétaro could not be expected to perish for the sake of his own dynastic pride.

"Negotiate," he said abruptly. And then, after a pause: "I demand certain terms, however. Let all my men be spared. I alone will answer to Juárez."

López bowed and departed. That night the Emperor communicated his decision to Salm and the generals. A stony silence met his first words. The *M*'s and Prince Felix were soldiers to the core; no language had as yet been invented wherein they could be told that surrender was not always cowardice.

"Your Majesty," Salm exclaimed, "will be taken prisoner. There can be no greater shame for a man who has held a scepter."

"Perhaps," said Maximilian, "I am not so sure of that——"

General Méndez, who had meanwhile recovered his breath, broke into the conversation. Like Salm, he felt certain that the Emperor would not escape capture. And furthermore, knowing the cold hatred of Benito Juárez toward all Mexicans who supported the Austrian, he foresaw only disaster to himself and the entire garrison if a compromise were effected.

"López will go to Escobedo to-morrow," Maximilian announced quietly.

At this the generals grew a trifle hectic. They held a council of war and determined to attempt a sally on the following day, April twenty-seventh. In the opinion of Méndez a concerted effort directed against one single spot in the surrounding enemy line would produce the necessary break through which the Emperor and his forces could retreat to Mexico City. With Puebla already in the hands of the Liberals, the defense of Querétaro had lost its meaning, since Maximilian had hastened north with only one purpose in mind—to keep the rebels from marching on his two most important cities. The fact that the Empire would stew for months in the bowl of Querétaro, while a gigantic Juarista flank stormed even Chapultepec, could not have been foreseen.

At any rate, on the morning of April twenty-seventh General Ramón Méndez enjoyed that superlative moment in a field-marshal's life, when the pin-pricks he has made on a paper chart the night before become the hazards over which his strategy will guide the Fates. The sortie worked splendidly up to a certain point. An advance patrol, with Méndez at the head, bored sedulously through the beleaguering wall. A great opening appeared, inviting further progress. And then the vast, cavernous maw closed as abruptly as it had opened. The little vanguard crumbled within those jaws. It was the last of Ramón Méndez.

Maximilian blanched at the news. His hopes fastened now on López, who had vanished during the night. If the young officer had got through to Escobedo—which, in view of his ingratiating person, seemed likely—all was not lost.

A week went by. López did not appear. It was May and the sun beating down on the stricken citadel brought new horrors

Swarms of flies rose with a deafening hum from stinking carcasses and the mounds of putrefaction that dotted the baked earth. Beating his head with pale feverish hands the Hapsburg prince paced madly along the convent parapet. Was this the reward of his dreams? This nightmare? Strange noises filled the darkness, and in distant adobe hovels there was the crackle of sacrificial fires. His imagination fought against the specters that haunted every waking hour. (Sleep had long ago become impossible, except in fitful spells of exhaustion.) He wondered what made the people of the town so quiet. Why hadn't they come and torn him to pieces for bringing upon them this Golgotha, this Hell? . . . He wondered what kept them so resigned, what kept them fed. . . . Those fires. Had this Aztec race gone back to ancient tribal rites? There was a dish—*tamali*—known in a dim historic past to have been made of infant flesh. . . . Oh, but he must be very ill to think such hideous ghoulish thoughts.

"Basch!"

"Yes, your Majesty."

"López is on his way. He has surely seen Escobedo by now."

"Yes, your Majesty."

"He thinks we shall get out of this all right. I am already looking forward to Miramar, where Carla will help me write a history of Mexico. King Leopold left us some money, you know, so we shall have leisure. And time to travel, of course, to the Grecian Islands, Naples, Turkey——"

"Of course, your Majesty."

"It's quite splendid, isn't it, Basch?"

"Quite, your Majesty."

The doctor's sturdy arm reached out to steady the monarch, whose entrails were wrenched in spasms of pain. Maximilian, the tallest of the Austrian Archdukes, leaned helplessly on the pudgy little frame of his court physician.

In distant gray adobe huts the murky fires burned low. A cloud of smudge spread upward against the dawn.

CHAPTER 4

COLONEL LÓPEZ confronted Escobedo at midnight on May eleventh, two weeks after the strategy of Méndez had terminated in disaster. The spruce young cavalier plunged into his perilous exploit with the agility of an eel. Waving a handkerchief which was not so exquisite as its fastidious owner would have wished it to be, Miguel stepped one day into a dugout occupied by the Juarista colonel, José Rincón-Gallardo. From then on he had to think fast.

It so happened that two Rincón-Gallardos formerly functioned at Chapultepec as ladies-in-waiting. López now hoped to establish a blood relationship between the enemy officer and the Señoras before a bullet got to him. He talked fast and volubly the while he slid down the embankment and into the foe's presence. As it happened, Rincón-Gallardo did belong to the same family as Doña Rosita and Doña Luisa, and there was no end to the questions he asked about his aristocratic kin. In fact, he strutted a little before his men at this opportunity to reveal his fine connections.

López was progressing famously when the menacing figure of General Francisco Arce, later Governor of Guerrero Bravo, approached. With practically no ceremony, the imperialist officer now felt himself seized by a coat-sleeve and led into the tent of the rebel commander, Mariano Escobedo.

General Escobedo, a former *arriero,* or mule-team driver, on the post roads to the Gulf, looked up sullenly. López saw at once that there was absolutely no small talk with which to beguile this warrior. He became subdued and pleaded now in moving words for the safety of his imperial master.

Escobedo listened in silence. He then asked a few questions in regard to conditions in the besieged town. López painted a dreary picture. When he had finished, Escobedo was perfectly oriented If matters were as bad as this, the general reflected, one could obtain a surrender on one's own terms. In fact, under the guise of offering a truce one might effect a decisive victory. López was jovially clapped on the back and told to remove the guards stationed about the convent of La Cruz, so that the Liberals might enter Querétaro by night.

"The guards at La Cruz?" López stammered. "They are the Emperor's lancers! I did not offer to surrender his Majesty's person—only the town, and that without sacrifice of lives."

Escobedo remained cool. "If you are not helpful we shall keep you here. With the information you have given us Querétaro will be ours in a day."

There was a boyish quiver on the face of López as he cried out in anguish: "What will you do to him? The Emperor is an innocent man!"

Escobedo nodded. "That is true, and I doubt that Señor Juárez will want to assume the responsibility for his death. So you see, on that score you need not worry."

López turned the ambiguous words over in his mind. It was reasonable to suppose that the Liberals might be embarrassed by a captive monarch on their hands. Surely this was Escobedo's meaning.

"There is a chance for the Emperor's escape?" he asked timidly.

Escobedo nodded again. "Perhaps, my friend. And there is also a purse of two thousand ounces in gold for him who removes the guards from La Cruz."

Colonel Miguel López was dismissed.

He returned to Querétaro and spent two days groping about as if in a dream. The miserable hovel where he kept himself in hiding was no more dismal than the dark cavern of his own conscience. Two thousand ounces in gold. And the Emperor would be quite safe. Would he? Certainly, Escobedo had said so. That was a lot of money, too. Miguel could go to Paris and lead the life of a great Don Juan—surely his little wife would let him go to Paris if he showed her all that gold. She loved him and always wanted him to do as he pleased. He had a way with women, her Miguel.

While he remained thus concealed from his comrades, things

were afoot in the citadel. Prince Salm-Salm, Miramón and Mejía were planning the ultimate coup which must bring them either victory or doom. A scheme was devised whereby the entire garrison would engage in action on one enemy front while at the opposite end of town the Emperor, in company of Doctor Basch, Secretary Blasio, and a few others, was to attempt an escape. As yet no definite conclusion had been reached, however, because Maximilian did not find it compatible with his honor to flee. Besides, every one would recognize his blond beard. Basch suggested a shave. But the imperial dignity would not bend to Thespian subterfuge. In an age when only mimes and balletmasters exposed their complexions, a prince must not be caught without his manly foil.

Before the argument progressed very far, López emerged from his cache and made contact with the Emperor, who received the officer in private. Carefully picking his words, López reported Escobedo's acceptance of the surrender, while, with rather less clarity, he glossed over the details concerning Maximilian's immunity and that of the garrison.

On hearing the young man's recital the Emperor was touched by so much pluck and devotion. Then and there, he sifted his own insignia and decorated López with the medal for valor. Blushing to the roots of his hair, the officer came to a rigid salute.

"If for any reason something goes wrong," Maximilian was musing, with a sober glance into the black night, "and they take me captive, I expect you—Miguel—to spare me this disgrace by sending a bullet through me."

Again López was dismissed.

He ran down a narrow corridor, confused and shaken. The Emperor's badge seemed to claw at his heart, but Miguel could pay no heed. There was no turning back, once the wheels of destiny were set in motion.

A guardsman answering to the incongruous name of Jablonski brushed past him. Jablonski was crooked and Miguel hated him, but now, as if driven forward by some demon, he took this man into his confidence. Together they moved ammunition cases out of sight and lured the sentinels from their posts. No one offered any opposition, for most of the men were too starved and listless to question orders. Several fell asleep in their tracks. But López, having completed his preparations, started out for the second time to the enemy camp.

Maximilian threw himself on his cot at one o'clock and tossed about in fitful slumber. At two-thirty he was seized with an attack of colic which caused him to cry out for Doctor Basch. The latter administered an opiate and remained at the Emperor's side almost a full hour before Maximilian found rest.

Shortly before dawn, gray shadows began to creep over the nearest hillock. Led by Miguel López, before whose uniform the imperial outposts were accustomed to present arms, two Juarista officers entered the citadel. They were General Vélez and Colonel Rincón-Gallardo who commanded the terrible *Supremos Poderes,* the enemy's shock troops, which to-day moved silently along without being challenged by a single shot.

To the very convent gates they advanced, when López parted from his sinister guests, for he must now change his rôle from that of accomplice to surprised victim. Yelling at the top of his healthy lungs, he tore through the hushed passages, spreading the alarm:

"Save the Emperor! The rebels are here in La Cruz!"

This was the cue for Jablonski to bolt from door to door, rousing Prince Salm-Salm, Doctor Basch and Secretary Blasio, all of whom rushed to Maximilian's side. Looking haggard from his wretched battle with insomnia, the Emperor was already dressed and in the act of buckling his saber. In a few minutes he would be ready to go down-stairs.

On the ground floor a handful of ruffians had begun to raise a tumult. As the Emperor and his companions descended, the disorder grew, and several troopers were about to lay hands on the monarch, when the voice of Colonel Rincón-Gallardo was heard bellowing above the uproar:

"Give them passage! They are *ciudadanos* [citizens]——"

With these words Escobedo's equivocal pledge concerning the sovereign's safe-conduct was redeemed in public. By all the laws of common sense Maximilian should now have made a dash for freedom, since the invaders were strenuously trying to ignore his person. But some one whispered the news that Miramón, coming to the Emperor's rescue, had been shot in the face and lay agonizing in a neighbor's courtyard. Mejía, the faithful Indian, waited on the Hill of the Bells with a remnant of straggling imperialists. . . . Something in Maximilian's make-up barred the dictates of common sense. He went first to the house where Miramón grappled with death. After that he climbed the Cerro de las Campanas and joined the dusky-faced Mejía. In doing this the Emperor sealed his own fate, for he knew that none of his Mexican followers could hope to escape.

The town, meanwhile, awoke to a frenzy of hysteria which had quickly communicated itself to Querétaro's docile citizenry. After weeks of terror and suspense, any change brought relief to pent-up emotions; a cheering populace now filled the streets, hailing the Liberal army. Bell ropes were pulled in the atrium of every church, while small urchins chirped the scurrilous rebel song attributed to Vicente Riva Palacio's muse:

"La nave va en los mares
Volando cual pelota. . . .
Adios mamá Carlota,
Adios mi tierno amor!"

("While bouncing o'er the ocean
The ship rocks like a pellet. . . .
Good-by, mama Carlota,
Good-by, my tender love!")

From the heights Maximilian could hear the rabble, and slow tears glazed his eyes. In the distance Juarista hordes, drunk with easy victory, were surging toward the foot of the knoll.

According to Blasio's diary, the Emperor inquired if it were possible to break through the blockade, whereupon Mejía, steeped in fidelity and utter consecration to a cause, answered with sublime disdain:

"Sire, to pass is impossible; but for your Majesty we shall try it. As regards my own person, I am here to die."

At this, Maximilian was unaccountably thrilled. He turned to the prince.

"Salm," he said, *"nun eine glückliche Kugel* [now for a lucky bullet]."

The tumult below had risen to a crescendo, but on high the Emperor stood motionless like a Viking, resting both hands on his sword. He was calm now. He could think of nothing more to do.

The finish, whatever it might be, was welcome.

There seemed to be no lucky bullet. The rebels, despite their wild uproar, were awed by that small group standing above them so quietly, so ready to be mowed down. It was no fun to shoot. Quite abruptly the firing stopped, followed by muddled indecision on the part of every one.

A faint smile flitted across Maximilian's face as he continued to wait. At last, a martial figure could be seen stamping up-hill with a squad of infantry. On reaching the top, the leader stopped for breath before advancing toward the Emperor. He paused, searching his memory for a helpful precedent. Finding none, he announced somewhat artlessly:

"I am General Echegaray."

"Yes?" Maximilian bowed politely.

"I am General Echegaray," said General Echegaray again, "and your Majesty is—er—my prisoner."

There was a sudden commotion as the Emperor's companions brandished their blades, but Maximilian checked them.

"Stop," he ordered curtly, "I do not wish it!"

He then mounted his Arab charger and rode down to the dusty clearing where General Escobedo and his staff awaited him. Jumping to the ground, he released his sword and handed it to the rebel chieftain who, visibly disconcerted, passed it on to a bystander, Lieutenant-Colonel Platón Sánchez.

As yet, not a word had been spoken. But now, remembering his fellow-prisoners, the monarch addressed Escobedo in halting Spanish.

"The officers of my following," he pleaded, "are guilty of nothing save their loyalty to me. I ask that they be spared all harm. If a sacrifice is needed, let the victim be myself; and may my blood be the last that will be spilled in this land."

He also begged for leniency toward his servants in the capital, and suggested that Salm, the doctor and all foreign officers be permitted to set sail for Europe. Escobedo replied evasively that Juárez must be consulted in all such matters and that the Emperor had best return to La Cruz until the necessary information arrived. The captives were assigned to Echegaray, who led them back to the convent through devious byways, for he wanted to save Maximilian from the jeers of the mob. This kindly impulse struck a response in the Hapsburg's breast. Upon arriving at La Cruz Maximilian leaped from his horse. He stood for a while rubbing the animal's nose. Then he turned quickly about and presented the lovely creature to his captor.

It was morning. A blazing sun ruled the heavens as the Emperor dropped heavily upon his bed. Throughout that day a never-ending stream of soldiery pressed through the passages. They came to take a look at this fallen giant who had resisted them in a siege lasting seventy-one days. But that was not all. They were souvenir hunters. At the close of their stampede the prisoner was bereft of all save the clothes on his body.

To prevent further pillage Maximilian asked to be removed elsewhere. A place was found for him in an abandoned convent of Discalced Carmelites where for a time he remained sheltered from view. But he had no money, and the absence of fresh linen, soap and other toilet articles caused him acute mortification. Also, he was forced to beg Escobedo for food, since no one had remembered about this minor detail. The Carmelite kitchens were in a state of almost prehistoric demolition.

When the news of the Emperor's plight trickled through the town the citizens of Querétaro experienced a wave of pity. Already the outburst of hysteria with which they had welcomed the break of the deadlock had subsided and given way to the pangs of remorse. Whatever had made them behave so nefariously? The townspeople were heartily ashamed. They now plundered the mess tents of the Liberal army and carried away victuals for the neglected prisoner. Steaming dishes of *frijoles refritos, enchiladas,* baked sweet potatoes, and thick white *atole* were prepared by tearful housewives and hurried to the Emperor's cell by rueful Indian husbands who burned their fingers and stubbed bare toes as they ran. Maximilian removed the atrocious doilies of bobbin lace which covered each container, and searched for the least peppered dish. The remaining delicacies were distributed among his fellow-prisoners who, not being afflicted with dysentery, did full justice to the merits of each tidbit.

But not at their hearths alone were the ladies of Querétaro busy. They now plunged into the depths of cupboards and clothes presses for shreds of homespun cloth. They cut up white cotton breeches prized by their spouses, and stitched intimate apparel for an emperor. They chipped bright opal rock from the Sierra Gorda hills into flat disk shapes. These were rubbed to a smoothness and pierced—for buttons. Rivalry sprang up in cozy sewing circles where trembling fingers plied the needle. One sophisticated minx embroidered monograms and coronets.

"I have never in my life had so much underwear," said Maximilian.

Chapter 5

The Princess Agnes zu Salm-Salm had come to Mexico with her husband and a short-haired terrier named Jimmy.

She was a buxom matron who displayed reticence on two subjects, her age and her antecedents. If the former foible is shared by many members of her sex the latter represents something of a phenomenon. Even when she wrote memoirs (and Agnes was a born memoirist), she began the story of her life with the year in which she married the prince. It happened in Washington, at the close of the Civil War. It happened also at a juncture in their lives when both Felix and his bride could look back upon years of precarious struggle, he as a vagabond hero and she as a circus rider of some weight.

But the princess refused all assistance to prying souls who longed to sketch her background. Her diary, verbose to the point of redundance, sheds no light on the circumstance of her birth, origin or profession. It is the saga of blue blood, in an abstract—and, to Agnes, manifestly thrilling sense. It offers a rare example of middle-class effervescence over an aristocratic theme.

Only in recent years have biographers gleaned a few scraps of information, released (with an unconcern of which the princess herself would have been incapable) by the Salms of to-day. To the present titled house literature owes the knowledge that Princess Agnes was an American of French extraction, a kind woman and a skilful equestrienne. Her diary admits that she was pretty.

Before her marriage she had used the name Agnes Leclercq and traveled with the "big top." After her marriage she roamed over the world with her rakish husband in search of adventure. They found it with Maximilian in Mexico.

Salm had brought credentials and letters of introduction from the Austrian Minister in Washington, Baron von Wydenbruck. According to all reports he had distinguished himself with the

Union armies in the north. Fighting was his *métier*. He loved it.

Maximilian was at first suspicious of this amiable scapegrace who had left Europe because of gambling debts. But before long Salm won the Emperor's affection and rose to the rank of aide-de-camp. He lived at Chapultepec and followed Maximilian everywhere.

The princess, meanwhile, skipped from one hotel to another in an endeavor to keep up with her husband and the sovereign. She settled now in Orizaba, now at Cuernavaca, and again back in Mexico City, always waiting for the moment when Maximilian would ask that she be presented to him. Circumstances had so far prevented the fulfilment of her wish. In the beginning Maximilian had not realized that his aide-de-camp was married. Also, the Salms had come to Mexico after the Empress's departure for France—and no ladies were received at the Castle of Chapultepec after that time. When, finally, Maximilian heard that there was a princess, that she spoke no Spanish and felt exceedingly lonely trekking from one strange town to the next, he offered to befriend her. It was arranged that Salm should bring his wife to a private reception on the evening of October 18, 1866. On the afternoon of that day a cable from Miramar brought the news of Carlota's illness. The reception did not take place.

There followed the Emperor's sudden decision to leave Mexico forever, his trip to Orizaba, and the return to La Teja. With no one left at Chapultepec save a few palace servants whom Maximilian did not want to discharge, the princess saw her goal receding into a problematical future. If ever she were to breathe *Hofluft* (the air of a royal Court), it would not be in Mexico. The Emperor's removal to Querétaro left no doubt about an impending climax. From her husband the princess had learned that everything was at stake.

She had never seen this Maximilian. But she had heard of him almost constantly ever since a day in late summer when she and the terrier Jimmy had been trawled up toward the Vale of Anáhuac in a ramshackle diligence. The enthusiastic Felix had painted so glowing a word picture of the noble Hapsburg that

Agnes, a most impressionable member of her sex, arrived in the Mexican capital tootling the same sentimental flute. She guarded in her rather athletic breast a lyric passion for the fair Emperor and, belonging to a generation that wallowed in superlatives, endowed him with a galaxy of virtues. With an adolescent schoolgirl abandon she pined for this paragon of her own imaginings and poured out on the pages of her journal the canonizing predicates which do him grave injustice. A charming and lovable man he was, but withal a very human person, enmeshed in the follies common to all mankind.

It was on the day Maximilian went to Querétaro that the princess began to take an active part in his fate. She had inspired her husband to disregard orders and follow the sovereign by means of any feasible ruse. After seeing Salm off (he was swathed in a huge muffler and an Indian poncho), she packed a small bag, lifted Jimmy into the post chaise, and set out briskly for San Luis Potosí and the headquarters of President Juárez.

Her journey was by no means easy. She was delayed, turned back, and twice frustrated in her attempts to see the Liberal war lord. Querétaro fell and still she had accomplished nothing. May fifteenth, the date of the capture, came as a crushing blow. "The very next morning," her notes report, "a gentleman called upon me. He told me that Querétaro had been sold to the Liberals for three thousand ounces by a certain López and a man from San Luis Potosí, named Jablonski, that the Emperor was a prisoner and my husband was wounded."

The news, inaccurate as regards the sum promised to López, stirred the princess to more daring efforts. She packed again and made for Querétaro, where without a tremor she forced herself into Escobedo's presence. This time her boldness bore fruit; she was allowed to visit the captives.

The great moment of her life had come. She was led into the cell where the Emperor lay ill on his cot. Maximilian rose to greet her. He bowed and kissed her hand. The heart of Agnes Salm quite melted.

In spite of the tender ministrations on the part of Querétaro burghers, she believed the imperial martyr shamefully neglected.

His comb and brushes, returned by contrite pilferers, lay on a bare rude table. The linen on his bed was coarse and gray. She hurried at once through the town, propelled by a feminine shopping urge; but her expedition netted little that the willing natives had not already given up.

Escobedo meanwhile had established himself on the near-by Hacienda de La Purísima where he agreed to receive Maximilian for a confidential talk. In company with the Salms the Emperor was driven in a surrey across the town to the meeting-place. Here, in a vast colonial hall supported by darkened beams, the monarch submitted a protocol which he had prepared during the days of his imprisonment. Pledging himself to abdicate officially, he asked again for the release of all foreign hostages who promised to leave Mexico at the earliest opportunity.

The news of this interview reached Juárez within the week and filled him with rage. By special courier General Escobedo was reproved for dealing so indulgently with his charges; stringent discipline would be exacted in future. Hereafter the townspeople were barred from further contact with the Emperor, and, in order to enforce this edict, it was decided to spirit the prisoners to another abandoned cloister known as *El Convento de las Capuchinas*. While a mason fortified the new cells, Maximilian was locked up temporarily in the monastery crypt. In this damp underground retreat, lined with sarcophagi, his Calvary began.

There were no more highly seasoned concoctions from the cuisines of Querétaro. The isolated monarch was put on coarse daily fare doled out by the Juarista army cook. This was especially galling to Tüdös, the Hungarian chef who had reigned over the kitchens of Chapultepec. Tüdös was not a prisoner; in fact, at Querétaro no one knew him. He had come from the capital as soon as the road lay open, and now he skirted the Capuchin convent, a frightened slinking figure, hoping to catch sight of his master. At times, when a tin pail expelling acrid vapors was carried past him, he shuddered. He could guess that the brew it contained made up the imperial menu.

Agnes Salm was not through fighting. She pursued Escobedo again. This time she pleaded with him—not for Maximilian's release, but for his removal from the death vault. The rebel general softened before her entreaties and, disregarding the command from San Luis Potosí, finally assembled all the prisoners in adjacent quarters on an upper floor of the building. But beyond this his mercy could not go, for it was clear that their doom approached. Each cell was equipped with a large crucifix and two silver candlesticks, an unmistakable warning that one must prepare for death.

In this, his latest abode, Maximilian lost all faith in the divine right of kings. The Empire of Mexico had shrunk to a floor-space twenty feet long by eighteen wide, with a spindling camp-bed for a throne.

From Mexico City, where the remnant of the imperialist forces still managed to hold Porfirio Díaz at bay, the news of Maximilian's capture was relayed to Europe. Great Britain, Belgium, France and Austria sent vehement appeals to Washington, urging President Andrew Johnson to take action and intercede with Juárez. As a result, Secretary Seward ordered the American Minister for Mexico, Mr. Lewis D. Campbell, to get in touch with the rebel authorities. The Envoy, appointed in May of the previous year, had never quite managed to present his credentials before either Maximilian or Juárez. Loath to step on bellicose territory, he had once got as far as the border town of Brownsville, where he had written a note: "The continued sickness of my daughter and other causes of a private and domestic nature render it very important in my judgment that I should make a short visit to my home." It was at his home, in New Orleans, that Mr. Campbell now learned of President Johnson's wishes. An interchange of telegrams ensued, for the Envoy wanted more explicit directions. If he must enter Mexico, could a battleship take him there? The White House replied that it could not. "Why not?" asked the official tartly, adding "Shall I go to the City of Mexico via Vera Cruz, or to San Luis Potosí via Monterrey?" Since he intended to do neither, the answer did not really matter.

But President Johnson was growing tired of the telegraphic duet. He curtly demanded obedience to orders. Thereat Mr. Campbell announced: "I have been confined to my room by a severe bilious attack. My physician says I can not go now without hazarding my life. . . ." And he tendered his resignation. Before the State Department could harass him for shirking his duty he had, however, dispatched a deputy, Mr. John White, to Foreign Minister Sebastián Lerdo de Tejada to fulfil the distasteful mission. White arrived in San Luis Potosí with the following statement in Campbell's writing:

> "To the Mexican Minister of Foreign Affairs:—My Government instructs me to make known to President Juárez its desire that, in case of the capture of Prince Maximilian and his supporters, they may receive the humane treatment accorded by civilized nations to prisoners of war."

Needless to say, Lerdo composed a polite reply stating that he would see what could be done. He promised nothing.

Princess Salm-Salm had meanwhile ferreted out an American lawyer, Mr. Frederic Hall, who longed to champion Maximilian's cause. Almost at once Hall arrived on the scene, armed with a tome of Henry Wheaton's *History of the Law of Nations,* wherewith he planned to confound the authorities at Querétaro. As he entered the Capuchin convent the diffident and professorial attorney noticed that, doubtless due to the extreme heat, the guards had relaxed their vigilance. The Emperor, the two generals and Prince Felix, whose left foot was bandaged, sat in the cool corridor playing dominoes. Hall introduced himself, whereupon Mejía immediately counted out a set of stones for him, while Salm and Miramón made room on the tiled floor between them. All smiled sheepishly.

"This is a stupid game, sir," said Maximilian, "but won't you join?"

Hall did. They played for an hour, talking the while of escape. The princess had money and she was bribing every turnkey in sight. Under cover of night the Emperor might flee in monk's clothing, hiding in the wilderness until the others could follow. But Maximilian shook his head. He had received word from Mexico City that the Prussian and Austrian Ministers, Baron von

Magnus and Baron von Lago, were engaging two eminent advocates for his defense. What a disgrace if on their arrival it were disclosed that the Emperor had taken to his heels. No, he preferred to stay.

The two lawyers, Mariano Riva Palacio (a cousin to the Juarista general) and Rafael Martínez de la Torre, reached Querétaro in June. Together with a local barrister, Jesús M. Vásquez, and the mouse-like but eager Mr. Hall, the gentlemen from the capital approached Escobedo, who made no bones about the fact that Maximilian faced a death verdict if his case came up for trial. At this it was decided that a committee must visit Juárez and beg for a pardon. The following diplomatic representatives agreed to plead in the Emperor's behalf: the Marqués de la Ribera (Spain), Monsieur Alphonse Dano (France), Baron von Magnus (Prussia), Monsieur Fréderic Hooricks (Belgium), Baron von Lago (Austria), Signor Francesco Curtopassi (Italy), and *Chargé d'Affaires* C. Middleton, who transacted the business of Great Britain during Sir Peter Campbell-Scarlett's leave of absence. The Resident German Consul at San Luis Potosí, Herr Bansen from Hamburg, also joined the petitioners. It was a stately array of names. But it won no pardon.

Agnes Salm, who had been left by herself, did not remain idle. The sovereign's freedom must be bought at any price, and she was resolved to pay it. General Vicente Riva Palacio, the bard, was said to have an eye for female pulchritude. In that case one would go to his tent. Pinning up her blonde curls, Agnes Salm lost no time in doing so.

The interview was fruitless, but this by no means exhausted a clever woman's resources. Peering out into the dark streets, the princess observed that it was evening and she could not return to her lodging house without an escort; surely her host——? The warrior acceded. He found himself presently in the lady's own bedroom. Although she was by now almost penniless, the princess offered to sign a promissory note for one hundred thousand pesos if Maximilian were released. Palacio wavered.

"Do you mean that is not enough?" she cried dramatically.

The officer's fingers itched, but he said nothing.

"Well, General, then here am I——" Agnes Salm shook her golden mane and began to undress.

Her white nudity lent a bizarre note to this night that was not made for love. There followed an awkward pause. The man did not respond to Eros. Like the entire rebel army he seemed to be in the grip of a strange power—Benito Juárez. Compelling, though unseen, the shadow of that presence snuffed even the searing flame of passion to ashes. Agnes Salm understood. A piteous smile curled her lips. To think that she had hoped to pit the lure of her woman's flesh against the spell of the Indian. . . . She felt neither embarrassed nor humiliated. Somehow, the stark seriousness of her purpose had lifted this episode above the plane of ridicule. She did not bother to cover herself, but merely went to the door and opened it. The officer walked out into the night.

On the following morning all foreigners who had no legitimate business in Querétaro were ordered to leave. A military guard was prepared to take Princess Salm-Salm to the nearest seaport, whence she might embark for the United States. The princess would greatly oblige the Liberal authorities by promptly complying with their demands.

Of course she did nothing of the sort. Pocketing the mandatory passport thus issued her, she set sail, but not over the waters of the Gulf. True, she allowed her armed convoy to chart the shortest way to Vera Cruz. But at the first stop, while the mules were being watered, she invited the guard for a bit of guzzling at the inn. The *pulque* was viscous and mellow; its effect upon the escort proved devastating. At the sound of the postilion's horn the princess rose, leaving the potion in her beaker untouched. But her companion's legs refused to stir, for a delicious palsy had stolen over them. Naturally, there was no denying that Agnes Salm must continue on her journey alone. This she did, in the opposite direction. One hundred and twenty miles inland she sped, across a sea of desert sands. To that stone idol she must go again, to Juárez. This time she would conquer. This time his granite mask would melt before the warmth of her appeal.

Even as she hurried to San Luis Potosí, Escobedo was notified by wire that Juárez wished the trial to open on June twelfth. Maximilian, Miramón and Mejía, as the outstanding culprits, would face justice at the first session of the courts martial, while Salm, Basch, Blasio and all other known imperialists waited for their turn. This meticulous arrangement was of course a mere formality, since the death penalty had been fixed for all at the moment of their arrest.

A provincial stage in the Teatro Principal de Querétaro was selected for the last scene in this sorry drama. The trial itself would provide a show wherein the court, the jury and a group of accused men performed on the boards, while boxes, stalls and gallery sold to the highest bidder. The star attraction behind those footlights would be an emperor fencing for his life.

But Maximilian disappointed his audience. He rejected the sardonic fitness of a theatrical setting and refused to be dragged under the proscenium arch. Escobedo had the tact to accept the monarch's illness as a valid excuse and went ahead with a trial by proxy. Since no foreigners were allowed to attend, Maximilian's counsel made use of lengthy briefs supplied by Mr. Hall and his Wheaton opus.

On January 25, 1862, Benito Juárez had once issued his terrorist decree threatening death to all who infringed the independence of the Republic or lent support to alien intervention. By this iron statute, which in its ramifications requited even robbery with capital punishment, the defendants were to be judged.

Escobedo had appointed his young aide-de-camp, Lieutenant-Colonel Platón Sánchez, as foreman of a jury whose members were the following six captains:

José Vicente Ramírez
Ignacio Jurado
José Verástegui
Emilio Lojero
Juan Rueda y Auza
Lucas Villagrán

As the proceedings opened, short shrift was made of Miramón and Mejía, but the absent sovereign was indicted on thirteen counts charging him with:

1. Serving as chief instrument of French intervention;

2. Accepting the crown from an unconstitutional minority;
3. Usurping the sovereignty;
4. Perpetrating violence against the lives, laws and interests of Mexicans;
5. Engaging in open warfare against the Republic;
6. Permitting filibusters from other nations to serve in his ranks;
7. Committing murder through the barbarous "Black Decree" of October 3, 1865;
8. Assuming in his preamble to this decree that President Juárez had left Mexican territory and established himself on United States soil;
9. Prolonging the civil war after the departure of the French troops;
10. Refusing to abdicate before being compelled to do so;
11. Demanding the considerations due a legal monarch, when in the eyes of the Republic he never possessed such rank;
12. Not recognizing the competence of the court and jury appointed to try him, averring that they represented a terrorist rather than a constitutional principle;
13. Having the audacity to voice this protest through his counsel.

The only inculpation to some degree irrefutable was contained under the eighth count. At various intervals throughout the campaign against the Empire, Juárez had entered Texas in search of supporters. Marshal Bazaine knew of this and worded the preamble to the effect that the Liberal Party was without a leader, omitting any inference that this might be only temporarily the case. At all events, there was no way of ascertaining whether or not the Frenchman had toyed with the truth when he persuaded Maximilian to sign the "Black Decree."

For the rest, the Emperor's counsel challenged all accusations. Documentary evidence brought forth by the defense showed: that French intervention in Mexico had occurred long before an empire was even thought of, that Maximilian and Carlota had landed at Vera Cruz without combat, and that they did so after having been summoned by a lawful monarchist group existing at this very moment in the country. Furthermore, no edicts proclaimed during their reign equaled in severity those passed by the Liberals themselves. Concerning abdication, Maximilian had twice offered to renounce the crown; twice he proposed a truce. Juárez alone had prolonged the war.

While these polemics went on in archaic legal phraseology, the jury sat munching sweet *chirimoyas* and *piñón* nuts. But the audience, mystified by the rotundities of academic diction, crouched in silent awe. Many eyes focused on the wounded Miramón who had been hailed—not so far back—with presidential honors. He was still in his prime, thirty-six years old, and had a sound military record to his credit. Yet now he swayed there before them, as if racked by unendurable suffering. Loss of blood had sapped his strength. Mejía, the Indian familiar and beloved in the Sierra Gorda region, supported his friend with infinite patience. Both officers had heard their sentence, yet both stood quietly throughout that day, waiting to learn their master's fate.

The Emperor's pundits had finished. Their perorations were jotted down by careless scribes and pushed into a portfolio entitled *"Memorandum sobre el proceso del Archiduque Fernando Maximiliano de Austria."* A copy of these records was later bound and stamped with a symbolic cross. Autographed by the defense lawyers, it was bequeathed to the Archduchess Sophie in Vienna.

The farce had lasted long enough. After the Emperor's vindication, to which no one paid the slightest heed, the jurymen filed out for a conference in the lavatory. They returned after some hours of general inertia, having accomplished exactly nothing. Their verdict was a tie, with three votes favoring death, and three lifelong banishment. It was Platón Sánchez who assumed the final responsibility. In clear crisp tones he passed the sentence formulated at the outset. Archduke Ferdinand Maximilian, self-styled Emperor of Mexico, would die on June sixteenth at an undetermined hour between sunrise and sunset.

The show was over and the court adjourned.

Chapter 6

Señor Benito Juárez examined his correspondence. It seemed that overnight he had become a man of universal importance. Were there not cablegrams addressed to him by almost every government in Europe? Not only that. A man named Victor Hugo had written him a long and stirring letter. He had praised the qualities which made Juárez a national hero; and he had finished with a strong plea for clemency to be shown to an Austrian princelet who was going to die. How gratifying that the world's mighty—of arms and intellect—had learned to grovel before the descendant of a crushed and crippled race. Juárez was pleased. The avenger of the Americas, history would call him.

Grimly his fingers unfolded another missive. It came from one Giuseppe Maria Garibaldi who termed himself a champion of liberty. In a manifesto to the entire Latin world this gentleman claimed to have fought Maximilian on the field of honor. He begged the freedom-loving Mexicans to deal kindly with his former foe.

A flock of women from San Luis Potosí and Querétaro signed petitions or came in person to the Liberal camp. Among them was Señora Miramón with a brood of children, pleading for her husband's life. Juárez remained speechless and unmoved.

Princess Salm-Salm arrived. She sank to the floor before the Indian President and wept. Her ardent tears brought an answer but it was a bootless one.

"I am grieved, Señora," Juárez said, "to see you on your knees before me; but if all the kings and queens of Europe were at your side, I could not spare his life. It is not I who take it away; it is my people and the law, and if I did not do their will, the people would take his life and my own as well."

With these words Juárez intended to fire that impersonal body, the mob, to a realization of its own power. Protesting his own impotence, he followed a precedent long established in the annals of absolutism. That impalpable, collective entity—the People—would shoulder the blame. Droves of humble citizens were sent away with the baffling words that the nation demanded Maximilian's blood.

Who constituted that monstrous tyrant *La Nación* the unhappy petitioners were unable to say.

Back in Querétaro, meanwhile, the Emperor and his companions were winding up a month's imprisonment. The doomed men continued segregated in the dark compartments assigned to them. Mejía sat in the chantry of Eleven Thousand Virgins—none of whom cared to perform a miracle; Miramón occupied Santa Rosa, while Maximilian drew Santa Teresa. Perhaps that pious namesake of his own ancestral grandam, Maria Theresia, prompted the hapless monarch to emulate Austria's great empress. For like Maria Theresia, whom the Archduke Max had delineated at length in his days of authorship—and who had "amused herself during her last hours, planning a coquettish tomb"—the Emperor of Mexico drew up dispositions regarding the embalming and removal of his body.

During the last week a false report had been spread, to the effect that the Empress Carlota had died at Miramar. Maximilian wrote at once to the Austrian Minister, Baron von Lago:

> "Only a moment ago I learned that my poor wife has been released by death from her misery. Such tidings, however much they may tear my heart, give boundless consolation to me, for I have now only one wish on earth, that my body may find burial beside the remains of my wife. With this mission, dear Baron, I entrust you as representative of Austria."

In another part of the letter he emphasized a point which caused him grave concern. "I am expecting you," he wrote, "to spare no effort in saving all Austrian officers and recruits still in Mexico, so that they may return at once to Europe."

As the time grew shorter the rumor concerning Carlota's death was denied and Maximilian, plagued with uncertainty, addressed a parting note:

"My beloved Carla! If God should allow you to regain your health, so that you may read these lines, you will learn how cruelly fate has dealt me blow after blow without respite since the day of your departure. Disaster has dogged my steps, breaking all my hopes! Death seems a happy solution. I shall go to my end as a soldier, a sovereign defeated but not dishonored. . . . Then, if your own distress becomes too great to bear, and God calls you to join me soon, I shall bless the hand which has been so heavy upon us. Farewell, Charlotte!

"MAXIMILIAN."

He spent the fifteenth of June writing from dawn till dusk, remembering all his close relatives and friends. That night, looked upon as his last on earth, he did not go to bed but engaged in final preparations. Taking stock of his personal effects, the Emperor distributed a few trifles among his followers. Basch was to have the scarf-pin sent by Franz Joseph to Miramar in those far-off days when the Archduke Maxl had needed a little prodding. . . . A pair of cuff-links went to Blasio, while the brushes and all remaining articles were to belong to the Salms. It was not until morning that the prisoner fell asleep.

Late the following day he was roused by a voice announcing that the execution would take place at three o'clock in the afternoon. An armed official stopped before each of the condemned men's cells and recited the sentence, after which the army chaplain, Padre Soria, appeared with censer and chalice. The Church offered redemption through the last sacraments, confession and holy communion. Maximilian accepted these ministrations with outward calm. Only a characteristic habit of stroking his chin betrayed that he labored under a nervous strain.

The small span of life which was now left him stretched out interminably. With sharpened senses the prisoners anticipated the striking of the fatal hour. At last a clock in a remote belfry chimed three, and Maximilian rose from his cot. He planted himself in the doorway of his cell, waiting five minutes, ten, half an hour. Why didn't they come? He felt he could not bear the torture. Time hung over him in an agony of suspense.

The bell in the tower rang out four o'clock and from somewhere there came the echo of a paternoster. Maximilian recognized the voice. It was Mejía, praying. Mejía was in no hurry. There was something that held him to life; something he would not explain.

The Emperor groaned in despair. Why couldn't they make an end of this? Had Latin procrastination combined with Indian lethargy to lend an added edge to his suffering? Surely the *mañana* habit did not make a fitting taunt for those awaiting death.

Footsteps sounded in the courtyard below. Now they approached, and in another moment General Riva Palacio stood in the corridor, jerking his arms and waving a piece of paper. It was a message from San Luis Potosí.

"Die Begnadigung," murmured Maximilian. ("The pardon!")

A faint radiance sparkled in his eyes and slowly lighted up his wan face. Suddenly the Emperor realized how fiercely he clung to earth, how desperate was his own love of living. Pride of origin and regal poise faded into nothingness beside that indestructible force—man's instinct for self-preservation.

Palacio had guessed Maximilian's meaning and shrugged apologetically.

"No pardon," he announced, shaking his head, "but the execution will be postponed for three days, because the wife of Comrade Mejía is in childbed. The prisoner will be allowed to visit his son."

"Alabado sea Dios!" finished the prayer from the next cell.

The time that followed was the most difficult of all. A restlessness filled the little town of Querétaro. Every one had misunderstood the telegram, and every one believed that Juárez, relenting at last, chose this devious way of granting mercy in order to save his own integrity before the law. Even the Liberal chieftains, Escobedo and Corona, were certain of Maximilian's immiment release. So were the remaining prisoners, who vaticinated thereby their own salvation. Felix Salm-Salm felt especially cheerful. He was already wondering where in the world a man could find another war. He had taken up heroism as a career.

At the old inn the diplomatic representatives, far less hopeful, were gathered in conclave. Their interview with Juárez had been fruitless. Neither the Indian President nor his Minister, Lerdo, was accessible to persuasion or bribery. The present delay in the execution plans might be puzzling but by no means reassuring. Baron von Magnus, the most skeptical of the group, dispatched a long telegram to San Luis Potosí. It ran:

> "On June sixteenth the condemned men have, figuratively speaking, already been led to their death. I beseech you, in the name of humanity and of Heaven, to give orders that their lives shall not again be threatened, that they shall not be forced to die a second time. And I repeat once again the assurance that my sovereign, his Majesty the King of Prussia, and all the monarchs of Europe related to the imprisoned Prince by the tie of blood—namely, his brother, the Emperor of Austria; his cousin, the Queen of Great Britain; his brother-in-law, the King of the Belgians; and his cousin, the Queen of Spain; as well as the Kings of Italy and Sweden—will readily agree to give his Excellency Señor Benito Juárez all guaranties that none of the prisoners will ever return or set foot on Mexican territory."

Baron von Lago also translated and passed on a message he had just received from Vienna. It appeared that at the eleventh hour, realizing his brother's danger, the Emperor Franz Joseph had reinstated Maximilian as heir presumptive to the Austrian throne. He now hoped that this measure would safeguard, if not Maximilian's position, at least his person, since it was unthinkable that a ranking member of a ruling house could be executed in cold blood by a foreign power. But Juárez was a son of the New World, which he considered far older than the Old, and he was totally unhampered by dynastic feeling. Furthermore, he refused to be cowed by the information that Maximilian was the "Cousin of Europe." On the contrary, it had been imprudent of Magnus and Lago to call the Indian's attention to this fact. Juárez was beginning to believe that the slightest move of his little finger would be heralded around the earth. It was a most satisfying thought.

A telegram from Maximilian himself, asking that he alone be

allowed to pay the penalty, while Miramón and Mejía returned to their families, met with equal cynicism. As for his two countrymen, Juárez would teach them the rewards of treason. No particular triumph in that. But the Hapsburg scion begging for favors—here was historic justice! Among Maximilian's ancestors was Charles V, white scourge of the Aztecs, while behind Juárez loomed the shadow of the Lord Motecuhzoma, whose name signified "Severe Man." . . . In the teeth of all the tyrants everywhere the dusky patriot would do this deed which was to him a sacred duty. He would do it and fear no one.

There were no replies to Magnus, Lago, or Seward in Washington (who had finally contrived a circumspect and polite letter). Maximilian of course expected none. He had already appealed to the Hofburg for a pension to be provided for the widows of his companions in death. It was the least that Austria might do, to acknowledge their sacrifice.

And so the morning of the execution arrived. During the night, while the prisoners slept, Maximilian had an extraordinary caller. General Escobedo, Commander-in-Chief of the garrison, stole into the convent to ask forgiveness for the ignoble part he must play. The Emperor was touched.

"Un abrazo, amigo," he said hoarsely, and the two men held each other for a brief second.

Escobedo's throat tightened so that he could not answer. To ease the strain Maximilian began to rummage among his effects, until he came upon a faded photograph of himself in coronation regalia (which he never actually wore). After inscribing the print he handed it to his captor.

The general left. But as he passed Mejía's cell a pang of self-reproach shot through him. In some earlier revolution he and Mejía had fought on the same side, and the latter had saved Escobedo's life. It was a debt, never repaid, which long pre-dated Maximilian's arrival.

Mejía stood erect behind the bars and he now saw Escobedo pass. In the gloom their eyes met. The Liberal commander stopped.

"I can save you, Tomás," he whispered, "if you are willing to escape alone. It was I who obtained the delay, that you might know your child."

Mejía flushed. "And the Emperor? And Miramón with his torn face?"

Escobedo made a sign of protest. "I can not help them too, without exposing us all. Besides, they would not survive the hardships——"

"Gracias, mi jefe," said Mejía without further interest. "I have seen my son. Now let me die with his Majesty."

Sick at heart, Escobedo departed.

It was three o'clock in the morning. The prisoners finished dressing, while at one end of the long corridor the priest Soria reappeared, wearing biretta and alb. He trundled a small campaign altar and began at once to read a low mass, gazing the while with pity upon his sparse congregation. While the monstrance was being raised during the consecration of the Host, Maximilian and his companions dropped to their knees to receive the blessing.

After the service the Emperor drew his wedding-ring from his right hand. He turned to Doctor Basch with a confused expression.

"Carla——" he began. Then: "Is there still no confirmation?"

"None, your Majesty." But a physician's faith in palliatives caused Basch to imply that the Empress had preceded her husband in death. This was the only real service he could now render the doomed monarch.

"Then—take it to my mother," Maximilian said, handing Basch the ring. *"Sie sollen ihn meiner Mutter bringen."*

A scapulary and a rosary which the kindly Father Soria had given to the Emperor were also destined for Vienna. But the small medallion of the Madonna—Eugénie's present, which was to have brought him luck—Maximilian bequeathed to the Empress of Brazil.

"She will need it," he said reflectively.

He turned now to Miramón and Mejía. "Are you ready, gentlemen? Have we done with everything?"

He clasped both generals and the members of his following

in turn. To the former he said: "We shall meet again in another world."

A detachment of infantry clattered through the passage. The officer in command announced that no foreigners were to accompany the Emperor from now on. This was a blow to Prince Salm-Salm, who continued to nurse mad schemes of possible escape during the drive to the scene of death.

Maximilian descended the stairs. He was in uniform. He wore a single order, the Golden Fleece. On reaching the street his eyes blinked at the unaccustomed brightness, for the sun was already high in the heavens.

"What a glorious day," he exclaimed. "I could not have chosen one better on which to die."

From far off there came the blare of a cornet. Maximilian turned to Mejía.

"Tomás, is that the signal for the execution?"

"I can not say, Sire; this is the first time I am being executed."

A smile from his master rewarded the brave cynic. Three carriages had meanwhile driven up and the condemned men climbed into them. Surrounded by a cavalry escort the procession started through the town, the firing squad marching at the rear. Even now the revolutionaries were taking no chances; a melodramatic dash for freedom would have ended in carnage.

But Maximilian had no such thought. He rode through the deserted streets resigned at last to his fate. The citizens of Querétaro did not see him pass, for the hour of the execution had been kept secret. Only here and there did a pair of dark uncomprehending eyes stare behind shuttered windows after the swift cavalcade.

At a safe distance a cloaked figure darted along, uttering strange Magyar sounds. *"Boldog Istenem!* [Good God!] I didn't believe it could come to this. I didn't believe——"

It was Tüdös, the cook, who had hovered about the Capuchin convent these many days and nights, waiting for his master. No one knew the black-haired, swarthy Hungarian, and no one stopped him now as he followed the gloomy train to the Hill of the Bells.

As the carriage neared the edge of the town a childlike wraith ran screaming from a doorway. It was Mejía's wife, with her newly born infant at her breast. She caught up with the vehicle which bore her husband away. Clutching one of the mudguards she let herself be dragged along until a sharp bayonet broke her grip.

Tomás Mejía saw her fall, and a great terror engulfed him. All his gallantry, his Indian fortitude—which was not unlike that of Juárez—suddenly withered. He felt the sickness that comes with a brutal blow in the stomach. On arriving at the foot of the Cerro he was almost insensate with grief and had to be lifted from the carriage.

The spot where Maximilian had been taken prisoner was chosen as the site of his immolation. With princely bearing, although his features had blanched at Mejía's agony, the Emperor walked uphill. Beside him went Miramón, equally staunch, for Miramón remembered that he had once ruled Mexico.

When they were near the top the firing squad lined up on three sides of a square opposite a low adobe parapet. The prisoners were stationed with their backs against this improvised elevation which had been constructed during the siege as a breastwork, guarding more important fortifications on the summit. In a mumbling monotone the firing parties were told off.

At this point a significant precaution appeared necessary. Obviously the troops could not be trusted, for the commandant in charge now read aloud to them a scathing pronunciamiento, threatening instant death to any one who raised a hand to save the Emperor. In the morning stillness four thousand soldiers, encamped at the foot of the hill, heard the message and pondered its meaning.

From the church of San Felipe Neri a bell rang out seven o'clock. Maximilian was asked if he had anything to say. He nodded. Walking up to the firing squad he distributed a few gold coins among the men, begging them to shoot well and not to aim at his head. In the event of his body being returned to Europe, he wanted to spare his relatives the sight of gory disfigurement. Had Juárez been present, this ultimate fastidiousness in the face of death would have drawn a smirk of derision from his impassive Indian countenance.

The soldiers, on the other hand, seemed abashed by an avowed emotion. A young captain stepped forward, stammering an excuse. The Emperor interrupted him.

"I understand, *amigo,"* he said simply; "it is your duty."

And now he saw the faithful Tüdös crouching behind the wall, his nervous fingers clawing at the unbaked clay. The presence of the servant, the last and only being out of a dear past, comforted Maximilian.

"Éljen Császár, veled!" cried the Hungarian. ("Hail Emperor, farewell!")

They embraced. Maximilian was unable to speak. A cold sweat had broken out on his face. He wiped it and, almost absently, left his hat and handkerchief with Tüdös, to take home. Yes, Tüdös was going home. But he, the gay, the urbane Maxl of other days, was not. He would never again need a hat....

The world was a great riddle. As if dazed, the Emperor took his place beside Miramón and Mejía. Before him lay the hamlet of Querétaro, drowsing peacefully in the sun. Looking up at a Mexican sky of ineffable blue, he made his last speech, in the best Spanish he had ever used:

"Muero por una causa justa. Perdono á todos y ruego que todos me perdonen. Espero que mi sangre corra por el bien de esta tierra. Viva México!" ("I die in a just cause. I forgive all, and pray that all may forgive me. May my blood flow for the good of this land. Long live Mexico!")

He had finished. The officer in charge raised and lowered his sword, while a volley of shots rang out. Maximilian collapsed, badly wounded. He had fallen face downward, and now they heard him groan: *"Hombres!* [Men!]"

Some one ran up to the twitching body and turned it over. The Emperor was still alive. Again, without a word, the officer swung down his blade. He was indicating the heart. Now a single shot was fired, which scorched Maximilian's tunic as it killed him. The servant Tüdös threw himself upon his master to extinguish the smoldering flames.

After the Emperor came his two knights errant, first Miramón, who stood in the place of honor which Maximilian had declined, and then Mejía. Before falling, Miramón spoke a few words in defense of his probity as an officer and a patriot. Mejía said nothing.

Of the manly paladins and their liege Mexican histories relate:

> "The victims met death with a dignity exacted by their chivalrous antecedents, the Emperor having said that men of their rank and of their race should die thus."

In a shabby hostelry that nestled along the outskirts of the town a woman wept. Princess Salm-Salm was back from San Luis Potosí. With carnal promises and assorted ducats she had stooped to tempt even the lowly jailer who might take pity on a captive Hapsburg. But an echo slashing through the morning stillness made known to her that she had failed.

It was the nineteenth of June, 1867.

Two days earlier, at a diplomatic dinner in Washington, Ambassador von Wydenbruck rushed up breathlessly to the Secretary of State.

"The Emperor Maximilian is in terrible danger. My Government implores you to do something!"

Mr. Seward crunched a radish. "His life is quite as safe as yours and mine," he said.

Chapter 7

The *New York Herald* of July 2, 1867, carried a story with a caption of startling informality:

"WHO ARE RESPONSIBLE FOR MAX'S DEATH?"

"Should the news published in the *Herald* of Sunday—of Maximilian's execution on the 20th of June—be finally confirmed, as there is every reason to believe it will be, the responsibility for his death will rest among several persons. First, of course, Napoleon and his henchman Bazaine; then Mr. Scarlet [sic], the British Minister, who, when the easily led Emperor was at Orizaba prepared to make a midnight skedaddle from the country, for which he had completed all his arrangements—persuaded him that it would be more dignified to remain and fight it out. Then Márquez, who dragged him into the Querétaro campaign and proved untrue to him after the expedition had been entered upon; lastly López, the final instrument of his betrayal. Whether some responsibility does not rest with the State Department at Washington for the muddle they have made of the Mexican legation, the country will determine. Had there been a United States Minister in San Luis Potosí on the 20th of June, as there might have been, and ought to have been, Maximilian's blood would never have been shed."

Historic events are seldom reported accurately at the time they happen, since view-points are clouded and means of communication highly precarious. The twentieth of June, while not the date of execution, marked the capitulation of Mexico City and the surrender of the remaining imperialist troops to General Porfirio Díaz. With the death of the Emperor the struggle had lost its meaning.

As regards the accusation against Sir Peter Campbell-Scarlett, it is doubtful whether Maximilian had any sort of "skedaddle" in mind. He was buoyed up by the British Minister's advice, but not swayed, for the break with Herzfeld preceded the Orizaba holiday and the Emperor had already made his decision before consulting Sir Peter.

General Márquez did not turn traitor. His failure to save Puebla was unfortunate, since he had had no instructions to go there in the first place. It has been established that he did so only to check the grim Porfirio's march on Mexico City.

About López the same issue of the *Herald* stated:

> "The fate of the officer who betrayed Querétaro and the Emperor is doubtful. He was seen at large in Querétaro the day after the surrender. That he had received his promised reward seems unlikely, since he made application to one of the leading Liberal officers for relief. Meeting Colonel Rincón-Gallardo (Pepe Rincón), he said: 'Colonel, I am not, like you, a rich man with many haciendas. I have nothing but my sword to depend upon. I hope you will recommend me to a position in the Liberal army.' Pepe Rincón (the same man who tried to let Maximilian escape) is reported to have replied: 'Colonel López, if I recommend you to any position it will be to a position on a tree, with a rope around your neck.' Colonel López has not been seen publicly since."

In after years Miguel López wrote and published a pamphlet entitled *La Toma de Querétaro—A mis compatriotas y al mundo.* In the hope of vindicating himself, he offered a supposedly exact account of his transactions with the enemy and stated that Maximilian had been consulted before the opening of such negotiations. He also complained that the Liberal chieftains, after making fine promises, had not paid him a single peso for his efforts as an intermediary, whereas the Emperor's gratitude took the shape of a medal.

Strangely enough, there is little actual proof against López. The most damning testimony is intangible in character; it lies in the attitude shown by both the Conservative and Liberal parties, as well as Miguel's own family and friends. When, after the fall of Querétaro, López hurried home to Puebla, his young wife wept behind the latticed door.

"How could you do this to our *compadre?*" she exclaimed, for Maximilian was fond of his officers and once acted as godfather to Miguel's child. "Unless you save him *no te conozco más* [I know you no more]." And she left her fallen angel standing in the street.

He was shunned and despised like Judas, although it is not impossible that López himself had become victimized by Juarista cunning and suffered doubly for his error. Certainly he had been made thorough use of and then discarded. He prowled about the provinces for some years as a lonely outcast. They tell in Mexico City that he was bitten one day by a mad dog and died of hydrophobia.

Fate dealt more kindly with Prince Salm-Salm. Of him the Emperor had said to Frederic Hall: "He is as brave as a lion, sir." Immediately after the monarch's death a wave of reaction swept over the country and Escobedo, who had refused to be present at the execution, entered a plea for mercy in behalf of the remaining prisoners still confined in the Capuchin convent. This being granted, Salm received a relatively light sentence which he served in the fort of San Juan de Ulúa at Vera Cruz, from where he was discharged on November 13, 1867. Two days later he sailed for Europe with his wife and the terrier Jimmy. They all enjoyed a good rest before Felix joined the war of 1870, against Napoleon III, which cost him his life. Thereafter Agnes Salm-Salm's hero-worship attained a new austerity. She spent the balance of her days penning a glowing memorial to the two beings who, she felt, had lifted her destiny out of the commonplace.

The release of the dead Emperor was not so easy to obtain as that of his fellow prisoners. At nine o'clock on the morning of the execution Baron von Lago had telegraphed to Juárez:

"Citizen President—

"I pray you to concede me the body of Archduke Maximilian, in order that I may convey it to Europe.

"Baron von Lago
"Tacubaya, Distrito Federal
"June 19, 1867."

But the Liberal government had other plans. It was desirous of obtaining recognition on the part of all the major powers in the world, including Austria. The Emperor Franz Joseph, on the other hand, might show himself lacking in the necessary enthusiasm.

For the time being, then, Maximilian would not travel. Lago received the following reply:

"Señor Baron von Lago—

"The President of the Republic has directed me to say to you, in answer to your telegram of yesterday, which was received this evening, that for grave reasons the right can not be granted you to dispose of the body of Maximilian.

"Sebastián Lerdo de Tejada

"San Luis Potosí,

"June 20, 1867."

Previous instructions had already reached Querétaro in regard to the remains of Miramón and Mejía, which were to be delivered to their respective families. The Emperor's body had been returned to the convent for embalming. It was carried from the Hill of the Bells in a rude coffin built by an army carpenter who had never seen Maximilian and thought him a man of average size. Consequently the Emperor's feet hung out over one end of the wooden box as the heavy burden was transported through the streets.

In an underground chamber of the monastery two Mexican doctors, Riva de Neyra, and Licea, made preparations for the embalming.

The distressed Basch had been allowed to witness the procedure, after promising that he would in no way interfere. Meanwhile exact body measurements—six feet, two inches—were sent to another carpenter for a new coffin.

The lifeless form had been placed on a table. At this point the work of preservation suffered a slight setback when it was discovered that no one had any naphtha. While Basch tore his hair in desperation the impromptu morticians reached for a flask of chloride of zinc. This they injected into the arteries and veins, an operation which lasted three days.

The torso, which showed four bullet holes in the left breast and one in the right, was next clothed in the blue campaign coat which the deceased had worn. A row of plain gilt buttons ran from the belt to the Emperor's throat, while his feet were encased in high military boots. Black trousers, necktie and kid gloves completed the burial costume.

Considerable difficulty was experienced with the arrangement of the hair, which had undergone severe chemical tests. It was also necessary to camouflage the ineptitude or nervousness of the Nuevo León infantry (which had served in three units of six men each) at the time of the execution. The first bullet that struck Maximilian hit his face, lacerating brow and temples. The saints in all the churches of Querétaro underwent inspection, but nowhere could a pair of glass eyes be found which resembled the Emperor's in color. At last a black set, taken from a Virgin in the cathedral, had to be inserted. Basch found his master's appearance painfully changed.

The new coffin was made of cedar and lined with zinc. Over the metallic lining another of cambric had been stretched. The Carmelite nuns provided a black velvet pillow edged with gold thread, and with gilt tassels at the corners. To this was added, by the good ladies of the town, a velvet cover ornamented with bands of gold lace.

In this resting-place Maximilian lay, his head made visible through a small glass window. Thus arranged, the catafalque was for some days displayed in one of the churches and thence removed to the Governor's quarters. Here it remained for two weeks, looking tolerably well, but after that time the body began to darken. No further evidence was needed to prove that the work of attempted preservation had failed.

Recognition of the Juárez government had meanwhile been wrung from the Emperor Franz Joseph, so that the demand for Maximilian's remains could once more be pressed by Austria. This time Baron von Magnus addressed himself to the Foreign Minister, Lerdo de Tejada:

"San Luis Potosí,
"June 29th, 1867.

"Sir:

"The prisoner Prince at Querétaro, on the evening before his death, expressed to General Escobedo the desire that his body be confided to us, his physician Doctor Samuel Basch and myself, for transportation to an Austrian vessel stationed at Vera Cruz. . . .

"I avail myself of this occasion to repeat to your Excellency the assurance of my high esteem and to beg for a prompt compliance with the above request.

"A. VON MAGNUS."

But the incipient decomposition of the corpse had now become a source of embarrassment to the authorities. In a careful dissertation Lerdo replied:

"I am pained to inform you that for various considerations the Government of the Republic believes it cannot permit the mortal remains of the Archduke to be carried to Europe."

President Juárez had stopped at Querétaro on his way to Mexico City. He had viewed the coffin and determined immediately that it must never leave the country. No one was henceforth allowed to see it; the keeper had strict orders to invent every possible excuse for turning away even those persons who were purported to hold permits.

On July 15, 1867, Juárez and his staff made their triumphal entry into the capital, after an absence of five years. This return signalized the rise of the new Republic and the culmination of the Indian patriot's own fame. The suspended Constitution of 1857 was made once more effective, and the national energies were directed toward repairing the waste caused by the long war. Austria and the sorrow of her imperial family had been almost forgotten when, on July twenty-seventh, Doctor Basch also wrote to the Citizen Minister:

"The fulfilment of my master's last request [he said] I

consider a sacred duty. . . . This solicitation is supported by the fact that the bodies of his companions in misfortune have been delivered to their families, and that never at any time has a government refused to deliver any corpse to the relatives who asked for it. I beg, finally, that you will condescend to answer my respectful plea, whatever that answer may be, so that on returning to my country I may justify myself before the family of the deceased Archduke. . . ."

To this Lerdo de Tejada replied with an added flourish:

". . . The Citizen President of the Republic has determined that for various and grave reasons the petition can not be granted.
Independence and Liberty!

"Mexico, July 29, 1867."

Several weeks went by and nothing happened. The dwindling number of Maximilian's followers despaired. One by one they drifted from the scene of their humiliation.

On the evening of August twenty-sixth an unexpected telegram arrived from the military commander of Vera Cruz. It was addressed to the Minister of War, and read:

"The Austrian Admiral Tegetthoff arrived this morning at Sacrificios with the war-ship of his nation, *Elisabeth*. He sent a message to this military command, stating that he wished to pass to the capital to ask a permit of the Supreme Government for carrying away the body of Maximilian. I desire to know whether I must prohibit his going to the City of Mexico.

"ZEREGA."

This was by no means a pleasing turn of events. With the Liberal army largely disbanded and no fleet at hand, the arrival of a foreign gunboat was distinctly annoying. Juárez wondered if, perchance, he had underestimated the resources of that ill-starred House of Hapsburg. Who could have believed that they would send an admiral bristling with guns! The reply dispatched to Vera Cruz during that same night of August twenty-sixth made a concession. "You can let him pass," it said.

With the utmost haste the corpse was now fetched from Querétaro to Mexico City and deposited at the Hospital San Andrés for reembalming. By immersion in great vats which held a solution of arsenic it was hoped that the advanced putrefaction might be arrested. This process took some time. The admiral, who had meanwhile paid his respects at Chapultepec, must be enmeshed in a certain amount of red tape while the gruesome business at San Andrés was completed. Accordingly Tegetthoff received a demand for an official document directed by the Government of Austria to the Government of Mexico, since the personal wishes of the imperial family were not sufficient to sway those invested with the dignity of a republic. Gritting his teeth, the admiral sent a cable and retired to his hotel. Since the desired document must bear the seals and signatures of Viennese officialdom the expected answer could come only by packet boat. Tegetthoff settled down to a protracted period of waiting.

A communiqué from the Austrian Chancellor of the Empire and Minister of the Imperial Household, Baron Friedrich Ferdinand von Beust, was received in Mexico City on November fourth. It had been formulated in the most cautious diplomatic language, referring to Maximilian's execution as his "premature demise," and pouring a stream of gratitude upon the heads of those who might aid in restoring the body to its rightful burial place. Obviously his Apostolic Majesty, the Emperor Franz Joseph, was concerned with only one thing—his brother's fitting interment.

Beust's dispatch pleased Lerdo de Tejada, to whom it had been addressed. It also coincided with the termination of the second embalming. Maximilian's body reposed on a table once used by the Inquisition Tribunals in signing an auto-da-fé. It had been clothed in a fresh suit of black and was now to be enclosed in a third coffin made of granadilla wood, elegantly polished and ornamented with a few carvings. A glass aperture seemed hardly requisite, since it was quite apparent that the body would not long be recognizable. The face had sunk in, and the features were gradually changing.

On November ninth Admiral Tegetthoff received his silent charge. Early the next morning he set out at once for the coast, accompanied by Doctor Basch, the servant Tüdös, and the remaining Austrian officers who had lingered in the country. A Mexican force of one hundred men escorted the funeral caravan, which was met at Potrero by the municipal authorities of Vera Cruz. On November twenty-fifth, at four P.M., the cortège reached the port.

The coffin was placed in the parochial church until six o'clock the following morning, when it was taken aboard the corvette *Novara*. The saloon of Maximilian's favorite ship was draped in mourning. In its center a table covered with black cloth supported the bier. At the head was erected an altar bearing a cross; the Austrian and the Mexican flags hung to right and left, framed by six large silver candlesticks with lighted wax tapers. The Emperor's sword lay on the coffin. The servant Tüdös and a sentinel stood by, day and night, holding the death watch.

After religious services had been performed at nine o'clock, anchors were weighed. Toward noon of that day the *Novara* steamed out of the harbor. On the same boat that had borne him to Mexico Maximilian now returned to the land of his birth. The *Elisabeth* and the mail steamer that had brought Beust's letter made up his escort.

As the small flotilla passed the castle-fortress of San Juan de Ulúa a specter out of the past seemed to beckon to the Austrian crew. They were all familiar with the legend concerning Charles V, whose viceroys had wheedled some four million pesos from the Crown for the building of this fort. Standing on the balcony of his castle in Granada the Spanish Hapsburg was seen one day, peering strenuously out to sea.

"At what is your Majesty looking?" inquired a courtier.

"I am looking for San Juan de Ulúa," the Emperor-King answered, "it has cost me so much money that I ought to be able to see it from here!"

From the presidio of this ancient pile of stone Prince Felix zu Salm-Salm saw the *Novara* bearing another Hapsburg home.

CHAPTER 8

MARIE ZU ERBACH-SCHÖNBERG, Princess of Battenberg, was still keeping up her girlish diary. It was biased and inaccurate, like most contemporary information on historical events.

On July 2, 1867, she made the following entry:

> "The Emperor Max was shot by the Mexican monsters on June ninth. The deed is hardly credible. Poor old Archduchess Sophie, and the poor Empress Charlotte! How will they break the horrible news to her? . . . It is asserted that a Mexican lady's maid gave the Empress a poison that causes insanity. How can such cruelties be practised in these days?"

On November twenty-second another paragraph was added:

> "During dinner we had to go to Mama's room to see the Archduke Karl. He told us his poor sister-in-law Charlotte as yet knows nothing of her husband's death. For that reason she did not, of course, wear mourning until the Queen of the Belgians went to Miramar. As the Court had just gone into mourning for the Queen of Naples, who died lately of cholera, the Belgian Queen was able to persuade the Empress to put on a black dress for the journey.—The body of the Emperor Max has at last been handed over to Admiral Tegetthoff."

The journey referred to above was Carlota's return to Laeken. Queen Henriette, once an Archduchess of Austria, had come to take the Belgian princess into her care. Doctor Bulkens—from Gheel, the village of the insane—had been hired to direct the royal progress.

Orders were sent ahead, forbidding receptions or demonstrations at railroad stations along the way, since Carlota became alarmed at the slightest noise. The Prince of Wales, later Edward VII, happened to be visiting incognito on the Continent; he saw the

Empress of Mexico as she crossed the Luxemburg border, but out of consideration for her health he did not speak.

In the little town of Groenendal, the waiting court carriage had driven up so close to the train that Carlota stepped into it unwittingly, and unnoticed. Anxious, watchful, Señora del Barrio did not leave her side.

They rode through Brussels in silence. With forlorn eyes Carlota gazed out of the carriage window at the park where, as a small girl, she had walked sedately with her brothers. They had always carried large hoops which they were not allowed to roll. Tutors and governesses were forever pointing out the unseemliness of such capers in children of royal blood. The Coburgs took themselves so seriously, perhaps because they had not been royal very long. . . . At any rate, it was all quite boring, Carlota had long ago decided.

At Laeken Léopold II gave her a tepid embrace. In truth, he did not know what to do with this deranged sister. He was busy with Africa and thoughts of colonial expansion; it was he who would put Belgium on the map. Wicked Léopold, who conquered the Congo cutting off hands. Carlota's inglorious return fitted ill with his schemes of territorial conquest.

She was given shelter, for a time, at the summer palace of Tervueren. Later the King ordered the medieval retreat of Bouchout to be restored for her occupancy. Here, in all its tragic witchery, the story of Mexico's phantom crown came to an end.

In the chill of mid-winter, the corvette *Novara* arrived with its sad burden at Trieste, whence Ferdinand Maximilian was borne to Vienna and the Kapuzinergruft—another crypt of Capuchin monks. A long line of Hapsburgs slumbered here, and he was laid quietly among them. Outside, in the sunlit streets, the bustle of a fruit and flower market reached the very portals of the old church while beyond, in the Eleganter Prater and in the less commendable Wurstl Prater, waltzing Vienna drank a toast to life.

The Archduke Maxl was at rest. On the marble sarcophagus lay a fan-shaped sprig of *siempre-vivas* placed there by his mother, to whom he had once sent them. The red and white blossoms had been tied to a palm leaf of faded green. Originally they had been given to Maximilian by the natives of Xocotitlán (Spanish: *naranjal,* the place of orange trees), a tiny hamlet outside Orizaba. With them had come a papyrus scroll, bearing a salutation in the almost extinct Aztec tongue:

> *"No mahuistililoni tlactocatzine, nican tiquimopielia mo icno masehual conetzihua, ca san ye ohualacque o mitzmotlacpalhuilitztinoto, ihuan ica tiquimomachtis ca huel senca techyolpaqui mo hualialitzin impampa itech tiqueta aco se cosamalotl quixiquintihuitz inon mexicolis mixtl nesi ye omochautiheaipan to thactocazotl. In senhuiltini mitztitlania, ma ye huatzin mitzmochicahuili ica titechmaquixtis. Nis tiquimopielia inin maxochtzintl, quen se machiotl in tetlasotla litzin, mitzmo maquilia mo xocotitlan coneztzitzihua."*

> ("Our honorable Emperor, behold your humble children, these Indians who have come to salute you; by this homage know that your coming much pleases their hearts, for in it they see a light that lifts evil shadows from our darkened Mexico. The God has sent you and it is He who gives you power over us. Here is this flower, it is our sign of friendship, and by this your sons of Xocotitlán bring you recognition.")

These words, once passed on to the Hofburg because of their oddity, have been treasured by greedy philologists. They also became the dead Emperor's epitaph.

Only once were the *siempre-vivas* disarranged by an armful of fresh roses. In 1870 the widowed Baroness von Bülow, formerly Countess Linden, visited Vienna. The aging Archduchess Sophie permitted the "little Linden's" floral tribute to rest for a week in the place of honor. Sophie had mellowed.

"Our Maxl gave us such trouble on your account," she said reminiscently, *"er hat Sie so gern gehabt!* [he was so fond of you!]"

For an instant a vision of her four roistering boys troubled the old lady. She could hardly realize that the Hofburg dancing parties, over which she had presided like a clucking hen, were gone forever. No one needed her clucking now. A new generation was growing up. Meister Strauss himself was dead, and the children of to-morrow would be whistling other tunes. Perhaps one day the very Kaiserstadt would change, and people would wonder about that giddy Vienna of the Archdukes. They would be unable to imagine what it had been like. Well, it was time for Sophie to tie up the strings of her bonnet. She had lost a son of whom friend and foe said: "It was a thing for reverence to see this Hapsburg die." A mother could not ask for more.

There were others who mourned as poignantly as she. In Paris the news from Querétaro ushered in a train of misfortunes. It was the year of the great Exposition and Eugénie prepared to distribute prizes to a group of winning participants when the tragic cable arrived. At first her senses left her.

"Louis," she gasped, "shall we cancel the festivities?"

Napoleon was as dismayed as his wife. Both were afraid to appear in public. But in view of the fact that the press had not yet printed a word on the matter it was thought prudent to carry on with the official program as if nothing had happened. All that afternoon and evening the Empress of the French bestowed her dazzling smile upon a sea of faces. Monarchs from all the Courts of Europe—save Austria—were present. Napoleon stood between the Tsar, the Shah, the Sultan and England's future King, and his blood ran cold, for above his brow he felt the sword of Damocles. When the show was over and the foreign visitors had left, Eugénie fainted, this time in earnest. They restored her with smelling salts, only to show her the head-lines in *Le Matin*.

"There remain now no sovereigns in Paris," wrote the famous journal, "except the Emperor Napoleon III and the specter of Maximilian at his elbow."

"They don't know," mused Eugénie with wan detachment, "how little—really—poor Louis had to do with it." She had been wrong about Mexico. She was right about Prussia. But the war she advocated against a Bismarck, who was only beginning to feel his strength in 1866, took four long years in coming. And when it came France could no longer cope with it.

How much of this did Carlota know? Did some one tell her that Maximilian had long ago returned to a world of which she had scarcely been a part? . . . In the Vienna of his youth he had found peace. And while he slept eternally, she roamed through the corridors of a distant Belgian castle, as far removed from him as their separate childhoods. At times it was as if it had never been.

She sorrowed. Slowly her once eloquent features grew distorted, her eyes dimmed by recurring cataracts. Nor would she find comfort. Her father lay dead of his gall-stone; her brothers shunned the dismal castle of Bouchout where for sixty years she was kept a recluse. They left her stranded on a planet of her own.

Her madness was not that of a maniac. She had many periods of apparent clarity, yet she was cautious of her words and never revealed the exact truth of her condition. She wrote many letters, some of them hinting at a strange awareness of things. Others were plainly unbalanced, teeming with references to Maximilian as "Lord of the Earth" and "Sovereign of the Universe." And she never forgot that she was an empress. It was the age of the Empresses! (Even Victoria's vanity was soon to dote upon a vicarious title supplied by a Jewish prime minister; the Queen transformed Disraeli into an Earl of Beaconsfield, but he made her Empress of India.) No, Carlota did not forget. To her end she remained an Imperial Highness, conversing briefly with a dignified imaginary Court—a prince, a baron, a handsome hussar. And at times she cried softly, *"Maximiliano, Maximiliano . . ."*

Five empires crashed while she sat in her garden munching *leche quemada,* the tasty caramel made in the region of Celaya and procured by Señora del Barrio from a new set of émigrés at Biarritz. The first to go was France—Eugénie had her *petite guerre* with Prussia. During the siege of Paris Monsieur Worth, the couturier, fled to safer markets (he chartered a balloon). But he returned after the peace to launch two symbolic colors: a virulent orange called *Bismarck enragé,* and a most topical gray, *cendres de Paris.* Also, for many years to come, he had a secret customer beyond the borders of France. At Farnborough Hill on the Blackwater near the Basingstoke Canal, or in the Villa Cyrnos at Cap Martin, the quondam Señorita de Montijo received once each year—even at ninety-five—a new robe from Paris and a bunch of imperial violets.

She had lost her husband prosaically after a surgical ordeal on a London operating table. She had sent her son to fight Zulus for England at Itelezi, calculating that heroism in any sort of campaign would once more revive in the world a moribund enthusiasm for the Bonapartist cause.

"Loulou will catch a Zulu!" chuckled a waggish press, while the prince rode on his horse "Fate" into a musty kraal on the Ilyotyosi. There was a rustle in the tall grass. Eighteen African spears shot through Loulou and of his face nothing was left when on the evening of June 1, 1879 (Whitsunday), a scouting squad picked up the ghastly form.... Yet Eugénie was to enjoy one triumph. She lived to see another Peace of Versailles, with Bismarck absent and the tables turned against his beloved German Reich.

On July 11, 1920, Eugénie died. In a secluded garden Carlota and her wizened lady-in-waiting talked over the funeral. Victoria, too, was gone. And Franz Joseph, Elisabeth, disastrous Otto. Rudolf at Mayerling—Franz Ferdinand at Sarajevo. Only Carlota of Mexico would view the entire panorama: the twilight of France, Brazil, Russia, Austria, Germany. Brooding in her armchair, she watched the sunset of five dynasties: Bonaparte, Braganza, Romanov, Hapsburg, Hohenzollern. Would there be a sunrise?

The world was shaken by its greatest war while thus she sat. During the German invasion of Belgium in 1914 a Prussian officer nailed a plaque above her gates. It bore the following inscription:

> "This castle, the property of the Belgian Crown, is occupied by Her Majesty, the Empress of Mexico—sister-in-law of our revered ally, the Emperor of Austria. German soldiers are ordered to pass by without singing, and to leave this place untouched."

Catastrophe thundered past her gates. The roar of cannon and the tramp of marching feet echoed against her walls, yet their din, resounding so close to her immediate abode, failed utterly to reach her ear. She could afford to ignore the destiny of Europe, as Europe had ignored her.

Now she alone was left—the last of the Empresses. She had witnessed the dissolution of her brother Léopold II, whose nephew Albert ruled since 1909 beside his cautious Bavarian queen. An octogenarian, she became contemporary with the automobile, jazz and radio. In the year of her death a boy named Lindbergh flew the Atlantic.

How mad was she? She would not tell. She would not let them know, for fear that they might rob her of what was now her last possession—her phantom crown. She would be Empress to the end.

Death came quietly on January 16, 1927. . . . A time so near that one can almost touch it. She was eighty-six, and her soft features had sharpened so that her shadow looked like the outline of a hawk. At her exequies, King Albert—himself soon a grandfather—was to behold once more what in his early childhood seemed but a nursery legend, a pale fantasy. Beside her incredible earthly shape he walked in a funeral procession both solemn and meaningless, entirely befitting an imperial myth.

Until that moment, however, hers was an epic hold on life. She knew herself to be a monument to Maximilian, and while she lived she would not allow men to forget him. To all who paid her visits she would whisper: "Let them remember the fair-haired stranger who gave his life for the ambitions of that grasping, unscrupulous Napoleon! Let them know that we acted in good faith; and may God grant that our memory be sad but never hateful. . . ."

The prayer was answered. Some years after the fall of Maximilian, the actress Concha Méndez appeared again in a Mexico City theater. The audience clamored for *La Paloma Liberal,* a parody on the song so loved by Carlota. The singer paled as she faced her public. She lifted her voice, but not in song:

> "Never shall I do what you ask, Señores. I wear on my wrist the bracelet given me by an unhappy princess who to-day weeps alone, widowed and mad, very far from our country. Neither I nor the Mexican nation, to which I am joined by my heart and my cradle, shall insult the memory of a prince mowed down at Querétaro, nor that of a noble lady who in place of a queenly diadem wears now the martyr's crown. . . ."

A great emotion swept over the audience. The courage of Concha Méndez met with the response gallant. Luster envelops the singer's name; never again was she importuned to render the ballad that had made her famous. With possible exception of those erratic haunts frequented by the tourist, *La Paloma* is not heard below the Río Grande to-day. To Carlota the modern Mexican accords a new chivalry. Without surrendering a single tenet of liberalism, without conceding an inch of ground to foreign meddlers from any portion of the globe, he speaks of that fair intruder as "the ill-fortuned Mexican Empress who was an innocent victim in the game of European politics. . . . She will remain engraved upon our history in her goodness, her nobility, and above all—as the most loving of women." Anáhuac may be justly proud of Benito Pablo Juárez for his signal fortitude in behalf of an ideal as he saw it. But Anáhuac is not proud of its deed against Maximilian, since pride is no measure for the rigors of implacable, impersonal fate.

Nor is there any vaunting spite north of the Río Grande. Representative Cox of Ohio and his tirades against the "Austrian Archdupe" have been forgotten. In their place shines the exquisite humanism of Gilbert W. Gabriel, before whose imagination the Maximilian drama looms as "the last grand, bewildered gesture of royalty on the American continent."

With fine generosity Mr. Gabriel pronounced in the *New York Sun* of September 18, 1926:

> "In the heroic dimensions and processional mood of al fresco painting this story unfolds itself before posterity. For Europe it bears the awful dignity of cactus thorns and martyrdom, for America it spells the victory of republican ideals. Secretary Seward's crisp and righteous dispatch to little Louis Napoleon, shooing the French army out of Mexico, placed the United States on Juárez's side. . . . Humanely and politely we asked them to spare Maximilian's life and they did not, and that was that. We were too busy planting peace lilies of our own, those 1860's, to worry of one wilting and rather incongruous orchid in the Mexican desert. . . ."

It is rather late for contentions of one sort or another. In death Maximilian of Hapsburg achieved a stature worthy of classic antiquity. There was that about him which drew forth self-sacrifice from his fellow men. Even in error he was strangely true. And he was loved. But most of all Carlota must have loved him. Carlota—for whom the final tableau was one of merciful darkness and peace.

> "I was to blame, my beloved darling, for everything. But now I am happy. You have triumphed! You are part of God's victory over Evil. . . . Your eyes look down at me from every place and I hear your voice everywhere. . . ."

Such were the letters she wrote during the sixty years when she had him no more.

THE END

THE STOREHOUSE

THE STOREHOUSE

Original Versions of Excerpts Translated in Text.

a. Napoleon's proposal for the hand of Eugénie. Page 60.

"Au Palais des Tuileries
Le 15 janvier 1853."

"Madame la Comtesse:

"Il y a longtemps que j'aime mademoiselle votre fille, et que je désire en faire ma femme. Je viens donc, aujourd'hui, vous demander sa main, car personne plus qu'elle n'est capable de faire mon bonheur, ni plus digne de porter une couronne. Je vous prierai, si vous y consentez, de ne pas ébruiter ce projet avant que nous ayons pris nos arrangements.

"Recevez, madame, l'assurance de mes sentiments de sincère amitié.

"NAPOLÉON."

b. Portion of the "Convention of Miramar." Pages 96-97.

"Article 1. Les troupes françaises qui se trouvent actuellement au Mexique seront réduites le plus tôt possible á un corps de 25,000 hommes, y compris la Légion Étrangère. Ce corps, pour sauvegarder les intérêts qui ont motivé l'intervention, restera temporairement au Mexique dans les conditions réglées par les articles suivants.

"Article 2. Les troupes françaises évacueront le Mexique au fur et à mesure que Sa Majesté L'Empereur du Mexique pourra organiser les troupes nécessaires pour les remplacer.

"Article 3. La Légion Étrangère au service de la France, composée de 8000 hommes demeurera néanmoins encore pendant six années au Mexique, après que toutes les autres forces françaises auront été rappelées . . ."

c. Manifesto contained in preamble to "Black Decree." Pages 214-15.

"Mexicanos!

"La causa que con tanto valor y constancia sostuvo D. Benito Juárez había ya sucumbido, no solo á la voluntad nacional sino ante la misma ley que este caudillo invocaba en apoyo de sus títulos. Hoy hasta la bandera en que degeneró dicha causa ha quedado abandonada por la salida de su gefe del territorio patrio.

"El Gobierno Nacional fué por largo tiempo indulgente y ha prodigado su clemencia para dejar á los extraviados, á los que no conocían los hechos, la posibilidad de reunirse á la mayoría de la Nación y colocarse nuevamente en el camino del deber. Logró su intento; los hombres honrados se han agrupado bajo su bandera y aceptado los principios justos y liberales que norman su política. Solo mantienen el desorden algunos gefes descarriados por pasiones que no son patrióticas, y con ellos la gente desmoralizada que no está á la altura de los principios políticos, y la soldadesca sin freno que queda siempre como último y triste vestigio de las guerras civiles.

"De hoy en adelante la lucha solo será entre los hombres honrados de la Nación y las gavillas de criminales y bandoleros. Cesa ya la indulgencia que solo aprovecharía al despotismo de las bandas, á los que incendian los pueblos, á los que roban y á los que asesinan ciudadanos pacíficos, míseros ancianos y mujeres indefensas.

"El Gobierno, fuerte en su poder, será desde hoy inflexible para el castigo, puesto que así lo demandan los fueros de la civilización, los derechos de la humanidad y las exigencias de la moral.

"México. Octubre 2 de 1865. "MAXIMILIANO."

d. Portion of "Black Decree." Pages 215-16.

"MAXIMILIANO, Emperador de México, oído nuestro Consejo de Ministros y nuestro Consejo de Estado, decretamos:

"Artículo 1. Todos los que pertenecieren á bandas ó reuniones armadas que no estén legalmente autorizadas, proclamen ó no algún pretexto político, cualquiera que sea el número de los que formen la banda, su organización y el carácter y denominación que ellas se dieren, serán juzgados militarmente por las Cortes Marciales, y si se declarase que son culpables, aunque sea solo del hecho de pertenecer á la banda, serán condenados á la pena capital que se ejecutará dentro de las primeras veinticuatro horas después de pronunciada la sentencia . . .

"Artículo 9. Todos los vecinos de un pueblo amenazado por una gavilla, que fueren de edad de diez y ocho á cincuenta y cinco años y no tuvieren impedimento físico, están obligados á presentarse á la defensa luego que fueren llamados, y por el hecho de no hacerlo serán castigados con una multa de 5 á 200 pesos, ó con prisión de quince dias á cuatro meses. Si la autoridad creyese más conveniente castigar al pueblo por no haberse de-

fendido, podrá imponerle una multa de 200 á 2,000 pesos, y la multa será pagada entre todos los que estando en el caso de este artículo no se presentaren á la defensa . . .

"Artículo 12. Los plagiarios serán juzgados y sentenciados con arreglo al artículo primero de esta ley, sean cuales fueren la manera y circunstancias del plagio . . .

"Artículo 14. Se concede amnistía á todos los que hayan pertenecido y pertenezcan á bandas armadas, si se presentaren á la autoridad . . ."

e. First letter from Carlota to Maximilian after her interviews with Napoleon. Pages 245-46.

"Paris, den 15ten August, 1866.

"Innig geliebter Schatz!

"Vor allem geht es mir vortrefflich und sei Dein Herz über diesen Standpunkt beruhigt. Zweitens ist es meine CONVICTION, *dass sich etwas wird erreichen lassen, weil ein Interesse dafür ist aber der schlechte Wille und die Hülflosigkeit in höheren Regionen ist gross und ich weiss aus sicherer Quelle von Metternich, dass seit zwei Jahren der Kaiser Napoleon sehr physisch und geistig herabgeht. Die Kaiserin ist nicht im Stande die Sache zu führen—bildet keinen Damm für die Minister und ruiniert mehr als dass sie nützt.* ON EST DEVENU VIEUX, *und beide kindisch. Dennoch weinen sie beide öfters; ich weiss nicht, ob es zu etwas führt. Ich habe alles erdenkliche geleistet und gleich das Ultimatum an den Kaiser gebracht. Jetzt habe ich müssen arbeiten, um die 500,000* PIASTRES *durch diesen Dampfer fortsetzen zu lassen, habe aber gewusst es war nicht zu erreichen. Es ist eine Pflichtssache.*

"Dennoch sind mit dem Kaiser Napoleon alle Karten nicht ausgespielt. Ich war nur zwei Mal bei ihm, das zweite Mal brachte ich ihm EXTRAITS *seiner Versprechungen, um ihn im Stillen zu nagen. Er sprach sehr viel von Mexico aber die Sache scheint ihnen längst vergessen. Er weinte mehr das zweite Mal wie das erste . . . Wenn es hier geht, so geht es auch in Rom und Washington.*

"Dieser Brief ist DÉCOUSU, *weil Poliakowitz gleich weggeht. Ich habe den ganzen Tag Leute, was alle Zeit nimmt.*

"Ich umarme Dich aus dem Tiefsten meiner Seele.

"CHARLOTTE."

f. Statement from the French volunteers who remained loyal to Maximilian. Page 297.

"Comme ces officiers (qui pendant tout le siège n'ont assisté à aucune affaire) sont Français, et que votre Majesté

pourrait croire qu'ils ont été les interprètes de nos sentiments, nous nous impressons, Sire, de rejeter toute participation à cet acte inqualifiable, qui a soulevé notre indignation."

g. Blasio's report of the Empire's last stand on the Hill of the Bells. Page 306.

"Preguntó el Emperador á Mejía si sería posible romper el cerco y éste, dechado de adhesión india y total sacrificio por una causa, hubo de responderle sublimemente—'Señor, pasar es imposible; pero si Vuestra Majestad lo ordena, trataremos de hacerlo, que en cuanto á mí estoy dispuesto á morir.'—"

h. Maximilian's words at the moment of his surrender to Escobedo. Pages 307-8.

"Los gefes, que me acompañan, no tienen más responsabilidad que la que les impone haber seguido mi suerte. Deseo que no reciban daño alguno. Si se necesita una víctima, yo quiero ser ella y que mi sangre sea la última, que se derrame en este país."

i. A Mexican paraphrase on the death of Maxmilian, Miramón, and Mejía. Page 331.

"Los fusilados murieron tan dignamente como exigían sus caballerosos precedentes, habiendo dicho el Emperador que los hombres de su rango y de su raza así habían de morir."

j. The plaque on the gates of Castle Bouchout. Page 346.

"Dieses Schloss im Besitz der belgischen Krone ist bewohnt von Ihrer Majestät der Kaiserin von Mexiko—Schwägerin unseres verehrten Bundesgenossen, des Kaisers von Oesterreich. Deutschen Soldaten ist befohlen, ohne Gesang vorbei zu gehen und diesen Ort unberührt zu lassen."

k. The tribute of the singer Concha Méndez. Page 347.

"Nunca he de cantar lo que me pedís, Señores. Llevo puesta en el brazo la pulsera que me regaló una infeliz princesa que hoy gime sola, viuda y loca, muy lejos de nuestra patria. Ni yo ni el pueblo mexicano, al que pertenezco de corazón y de cuna, hemos de insultar la memoria de un príncipe ajusticiado en Querétaro, ni de una dama virtuosa

que en vez de la corona de reina ciñe ahora la corona del martirio . . ."

1. The words of Don Matías Elizondo y Zamora (addressed to the author in May, 1934). Page 348.

> *"La desafortunada Emperatriz Mexicana que fuera víctima inocente de la política europea. . . . En nuestra historia quedará grabada como una mujer buena, noble, pero por sobre todo—amantísima."*

Nota Bene on Accents

Throughout the text particular care has been exercised in rendering all foreign terms with complete accuracy. In thus according each language its due, inconsistencies are met with. These are apparent, not real. To wit:

María, accented in Spanish.

Maria, not accented (as in the Pope's name) in Italian.

Sebastián, accented in Spanish, but not in German.

Napoleon, of Italian origin, accented only where the name is quoted specifically in French.

Leopoldine, Empress of Brazil (born an Archduchess of Austria) used no accent. The same is true of her daughter who, as a Braganza, did not require it.

Léopoldine, patronymic of Princess Charlotte of Belgium, given in French.

Leopold I, although King of the Belgians, was a born German and a naturalized Briton, therefore never used the accent except on official documents.

Léopold II, Belgian by birth and upbringing, always used it.

Since accent marks are not mere quirks but rational keys to pronunciation in the languages endowed with them, it was deemed necessary to include them here.

Variable Spelling

1. In Spain, *Méjico* is correct. The Mexican expatriates in Europe obeyed this pattern.

2. The Aztec passage on page 343 was transcribed according to Spanish phonetics, *qu* before *i* being equivalent to the English *k*. No attempt was made to impose modern accent rules or capital letters, which accounts for *xocotitlan* in its first orthographic form.

3. In Maximilian's day the word *jefe* (chief) was spelled with a *g*. (See preamble to "Black Decree.")

4. Castle Bouchout is sometimes known to Teutonic Flemings as Bukhote, and to Celtic Walloons as Bouchoute.

5. Bosporus, as pronounced by the Turks, has been given preference over the Greek Bosphorus.

Quotations

All material here reproduced is necessarily fragmentary and condensed, since the scope of this narrative did not permit a greater mass of detail. Some of the sources used have since been destroyed by communist incendiarism, although most of the letters quoted may be compared with originals in the *Haus-, Hof- und Staatsarchiv* of Vienna, the *Museo Nacional* of Mexico City, and the private archives of the Alba family in Madrid.

The dialogue is based on memoirs of the period (see Bibliography). In addition, the author is indebted to many private sources for such items as the note to Pepita, the menu cards, programs, songs and invitations to Chapultepec.

The Empress Carlota made a careful copy of all her writings which, translated into Spanish, fell into the hands of collectors in the Aztec capital; a second transcript into English was required before their addition to the body of this book. Likewise, portions of the famous "Black Decree" were translated by the author from a copy so small and faded that it could scarcely be deciphered through a magnifying-glass.

Wherever possible, important passages are offered in their original language and form, for the special scrutiny of purists. There are times when the most meticulous interpretation falls short and fails to convey a subtle shading. With the actual text at hand no flavor is lost. This is especially valuable where quotations—whether in correspondence or dialogue—have at some historical moment been corroborated by witnesses.

Grateful acknowledgment is here accorded to all whose unstinted help gave impulse to this work:

The music master, Don Daniel Zambrano-Lafont, of Monterrey.
The critic, Henry Bornhoeft; the artist, Hugo Brehme; the laundress, Adelaida Cruz, of Mexico City.
Court Photographer Raoul Korty in Vienna.
Baron Oskar von Mitis (in charge of the Vienna Archives from 1919-1925).
Hofrat Pick, Director of *Wiener Nationalbibliothek.*
Her Excellency, Jenny von Rónai-Horváth, Budapest.
The curators of Castle Schönbrunn, and the Erzsébet Museum (Budapest Royal Palace).
The *New York Herald Tribune,* for permission to reprint the report of Maximilian's death. Pages 332, 333.
The *New York Sun,* for excerpts by Gilbert Gabriel. Page 348.
J. B. Lippincott and Co., for quotations from *Porfirio Díaz: Dictator of Mexico* by Carleton Beals. Pages 137, 276, 322.
M. Gaston Gallimard, Editor of "La Nouvelle Revue Française," for Napoleon's proposal and Eugénie's reports to Paca. Pages 25, 33, 60, 112, 353.
(*Publié pour la première fois dans son texte intégral par Robert Sencourt—"La Vie de l'Impératrice Eugénie"—Librairie Gallimard, Paris.*)

In addition, the American edition of Count Corti's *Maximilian and Charlotte of Mexico,* published by Alfred A. Knopf, proved of outstanding value while verifying important points in translation.

Heirlooms

In the summer of 1909 a Hungarian lady left Mexico City with three children, a governess and a mysterious black trunk. Ostensibly on a pleasure trip, she arrived in Europe with an ambassador's seal on her special passport. She directed her steps toward Vienna and the Hofburg, where the Emperor Franz Joseph—white-haired and a trifle bent with age, yet still a man of extraordinary elegance—awaited her. In a private audience Sarolta Posztl-Károly de Leonarz (wife of Don Emilio Leonarz) returned to Austria's state coffers the priceless baubles that once adorned an emperor and his consort. Into the hands of Franz Joseph she placed those gems, decorations and insignia which were worn by Maximilian and Carlota, and which belonged originally to the House of Hapsburg. On this occasion she received the distinguished Signum Laudis, awarded for service to the Crown. It is to-day in possession of the author, whose mother was that lady. . . .

Through the long years popular fancy has woven the inevitable fabric of fantastic legend about a mystifying subject—the lost imperial heirlooms. Much speculation centered around the caravan of packing cases which were taken to Vera Cruz by Herzfeld. It is almost certain that, with the exception of a few things still in the Emperor's possession, such effects reached Europe intact. Among the objects that remained behind was the small individual coffee set and a portion of the silver flatware. The former, presented to the author by an uncle, is shown frequently in exhibits. The sugar bowl, large and out of proportion to the other pieces, may have belonged to the banquet set. Its gold lining is unmarred, whereas coffee pot and cream pitcher show the scars of daily use.

Mr. J. Chester Cuppia, of New York, whose Italian grandfather served as a general in gold-braided imperial Mexico, has the flatware There are also in Mr. Cuppia's possession three small coffins, toy imitations of the makeshifts used during Maximilian's protracted obsequies. These macabre trophies, each about three feet in length, were probably manufactured for one of those bizarre fiestas of the dead held throughout Mexico on a sunny day in November, when Indians picnic on sepulchres and make a condiment of shivers. . . . Each of Mr. Cuppia's coffins shows a wax figurine of the Emperor, in a loin-cloth, an elaborate uniform and a dress suit, respectively. The owner keeps this strange exhibit in his attic. With Lord Dunsany one is moved to say:

> "Indeed, it is a piteous thing to see lie thus
> one who has held a sceptre. . . ."

In 1878 an American, General Jefferson C. Davis, visited Mexico City on official business. Making the rounds of the *Monte de Piedad* pawnshops he came upon the Miramar scarf-pin which first lured the Archduke Maximilian to his doom. Doctor Basch had received it at Querétaro as a keepsake, but the confusion which attended the last days of the Empire proved too much for the physician. He lost the pin and most of his baggage while tearing from one official to another, pleading in vain for his master's body. In the form of a pendant the heirloom is now the property of Mrs. Marietta Finley Hahn, of Indianapolis and New York, a descendant of General Davis.

Maximilian jewels of French and Mexican workmanship continue to crop up from time to time, since to these the Emperor Franz Joseph laid no claim. Court attendants, ladies-in-waiting, erstwhile palace servants, all cherished gifts and mementoes from their former masters. Through these channels the author was able to acquire a salver, a fan, a comb, a decoration of the Order of Guadalupe, as well as a few letters and photographs. Were the story of each inanimate piece told in these pages the manuscript would have assumed forbidding proportions.

In 1911, during the outbreak of the Madero revolution against Díaz (who had ousted Juárez's successor, Lerdo de Tejada), the Ward liner *Mérida* was rammed and sunk off the Virginia Capes by the United Fruit Company steamer *Admiral Farragut*. Six million dollars in bullion and gems were said to have gone down in her hulk, for the ship was crowded with Mexican aristocrats and their belongings, exile bound. A reputed Maximilian collection lies in thirty fathoms of water awash Cape Hatteras. It is said to consist of loot from a Burmese shrine which was raided in the sixteenth century by an adventurous Hapsburg, one Count Herrmann, and a set of gorgeous emeralds from the Aztec temple of Quetzalcoatl. Relatives of the poet, Alan Seeger, who survived the *Mérida* disaster, do not confirm such tales. To date the fabled treasure has stubbornly eluded all efforts expended by ever-hopeful salvage crews.

Meanwhile the month of October, 1932, witnessed the appearance in London of the customary unknown heir to vanished royalty. William Brightwell, a fishmonger who supplies excellent kippers to the small public houses along the Thames, claims to have been born—of all times—during Carlota's unorthodox sojourn at the Vatican. The distraught Empress (who was never for a moment uncompanioned) is supposed to have left him on a church door-step, a door-step which led somehow to London and adoption by a cockney greengrocer.

That the House of Hapsburg, never warlike but always ardent in ferreting out the profitable claims of birthright, should abandon—nay, disown—so precious a twiglet is noteworthy indeed. Few factors are more potent in the restoration of fallen dynasties than the existence of legitimate or illegitimate offspring. When revolutionary cycles have run their course, these hardy prototypes of the once mighty have a surprisingly facile aptitude for returning to public favor.

Mr. Brightwell, notwithstanding, upholds the truthfulness of his extraordinary tale. His solicitors, who concede him at least three shining names in Hapsburg history, Rudolph Franz Maximilian (after the founder of the dynasty, the Biedermeier Emperor, and the victim of Querétaro, in turn), have posted their claim to the *Mérida* treasure when, if and by whomsoever it may be retrieved. This leaves the matter open to philanthropy. Any sort of expedition inspired with generosity toward Mr. Brightwell—who should now be near seventy, though he makes no point whatever of his age—will be greeted by the London solicitors with unrestrained enthusiasm.

Suffice it to say that for generations yet to come the fascinating chase for scattered valuables is destined to continue. In 1922 the wife of Signor Cusi, Italian Minister to Mexico, discovered the crimson brocades of Carlota's private chapel fading in the glare of the *Volador* (Thieves' Market) and lined therewith the walls of her husband's study in the turreted house on the Paseo de la Reforma.

In a forsaken spot of the Buena Vista railroad station there stood for a while the imperial couple's old-fashioned *wagon-lit,* its blistered varnish peeling in the dry air. Equally gaudy, though not so weather-beaten, the gilded state-coach has found shelter in the *Museo Nacional.* This vehicle, once the wonder of rustic passers-by, has become the delight of American tourists who in the absence of a guide scramble triumphantly into its cushioned interior, there to favor their democratic haunches with a unique contact. . . .

Nor is this all. Second-hand china shops are known occasionally to offer for sale a cast-off and tarnished medal of San Carlos, the patron saint of an empress who was never chastened, or to hide amid the grime of worthless pottery yet another chipped and florid plate, tureen, or porringer bearing the imperial cipher beneath a crown.

Also there is still to be found the Maximilian peso. It is stamped on one side with the profile of a prince who found greatness in death, and on the other with the regardant double griffin of the Hapsburg arms crossed by an Aztec serpent.

And more there is not.

Happy ending? Hardly. This is a story of persons in high places.

> "They that stand high have many blasts to shake them;
> And if they fall they dash themselves to pieces."

Addenda

1. Carlota's retinue had been discharged in Rome. Señora del Barrio, whose husband took up temporary residence in Paris, aided the Empress in her transfer from Miramar to Brussels. She visited Carlota at intervals thereafter and remained at her side until she was replaced by an aged Belgian waiting-woman whom the Empress continually mistook for her former friend.

2. Since the actual eye-witnesses to Maximilian's execution were not of a literary bent, the most conflicting descriptions exist in regard to the costume he wore at the end. The bullet-riddled garment (on page 328), known in Mexico as a *levita,* had long been used by the Emperor as a campaign coat. With boots, buttons and the Golden Fleece, Lawyer Hall considered it a uniform. Blasio cautiously avoids the issue by stating that the monarch "wore black."

BIBLIOGRAPHY

BIBLIOGRAPHY

In German

Almanach, Gotha, 1871-1872.

ALVENSLEBEN, MAXIMILIAN FREIHERR VON: *Mit Maximilian in Mexiko.*

BASCH, DR. SAMUEL: *Geschichte der letzten zehn Monate des Kaiserreichs. Tagebuch. Leipzig, 1868.*

CORTI, EGON CAESAR, GRAF: *Maximilian und Charlotte von Mexiko. 1924. Amalthea-Verlag, Wien. Most complete German letters.*

KOLLONITZ, GRAFIN PAULA: *Eine Reise nach Mexiko. Wien, 1867.*

LINDEN, EXZELLENZ PAULA VON BÜLOW, GEB. GRAFIN: *Aus Verklungenen Zeiten. 1833-1920. Koehler und Amelang Verlag, Leipzig.*

LINSERT, RICHARD: *Kabale und Liebe, Dafnis Verlag, Berlin, 1931.*

MAURENBRECHER, MAX: *Die Hohenzollernlegende. Verlag des Vorwärts, Berlin, 1905.*

MONTLONG, WILHELM VON: *Authentische Enthüllungen über die letzten Ereignisse in Mexiko. Stuttgart, 1868.*

SALM-SALM, AGNES, PRINZESSIN ZU: *Zehn Jahre aus meinem Leben. Stuttgart, 1877.*

SALM-SALM, FELIX, PRINZ ZU: *Blätter aus meinem Tagebuch in Mexiko. Stuttgart, 1868.*

SALM-VAN HOOGSTRAETEN, LUDWIG, GRAF ZU: *Mein lieber Peter.*

TSCHUDI, CLARA: *Elisabeth, Kaiserin von Oesterreich, Leipzig.*

TSCHUPPIK, KARL: *Kaiserin Elisabeth, Wien, 1930. Epstein Verlag.*

TSCHUPPIK, KARL: *Franz Joseph I, Avalun Verlag, Dresden, 1928.*

TAVERA, DR. ERNST SCHMITT, RITTER VON (BARON VON LAGO'S ASSISTANT): *Die mexikanische Kaisertragödie. Wien, 1903.*

ULICZNY, JULIUS: *Geschichte des österreichisch-belgischen Freikorps in Mexiko. Wien, 1868.*

WIEGLER, PAUL: *Wilhelm der Erste. 1927.*

WERFEL, FRANZ: *Juárez und Maximilian, Tragödie. 1926.*

In French

CARETTE, MADAME, NÉE BOUVET: *Souvenirs intimes de la Cour des Tuileries. 1861-1870.*

HUGO, VICTOR: *Napoléon-le-Petit. 1852.*

KÉRATRY, ÉMILE, COMTE DE: *L'Empereur Maximilien—son élévation et sa chute, Leipzig, 1867.*

LICHTERVELDE, COMTE LOUIS DE: *Léopold II, Roi des Belges.*

LOLIÉE, FRÉDERIC: *La Vie d'une Impératrice, Eugénie de Montijo, Paris, 1907.*

MÉRIMÉE, PROSPER: *Lettres à M. Panizzi (1850-1870) 2 vols. Paris, 1881.*

OLLIVIER, ÉMILE: *L'Empire Libéral. 17 vols. 1895-1915. Most complete French letters.*

OLLIVIER, ÉMILE: *Papiers Secrets et Correspondance du Second Empire. 1877.*

TAISEY-CHATENEY, MARQUISE DE: *A la cour de Napoléon III.*

TASCHER, STÉPHANIE, COMTESSE DE LA PAGERIE: *Mon séjour aux Tuileries. Paris, 1900.*

VIEL CASTEL, COMTE H. DE: *Mémoires sur le Règne de Napoléon III. 1884.*

In English

ASHLEY, THE HONOURABLE EVELYN: *Life of Viscount Palmerston (1846-1865) 2 vols. London, 1876.*

BANCROFT, HUBERT HOWE: *History of Mexico. San Francisco, 1888.*

BARKER, RUTH LAUGHLIN: *Caballeros. (The Romance of Santa Fé and the Southwest). D. Appleton & Co. New York, 1931.*

BATTENBERG, PRINCESS MARIE OF: *Reminiscences. London, 1925. Unwin Brothers, Ltd.*

BEALS, CARLETON: *Porfirio Díaz. J. B. Lippincott, New York, 1932.*

BOLITHO, HECTOR: *Albert the Good. D. Appleton & Co. New York, 1932.*

BRENNER, ANITA: *Idols Behind Altars. New York, 1929. Payson & Clarke Ltd.*

CHASE, STUART: *Mexico—A Study of Two Americas. Macmillan Co. New York, 1931.*

CORTI, EGON CAESAR, COUNT: *Maximilian and Charlotte of Mexico, translated by Catherine Allison Phillips. Published by Alfred A. Knopf, New York, 1928.*

DRAPER, JOHN WILLIAM: *History of the American Civil War. 1870.*

GUEDALLA, PHILIP: *The Second Empire. G. B. Putnam's Sons, 1922.*

HALL, FREDERIC: *Mexico and Maximilian. Hurst & Co. New York, 1867 (written before Maximilian's body reached Europe; probably earliest record of trial).*

MARTIN, PERCY F.: *Maximilian in Mexico. London, 1914.*

SENCOURT, ROBERT: *Napoleon III, The Modern Emperor, New York, D. Appleton-Century Co. 1934.*

SMITH, ARTHUR D. HOWDEN: *Conqueror. J. B. Lippincott, 1933.*

STORM, MARIAN: *Prologue to Mexico—The Story of a Search for a Place. Knopf, 1931.*
STRACHEY, LYTTON: *Queen Victoria.*
TREVELYAN, G. M.: *Garibaldi and the Making of Italy. 1911.*
TUER AND FAGAN: *First Years of a Silken Reign. London, 1887.*
VAN LOON, HENDRIK WILLEM: *The Story of Mankind. Horace Liveright, Inc. 1921.*
WHITE, JAMES: *The Republic of Mexico Restored. 1867.*

In Italian

ANELLI, FRANCESCA, E BICE CAMPOLONGO: *Coscienti e Buone—Antologia. Milano, 1907.*
BONFIGLI, F. SALVERIO: *Pagine sull'Italia di Massimiliano d'Absburgo. Firenze, 1868.*

In Spanish

BAZ, GUSTAVO: *Vida de Benito Juárez. México, 1874.*
BLASIO, JOSÉ LUIS: *Maximiliano Íntimo.*
CASTRO, JUAN DE: *El Emperador Maximiliano y su augusta esposa Carlota. Madrid, 1867. Most complete Spanish letters.*
CAMPOS, RUBÉN M.: *El Folklore Literario de México. 1929.*
CASTILLO, BERNAL DÍAZ DEL: *Historia de la Conquista. 1517-1519.*
IBÁÑEZ, VICENTE BLASCO: *Los Enemigos de la Mujer.*
POLA, ÁNGEL: *Los traidores pintados por sí mismos.*
RIOS, ENRIQUE DE LOS: *Maximiliano y la toma de Querétaro.*
SAHAGÚN, BERNARDINO DE: *Historia General de las Cosas de Nueva España. México, 1829.*
SEPTIÉN Y LLATA, J. A.: *Maximiliano, Emperador de México, no fué traidor. 1907.*

Government Documents, Pamphlets and Periodicals

DIARIO DEL IMPERIO. *Ciudad de México 1865-1866 (contains Black Decree).*
CAUSA DE FERNANDO MAXIMILIANO DE HAPSBURGO, *que se ha titulado Emperador de México, y sus generales Miguel Miramón y Tomás Mejía, sus cómplices, por delitos contra la Independencia y Seguridad de la Nación. México, 1868.*
CORRESPONDENCIA DE LA EMPERATRIZ CARLOTA, *Museo Nacional de México.*
JOSÉ MANUEL HIDALGO Y ESNAURRIZAR, *"Notas Secretas."*
CONVENTION DE MIRAMAR, *Paris, 1864.*
PAPIERS ET CORRESPONDENCE DE LA FAMILLE IMPÉRIALE, *Paris, 1871.*
REVUE DES DEUX MONDES, *15 Juillet, 1932. "Les Fiançailles de L'Impératrice" (Lettres à la Duchesse d'Albe.* Madrid Archives.)

MAXIMILIAN UND CHARLOTTE VON MEXIKO, *Korrespondenz. Staatsarchiv, Wien. 1926.*

RAPPORTI DELLA CORTE DI ROMA COL GOVERNO MESSICANO. *Roma, 1867.*

RECORDS PUBLISHED BY ARCHIVES OF QUAI D'ORSAY.

RECORDS PUBLISHED BY VIENNA NATIONAL ARCHIVES.

INDEX

INDEX

Adriatic Sea, 22, 48, 120, 227, 253, 254
Africa, 146, 213, 342
Aguilar, Ignacio, 95
Aix-les-Bains, 252
Ajaccio, 72, 73
Albert of Coburg, 28, 29, 34, 35, 46, 49, 81, 347
Alexander I, 28
Alexandrine, la Belle Sabotière ("Madame Sans Gêne"), 59
Alfonso XII, 31
Alleau, Abbé, 170-71
Almonte, Juan Nepomuceno, 78, 94, 136, 137, 139, 172
Alsace-Lorraine, 221
Amazon River, 72
American Civil War, 169, 191, 290, 310
Anáhuac, 66, 140, 143, 311, 348
Ancona, 127, 271
Andalucía, 56, 63, 182
Andrássy, Count Julius, 23, 180
Antonelli, Cardinal Giacomo, 261, 266, 268
Aragón, 72
Arango y Escandón, Alejandro Don, 276
Arangoitia, Rodríguez, 149
Arangoiz y Berzabal, Francisco de Paul, 118
Arce, General Francisco, 302
Arquinto, Count, 41
Arroyo, Señor Luis de, 168, 286
Arteaga, General, 217
Ashmore, General, 135
Asia Minor, 24
Asturias, 72, 177
Atlantic Ocean, 65, 77, 83, 94, 131, 204, 229, 251
August, Prince (of Saxe-Coburg-Gotha), 184
Austria, 45, 47, 49, 80, 86, 128, 138, 175, 183, 225, 226, 231, 235, 241, 254, 322, 326, 337, 344, 346
  Ambassador Linden and daughter leave, 24
  and the Mexican enterprise, 134
  appeals to Andrew Johnson in Maximilian's behalf, 314, 316
  demands Maximilian's renunciation of rights to throne, 104-6
  friends from, at Maximilian's coronation, 116
  Maximilian leaves, on diplomatic visits, 28-40
Austria—*continued*
  Maximilian reinstated as heir to throne of, 325
  Maximilian's body returned to, 338-40, 342-44
  Mexican liberal government desires recognition by, 335-36
  Mexican social questions compared with those of, 176
  shadow of Bismarck over, 220-22

Bansen, Herr, 316
Barrio, Marquesa Neri del, 230, 242, 245, 260, 261, 263, 264, 265, 266, 268, 270, 271, 342, 345
Basch, Dr. Samuel, 227, 280, 291, 293, 301, 304, 305, 318, 323, 327
  petitions return to Austria of Maximilian's remains, 337-38
  returns to Austria, 340
  witnesses embalming of Maximilian, 335
Bazaine, Josefa Peña y Azcárate de, 169
Bazaine, Marshal François Achille, 85, 97, 137, 147, 153, 157, 171, 173, 193, 203, 225, 287, 319
  and the "Black Decree," 214-17
  curb put on large expenditures of, 181
  eludes Emperor on subject of military command, 167
  leaves Mexico, 275-76
  marriage of, at Chapultepec, 167-69
  ordered to evacuate Mexico, 195-99, 211
  responsibility for Maximilian's death, 332
  state dinner in honor of, 161-62
Beauchamp, Pliny, 29
Beauharnais, Josephine, 61, 62, 84
Belgium, 35, 42, 92, 116, 198, 234, 342, 346
  appeals to Washington in Maximilian's behalf, 314, 316
  Léopold II ascends throne of, 213
  Maximilian's visit to, 1856, 36-38; in 1864, 114
  refuses aid to Mexico, 227
Bellona, Austrian gunboat, 122
Berlin, 38, 149, 164, 221
Berwick and Alba, Duke of, 57
Beust, Baron Friedrich Ferdinand von, 339
Biarritz, 62, 225, 345
Bigelow, John, 194, 278
Billarderie, General Count Auguste Charles de Flahault de la, 114
Binther, Baron de, 116

Bismarck, 220, 221, 232, 235, 250, 344, 346
"Black Decree," 217, 281, 319
  manifesto contained in preamble to, 214-15, 353-54
  portion of, quoted, 215-16, 354-55
Blasio, José Luis, 230, 259, 280, 285, 289, 304, 305, 318, 323
  reports Empire's last stand on Hill of the Bells, 306, 356
Bohemia, 231
Bohuslavek, Doctor, 248, 249, 251, 253, 263, 270, 280, 285, 289
Bologna, 260
Bombelles, Count Heinrich, 16, 21, 22, 23, 28, 38, 116
Bombelles, Count Karl, 116, 230
Bonnefond, Monsieur, 174
Booth, Edwin, 189
Booth, John Wilkes, 189-90
Booth, Junius Brutus, 189
Borromeo, San Carlos, 160
Bosporus, the, 24
Bosse, Rear-Admiral, 136
Bossi, Colonel, 266
Botzen, 258
Bouchout
  Carlota spends last days at, 342
  plaque on gates of castle, quoted, 346, 356
Brabant, Duchess of
  see Henriette of Austria
Brabant, Duke of, 36, 37, 114, 201
  see Léopold II
Braganza, Princess of, 30
  Maxl's engagement to, 27
Brazil, 184, 346
Brincourt, General, 142
Bringas, Luz Robles de, 151
British Isles, 49
Brussels, 36, 37, 41, 59, 75, 92, 101, 104, 114, 121, 168, 213, 223, 227, 268, 342
Buckingham Palace, 45
Budapest, 50, 180
Bulkens, Doctor, 341
Bülow, Baroness von, 39, 40, 343
  see Countess Linden
Buonaparte, Donna Lætitia Ramolino, 72

Cádiz, 112
Calais, 59
Campbell, Lewis D., 314
Campbell-Scarlett, Sir Peter, 175, 227, 286, 316, 332
Campero, María Barrio de, 150
Canary Islands, 132
Cape St. Vincent, 131
Carette, Madame, 237, 243
Carlota, Empress of Mexico (also Charlotte and Carlotta)
  a natural linguist, 177
  and Maxl's visit to Belgium, 1856, 36-38
  audience with Pope Pius IX, 260-66
  audiences with Napoleon, 238-41, 242-44, 247-48
  becomes Empress of Mexico, 119
  changes name to Italian, Carlotta, 44
  chooses court of honor, 150-51
  consults her father on Mexican venture, 92, 105-6
  description of, in 1856, 37-38; at coronation, in 1864, 116
  draws up her testament, 268
  establishes a reading circle, 151
  fears being poisoned, 243-44, 259, 263, 266, 269-71
  filches tumbler from the Vatican, 270-71
  goes abroad to secure aid, 229-35
  interviews the nuncio on the Church question, 157
  last days of, 341-49
  letters to the Empress Eugénie quoted, 140, 142, 143, 157, 158, 166, 167, 192, 193, 195, 211, 219
  letters to Maximilian quoted, 241, 245-46, 249-51, 252-54, 355
  literary aspirations of, 89
  love of music of, 151-52
  marriage to Ferdinand Maximilian of Austria, 1857, 41-43
  portraits of, 212
  pronounced incurably insane, 269-71
  quoted on Maxl's decision to abdicate, 228
  receives personal call from Eugénie, 236-37
  receptions and soirées of, 164-66
  rumors of death of, 322
  spends night at the Vatican, 266-67
  sponsors *Orden Imperial de San Carlos,* 160
  uses Spanish spelling of her name, Carlota, 120
  visited by French Minister in Paris, 246-47
Castiglione, Countess, 33
Castilla la Vieja, 177
Castillo, Bernal Díaz del, 69
Castillo, Don Martín, 230, 238, 239, 247, 258, 259, 260, 263
Castle Claremont, 35, 111
Cavour, Count Camillo Benso di, 47
Cerro de las Campanas, 293, 306, 328, 329, 335
  Blasio's report of Empire's last stand on, 306, 356

Cerro de las Cruz, 293
Cervantes, Soledad Vivanco de, 150
César, Francisco de Paul, 217
Chapultepec, 67, 170, 173, 175, 191, 192, 198, 204, 206, 207, 208, 209, 222, 224, 230, 231, 232, 234, 239, 244, 257, 258, 278, 279, 281, 287, 295, 296, 298, 300, 302, 311, 339
  Court takes residence at, 148-54
  Marshal Bazaine's marriage at, 169
  Maximilian describes routine at, 159
  palace functions at, described, 159-66
Charles V, 29, 34, 119, 290, 326, 340
Charles VI, 29
Charles X, 78
Charleston, 88
Charlotte, Princess (daughter of George IV, and first wife of Leopold I of Belgium), 35
Charlotte, Princess (daughter of Leopold I and Louise Marie, of Belgium)
  see under Carlota, Empress of Mexico
Chihuahua, 191
China, 241
Cholula, 143, 144
Christian IX, 13, 221
Cittadella-Vigodarzere, Count, 254
Ciudad Juárez, 97
Civitâ Vecchia, 128
Claremont
  see under Castle Claremont
Clémentine, Princess (daughter of Queen Marie Amélie of France), 112, 113
Clímaco, Juan
  Escala Espiritual, 69
Cloué, Captain, 233
Codrington, General, 130
Collantes, Calderón, 88
Comonfort, 75
Compiègne, 62
Constantin zu Hohenlohe-Schillingsfürst, Prince, 13
"Convention of Miramar," 119-20, 173, 243
  portion quoted, 96-97, 353
Córdoba, 83, 140, 232, 233
Corio, Marquis, 116, 118
Corredor de la Vitrina, 169
Corsica, 72, 130
Cortés, Hernán, 66, 68, 69, 70, 132, 138, 223
Corti, Count, 50
Cossé-Brissac, Count, 236
Coyoacán, 223
Creevey, Mr.
  diary quoted, 111
Crimean War, 32
Crivelli, Count, 88
Cruz, Adelaida, 231
Cuautitlán, 144
Cuautlálpam, 144
Cuautlatohua, 144
Cuba, 83
Cuernavaca, 153, 182, 213, 217, 223, 225, 229, 231, 253, 257, 311
Curtopassi, Signor Francesco, 316
Cuzco, 72
Czismandia, Baron, 227

Dandolo, Austrian corvette, 281, 283
Dano, Monsieur Alphonse, 171, 316
Danube River, 14, 25, 89, 220
Daudet, Léon, 200
David, Baron Jérôme
  quoted, 277
Dayton, William Lewis, 103, 210
Degollado, Don Mariano, 191
Denmark, 13, 220
Derby, Lord, 78
Díaz, Porfirio, 85, 97, 222, 289, 295, 296, 297, 298, 314, 332
Dietrichstein, Countess Gaby, 17, 164
Doblinger, Fräulein Mathilde, 230
Dolores, 153
Dover, 59
Dunlop, Admiral Hugh, 82, 84
Dupin, Colonel, 153

Echegaray, General, 307, 308
Edward VII, 129
Egypt, 24, 48, 66
Elba, 61, 73
Elgüero, Dolores Germandín de, 151
Elisabeth, Empress of Austria and Princess of Bavaria, 27, 50, 89, 113, 149, 212, 346
  marriage to Franz Joseph, 26
Elizondo y Zamoro, Don Matías
  quoted, 348, 357
El Nevado de Toluca, 154
Eloin, Felix, 132, 213, 229, 230
El Paseo de la Reforma, 150
England, 26, 28, 32, 35, 45, 49, 58, 75, 79, 80, 81, 82, 83, 87, 91, 101, 103, 111, 129, 130, 137, 149, 175, 286, 346
  Maximilian visits in, 1856, 34
  protests against Mexican venture, 102
Erbach-Schönberg, Marie zu (Princess of Battenburg)
  diary quoted, 272, 341
Escandón, Antonio, 95
Escandón, Carolina Barrón de, 150
Escandón y Landa, Francisca, 150
Escobedo, General Mariano, 289, 293, 297, 300, 301, 302, 304, 312, 313, 316, 317, 318, 324, 326, 337
  enters plea in behalf of prisoners, 334
  Maximilian surrenders to, 307-8, 356

Escudero, Pedro, 156, 157, 217
Esher, 35
Esteva, José María, 217
Estrada, José María Gutiérrez de, 74, 86, 87, 89, 90, 91, 92, 94, 110, 118, 119, 170, 219, 229
Estremadura, 144
Eszterházy, Prince, 116
Eu, Count of, 184
Eugénie, Empress (wife of Napoleon III), 31, 74, 80, 85, 86, 87, 88, 91, 100, 105, 114, 130, 137, 168, 238, 240, 242, 245, 257, 263, 327, 344, 345
  and the Mexican plot, 63-71, 77-95
  becomes a politician, 61
  birth of son of, 33
  Carlota's letters to, quoted, 140, 142, 143, 157, 158, 166, 167, 192, 193, 195, 211, 219
  descriptions of, 32-33, 212
  last days of, 345-46
  makes personal call on Carlota in Paris, 235-37
  marriage to Napoleon III, 60-61
  presents Carlotta with Spanish mantilla, 112
  studies history of Mexico, 61-76
  warned against Mexican venture, 102-3
Europe, 14, 15, 16, 21, 24, 36, 40, 42, 66, 67, 73, 74, 79, 80, 81, 85, 88, 89, 102, 110, 120, 132, 134, 138, 141, 143, 149, 158, 164, 170, 176, 179, 181, 197, 200, 208, 209, 213, 217, 218, 221, 224, 228, 229, 232, 234, 239, 244, 250, 254, 256, 281, 285, 289, 291, 311, 314, 321, 322, 325, 327, 337, 344, 346, 348
Eyre, Edward John, 135

Ferdinand I, 15, 132
Ferdinand Maximilian, Archduke
  see under Maximilian I, Emperor of Mexico
Ferretti, Count Giovanni Maria Mastai, 127
Fischer, Father Augustus, 203, 204, 205, 206, 226, 227, 228, 283, 284, 286, 295
Flanders, Count of, 114, 270, 271
Foligno, 260
Fontainebleau, 62, 80
Foreign Legion, 97, 243, 277
  protestation of loyalty from, 297, 355-56
Forey, Elie Fréderic, 85, 94, 110, 119, 120, 198, 214, 215
Fould, Monsieur Achille, 97, 98, 101, 105, 113, 173, 238, 239, 240
France, 28, 35, 47, 59, 61, 72, 74, 75, 77, 78, 79, 81, 82, 83, 88, 93, 94, 96, 97, 98, 101, 103, 107, 114, 120, 128, 137, 149, 168, 170, 173, 179, 183, 194, 195, 196, 205, 209, 210, 211, 220, 229, 235, 239, 241, 243, 248, 250, 276, 278, 281, 311, 344, 345, 346
  abandons Mexican Empire, 222, 248
  appeals to Washington in behalf of Maximilian, 314, 316
  Carlota and party leave (August 23, 1866), 252
  Carlota unwelcome in, 234, 236
  celebrates Forey's occupation of Mexico City, July, 1863, 85
  Maximilian makes diplomatic visit in, 1856, 32-34
Francis, Duke of Lorraine, 29
Francisca, Duchess of Alba, 25, 56, 57
Franz Ferdinand, Archduke, 292, 346
Franz Joseph, Emperor of Austria, 15, 16, 18, 19, 20, 25, 26, 27, 28, 31, 42, 47, 50, 86, 92, 93, 99, 100, 101, 113, 179, 180, 182, 184, 195, 208, 220, 221, 224, 227, 232, 235, 246, 260, 323, 335, 339, 346
  at Miramar Convention, 115-17
  demands Maximilian's remains, 336
  demands Maximilian's renunciation of rights to Austrian throne, 104-6, 108-9
  enthusiasm for Mexican venture, 89-90, 104
  marriage to Princess Elisabeth of Bavaria, 26
  plans cure for his love-sick brother, 23
  provides troops for Maximilian in Mexico, 103-4, 227
  reinstates Maximilian as heir presumptive to Austrian throne, 325
Franz Karl, Archduke (husband of Dowager Archduchess Sophie), 15, 16, 50
Frederika Sophie, Archduchess
  see under Sophie
Frossard, General Charles August de, 107, 109, 116
Funchal, 89

Gabriel, Gilbert W., quoted, 348
García, Antonio, 288
Garibaldi, Giuseppe Maria, 321
Garza, Juan José de la, 85
Gaulfrèrons, Xavier, 298
Gautier, Théophile, 32
Genlis, General Waubert de, 236
George, Prince, of Saxony, 111
Germany, 115, 220, 235, 346
Gibraltar, 133

Gisela, Archduchess, 50, 208, 292
Gloria, Maria da, 36
Gomez, Father Tomás, 119
Granada, 56, 90, 340
Grasshopper Hill, 67
Gravière, Vice-Admiral Jean Pierre Edmond Jurien de la, 81
Great Britain, 101, 314, 316, 325
Greece, 92
Groenendal, 342
Grünne, Count, 117
Guadalajara, 76
Guadalupe, 144, 159, 233, 289
Guadalupe, Marquesa de, 232
Guadalupe, Nuestra Señora de, 144
Guadalupe, Pocito de, 145
Guerrero, Vicente, 73
Günner, Rudolf, 294

Habana, 135
Hacienda de la Teja, 287
Hadik, Count, 227
Hall, Frederic, 315, 318
Ham, 58
Hamburg, 101, 316
Hammerstein, Lieutenant-Colonel Baron, 287, 289
Hanover, 38
Harvey, James E.
quoted, 278
Hatzfeld, Countess, 33
Hautecombe, 252
Heiligenberg, 271
Henriette of Austria, Archduchess (Duchess of Brabant), 36, 37
takes Carlota into her care, 341
Héraud, Théodore, 298
Herbet, Monsieur d', 96, 98, 99, 105, 113, 116, 119
Hérillier, General d', 166, 173
Herzfeld, Stefan, 116, 283, 284, 286, 287, 333
Hidalgo y Costilla, Miguel, 73, 153, 154, 229, 285
Hidalgo y Esnaurrizar, José Manuel, 63, 64, 65, 66, 68, 74, 77, 78, 86, 87, 95, 114
Hidalgo y Terán, Dolores Quesada de, 150
Hildreth, Richard, 102
Hill of the Bells
see Cerro de las Campanas
Hofburg, the, 15, 20, 22, 26, 37, 40, 41, 42, 49, 50, 87, 89, 90, 99, 103, 104, 106, 109, 115, 149, 180, 182, 208, 222, 228, 291, 326, 343
Holland, 38
Hoorícks, Monsieur Fréderic, 316
Hope, Admiral Sir James, 135
Hortense, Queen, 33, 59, 114
Howard, Miss, 59
Hradschin, 15
Hugo, Victor, 167, 321
Hülsemann, Ritter von, 88
Hungary, 25, 42, 118, 281
Hunyadi, Countess Julia, "Juppy," 18

Iglesias, Señor Ángel, 95, 120
Iguala, 73
Innsbruck, 15
Ireland, 244
Isabella II, 31, 56, 78, 81, 110, 132
Italy, 44, 47, 48, 78, 86, 128, 129, 224, 227, 254, 257, 260, 316, 325
Itelezi, 346
Iturbide family, 205-9
Iturbide, Agustín de (Crown Prince of Mexico; adopted heir of Maximilian and Carlota), 217, 225, 231, 279
sent to Europe, 281-82
Iturbide, Emperor Don Agustín de, 73, 160, 205
Iturbide, Alice de, 206, 209, 279, 281
Iturbide, Ángel de, 205, 206, 209
Iturbide, Cosme de, 205, 206
Iturbide, Josefa de, 205, 207, 209, 213, 281
Iturbide, Salvador de, 206, 207
Ixtaccihuatl, 143

Jablonski (guardsman), 304, 305, 312
Jamaica, 134
Jecker, Jean Baptiste, 75, 81
Jecker, Louis, 75, 81
Jecker, Torre and Company, 75
Jerome of Westphalia, King, 31
Jilek, Doctor, 120, 121, 176, 253, 270
Johnson, President Andrew, 191
Joseph, Archduke, 117
Juárez, Benito Pablo, 77, 78, 82, 83, 84, 97, 127, 128, 137, 138, 153, 155, 156, 169, 181, 192, 193, 199, 200, 214, 215, 217, 222, 223, 224, 226, 227, 259, 285, 287, 288, 289, 300, 303, 308, 312-26, 329, 334, 338, 348
abandons Mexico City to French, 85; reenters, 337
declares moratorium on all foreign loans (1861), 79, 81, 173
receives pleas in Maximilian's behalf, 321
recognized by United States as president of Mexico, 76, 191
Jurado, Ignacio, 318

Karl Ludwig, Archduke, 21, 23, 37, 117, 154, 155, 208, 292, 341
Karlsbad, 102

Károlyi, Count, 227
Kendall, Captain J. J.
quoted, 276
Kératry, Count Émile de, 120
Khevenhüller, Colonel Karl von, 227, 283, 287, 289, 291
Kieffers, Felix, 298
Kinsky, Princess Cara, 20
Kirkpatrick, Mr., 55
Kodolitch, Alfons von, 227, 283, 295
Kollonitz, Countess Paula, 99, 100, 118, 131, 152
Königgrätz, 232
Kossuth, Louis, 25
Krüdener, Baroness von, 15
Kuhacsevich, Frau von, 230
Kuhacsevich, Jakob von, 48, 171, 172, 230, 236, 258, 259

Labastida y Dávalos, Monsignor Pelagio Antonio, 77, 127, 156, 158, 200, 218
La Bombilla, 75
La Cañada, 140
Lacroma, Abbot of, 119
La Cruz de la Constancia, 160
Laeken, 36, 37, 46, 111, 114, 115, 141, 178, 181, 202, 213, 341, 342
Carlota returns to, 1867, 271
Lago, Baron von, 316, 322, 325, 326, 332
asks for body of Maximilian, 334-35
La Guadalupana, 146
La Habana, 233
L'Aiglon, 14
Lake Como, 252
Lake Texcoco, 143
La Paloma, 151, 347, 348
La Patrie, 84, 168, 170
La Plata River, 72
La Puebla de los Ángeles, 76, 84, 85, 142, 143, 232, 287, 289, 295, 296, 297, 300, 333
Lares, Teodosio, 285
Larousse, Pierre Athanase, 98
Las Cumbres, 142
La Soledad, 83, 137
La Teja, 311
Latin America, 70, 72, 191, 277
La Villa Rica de la Vera Cruz, 68, 138
Leclerq, Agnes
see Princess Agnes Salm-Salm
L'Empereur, 28, 32, 64, 66, 80, 91, 96, 107, 113, 194, 198, 222, 234, 235, 241, 255
see Napoleon III
León, 153
León, Señor Joaquín Velásquez de, 95, 120
Leopold I, King of Belgium, 25, 35, 36, 37, 38, 41, 42, 49, 92, 99, 103, 106,
Leopold I—*continued*
108, 111, 114, 132, 167, 168, 223, 225, 230, 236, 301
death of, 213
final counsel to Maxl, 213
quoted on Mexican venture, 93, 96, 101, 105-6
refuses dowry for daughter, 42, 99
Léopold II, 36, 114, 342, 347
ascends Belgian throne, 213-14
Leopold, Otto Eduard (Prinz von Bismarck-Schönhausen), 115
Leopoldine, Princess (of Brazil), 41, 184
Lerdo, Toluca de, 154
Lhuys, Drouyn de, 238, 239, 278, 280
Libényi, János, 25
Lincoln, President Abraham, 190, 191
Linden, Ambassador
see Franz de Paula
Linden, Countess Paula von, 18, 19-23, 27, 36, 38, 39, 41
see also Baroness von Bülow
Lojero, Emilio, 318
Lombardy, 42, 47, 86, 143, 252
London, 34, 38, 49, 56, 58, 59, 63, 75, 103, 110, 121, 164
López, Colonel Don Miguel, 139, 298, 299, 302, 303, 304, 305, 312, 332, 334
fate of—*New York Herald* quoted, 333
La Toma de Querétaro—A mis compatriotas y al mundo, 333
Lorencez, General, 84
Louis IX, 242
Louis XIV, 106
Louis XVI, 205
Louis XVIII, 78
Louis of Holland, King, 58
Louise Marie (second wife of Leopold I, and mother of Princess Charlotte (Carlota), 35, 92, 113
Louis Philippe, 36, 59, 112
Loulou (son of Napoleon III), 67, 77, 85, 238, 239, 346
Loysel, Major, 213, 257
Ludwig Viktor, Archduke, 21, 117, 184

Madrid, 31, 38, 56, 57, 64, 78, 80, 88, 110, 112, 121, 122, 278, 290
Magenta, 47, 86
Magnus, Baron von, 175, 227, 316, 326, 336
petitions for Maximilian's life, 325
requests Maximilian's body, 337
Málaga, 24, 130
Malmaison, 84
Malmis, 96
Mantua, 259
Manzanares, 64

Marescotti, Palazzo, 128
Maria Anna (wife of Ferdinand I), 16
María Eugenia (mother of the Empress Eugénie), 56
Maria Theresia, 29, 149, 322
Marie Amélie (wife of Louis Philippe), 59, 112
Marie Antoinette, 29, 48, 62, 72, 89, 205, 219, 253
Marin, Monsieur, 233
Márquez, Leonardo, 287, 288, 293, 294, 295, 296, 297, 332, 333
Marseilles, 93
Martin, Percy F., 122
Mathilde, Princess, 33
Maximilian I, Emperor of Mexico (also Archduke Ferdinand Maximilian)
accepts Mexican Crown, 116-19
accorded honors at Gibraltar, 130
addresses citizenry of Dolores, 154
addresses parting note to Carlota, 323
adopts heir, Augustín de Iturbide, 204-8
and Countess von Linden, 19-23, 39-40
and the ecclesiastical problem, 155-59, 201-5
arrival at Vera Cruz, 136
arrives at Mexico City, 148
becomes engaged to Portuguese girl, 27
"Black Decree" of, 217, 281, 319
Manifesto contained in preamble to, 214-15, 353-54
portion of, quoted, 215-16, 354-55
comments on beauty of Mexican ladies, 182
decides to abdicate, 227-28
defense of, 319-20
describes routine at Chapultepec, 159
diplomatic representatives plead in behalf of, 316
diplomatic visits to foreign parts, in 1856, 30
embalming of body of, 335-36, 339
epitaph of, quoted, 343
equestrian passion of, 28
execution of, 323-31
flees from Italy to Miramar, 1859, 47
Franz Joseph reinstates, as heir to Austrian throne, 325
granted trial by proxy, 318
greets Italian royal family, 129-30
indictment and sentence of, 318-19, 320
learns of Carlota's illness, 280-81
letter to Archduke Karl quoted, 155
letter to Doctor Jilek quoted, 176
letters to his mother quoted, 227-28, 232
letters to Napoleon III quoted, 196-97, 225-26
literary inclinations of, 49
Maximilian I—*continued*
marriage to Charlotte of Belgium, 1857, 41-43
moves to Chapultepec, 148-49
Napoleon's reply to telegram of congratulation from, 255-56
observes Catholic Holy Thursday ritual, 183-84
paraphrase on death of, quoted, 331, 356
petitions for body of, refused, 335, 337, 338
plans cultural expansion in Mexico, 223-24
pleads for safety of his officers and servants, 307-8, 313, 322
pledges himself to abdicate officially, 313
prepares to leave Mexico, 283-86
receives false report of Carlota's death, 322
receives threat from a messenger of Juárez, 137
receives threat from Austrian anarchist, 133-34
receives warnings against Mexican venture, 101-2
reception for, at Puebla, 142
relinquishes rights of Hapsburg succession, 104-9, 117, 122
reports as to sexual impotence of, 170, 204
responsibility for death of—*New York Herald* quoted, 332
sails for Mexico on *Novara,* 122-23
selects natives as Cabinet members, 168
sends Napoleon telegram of congratulation, 244
speculations of conquest, 184
states wishes as to disposition of his body, 322, 329
surrenders to Escobedo, 307-8, 356
travels in summer of 1850, 24
Venetian honeymoon of Carlotta and, 44-47
visited by Princess Salm-Salm, 312-13
visits in Belgium in 1856, 35-38
visits in Berlin in 1856, 38-39
visits in France in 1856, 31-34
visits in Spain in 1856, 30-31
visits in Vienna in 1860, 49
Maximilian II, 113
Meglia, Monsignor, 155, 156, 157
Mejía, Tomás, 287, 288, 293, 304, 306, 315, 318, 320, 322
disposition of body of, 335
execution of, 324-31
paraphrase on death of, quoted, 331, 356

Méndez, Concha, 151, 347, 348
  tribute of, quoted, 347, 356-57
Méndez, Ramón, 287, 288, 293, 300, 302
Mérimée, Prosper, 56, 58, 238, 241
Metternich, Prince Richard, 241
  quoted on Mexican venture, 87
Metternich-Sándor, Princess Pauline, 118
Mexico
  departure of royal party for, 120-23
  difficulties of travel in, 138-43, 232-33
  France abandons Empire in, 222, 248
  history of, through 1858, 68-76
  Maximilian accepts Crown of, 116-19
  Maximilian plans cultural expansion in, 223-24
  Maximilian prepares to leave, 283-86, 311
  negotiations for establishment of Empire in, 83-115
Mexico City, 74, 75, 82, 85, 94, 120, 127, 137, 142, 143, 144, 147, 148, 152, 154, 158, 165, 167, 173, 191, 192, 195, 199, 205, 213, 218, 223, 276, 287, 288, 290, 293, 294, 295, 300, 311, 314, 315, 332, 333, 334, 337, 339
Meyer, Pater, 116
Michoacán, 73, 76
Middleton, C., 316
Mikosch, Baroness, 282
Milan, 43, 44, 45, 47, 121, 129, 131, 151, 212, 249, 252
Miramar, 47, 50, 51, 89, 92, 94, 96, 99, 100, 102, 103, 104, 105, 106, 107, 108, 109, 110, 113, 115, 116, 118, 120, 137, 144, 149, 152, 159, 171, 172, 176, 179, 180, 190, 220, 230, 248, 249, 252, 253, 256, 258, 259, 270, 280, 285, 289, 301, 311, 323, 341
  Carlota removed to, 271
  "Convention of"
    see under "Convention"
  description of palace of, 47-48
Miramón, Miguel, 75, 76, 78, 81, 98, 287, 288, 293, 304, 306, 315, 318, 320, 321, 322
  disposition of body of, 335
  execution of, 326-31
  paraphrase on death of, quoted, 331, 356
Miranda, Francisco, 95
Modena, 45, 134
Modena, Duke of, 86
Monier, Monsieur, 116
Monroe, President James, 79
Mont Cenis, 252
Montebello, Countess of, 237
Monterrey, 154, 176, 191, 314
Montezuma, 66, 71, 84, 143, 149, 196, 223, 326
Montholon, Marquis de, 147, 168, 170, 171
Montijo, Eugenia de, 30, 345
  bad reputation of, 24-25
  see also Empress Eugénie
Monza, 49
Morán, Guadalupe Cervantes de, 150
Morel, Henri, 298
Morelia, 73, 153
  see Valladolid
Morelos, José María, 73, 78
Morny, Duc de, 33, 75, 114
Morphy, Tomás, 95
Moscow, 14, 45
Motecuhzoma
  see Montezuma
Moustachu, 63, 80, 198, 226
  see also Napoleon III
Moya, Marquesa de, 55
Munich, 113

Nantes, 234
Naples, 129, 130, 301
Napoleon I, 14, 28, 33, 41, 45, 56, 62, 73, 113, 167, 194
Napoleon II (Duke of Reichstadt), 194
Napoleon III, 24, 25, 28, 32, 33, 47, 58, 59, 73, 78, 80, 84, 85, 88, 89, 91, 93, 96, 97, 100, 103, 108, 112, 113, 128, 129, 133, 168, 169, 170, 179, 185, 194, 195, 196, 197, 198, 200, 203, 210, 220, 222, 225, 227, 229, 234, 235, 237, 247, 249, 252, 260, 261, 262, 272, 277, 279, 291, 334, 344, 347, 348
  and responsibility for Maximilian's death, 332
  and the Mexican plot, 65-71, 77, 80-81, 86-95
  grants audiences with Carlota, 238-41, 242-44
  letter to Maximilian quoted, 257
  marital rift between Eugénie and, 33-34
  meeting with Carlota at the Grand Hotel, 247-48
  orders Bazaine to evacuate Mexico, 195-99, 211
  proposal for hand of Eugénie quoted, 60, 353
  receives telegram of congratulation from Maximilian, 244
  replies to Maximilian's telegram of congratulation, 255-56
  telegram of congratulation quoted, 121
  telegram to Carlota quoted, 234
Napoleon, Prince ("Plon-Plon," cousin of Napoleon III), 31

Narváez, General, 56, 57
Netzahualcoyotl, 143
New England, 69
New Orleans, 193
New York, 66
New York Herald
quoted on fate of López, 333
quoted on responsibility for Maximilian's death, 332
New York Sun
quoted on the Maximilian drama, 348
Nicaragua, 66
Nice, 47
Nicholas, Tsar, 29
Nomel, Victor, 298
Noriega, General, 295
North America, 74
Notre Dame, 25
Novara, corvette, 48, 103, 122, 123, 130, 131, 132, 133, 190, 342
Maximilian's body returned to Europe on, 340
Novella, Don Francisco de, 73

Oaxaca, 76, 97, 140, 289
Obregón, General Álvaro, 75
Obrenovitch, Prince Milosh, 18
Oca, Dr. Ignacio Montes de, 119
Ocotlán, 146
Olmütz, 232, 292
Orden Imperial de San Carlos, 160
Order of Guadalupe, 160
Orizaba, 83, 136, 182, 232, 284, 286, 311, 332, 333, 343
Ortega, Don Jesús Gonzales, 222, 224
Oswiecim, 231

Paca (Duchess of Alba), 25, 56, 112
see Francisca
Pacca, Monsignor Bartolommeo, 266, 269
Padua, 254
Palacio Nacional, 148, 173, 223
Palacio, General Vicente Riva, 289, 316, 324
Palmar, 140
Palmerston, Lord, 25, 102, 111, 221
quoted, 47
Pamplona, 62
Panamá, 184
Panizzi, Sir Anthony
quoted on Carlota's visit to France, 241
Paris, 25, 31, 32, 33, 38, 45, 56, 59, 62, 63, 72, 75, 78, 79, 80, 84, 85, 86, 87, 93, 95, 102, 105, 107, 109, 112, 113, 114, 118, 121, 136, 142, 147, 158, 164, 169, 181, 205, 210, 220, 222, 234, 235, 238, 241, 242, 244, 248, 251, 252, 253, 254, 255, 256, 258, 260, 277, 278, 303, 344, 345
Paso del Macho, 233, 234
Paso del Norte (Ciudad Juárez), 97, 191, 222
Patti, Adelina, 32
Paula, Franz de (Ambassador Linden of Württemberg), 19, 24
Pedro de Braganza, Dom (Emperor of Brazil), 41, 184
Pedro V, King of Portugal, 111
Péjun, Émile, 298
Peñaranda, Don Manuel Fernández de (Count of Teba and Montijo), 56
Peñaranda, Duquesa de, 55
Peraz, María Muñoz de, 150
Peza, Juan de Dios, 216
Pezuela, Luis Robles, 216
Phantasie, imperial yacht, 122
Philip II, 29, 30
Philip, Count of Flanders, 271
Philip, Duke of Anjou, 106
Pius IX, Pope, 127, 128
grants audience to Empress Carlota, 260-66
letter to Carlota quoted, 270-71
Plaizora, Manuela de, 150
Plaza Mayor, 147, 148
Plon-Plon, 32, 33
Poland, 221
Poliakowitz, Señor Montalba, 230, 245, 246
Popocatepetl, 143
Po River, 45
Port Royal, 135
Portugal, 35, 130, 183, 278
Possenhofen, 26
Potosí, San Luis, 97, 194
Potrero, 340
Pour le Mérite, 160
Prague, 15, 50
Prim, General Juan (Count of Reus), 81, 83, 84, 250
Promenade of Carlota, 150
Prussia, 29, 115, 220, 221, 231, 235, 242, 316, 344
Puebla
see La Puebla de los Ángeles
Puente Colorado, 142
Pyrenees Mountains, 78

Quai d'Orsay, 234
Querétaro, 64, 287, 288, 289, 290, 291, 292, 294, 295, 296, 300, 303, 306, 308, 309, 312, 313, 315, 316, 317, 321, 324, 328, 330, 332, 333, 335, 336, 337, 339, 344, 347
trial of imperialists held in, 318
Quetzalcoatl, 154

Radonetz, Prefect, 253, 258
Rainer, Archduke, 117

Ramírez, José Vicente, 216, 318
Randon, Marshal, 235, 238
Reggio, 260
Régules, Corona, 289
Reichstadt, Duke of, 14
Reine Hortense (French imperial yacht), 34
Rhine River, 161, 235
Rhone River, 161
Ribera, Marqués de la, 178, 316
Richthofen, Baron Emil von, 101
Ricot, Jean, 298
Riedel, Professor, 271, 280, 291
Rincón-Gallardo, Ana Rosa de, 150, 302
Rincón-Gallardo, Colonel José, 302, 305, 333
Rincón-Gallardo, Luísa Quejano de, 151, 302
Río Grande, 70, 72, 79, 81, 169, 185, 223, 278, 287, 348
Río, Pablo Martínez del, 118
River Chiquihuite, 139
Riviera, 56
Robespierre, 72
Robles, Luz Blanco de, 150
Robles, Rocha de, 151
Rome, 105, 121, 155, 158, 170, 184, 201, 203, 226, 246, 248, 258, 259, 260, 261, 268, 270
Romero, Matías, 191
Rouher, Monsieur Eugène, 246-47
Rovigo, 254
Rowles, Miss, 60
Rozeville, Ernest de, 298
Rudolf, Crown Prince, 19, 50, 104, 106, 208, 292, 346
Ruedo y Auza, Juan, 318
Russell, Lord John, 49, 50
Russia, 32, 87, 260, 346

Sachsen-Weimar, Gustaf von, 291
Sadowa, 232, 235
Sainte-Beuve, 32
Saint Nazaire, 234, 235
Salas-Varela, Josefa Cardeña de, 151, 232
Salazar, General, 217
Salm-Salm, Prince Felix zu, 290, 291, 293, 294, 299, 300, 304, 305, 306, 307, 308, 310, 311, 312, 315, 318, 324, 328, 340
  fate of, 334
Salm-Salm, Princess Agnes, 146
  characteristics of, 310-11
  quoted, 138-39
  resolves to buy Maximilian's freedom, 316-17
  visits Emperor Maximilian, 312-13
  writes memorial, 334
Saltillo, 191
Salvator, Archduke, 117
San Ángel, 75
Sánchez, Lieutenant-Colonel Platón, 307, 318, 320
Sánchez-Navarro, Otea de, 151, 166, 203
San Gregorio, 293
Sangremal, 293
San Luis Potosí, 287, 312, 314, 315, 316, 317, 321, 324, 325, 331, 332, 337
Santa Ana, Antonio López de, 74, 75, 78, 160
Sarajevo, 292, 346
Savoy, 47
Schaffer, Karl, 294
Scherzenlechner, Sebastian, 102, 131, 132, 133, 154, 179, 180
Schleswig-Holstein, 220, 221
Schmidt, Charles, 298
Schneider, Count von, 116
Schönbrunn, palace of, 14, 45, 182
Seward, William Henry, 190, 194, 211, 243, 277, 278, 279, 314, 326, 331, 348
  quoted, 210
Siliceo, Manuel, 217
Sisi (Franz Joseph's consort, Elisabeth), 33, 117, 292
Smith, General Kirby, 169
Smyrna, 24
Solferino, 47
Solitude, 137
Sonora, 168
Sophie, Archduchess (mother of Maximilian I), 15, 16, 21, 22, 26, 27, 30, 37, 50, 89, 113, 208, 228, 320, 341, 343, 344
  letter to Maximilian quoted, 291-92
  telegram of farewell quoted, 122
Soto la Marina, 73
South America, 41
Spa, 59
Spain, 30, 31, 56, 57, 65, 70, 72, 74, 79, 81, 82, 83, 85, 90, 91, 93, 101, 103, 110, 122, 130, 137, 144, 181, 183, 316, 325
St. Cloud, 31, 62, 112, 226, 230, 234, 236, 237, 242, 246, 255, 257
St. Helena, 14, 56
St. Petersburg, 29, 33
Strauss, Herr Johann, 13, 14, 15, 18, 21, 164, 221, 344
St. Sulpice, 114
Sweden, 325

Tacubaya, 176
Tamaulipas, legislature of, 73
Tatra Mountains, 48
Teatro Principal de Querétaro
  trial of imperialists held in, 318
Teba, Condesa de, 55, 60

Tegetthoff, Admiral Baron Wilhelm von, 253, 341
sails with Maximilian's remains to Europe, 338-40
Tehuacán, 83
Tejada, Sebastián Lerdo de, 315, 339
refuses petitions for Maximilian's body, 335, 337, 338
Tenochtitlán, 66, 143, 144
Tepeyac, 144, 146
Texas, 74
Texcoco, 143
Themis, French gunboat, 116, 122, 133
Thun, Count Guido, 175
Tlálpam, 177
Tlaltelolco, 144
Tlaxcala, 143, 146
Tomalto, 138
Tonantzín, 144, 146
Torre, Rafael Martínez de la, 316
Torreón, 191
Tosti, Sir Francesco Paolo, 44
Trieste, 22, 47, 89, 102, 105, 115, 121, 123, 152, 171, 173, 227, 232, 253, 254, 258, 270, 342
Tronin, Émile, 298
Troubetzkoi, Princess, 33
Tüdös, chef at Chapultepec, 162, 313, 328, 330, 340
Tuileries, 25, 78, 86, 91, 103, 195, 210, 219, 225, 247, 255
Turin, 252
Turkey, 301
Tuscany, 134
Tyrol, 47
Tzintzuntzan, 200

Ugarte, Countess, 19
Ulúa, San Juan de, 81, 136, 334, 340
United States, 65, 66, 74, 77, 78, 79, 80, 191, 193, 210, 214, 244, 249, 277, 278, 279, 317, 319, 348
orders Minister to leave Mexico, 135
Uraza, Rosa Obregón de, 150
Uruápam, 200

Valladolid, 73
Valle, Concepción Lizardi del, 151
Valle, Count de, 230, 238, 247, 263
Vásquez, Jesús M., 316
Vatican, 75, 78, 127, 155, 156, 203, 226, 228, 252, 270
Carlota visits, 261-68
Vélez, General, 305
Venice, 253, 257, 258
Vera Cruz, 76, 80, 81, 82, 83, 84, 95, 97, 98, 136, 173, 174, 192, 196, 222, 233, 234, 276, 281, 283, 284, 286,
Vera Cruz—*continued*
287, 289, 314, 317, 319, 334, 337, 338, 339, 340
Verastegui, José, 318
Vetsera, Countess, 19
Vichy, 234, 235
Victor Emmanuel II, 129
Victoria, Queen ("Vicky"), 26, 28, 34, 35, 45, 49, 110, 111, 112, 130, 134, 212, 260, 345, 346
Vienna, 13, 14, 16, 18, 19, 24, 25, 26, 27, 30, 31, 32, 36, 37, 40, 42, 45, 50, 87, 89, 101, 103, 106, 108, 115, 117, 133, 149, 163, 164, 180, 181, 184, 208, 221, 223, 225, 227, 228, 232, 237, 270, 271, 280, 320, 325, 327, 342, 344, 345
Carlotta and Maxl's visit to, in 1860, 49
Villagrán, Lucas, 318
Ville Lumière, 31
Ville, Marquise de, 118
Vleeschouwer, Mynheer
quoted, 198
Volga River, 78

Wales, Prince of (Edward VII), 341
Walewska, Countess, 33
Washington, 72, 76, 88, 171, 194, 195, 243, 246, 275, 277, 278, 279, 310, 314, 331, 332
Weckerle, Franz, 180
Wenzel, Prince Clemens Lothar, 15
West Indies, 234
White, John, 315
Winterhalter, François Xavier, 61
Wittlesbach, House of, 113
Woll, General Adrian, 95, 120
Worth, Charles Frederick, 31, 235, 345
Württemberg, Ambassador of, 19
see Franz de Paula
Wyckenburg, Count Edmund, 287
Wydenbruck, Baron von, 195, 310, 331
Wyke, Sir Charles, 102, 110

Xinantecatl, 154
Xochimilco, 176
Xocotitlán, 343

Yucatán, 234

Zaragoza, General, 85
Zerman, Vice-Admiral, 116
Zichy, Countess Melanie, 122, 131, 152, 237
Zócalo, 148
Zuloaga, 75
Zumárraga, Fray de, 145, 146
Zwickau, 231